Meaning and Embodiment

Meaning and Embodiment

HUMAN CORPOREITY IN HEGEL'S ANTHROPOLOGY

nicholas mowad

Cover art: Carl Randall, *Tokyo Portrait No. 4*

Published by State University of New York Press, Albany

© 2019 State University of New York

All rights reserved

No part of this book may be used or reproduced in any manner whatsoever without written permission. No part of this book may be stored in a retrieval system or transmitted in any form or by any means including electronic, electrostatic, magnetic tape, mechanical, photocopying, recording, or otherwise without the prior permission in writing of the publisher.

For information, contact State University of New York Press, Albany, NY
www.sunypress.edu

Library of Congress Cataloging-in-Publication Data

Names: Mowad, Nicholas, 1979– author.
Title: Meaning and embodiment : human corporeity in Hegel's anthropology / Nicholas Mowad.
Description: Albany : State University of New York, 2019. | Includes bibliographical references and index.
Identifiers: LCCN 2018043674 | ISBN 9781438475578 (hardcover) | ISBN 9781438475585 (pbk.) | ISBN 9781438475592 (ebook) Subjects: LCSH: Hegel, Georg Wilhelm Friedrich, 1770–1831. | Human body (Philosophy)
Classification: LCC B2948 .M69 2019 | DDC 128.092—dc23
LC record available at https://lccn.loc.gov/2018043674

10 9 8 7 6 5 4 3 2 1

To Dylan, Felix, and Leo

Contents

Acknowledgments	xi
Introduction	xiii
Abbreviations	xxvii
Chapter 1. That the Term "Body" Is Equivocal	1
The Essence of Embodiment	2
Dimensions of Embodiment	5
The Materiality of the Soul	16
Multidimensional Embodiment	17
Chapter 2. The Concept of Spirit	25
The "Idea" and Hegel's "Idealism"	25
The Idea in Nature: Life and Death	31
The Concept of Spirit as the Idea Knowing Itself in Its Other:	
A Close Reading of §381	35
Revelation	43
The Soul as Natural Spirit	45
Whether the Anthropology Is Normative	50
Chapter 3. Immersion in Nature	55
What Hegel Means by "Soul [Seele]"	56
The Soul of the World; or, That Meaning in Nature Is Not	
Fabricated Arbitrarily	59
Reconciling Different Explanations of the Same Phenomenon	61
Anthropological Description Is Interpretation, Not Classification	64
Examples of Finding Meaning in Nature	69
What "Race" Is Not, and What It Means for Hegel	73
What Can Be Salvaged in Hegel's Philosophy of Race?	81

The Extent to Which Race Can Be Transcended	87
The Individual Soul	92
Chapter 4. The Inner World of the Soul	**97**
The Ages of Life	100
Life and Death	102
What Lies on the Surface of Hegel's Theory of Gender	109
The Law of the Netherworld and Radical Guilt	113
Waking from Sleep and the Masculine Pathos	116
Sleep as a Transcendental Condition of Waking Experience	120
Chapter 5. Sensation and the Oblivion of the Body	**127**
Seeking a Middle Term	128
The Five Senses	130
Setting the Stones in Motion	136
The Soul as "Mixed" with Its Body	142
The Embodiment of the Emotions	145
Chapter 6. Perverse Self-Knowledge	**151**
From Sensation to Feeling	151
The Displacement of the Self	157
Examples and Analysis	160
Chapter 7. Mental Illness and Therapy	**169**
What It Means to Say That Mental Illness Is Pathological	170
Mental Illness as "Self-Feeling" and Sickness of the Soul	172
Mental Illness as Excessive Attachment	177
Habit as Therapy	179
Hegel and Foucault	184
Chapter 8. The Social Dimension of Human Embodiment	**191**
Habit as a Social "Sense" with Unlimited Scope	192
Internalization, Imagination, and Ethical Life	196
The Enduring Ambiguity of Nature	200
Assigning Meaning to the Human Body	202
"Double Consciousness": Feeling in Its Immediacy as Ideology	204
"The nation is sick, trouble is in the land, confusion is all around"	212
Habit and the Unmooring of a Reified Culture	214
Racial Politics and Democracy	220

Conclusion	227
Notes	231
Bibliography	297
Index	311

Acknowledgments

I would like to extend my sincere gratitude to the Arthur J. Schmitt Foundation for the support I received while working on this project as a Schmitt fellow. My greatest debt is to my professor, Adriaan Peperzak, who illuminated Hegel's philosophy for me and first encouraged me to write about the anthropology. Though I have in some cases departed from his interpretation, my understanding of Hegel has been guided by him more than anyone else. I remain deeply grateful for the unwavering support. I also thank the other faculty at Loyola University Chicago with whom I studied, especially Ardis Collins, who first introduced me to Hegel and showed me how to follow the path he takes in his arguments, and Hugh Miller whose helpful comments have improved my understanding. I thank Karin De Boer, Allegra De Laurentiis, Alfredo Ferrarin, Angelica Nuzzo, Adriaan Peperzak, and Richard Dien Winfield for reading parts of this book and offering helpful comments. I further extend my thanks to the anonymous reviewers whose comments have helped me improve this book considerably.

In many cases I took the advice offered by those generously giving the time and effort to read my work; what merit this book has was augmented as a result. I would not be surprised if the audience for this book will find places here where I have been too verbose, made a point inadequately, or veered off in the wrong direction. Hegel scholars will know the difficulty in writing a book on Hegel that gives enough background explanation while remaining on point and still making some worthwhile contribution, so I humbly ask for the reader's charity. In any case, it should go without saying that what weaknesses this book has, it has despite the advice of those who have offered their comments, which have only improved it.

Finally, I thank my wife, Erin Mowad, for her limitless patience with me as I brought this book to completion.

Introduction

This is a book about human embodiment. My thesis is that although the corporeal dimension of the human being can be accurately described in biological (and physical and chemical) terms, to understand it adequately requires transcending the categories used in analyzing animal and other merely natural forms of life. Only then can we see that what is most properly called "the human body" is not a body given by nature, but one produced by spirit (or human subjectivity[1]) for itself.

The body is one of the rare topics in philosophy that is both of perennial interest and of heightened contemporary concern. However, the attention paid to the body is both a blessing and a curse: while the contemporary reader can be grateful for the breadth of work on this topic, she may also be daunted by the sheer mass of arguments and doctrines concerning the body that have accumulated over the centuries. Gaining familiarity with the contributions of past philosophers on this topic is made especially difficult in the case of systematic philosophers like Hegel, whose writings on the body are hard or impossible to separate from the rest of his theory. Yet the accounts of human embodiment offered by other prominent philosophers of the past century as well as the general trend toward understanding human life and experience holistically suggest that many today would be interested in and sympathetic to Hegel's theory if they were familiar with it.

Hegel's theory of human embodiment is mostly contained in a section of his *Encyclopedia of the Philosophical Sciences in Outline* that he calls "the anthropology."[2] Because few, even of those with doctorates in philosophy, are familiar with Hegel's anthropology, some might suppose it resembles Kant's better-known "pragmatic anthropology." The two are similar in that both attempt to explain the peculiar corporeal existence of humanity, which is often characterized by its transcendence of embodiment. Yet different methodological commitments make Hegel's deduction and organic development of humanity out of nature different from Kant's curious descriptions of the natural variety in which humanity finds itself. A better analogy (and one that Hegel himself makes) would liken the anthropology to Aristotle's *De Anima*. Like the latter, Hegel's anthropology is investigation of "the soul," which, as he understands it, is what makes the human body different from other bodies.[3] Hegel's anthropology is thus a study of the intersection or overlapping of what is distinctly human and what is corporeal, or of the specifically human form of embodiment.

Some prefer to leave this topic to natural scientists, who know best how a human brain differs from that of an ape, or how the genome of the human species is unique. But while the natural scientist is the one to consult if one wants to know how the biological system of the human species differs from those of other species, the question of whether the corporeal dimension of the human being is best understood as a biological system at all is not one natural science is prepared to ask much less answer, unless we classify anthropology as a natural science. Yet within the field of anthropology itself there is vigorous debate about whether it should associate itself more with the sciences or the humanities, and how one answers this determines whether anthropology really is capable of answering whether humanity should be defined strictly as a biological species. It is telling that the one discipline (other than philosophy) that aims to understand humanity in all of its complexity has ended up divided into subdisciplines whose partisans often see little in common with each other: those studying "physical" (or "biological") anthropology present humanity as simply an anatomical system developing under evolutionary pressure in the same way other species do, while "cultural" (or "social") anthropologists—while acknowledging the biological side—present humanity as above all an agent for recognizing and establishing meaning in the natural world and its own institutions.

Given these apparently separate and independent methods, it is not clear how we are to understand what Marcel Mauss called "techniques of the body"[4] like walking or swimming. These actions do not come from instinct (and so are not purely "natural") but rather have their foundation in this or that particular culture, such that there is no such thing as regular *human* walking, but only a way of walking that is French, Somali, Japanese, and so on (notwithstanding that these differences are increasingly covered over by cultural homogenization through mass media). Yet, these techniques appear to exist in some form across all, or nearly all, cultures and to have not only been made possible by the unique trajectory of our evolution, but to have played a role in guiding it. It is by refusing to ignore or to minimize either the obvious naturalness of humanity or the equally clear discontinuity between humans and all other species (including our closest evolutionary relatives) that the best anthropologists distinguish their discipline as one of almost unparalleled depth and sensitivity.

A philosophical understanding of humanity and human embodiment must likewise come to grips with our biological constitution and that in us that is not and cannot be captured by biological explanations, without sweeping either under the rug. But, to compare philosophy with anthropology, what the philosophical enterprise lacks in ethnological fieldwork and empirical detail, it more than makes up for in its comprehensive scope (integrating questions of human identity with moral, political, epistemological, and ontological questions, all rigorously interrogated in their own right) and its especially critical methodology (though anthropology is certainly more reflective about its method than most other disciplines).

To capitalize on philosophy's strengths, one could hardly find a thinker whose work is wider ranging and who more thoroughly sorted out methodological problems than Hegel. His writings on the body bear this out, as he is keen to show that "body" is not a univocal word denoting a certain biologically determined way of existing and experiencing the world, and that we cannot understand the human form of embodiment by analysis and interpretation using only evolutionary-biological concepts.[5] Studying human embodiment entails studying not just the physical stuff composing humans, nor even human behavior in pursuit of ends having material origins in the human biological constitution, but also and primarily how a mind that can seem independent of the corporeal world is yet situated in a body that is very much *its own*, even as this mind thinks actively and spontaneously. Although studies of the mind or body in isolation from the other yield fascinating results, in the process the mind and body tend to recede further and further from each other, making the human experience of embodiment more, not less, baffling. On the other hand, taking human embodiment as a topic is to focus on where the rubber meets the road: whatever is involved in the complex relationship between thinking subjectivity and corporeal objectivity will have to show itself in the embodiment of the thinking human being.

Yet research into this topic is often stymied by the common assumption that there is a certain essential nature that all bodies share. This approach to embodiment seems to go hand in hand with the idea that the mind and body are substantially distinct and may be treated separately. Accordingly, it is not surprising that the reduction of all bodies to one shared essence can be traced back to Descartes, the most famous modern dualist. According to Descartes, corporeity is essentially extension, parts outside of parts, such that all differences between bodies boil down to different ways of being extended.[6] For instance, living and nonliving would be mere modes of extension, differing only based on complexity of parts (organic matter being more complex than but essentially the same as inorganic matter).

Descartes's conception of human bodies as complex machines has since been both celebrated and condemned for bringing the methods of modern natural science to bear in investigations into human identity. This push to make philosophy scientific has gained momentum throughout the modern era, but its direction was altered decisively in the work of the German Idealists, who drew their inspiration from an admirer and a critic of the scientization of philosophy, Immanuel Kant. Kant legitimized science's exploration of corporeal nature by limiting the extent of its claims, arguing that whatever falls within the bounds of possible experience must be determined in certain ways and hence obey certain basic laws (given by the conditions for possible experience). Kant thus granted to natural science a broad scope but denied it standing regarding questions concerning objects beyond all possible experience (God, immortality, freedom, etc.). Kant can easily give the impression that human embodiment as well is a part of nature and hence falls within the field consigned to natural science. However, his notion of human embodiment was much more nuanced, as Angelica Nuzzo has recently highlighted.[7] Rather than being a mere object of experience, the body (and not just a nebulous transcendental ego) must be considered a transcendental condition of all experience and thus cannot be treated as having the same nature as other sorts of bodies.

The claim that the natural sciences are not in the best position to understand human embodiment (which is not to say that the sciences are "wrong," provided they restrict their claims to what is visible according to their methods) has also received support in the twentieth century, most notably from Martin Heidegger, Maurice Merleau-Ponty, and Judith Butler.[8] Despite their admitted differences, all three offer arguments resembling that of Kant in significant ways. All argue that the problem in trying to understand human embodiment purely through natural science lies in the way natural science constructs a theory of what embodiment is, and subsequently hypostatizes this theoretical construction to the experiencing self, which is not an object but rather a condition for the experience of objectivity. In this way, subsequent experience gets distorted and "confirms" the scientific account of embodiment in a question-begging way.

There are passages in the works of these philosophers that seem to indicate a different approach to the body. For instance, Heidegger sometimes seems to accept the idea that the human body is merely one object among others in the world and is defined by extension. In articulating his notion of being-in-the-world for instance, he distinguishes the being-in proper to Dasein from the spatial insideness that a body (including the human body) can have relative to a larger body. Yet his point in making this distinction is to show that Dasein's spatiality (the spatiality proper to humans) is not founded on its being "in" a body that is extended. Rather, Dasein's spatiality is founded on Dasein's having care (being outside of oneself in the sense of being preoccupied with and absorbed in one's surroundings) as its fundamental existential structure: all experience of corporeal bodies and their extension is posterior rather than prior to the immediate experience of being immersed in a world.[9]

Merleau-Ponty offers a similar argument. Thus for example I may read in a psychology textbook about the so-called "law of effect," namely, that as a rule, people seek to recreate pleasant experiences and avoid painful ones, such that a person's experience is ordered toward the end of egoistic survival, or crude pleasure. According to Merleau-Ponty, this conception of human embodiment can then act as a filter by which I determine what is real in my experience and what is illusory, that is, what counts as valid scientific data and what is irrelevant, perhaps a suitable object for literature but not science. With this approach, the unreflective feeling of empathy I have toward another person I see suffering would be dismissed as unreal, as in truth only disguised egoism insofar as my anxiety at seeing another suffer lies in my fear that I too may suffer. Empathy would then be rejected as an imaginative ideal celebrated in art and religion but not part of genuine (i.e., quantifiable and empirically observable by a third party) human experience. However, my immediate experience of the psychology textbook—and indeed, the immediate experience of the psychologists who wrote it—is prior to any theoretical construction, including the notion of humans as biologically determined to seek pleasure even at the expense of others. Such theoretical constructions may be valid for some purposes, but they can never legitimately reach back, rearrange, and violate the original and undeniable reality of the immediate experience on which they were founded; nor may these theoretical constructions delegitimize my equally original and immediate experience of empathy.[10]

Her different aims notwithstanding, Butler presents a similar argument in opposition to the idea that the body (and its supposedly determinate sex) is a stable, material, and extra-discursive foundation on which cultural products like gender may be constructed. Rather, she argues, the so-called purely material part of embodiment (e.g., "sex") is assigned this character (as extra-discursive) through our discursive activity (from which it is thus never truly independent). Moreover, drawing on Freud and Lacan, Butler argues that our experience of our bodies (as something ostensibly foundational and independent of thought, culture, and experience) is phenomenologically co-originary with our experience of (sexual) pleasure and pain, and the latter always already involve a certain gendered way of experiencing.[11] Thus the material body cannot be the foundation for cultural products like gender and sexuality. Rather, what counts as the body is from the beginning influenced by our own gendered and sexually oriented subjectivities.

Thus Kant, Heidegger, Merleau-Ponty, and Butler all object to the way natural science (and philosophy inspired by it) tends to lump the human body in with other bodies in nature. And the underlying reason for their objections is that human embodiment is in some sense a condition for the possibility of the experience of natural bodies (or the experience of bodies as "natural," and independent of the experiencing subject). In this, all four resemble Hegel as well, though Kant could not have known Hegel's position, and while the other three are certainly well versed in Hegel, none to my knowledge gives any indication of familiarity with Hegel's "anthropology." Indeed, the philosophical public generally is largely unaware that Hegel's anthropology exists, or why it is important.

Yet Hegel's theory is important, not least because it offers something unavailable in the works of those other profound thinkers. That is, not only does Hegel show how human embodiment cannot be understood simply according to the concepts of the natural sciences, he also shows remarkably well how the specifically human form of embodiment relates to mechanism, chemical polarity, and biology (the forms of embodiment recognized by the sciences as characterizing other parts of nature and, to a limited extent, the human body itself). In other words, Hegel shows how human embodiment is genuinely built upon the more abstract forms of embodiment (like spatial extension, chemical relations, and organic processes), yet also that the human form of embodiment goes beyond these, profoundly changing how they must be understood in the human body. Hegel's argument thus allows us to show both: (1) the precise way in which the human body does indeed display "merely natural" characteristics (such as extension), and (2) that the concepts natural science uses to understand merely natural bodies are of limited use in understanding human embodiment.

Granted, of the aforementioned philosophers, Heidegger and Butler have not taken as their precise theme the way human embodiment bears mechanical, chemical, and biological determinations and yet is not reducible to them. It would be unfair to blame them for not providing an answer to a question Hegel asks. Merleau-Ponty on the other hand has devoted a great deal of attention to this ambiguity in human embodiment.[12] Merleau-Ponty's extraordinary contribution in this area is generally acknowledged, in contrast with Hegel's largely unknown contribution. Yet even granting the value of Merleau-Ponty's work on the topic, Hegel's anthropology should command our attention, because the methodological difference between the two means that however much we may legitimately get from Merleau-Ponty on this question, we cannot get from him what we can from Hegel. Merleau-Ponty's method (which he assiduously defends) involves remaining within a prereflective way of apprehending bodies and describing the experience without the interposition of any "reflective" theory.[13] In contrast, Hegel's method is to carry out an immanent critique of concepts of embodiment: that is, to analyze a concept of embodiment, drawing out its presuppositions and implications to show how it already contains within itself other concepts of embodiment or points beyond itself toward them. In this way he can show how the meaning and applicability of extension is qualified and reinterpreted in the context of a living body, and how extension *and* life are reinterpreted by their integration into human or "anthropological" embodiment.

While it may seem that Merleau-Ponty would consider Hegel's approach to be "reflective" in the damning sense, one should not jump to this conclusion: Hegel was nothing if not critical of the "reflective" approach, which he associated with the machinations of the abstract understanding (the *Verstand*, conceived as a bare subject waiting to encounter bare objects). Rather than this kind of "reflection" (which Hegel associates with Kant and derisively likens to the attempt to learn to swim before getting in the water[14]), Hegel's method of immanent critique involves making no assumptions about what experience is, what does the experiencing, or what may be experienced, but rather taking experience as it presents itself and persistently drawing out its presuppositions and implications. He never crosses the threshold into "reflection" in the pernicious sense because the implications drawn out dialectically do not reach back to substantially revise or categorically invalidate the original experience, but only integrate it into its proper context (in which it must be integrated given *other*, equally valid experiences).[15]

Yet suppose that Merleau-Ponty would have called Hegel's approach "reflective," and suppose further that this accusation is just. Still, there would be good reason to study Hegel's anthropology. Merleau-Ponty renounces reflection from the beginning because of the insoluble problems he says it leads to: a subject only accidentally and inexplicably located in a body; the encounter with bodies in nature that appear to reflection as independent and indifferent to knowing subjectivity and consequently alien to any kind of value or significance—such that value judgments are considered mere subjective opinions. Yet if Hegel's dialectical method is "reflective," then by delving straight into such "reflection," Hegel shows how the conclusions Merleau-Ponty thinks reflection leads to are not only not inevitable, but patently false. In other words, *even if* Hegel engages in "reflection" in the pejorative sense (and I maintain that he does not), his approach would still be very worthy of study insofar as where Merleau-Ponty would fear to tread, to prevent "cutting up what is lived into discontinuous acts" and thus being drawn into "impasses we are trying to avoid,"[16] Hegel would boldly go and lead the way out of the apparent impasse. I do not claim that we can give Hegel's account as he wrote it a full-throated endorsement, and I will make clear where Hegel's approach errs in being inconsistent, outdated, bizarre, or otherwise unhelpful. Yet I do contend that his approach can shed a great deal of much-needed light on human embodiment. Accordingly, I intend this book to be not just a commentary on Hegel's anthropology, but a criticism, a qualified defense, and a creative extension of it.

Despite the renewed interest in Hegel in recent decades and the increasing attention devoted to embodiment in philosophy generally,[17] the theory of human embodiment Hegel presents in the anthropology remains fertile ground for study. Russon has provided a welcome study of the place of embodiment in Hegel's *Phenomenology of Spirit*, showing correctly for example that Hegel understands the body must be understood as the expression of spirit (i.e., thinking human subjectivity):[18] a commentary on the anthropology, where Hegel gives his most detailed and sustained study of embodiment, can supplement this work. Wolff has written an admirable book devoted to explaining the relation between the corporeal world and human subjectivity as distilled through a single paragraph of Hegel's anthropology.[19] It is difficult to praise this book highly enough, but there remains something to be gained by presenting a study of the anthropology as a whole. I have been fortunate to benefit from many books and articles that treat embodiment in Hegel, or parts or aspects of the anthropology, but I mean my contribution here to rectify the absence of a book-length study focused on the anthropology and treating the whole of it.[20]

In order to show what is distinctive about anthropological embodiment, I begin in chapter 1 with a discussion of the different ways in which something can be embodied according to Hegel: mechanically, chemically, biologically, and anthropologically. This discussion is meant to lay bare some of the ambiguities surrounding the idea of a body and to introduce the forms of embodiment that Hegel distinguishes, as well as the relations between them. In this chapter I also develop in a preliminary way the thesis of the whole book, namely, that the human form of embodiment is different in kind from that of animal life, because the human body is a body of spirit rather than a merely natural body.

Chapter 2 is devoted to Hegel's concept of spirit (*Geist*) and the place of the anthropology in his philosophy of spirit. After a more general explanation of this concept, I offer a close reading of the four paragraphs outlining the "concept of spirit" in the *Encyclopedia*. Hegel's conception of spirit is multifarious: not only the human body and the inner life of the human being (desire, thought, will, language, memory), but also things like property and contracts; moral codes and acts; as well as familial, economic, and national ties are forms of spirit. Indeed, even the most horrendous things such as crime, moral evil, and war are forms of spirit, along with the most divine things, like fine art, religion, and philosophy itself. I have made use in my explanation of spirit of many such examples, while also identifying the shared structure that makes them all forms of spirit. I intend this book to be helpful both to Hegel experts interested in a thorough study of the anthropology and to those educated in philosophy but unfamiliar with Hegel. Readers conversant in all three volumes of the *Encyclopedia* may decide to skip this chapter.

Chapters 3 through 7 are devoted to different parts of the anthropology. In these I show how our anthropological embodiment entails three different cognitive relations to other bodies and our own embodiment. The precise themes of the anthropology's different sections are not always clear from Hegel's subtitles (e.g., "natural qualities," "natural changes"), but I make clear what justifies the lines along which the anthropology is articulated. For instance, my third chapter is called "Immersion in Nature," because Hegel understands the phenomena he groups under the name "natural qualities" to be ways in which the soul unreflectively identifies with and finds meaning in external nature: this is the first of the three cognitive relations to embodiment I examine. This immersion also involves the various racial and national characters that according to Hegel correspond to differences in land and climate. While not letting Hegel off the hook for his shortsightedness here, I place his controversial remarks in context and draw on other parts of his work to begin to present a more critical account of race and nationality.

Chapters 4 and 5 continue examining ways we unreflectively find meaning in nature, while steadily showing how other ways of relating to nature are developed out of this naïve absorption. The themes of chapter 4 are: growth (including not just physical but psychosocial development), aging, and death; gender; and sleep and waking life. This chapter is called "The Inner World of the Soul," because it is in the section that Hegel calls "natural changes" that he articulates the difference between the soul's immediate absorption in its body and its apprehension of external nature and the implicit dependence of the latter on the former. Because we have access to external nature only through immediate absorption in our own body, the interiority of the soul begins to come into view, but only as something dark and mysterious.

Chapter 5, "Sensation and the Oblivion of the Body," explores further the dependence of perception of external nature on the failure of apperception. Hegel relies heavily on *De Anima* for his theory of sensibility but he does not merely rehash Aristotle: Hegel's account overflows traditional boundaries between mind and body, spontaneity and receptivity. Just as Hegel presents sensation as knowing that which is incarnate, he presents nature not as dead, inert matter but as corporeity that raises itself up to intelligibility. Hegel's romanticism is most clearly seen in his theory of the emotions, also treated in this chapter. It is in emotion that the embodied spirit first senses its own self.

Chapter 6, "Perverse Self-Knowledge," concerns "feeling [*Gefühl*]," which is a precise, technical term for Hegel without the broad sense it has in everyday English. *Gefühl* is affective self-knowing that is immediate. Emotion belongs to chapter 5, but in some ways it seems more like a feeling than a sensation. In emotion the soul knows itself (rather than an external object) but still does so by way of some part of the body (as anger is felt in the chest, embarrassment in the face). Genuine feeling involves the second of the three ways of relating to embodiment: circumventing the naturally given body altogether and feeling immediately in a way that can appear miraculous, but for spirit feeling is in most cases rather a sickness of the soul.

Feeling relates to its content immediately, such that it is unable to distinguish itself from what it knows to be a mere contingent object: this is how Hegel understands mental illness, the subject of chapter 7, "Mental Illness and Therapy." The therapy that cures mental illness may be prompted by a psychiatrist, but whether such a professional is present or not, therapy according to Hegel is the inculcation of "habit," which creates for the soul a new form of mediation between itself and its contents. I situate Hegel's theory of mental illness and therapy in relation to Foucault's influential presentation of the modern misunderstanding of madness, showing that although Hegel's theory bears some superficial similarities to what Foucault criticizes, there is no reason to think Foucault was even aware of the anthropology and his criticism is generally inapplicable to Hegel's account. Habit is the third and final way the anthropology gives of relating to embodiment: in habit, the soul wrests itself from its attachment to any particular content in order to identify instead with the continually forming and reforming broader pattern characterizing its experience. Habit provides a way to order not just the content of an individual soul (which I cover in chapter 7) but also individual humans into a larger social community, the theme of chapter 8.

In chapter 8 I extend what Hegel's analysis of habit gives us to return to unresolved questions from chapters 3 and 4, attempting a critical theory of race and gender. What I give there is not Hegel's own account, but I submit it as: (1) an interpretation of Hegel's analogy between individual habituation and social integration; and (2) an extension of this analogy, an exploration of social analogues for other ways individual selfhood is constituted. Habit lies at the heart of acculturation because it assigns the meaning that legitimates social identities and rules. Racism and sexism can be understood as social pathologies that persist to the extent that the culture, the social body through which its members experience their social world, is organized according to one of the lower, more abstract levels of development belonging to earlier parts of the anthropology. Hegel's anthropology can thus point a way forward today for us, who live in a fundamentally unjust culture.

A Note on the Text

The anthropology consists of a mere twenty-five short paragraphs, some also with short remarks (*Anmerkungen*) appended to them (added by Hegel in the *Encyclopedia*'s second and third editions). These original paragraphs with the added remarks constitute the *Haupttext* or main text. I will also however make careful use of the *Zusätze*, the additions from Hegel's lectures collected and published by Boumann (one of Hegel's students) after his death. Hegel intended the *Encyclopedia* to be a handbook for use in his classes and therefore expected that its readers would also get the benefit of hearing his lectures. As one might expect, the lectures give more examples and the language is generally more down to earth. This can of course be very helpful in understanding Hegel. However, because these additions were never actually published by Hegel, one must always take what is attributed to Hegel there with a grain of salt, seeking corroboration in the *Haupttext*: a student might always insert his own interpretation. Even if a point appears in the notes of several students, or in the lectures given over different semesters—that is, even if it is extremely likely that Hegel did actually make a certain point in his lectures—it must be acknowledged that Hegel no doubt spoke with greater latitude in his lectures than he would have allowed himself in his written, published work.

Boumann's *Zusätze* also conceal any divergence among the various transcripts of the "circle of friends" from which they are composed. Thus any changes Hegel may have made over the course of his lectures on subjective spirit from the summer of 1820 to the winter of 1829/1830 are also concealed in these *Zusätze* for the sake of achieving a speciously authoritative status. Recently however, the transcripts of Erdmann and Walter from the winter semester of 1827/1828 have been published by Felix Meiner Verlag. Editors Hespe and Tuschling confirm the unprecedented reliability of the Erdmann transcript, especially as it can be cross-checked with Walter's version[21] (both are published together but not merged into one version that glosses over the differences between them).

Yet any exegetical work on Hegel's anthropology must begin by plainly acknowledging that Boumann's *Zusätze* contain much more material on certain parts of the anthropology than do Erdmann's or Walter's transcripts. Accordingly, the presence of the *Zusätze* in some of what follows is more pronounced. However, I still make every effort to use the *Zusätze* critically, for example, giving preference to remarks that also appear in Erdmann's and Walter's transcripts. I will rely more heavily on Boumann's *Zusätze* only when Erdmann's and Walter's transcripts do not cover a certain aspect of the *Haupttext* or cover it minimally. Furthermore, any lecture notes are used only for the sake of illustration of or elaboration on a point made in the *Haupttext*. Thus while the *Zusätze* should not be neglected, one must be very careful in making use of them to interpret

Hegel. One must always allow Hegel's published material to have the final word, and when a *Zusatz* makes a point on which his published material is silent, one must discount what is said in the *Zusatz* accordingly. The only writing of unimpeachable authenticity therefore are the twenty-five paragraphs and their occasional remarks that constitute the *Encyclopedia*'s anthropology "in outline."

I have found that I could not substantially improve on Petry's authoritative translation of the anthropology, and so unless otherwise indicated I use it throughout the book. However, even as I use it I will render *Begriff* as "concept" (rather than "Notion" as Petry does) in order to preserve a closer etymological connection (as *greifen* and *capere* both mean "to grasp"). I will also avoid capitalizing Hegel's technical terms (like "idea" or "concept"). Hegel only capitalized these because all nouns in German are capitalized. Capitalizing them in English can remind the reader that the term means something special for Hegel, but I prefer to accomplish this through an explanation of such terms and proceeding with the normal style in English. Finally, I will render *Selbstgefühl* as "self-feeling" rather than "self-awareness," as Petry does, first because this preserves the connection between self-feeling and other forms of the feeling soul; second, though it has an important role to play, *Selbstgefühl* is in an important sense a perversion of spirit—not just an abstract, early stage, but a disease spirit sinks into—"self-awareness" sounds too innocuous to convey this. I have preserved Petry's use of boldface to show text added in the second or third editions of the *Encyclopedia*. For all of Hegel's texts, where numbers for section or paragraph (§) are given, I will cite them. And since these are usually more precise and hence preferable, I will use them as well in citing the *Phänomenologie des Geistes*: these are not given in the German, but they are familiar among Anglophone readers of Hegel from A. V. Miller's translation (published by Oxford University Press) of the *Phänomenologie*. I will refer to Hegel's works using the abbreviations given following this introduction. For those *Zusätze* that span several pages, I have also given the page number.

Abbreviations

EPW   *Enzyklopädie der philosophischen Wissenschaften im Grundrisse* (1830)

GPR   *Grundlinien der Philosophie des Rechts*

PG   *Phänomenologie des Geistes*

VA   *Vorlesungen über die Äesthetik*

VPG   *Vorlesungen über die Philosophie des Geistes*

VPGes *Vorlesungen über die Philosophie der Geschichte*

VPR   *Vorlesungen über die Philosophie der Religion*

WL   *Wissenschaft der Logik*

A   *Anmerkung*

Z   *Zusatz*

1

That the Term "Body" Is Equivocal

[T]he external human form is alone capable of revealing the spiritual in a sensuous way. The human expression in face, eyes, posture and air is material and in these is not what spirit is; but within this corporeality itself the human exterior is not only living and natural, as the animal is, but is the bodily presence which in itself mirrors spirit. Through the eye we look into a man's soul, just as his spiritual character is expressed by his whole demeanor in general. If therefore the bodily presence belongs to spirit as *its* existence, spirit belongs to the body as the body's inner being and is not an inwardness foreign to the external shape, so that the material aspect neither has in itself, nor hints at, some other meaning. The human form does carry in itself much of the general animal type, but the whole difference between the human and the animal body consists solely in this, that the human body in its whole demeanor evinces itself as the dwelling-place of spirit in nature.

—Hegel, *Hegel's Aesthetics: Lectures on Fine Art*

In this chapter I analyze the different forms of embodiment according to Hegel: mechanical, chemical, biological, and anthropological (or human, ensouled). I show how these constitute a series of ascending complexity such that higher determinations a body may possess limit the applicability of its lower determinations. I use the metaphor of dimensions, since higher spatial dimensions contain lower ones, but dramatically change how they must be understood. Thus while a human being retains mechanical, chemical, and biological determinations (being extended, chemically reactive, and needing to consume and respire), not only can the human not be adequately understood through those concepts, but also, the meaning of a biological determination such as consumption changes with the addition of anthropological embodiment. I also give a preliminary sketch of human embodiment as involving the soul's ability to distinguish itself from its body and from corporeity generally, and to create for itself a form of mediation (or a "body") between itself and its object, thereby liberating itself (at least somewhat) from those forms of mediation given by nature. This chapter is meant to show that embodiment is not univocal, that there are different sorts or grades of natural bodies, and also a body that belongs to "spirit," that is, human subjectivity, or what is distinctively human.

The Essence of Embodiment

That bodies are essentially extension, that is, divisibility, constitution by multiple parts, occupation of distinct but contiguous spaces, is a thesis with a long history. One should be wary of being too cavalier in rejecting such an ancient and enduring position. Certainly, it would be foolish to deny that all bodies are extended (as Kant said, extension belongs analytically to the concept of a body[1]), and Hegel does not deny it. But holding that extension belongs to all bodies, even that extension *necessarily* belongs to all bodies (both of which Hegel would accept) is not the same as holding that extension is the *essence* of a body. It is only the latter point that Hegel rejects. It would be worthwhile however to elaborate on this position before examining why Hegel's rejects it.

One might offer the following justification for the thesis that extension is the essence of embodiment. Bodies seem to be of infinite variety. They vary in color, texture, weight, shape, density, and tensile strength. They also vary in the sounds they make when they collide, the temperature at which they melt, and whether or to what extent they conduct electricity. Furthermore, bodies vary insofar as some have life, some had life but lost it, and some appear presently, formerly, and in perpetuity incapable of life. However, one must not allow oneself to be overwhelmed by this variety. By finding order in it, one can see which properties are more basic, and which are derivative of these basic properties. The most basic property or properties, those inseparability from embodiment as such, will be the essence of embodiment.

For example, consider the sonorousness of bodies, their ability to make distinct sounds when they collide with other bodies. Might this be one of the more basic properties of embodiment? Might it even be the essence of embodiment? If so, it should be immediately linked with embodiment as such, so that anything corporeal must be sonorous, and anything sonorous must be corporeal. But that is clearly not the case. Some bodies are so soft that they make no discernable sound when colliding with another body. More importantly, sonorousness seems to presuppose other properties, like a certain shape and cohesion of parts in bodies, as well as the ability of bodies to be put into motion. Without these latter properties, sonorousness would not be impossible. This would indicate that shape, cohesion, and mobility are *more basic* properties of bodies than sonorousness.

Is shape then the essence of embodiment? It would seem that all bodies have a shape. But shape still presupposes another property "intervening" as it were between it and embodiment: namely, extension, insofar as to have a shape is only to be extended in a certain way (i.e., shape is a mode of extension). Indeed, color, texture, density, conductivity, even life, all seem to be properties a body can have only insofar as it is extended. Extension on the other hand is not something a body has only insofar as it has some other property, but rather simply insofar as it is a body. And, it appears that properties that are not reducible to extension, for instance, deductive validity, are not properties of bodies at all. In other words, extension seems to be the *essence* of corporeity.

Hegel would argue however that while it is true that all bodies are extended, extension is not the essence of embodiment, if "essence" is taken as it is in the preceding discussion, such that all other properties of bodies would have to be modes reducible to extension. There are other ways of being corporeal besides being extended. These "other ways" (what I called the other "forms of embodiment") are not simply properties *specifying* extension (as are, e.g., movement, speed, acceleration). Nor do these other ways of being corporeal exist "alongside" a body's extension, endowing the body with certain other properties that are unrelated to and do not affect those properties following from the body's extension. Rather, these other forms of embodiment qualify and determine the meaning and applicability of the concept of extension to a body. Thus although extension belongs to each body, the concept of extension, taken by itself, gives a very poor understanding of what embodiment is, and for that reason should not be thought of as the "essence" of embodiment.

Bodies can take forms that are: (1) extended or mechanical; (2) chemical; (3) biological; or (4) anthropological.[2] One can also call these "dimensions" of embodiment because, like spatial dimensions, each supersedes the previous one, containing it, but also making it more complex, enriching it, and changing how it must be understood. These dimensions of embodiment are listed in ascending complexity, such that for example while all bodies are extended, some are also chemical; and of these chemical bodies, some are also biological; and of these biological bodies, some are anthropological, or have souls.[3] The use of the word "also" in the last sentence would be misleading however if it were taken to mean that, for example, a body's humanness is internally unrelated to its biology, its chemical nature, or its extension.

Thus while one and the same body can "have" many of the dimensions listed, understanding such a body requires not only knowing the various ways in which it is corporeal but also how its higher dimensions of embodiment necessitate the reinterpretation of the lower ones. For example, the living body of a plant or animal is extended and does bear certain mechanical relations to other bodies, and it does have some definite chemical composition. However, it can only be adequately understood by understanding it biologically, as a living body, and understanding how its extension and chemical structure (and what follow from these, e.g., its movement and its interaction with oxygen and carbon dioxide) must be conceived in light of its life.[4] Thus we understand the plant correctly only when we see that it performs a mechanical act like movement (turning toward the light), or displays chemical properties (taking in carbon dioxide to release energy stored in carbohydrate form) *for the sake of* better fulfilling its vital drives. Likewise, there remains something mechanical, chemical, and biological about the human body, but the human body can only be properly understood as an *ensouled* body whose mechanical, chemical, and biological dimensions are not comparable to those of bodies limited to any of these.

Thus if there is an essence of embodiment,[5] it is not the lowest dimension, extension, because it gives too poor an idea of what bodies are or can be. Analogously, a (one-dimensional) line or ray does not give an adequate picture of what space is. Yet the essence of embodiment also cannot be the highest determination (having a soul) because then most bodies would not even have the essence proper to them. Nor, of course, could it be an intermediate determination insofar as these are relatively both "higher" and "lower," and so would have both of the problems given here. Instead, according to Hegel the essence of embodiment, what belongs to a body simply because it is a body, is "*externality* [Äußerlichkeit]."[6] This "externality" must be understood not simply as a body's externality to other bodies, but a body's externality to *itself*.

The idea of such "self-externality" may seem initially to be utterly incoherent. After all, externality involves separation, and how can something be separated from itself? As is so often the case with Hegel, there is no one place in his work to which a reader can turn for an easy answer, because there is no one place where he gives a clear and exhaustive explanation of what "self-externality" is. However, a close reading of the way he treats embodiment throughout his *Philosophy of Nature* and the anthropology section of the *Philosophy of Spirit* (the results of which will be outlined in this and subsequent chapters) shows that "self" here means "principle of identity." Thus to be "self-external," as Hegel thinks all bodies are, is to have the principle of one's identity "outside" of oneself in some sense.

One might allege that this explanation hardly renders the term "self-externality" coherent. If the principle of X's identity (let us call it Y) is "external" to X, in virtue of what exactly would anyone call Y the principle of X's identity? It is impossible to answer this question in the way it is stated, that is, by lumping all bodies together in one class and denoting them each by the same letter X. That is, it is impossible to say why the principle of a certain body's identity is what it is (and why it is external to the body in question) without knowing which body is under investigation. Without further ado, let us proceed therefore to examine these dimensions of embodiment in turn, beginning with the lowest.

Dimensions of Embodiment

A preliminary note: in this exposition bodies will be designated according to their highest dimension. Thus when I refer to "extended bodies" I am referring to bodies that are determined by *mechanism alone*; and when I refer to, say, organic bodies, I am referring to bodies that are determined biologically, though this should not be taken to negate the fact that such a living body is still *also* extended (determined mechanically) and chemical. The following account will make clear how bodies can be determined according to different "dimensions of embodiment" as I have called them.

An extended body is simply one that takes up space. The identity of such a body lies in its extension, and, posterior to its extension, its figure, and (possibility of) local motion. In other words, to be such a body is first of all have a certain length, width, and depth. That the spatial dimensions of a body are certain means that the body has a determinate figure. A consequence to the occupation of a determinate space is the necessary expulsion of other bodies from the space occupied by the body in question (i.e., the putting of other bodies into *motion* through contact with them or being so put into motion).

What then is the mechanical body "in itself," that is, what is its self, the principle of its identity? Answering this question requires stripping away the inessentials of the thing, leaving only that which makes the thing what it is. Consider for example a body exhausted by mechanical determinations: the gear of a clock. Imagine you have disassembled a clock and, like Descartes with his wax, you have picked up one gear and are examining it, turning it over in your hand and asking yourself, "What *is* this thing?" You may first answer that it *is* gray, hard, and smooth. Yet while these sensible properties inhere in the thing, they are not the thing itself. These are the inessentials that we must strip away in thought to get at the thing itself. The thing itself is what underlies and supports these properties, the substance. In other words, the self of the thing is extension: that is, the gear's self is the space that it takes up.[7] The extension of the gear (what the gear *is* most fundamentally) is what allows the gear to *be* what it is in a derivative sense (i.e., to be its predicates: gray, hard, and smooth).

But there is a problem in making occupation of space the criterion of a thing's identity. To take up space means only to be present at different points, that is, to take up different discrete spaces. Thus the self of the gear would be divided into infinitely many selves, as the gear itself can be infinitely divided with respect to space.[8] One might respond however that the self of the gear is its precise figure, thus determining it as having certain limits: extending in diameter one inch, being present in this whole inch, but no farther. But again, defining the thing's identity in this way raises a new problem. For a thing to be limited is only for it to have a relation to that which is *not* itself. Again, the self of the gear has multiplied: it is "in," or it simply *is* these dimensions (these are what make the body what it is, and not something else), but it is also outside of these dimensions, insofar as its spatial determination makes its relation to its other (i.e., that which lies beyond its limit) not incidental to its identity but rather necessarily constitutive of it.

The mechanical body appears doomed to be separated from the principle of its own identity, to be "self-external" as Hegel says. This body is not to blame for this condition: it is not that it failed somehow to live up to the standards for being extended. In fact, the self-externality in question is a consequence not of any defect in this gear in particular but of the concept of extension itself. Thus no extended body qua extended body can ever seize the principle of its identity: if the gear (or any mechanical body) were to "try" to overcome this self-externality, coming into contact with the other that determines it in its identity, it instead would *repel* that other.[9]

That the concept of mechanism makes the criterion of a body's identity something that the extended body as such can never possess is an example of the infamous Hegelian dialectic, which proceeds by "contradictions." The "contradiction" here (between how the concept of mechanism would make occupation of space the criterion for identity, and how occupation of space actually deprives any extended body of the principle of its identity) is not one that renders both terms null, as contradictions are usually understood. Rather, the emergence of this conflict within the concept of mechanism is implicitly the emergence of a new criterion of a body's identity. This new criterion is realized in the chemical, which lives up to what the mechanical body *ought* to have been according to its concept but failed to be: namely, a body for which spatial extension and separateness is no barrier to its identity. Chemicals are determined in their identity by other chemicals, with respect to which they are polar; and in bonding, each chemical unites with the "self" that was external to it, forming a new substance.[10]

The upshot is that Hegel's analysis of mechanical bodies shows this concept to be of only limited value in understanding embodiment. This concept seemed to give us the simplest, least problematic account of embodiment, defining it by its dimensions and figure. An extended body seemed completely self-contained, substantial in its own self, having no necessary relation to any external object. However, analysis of the concept of mechanism showed that such a body's identity is *nothing but* relation to other bodies that limit the body, thereby constituting its identity, such that embodiment is better understood through the concept of the chemical.

The chemical has a superior concept for understanding embodiment because unlike the merely mechanical body, the chemical is able to *seize* (rather than repel) the other that determines it in *chemical bonding*, wherein two chemicals that are polar relative to each other combine to form a new substance.[11] This new substance is *neutral*, at least relative to the polarity that determined its constituents: this *neutrality* constitutes the identity of the chemical, just as dimension and figure constituted the identity of the extended body. Thus the chemical is *in fact* what the mechanical body only strives to be, namely, a body for which the privation of its own self by a spatial separation is nothing it cannot overcome.

Yet when one recognizes that the character of this "self" has changed, that the criterion of selfhood is here no longer (spatial) extension and figure but rather chemical neutrality, it becomes clear that the chemical *still* has its own self outside of it, insofar as though the new substance is neutral relative to its constituents, it is *still* polar relative to *another* chemical.[12] Moreover, no matter how many combinations and dissolutions a chemical undergoes, it remains merely *relatively* neutral (i.e., neutral relative only to its constituent chemicals): the prospect of *absolute* neutrality (i.e., nonpolarity) is only ever a phantom for the chemical, never actually achievable.[13] Since in combination a chemical fails to enter on possession of itself (achieving not neutrality but only yet another version of polarity), one could say (were one to speak metaphorically) that even in its bonding, the chemical sees its own self recede from its grasp at the very moment when it would take possession of it. Indeed, such independence is impossible on the chemical level: that is, on a chemical level a body simply cannot *be itself*.

This failure of the chemical indicates the dissolution not only of a certain chemical compound but of the very concept of chemical relations.[14] The coherence of this concept depends on the possibility of reaching some point at which a chemical is simply *itself*, and not constantly at risk of being converted into something completely different by interaction with another body (which had always been covertly determining the first). However, that condition *in principle* cannot be achieved—at least not on chemical terms. The concept of the chemical thus has at its heart a contradiction just as the concept of mechanism did. And here again, the emergence of this contradiction is also the emergence of a new criterion of a body's identity: a form of embodiment is required in which the "thing" in question maintains its identity with itself throughout indefinite chemical combination and dissolution. The chemical cannot satisfy this requirement, but the living body can.

Because the living body is able to maintain its identity throughout chemical combination and dissolution, it is *in fact* what the chemical only strives to be, just as the chemical is in fact what the mechanical body only strives to be. The living body is a system of processes that maintains itself throughout the combination and dissolution of chemicals that constitutes its intercourse with nature (consumption, respiration, etc.).[15] The animal (and likewise the plant) is not strictly speaking a material thing but rather the constant consumption of matter, and the transformation of this matter into energy for the continuation of the same assimilative processes.[16] The animal *appears* to be simply an extended, material thing only because instead of transforming the objects of its consumption directly into energy, it transforms them first into the material of its own organic body: muscle, fat, and so on. This organic matter is however only something transitory, which will later be transformed into energy for the continuation of the animal's life—and it is this *life* of the animal that really constitutes its identity.[17]

Yet even in its transcendence of chemical relations, life remains determined by an opposition, and to that extent it remains merely natural. Biological life is power over nature insofar as it is the constant consumption of nature and the constant transformation of nature into energy for the processes that both *are* this life and *maintain* this life. But though biological life depends on the prior presence of nature as the material for its vital activity, this form of life is not in a position to become aware of its dependence and one-sidedness. As a result, the animal's and the plant's power over nature is defeated from the beginning: it never experiences nature as meaningful and so is never at home in nature, any more than a despot is at home among those he dominates. To be sure, the features of its environment *matter* for the living thing and are experienced as means for the achievement of the living thing's own ends, but if we restrict the term "meaning" to the significance nature can have above and beyond being a resource for life (to be used up and destroyed for the sake of something else), then biological life lacks a way to recognize any meaning in nature, since it cannot see nature except through its own vital drives.[18]

Before illustrating the difference between the biological and the anthropological, however, I must note that while what I describe can be empirically observed in human and animal behavior, it might easily escape observers who do not bring with them the proper concepts for understanding and interpreting different kinds of embodied life. In what follows I aim to isolate and elaborate upon the principles governing what makes one experience biological and another anthropological, leaving out all of the details not pertaining to this distinction. This focus will sharpen the distinction between human and animal life, and though a case of immediate observation may not present these differences so starkly, as a way to highlight the different principles involved this description is accurate on its own terms.

Furthermore, because human beings are biological as well as anthropological, human experiences are more complex, ambiguous, and difficult to understand than animal ones. In analyzing human experience, I am depicting human experience *as such*, that is, in its humanity. This should not be taken to mean that in *all* human experiences this anthropological richness must be immediately apparent to everyone. That, properly speaking, human consumption is about more than just assimilating nutrients for the continuation of biological life (that it may be about sharing food with family and friends, providing an opportunity for social exchange) does not mean that we do not sometimes eat alone, or that we are never so hungry that the act of eating is so ravenous that an observer might be at pains to distinguish it from animal consumption. It means only that in these cases eating is not executed in a way that makes apparent its properly human meaning, though the eater is not thereby stripped of his or her humanity, just as being blown over by the wind (to which one is susceptible simply by being extended) does not reduce one to a merely mechanical object. Accordingly, there is a normative aspect to this account insofar as human experience proper is anthropological and not merely biological or mechanical. In later chapters we will have occasion to examine the ethical side of this, and how a human being should, given the right external circumstances, eat, walk, and love in a human way rather than a merely animal way. Here however, I intend only to show how what can deceptively present itself as one phenomenon (desire) is experienced biologically, in some cases, and anthropologically in others.

To see how the animal has a limitation humans do not have, reflect on the animal's feeling of desire.[19] As animal life is the assimilation of nature (as, e.g., through consumption), animal desire is the feeling in the animal that a part of nature is only *apparently* independent but in truth is the animal's own self. For example, a cow in a field does not apprehend the grass as something objective, having its own independent existence. Rather, the cow apprehends the grass as its own bovine self, which however inexplicably has the appearance of something external. Obviously, the cow does not apprehend the grass as itself by seeing the colors marking its own exterior, as well as its horns, snout, ears, and so forth, in the grass. Rather, the cow apprehends the grass as something answering a lack that it feels acutely and thus as something that *ought* to be brought into itself. This is the feeling of desire, according to Hegel. In accordance with this feeling, the cow without hesitation consumes the grass, destroying its appearance of independence and transforming the grass *in fact* into what it always was *essentially* (viz., the cow's own self).[20] The cow does not wonder at the fortuitousness of the presence of its food in nature because it does not begin to grasp nature as anything other than a resource for life.

That the animal is unaware of and cannot be reconciled with nature's ultimate indifference to life means that the animal never confronts its own mortality. Hegel argues that the germ of death is always contained within life because vital assimilative processes stand external to the material they assimilate: they do not generate their own content, as "spirit" or human subjectivity does,[21] and as a result, one organ can always begin to operate at variance with the biological processes of the whole animal.[22] In contrast, being human involves being able to experience nature apart from vital drives, and consequently being able to appreciate (nonbiological or suprabiological) meaning in nature. Thus not only does nature's meaningfulness for us not preclude nature's foreignness to us and our needs: the presence of meaning in the human sense requires this indifference. The significance nature has for an animal (insofar as some things are recognized as conducive, others as harmful to life according to given instincts) is strictly biological, whereas the deeper meaning the corporeal world can have for us involves experiencing it outside the bounds of our biology.

No matter what kind, all bodies have the principle of their identity outside of themselves, but neither a merely extended object like the gear of a clock, nor a chemical, nor even an animal *knows* this (though animals do *feel* it). The human being in contrast is able to grasp that its own self appears to it as something external. This knowledge of oneself in the other (in what is not oneself), but in such a way that the foreignness of the appearance is not destroyed, is one formula for expressing what Hegel means by "spirit," that which is distinctively human. This "being with oneself in the other" can also be seen in love, which Hegel sometimes equates with spirit. In contrast with love, possessiveness or lust (which is more like animal desire) means seeking to make oneself whole again by undermining the jarring appearance of oneself as something external: the animal feels itself outside of it but cannot bear the tension. In love however, the human being shows the ability to endure this loss or alienation of itself in its other because the human self is one that incorporates difference within it: it is other to itself, so that it spans the gap between itself and another without collapsing from this tension. The endurance of this tension is what Hegel calls in the preface to the Jena *Phenomenology of Spirit* "tarrying with the negative," that is, "holding fast to death," "enduring" it, "not averting one's gaze," but instead "looking death in the face."[23]

In other words, we differ from animals insofar as we may be confronted by our own impending deaths: this destiny enters into our consciousness and greatly alters how we experience the world by showing it to us as something not ultimately devoted to maintaining life and pointing us toward something beyond mere life. The influence our knowledge of death has on our experience allows us, in contrast to mere animals, to be reconciled with death, incorporating it into life such that for us death is not the annihilation of life because the properly human life is always already in the shadow of death. Of course, to say that our life is not defeated by death is not to say that we live biologically forever.[24] Insofar as the human being is also biological, it is subject to biological death just as the animal is, but what is human in our life is always beyond the opposition of life and death that defines animal life. Subsequent chapters will explore the unique character of human embodiment at length, but its difference from biological embodiment can be intimated by considering the difference between human and animal desire.

Often human desire can seem not to differ greatly from animal desire, but there is a dimension that can (and probably to a certain extent always is) involved in human experience that is impossible for mere animal life. The animal experiences the world through the medium of its natural body and naturally given instincts:[25] the field mouse can be aroused by a nearby potential mate and the prospect of reproduction, at the same time that it is aroused by the smell of food in the other direction and is stimulated by the fear of being exposed to predators whenever it is in the open. Three competing desires arise in the mouse: sexual desire, desire for food, and desire for safety. Yet all of these are but three different expressions of one and the same vital drive: to safeguard and promote the life that animates it long enough to reproduce this life as much as possible. The mouse's desires appear as three and not one only because this single drive relates to various objects in its environment differently. The mouse is not presented with a tragic choice of satisfying the demands of life by risking death, but it rather always acts for the sake of its own dominating end, promotion of life. If the mouse ends up fleeing from the mate and the food, scurrying back to safety, it is only because the one vital drive was stimulated the most strongly (a quantitative difference) by the sensed danger rather than the enticing prospects of food and sex. The mouse is not the least bit removed from its body and instincts: it is so thoroughly immersed in these media by which the world is presented to it that it could never conceive of any other possibility.

In contrast, our desires are not only varying degrees of intensity of one and the same drive. Thus for us, there may be no way given by nature to resolve conflict between competing desires. Discussion in ethics often focuses on why we should not act on desires we already suspect are bad, like murder, theft, lying, and so on. But negotiating the field of our desires is more mundane and more complicated than resolving the familiar ethical problems posed by clearly vicious acts. And humanity prevents us from responding as animals do: when deciding whether to marry or not, to have two children or three, to visit a friend or stay home and read, biological drives provide scant help. Grand ethical theories of modernity like Kantian ethics and utilitarianism promise to sort out even questions like these, but whether they succeed or not, these situations involve weighing social customs, family traditions, interpersonal obligations, and authenticity to one's chosen identity—none of which are present in the merely biological form of embodiment.[26]

Because we know nature's fundamental indifference to our needs, forms of interpretation and meaning-bestowal proliferate in our lives and cultures. In the field of anthropology it has long been known that the emergence of human culture was not the effect of biological changes following evolutionary-biological patterns. Rather, it is the reverse: the precise biological form of the human being (the well-developed forebrain and the neocortex that sets us apart physiologically from other primates) were *the effect* of the adoption of the symbolic systems and social organization characterizing culture.[27] The precise path our development has taken (as acculturation leads to biological changes that in turn reaffirm the centrality of culture to human life) leads also to an "information gap"[28] between what our enduring instincts impel us to do and what we need to know to actually carry it out (for which we rely on culture), making reliance on biological determination of our behavior impossible. For instance, our biological constitution compels us to eat, and to flee danger, but our biology does not provide a method of eating or fleeing: this gap must be filled in by culture.[29]

Accordingly, we can—indeed, we cannot help but—place some distance between ourselves and the object of our desire, and between ourselves and our desire. And there is neither a rule determining how we must interpret nor a limit to how many ways we may interpret what happens around us: we can feel something as at once intensely pleasant though socially frowned upon and professionally imprudent, even as it is politically obligatory (vehemently calling out racism in a powerful colleague for example). The social forms we have fashioned for ourselves, and through which we feel our world (e.g., the sounds coming out of our colleague's mouth) are independent of what our biological makeup would have us feel as pleasant and appropriate, or painful and uncomfortable.

To take another example, whereas an animal consumes nature when it is seized by a desire to do so, such that once the desire ceases to animate the animal, the erstwhile object of its desire vanishes from the animal's attention, for us nature can mean something regardless of how it relates to us biologically. If I eat until I am sated, what remains of my food is still *something* for me, not just colors in a certain pattern: it can be a warning against gluttony, the subject of a painting, one factor in a commercial calculation, among others. Likewise, an oncoming flood, a crashing avalanche, a sudden earthquake all portend grave danger when interpreted biologically. Yet each of these can be the object of sublime admiration. Perhaps in none of these cases will I consciously reflect on my mortality, but I am reflecting on the inexhaustible and multifarious ways that nature can appear to me, and this way of relating to nature is possible only by suspending the reduction of nature to what helps and harms my vital drive and recognizing it as something whose meaning is not confined to how much it hurts or helps me. To recognize nature as independent of our biological processes is to implicitly recognize the ever-present possibility of organic dysfunction and death. This abiding with death is necessary for nature to appear to us as meaningful beyond utilitarian calculation.

Thus for Hegel, the human condition can be described equally well as enduring the loss of self and as knowing death. If "death" is taken in a broad, metaphorical sense as including not only the cessation of organic processes but generally any corruption, decay, dissolution, or loss of identity on the part of a body, it would appear that all bodies are by nature subject to death. Recall, it is the essence of all bodies to be "self-external," and so to be subject to precisely the kinds of degeneration listed earlier. At its most primitive level, to be corporeal means to be extended; and to be extended means only to be divisible,[30] to be capable of being sundered, and "dying" in that sense. But in a deeper sense, all bodies are subject to "death" since anything corporeal, insofar as it is a body, is not in possession of its own self, the principle of its identity.

Not everyone is troubled by this. For a naturalist like Epicurus (for whom a person is simply a body, and no soul) "death is nothing to us,"[31] insofar as death is the destruction of the body and what no longer exists cannot suffer. Of course, one can suffer pain from, say, an injury, but pain is not death. Even if the injury were exacerbated to the point of death, one would still feel pain only insofar as one is alive. With the arrival of death the body is destroyed, and pain loses the condition for its existence. Death itself, the very destruction of the body, is therefore (according to Epicurus) that which most assuredly escapes our knowledge.

It is true that *biological* death cannot be experienced in a biological way. Yet both Plato and Hegel would respond to Epicurus by noting that if there were a body that had a notion of death, a body for whom death was not nothing, then ipso facto such a body would not be *merely* a body: it would be a body with a *soul*. For Plato, death is not simply the destruction of the body but is taken more broadly as denoting the separation (in some sense) of the body and the soul,[32] or the emergence of the soul in its own right; philosophy is "practicing death"[33] because philosophy is the soul's communion with immaterial forms and thus is the expression of the soul's transcendence (in some sense) of the body. Seen in this context, it is clear that Epicurus's position that death is nothing to us, that it is beyond our capacity to experience the separation of the soul from the body, is nothing short of a denial of the possibility of (Platonic) philosophy. Epicurus would deny the possibility of philosophy because philosophy would be *the experience of death*—not the physiological sensation of the cessation of one's own metabolic processes (death in the biological sense), but still the experience of the limitations of the body (insofar as it is something biological) and hence the transcendence of these limits. However, it is this metaphorical experience of death (i.e., the activity of philosophy, self-knowledge) that constitutes the human vocation, both for Plato and for Hegel (though they understand this in very different ways).[34]

Moreover, the experience of death (understood in this metaphorical way as an experience of the limitations of organic embodiment) is the same as what was referred to earlier as the endurance of the loss of self. Recall, all bodies are determined from without in different ways, and for that reason nothing corporeal, insofar as it is corporeal, is in possession of that which gives it its identity, that is, is not in possession of its own self. Each body however is impelled to unite with that which is essentially its own self but factually external in order to be in possession of its own self, or to be the principle of its own identity. Yet all merely natural bodies fail in this endeavor. A mechanical body, for instance, repels the external body determining it, thereby ensuring its continued spatial exile from its own self. Similarly, every time a chemical bonds with its polar opposite and by this means achieves a qualified neutrality, it at the same time displaces the principle of its identity into yet another external chemical, with respect to which it is thenceforth polar. Most unfortunately of all, the animal fails to come to grips with the fact that it is wholly dependent on external nature to furnish it with material on which its assimilative processes may work. The human being alone is capable of experiencing the externality of its self to itself, and to *endure* this externality through the knowledge that it belongs to human nature to be self-differentiating in this way. Such an experience would mean knowing oneself as beyond one's merely animal body, transcending the conditions of organic embodiment. It would be to know oneself as soul, to initiate the separation of the soul from the (biological) body and thus to "practice death" in a sense analogous to the Platonic sense.[35]

Epicurus is therefore correct only in that for a *mere* body, one without a soul—that is, for a nonhuman body—death would be nothing. I am not claiming that the human being "transcends the conditions of organic embodiment" by continuing to have physiological sensation when biological death has set in. I am claiming only that humans can experience themselves and the world in a way independent of biological exigencies: this is precisely what it is to live *as* a human. This can be accomplished in many ways. For instance, objects in nature that do not answer to a biologically given instinct on the part of the animal escape the animal's experience, that is, are "nothing" for the animal. Yet because the human being is not limited to such a biological way of experiencing the world (or, because the human being transcends animal embodiment), biologically insignificant nature can still be "something" for the human being. To take another example, the feeling of love (as opposed to bestial lust), as described previously, similarly constitutes the transcendence of embodiment in its animal dimension. In love, the human being knows that its own self exists external to it, in another person. The animal would no more be able to endure this loss of self than it could endure having its own heart beating in the chest of another animal.

The Materiality of the Soul

The human self, the soul, is by its nature an object for itself, knowing itself as other to itself. In the soul's transcendence of the animalistic dimension of embodiment, which is at once philosophical self-knowledge and a metaphorical "death," the soul knows that its appearance to itself as something other is not an experience that violates its identity, but rather one that reveals it as that which is an object for itself. Indeed, a human life is precisely a life lived in acknowledgment of and meditation on the externality of oneself to oneself. That is, a human life is lived in what is from the perspective of what is merely natural, *death*, the loss of self.[36] All bodies suffer a kind of death, this externality of their selves to themselves: but for the human being, the soul, this self-externality involves no "contradiction." That is, in the case of the human, its self-externality does not undermine what it is supposed to be according to its essence (or concept, as Hegel says). In contrast, the mechanical body's very spatiality deprives it of the principle of its identity, just as the chemical's specious neutrality deprives it of the principle of its identity, and the animal's very assimilation of nature underscores the animal's dependence on nature. The human being in contrast is able to *endure* this externality to itself through self-knowledge, thereby being in fact what it is essentially.

The human being has this remarkable status only because it can discern the fractured state of its own selfhood, knowing itself as an other to itself. In other words, the human being can recognize that its self is split, not just in fact but in principle, such that being external to itself (and overcoming this externality by knowing this externality as oneself) is the human condition. Indeed, it is because human nature is to be outside of itself in this way, to be an *object* for itself, that the world generally can appear to humans as meaningful. Far from being alienated from the world, human beings can thus take possession of the world in a way that a mere animal cannot (for want of the ability to tolerate its separation from itself).

The correlate of the human self's identification with externality is the externalization of the human self. The human being is unique according to Hegel in knowing itself as an object. The animal has some sort of self-awareness, but only to the extent that it can dimly recognize that certain parts of external nature (which answer to its instincts) *ought* to be assimilated to its own self. The animal thus suppresses any awareness of its self as an object insofar as whenever in its experience it appears to itself in objectivity (e.g., in the object of desire), the animal annihilates the objectivity of this appearance. That the soul knows itself as an object, and knows this aspect of objectivity to legitimately belong to it, is an indication for Hegel that the soul necessarily has what one might call "a material aspect," insofar as the soul is necessarily absorbed and invested in the material world in which it finds itself. By "soul" Hegel does not therefore mean an immaterial, nebulous awareness floating around objects, knowing them but substantially distinct from them. Instead, the soul for Hegel knows itself *as* objective, *in* the objectivity of the world.

Multidimensional Embodiment

This is only a skeletal sketch of the way human embodiment must be understood, to be fleshed out in the rest of the book. It is worth pointing out here however that the foregoing remarks on some differences between animal and human perception is an example of how the applicability of a "lower" (biological) dimension of embodiment is qualified by the presence of a "higher" (anthropological) dimension. One should thus not be misled by the *biological* similarities between, say, a human eye and a cow's eye. A human eye is an organ determined anthropologically, which means it is set free from the exigencies of life, which determine the cow's eye. The human eye experiences (or can experience) the world independently of the vital drives to consume and reproduce the genus, drives in the thrall of which the cow must remain. Similarly, one should not take the fact that the human body does indeed have some chemical composition (as shown, e.g., in flesh's reaction with hydrogen sulfate), or that the human body does have definite spatial dimensions to mean that the human body is just a mix of chemicals, or that it is mere extension. Nor, for that matter, should one believe that the only thing distinguishing a human being from an animal is some specific biological property (such as a larger brain) possessed by humans but not by other animals, or that the only thing distinguishing a human *or* an animal from a stone is the human's or animal's possession of ways of being extended not shared by the stone.

To take another example, consider how "movement" is an equivocal term, referring possibly to a *mechanical event*, or to, say, a *teleological act* on the part of an animal. To be sure, for a living being there can also be a kind of "movement" that is merely mechanical: for example, if a coyote limps, dragging its wounded leg along with it, the wounded leg qua moved object has a merely mechanical relation to the healthy, living body that moves it. Animal movement proper on the other hand is self-movement insofar as the principle of movement comes (in a nonincidental way) from within the very body that is to be moved. This self-movement is what the animal displays when it walks, swims, or flies, in order to satisfy its desire.

Self-movement is traditionally considered a sign of freedom, and while the self-movement that the animal displays when it sets itself in motion in order to satisfy an appetite is not a free act in the strongest sense of the term (since it does not display properly human freedom, which is not impelled by vital drives), nor is it merely mechanical movement. Imagine a coyote sees a hare foraging in the brush: this sight arouses the coyote's instinct, and to that extent determines the coyote to act.[37] The coyote merely *reacts* to the presence of the desired object, and so does not engage in a free act in the strongest sense. Yet the coyote's movement, crouching and stalking the hare, is not a movement toward a mechanical force pulling it (as, e.g., an engine mechanically pulls a train). The hare affects the coyote only by being present and answering a desire already within the coyote,[38] and the presence of this desire is distinctively *biological* and not mechanical, though for all its purposive behavior, the coyote remains an extended object subject to physical forces.[39]

Mechanical relations involve two terms, each of which is and remains simply external to the other.[40] The coyote's desire however indicates that the hare is not ultimately something separate from or opposed to the coyote. The hare appears external to the coyote and so *seems* to be so opposed, but the coyote's consumption of the hare, its factual transformation of the hare into the coyote's own self, is the explicit proof for the fact (of which the desire is already implicit proof) that the hare was always essentially the coyote's own self. Thus in time, the coyote shows itself to be in possession even of the *occasion* of its own movement.[41] Therefore the two terms (the coyote and the hare) do not remain separate before, during, and after the establishment of the relationship (as would be the case were the relationship merely mechanical, such as the relation between the parts of a clock, or the engine and its train). The coyote's consumption of the hare is not merely the alteration of the position or velocity of the hare, as might happen in a merely mechanical exchange. Here in contrast, the hare is *destroyed* (insofar as it is independent) and transformed into a part of the coyote's own self. The two terms (coyote and hare) become one as the coyote transforms the hare into itself.[42]

The animal body thus transcends mere mechanism insofar as its movement toward its food, spurred by appetite, is not a mechanical movement. Moreover, even the animal's susceptibility to mechanical movement is qualified insofar as the animal will resist any imposed mechanical obstacles to move toward its desired object. Animal movement, and everything belonging to it as such (hunger, consumption, and satiety for example) are possibilities unique to biological bodies (including human bodies). Merely mechanical bodies (gears and billiard balls, for example) are unable to consume. Nor can they feel hunger or satiety—these cannot be the cause for their movement or their lack of movement.

Someone might object that a machine can be nourished (by fuel or electricity) and can seek this nourishment (if programmed to do so). Consider for example a machine whose operation consists in shining a light, and which seeks out electrical outlets to charge its battery in order to continue to shine its light. Such a machine might even construct a new machine out of available parts and thus "reproduce." Yet such a machine would not exhibit teleological action as living things do. The shining of a light and construction of a new machine are not the ends of the machine itself, but the ends of the creator who made its program. The machine does not seek out electricity to achieve its own *telos* but rather to achieve its creator's *telos*: the machine has no *telos* of its own.[43] Alternately, someone might object by likening an animal to a machine rather than a machine to an animal: this objection would allege that our coyote is still in this case simply determined to act mechanically: the movement toward the hare would then be understood not as a purposive act but as the rhythmic tightening and relaxation of certain muscles in the coyote's legs. This tightening and relaxation of the leg muscles would mechanically propel the coyote forward as belts might function to mechanically propel a machine. Moreover, this tightening and relaxation would itself be explained by a prior mechanical cause (perhaps some mechanical event in the coyote's brain that stimulates nerves in the legs, mechanically determining the muscles to tighten and relax in just the right way). Light reflected from the hare on to the coyote's optic nerve (producing in the coyote's brain an image of the hare) would be cited as a mechanical cause for the electrical activity in the brain that in turn stimulates nerves in the legs.[44]

Admittedly, it is possible for an animal body to be moved mechanically in this way and thus to carry out what for an observer would appear to be the same action. The movement of the animal's legs propelling it forward and the movement of its jaws and throat chewing and swallowing the food can possibly be effects of mechanical causes. This account is not in principle impossible, but were it true then the animal would simply not be behaving as an animal. The animal body is indeed extended: as such, it can be divided into parts, and it is possible for these parts to act on each other mechanically in the way described above[45]—but this (viz., that an animal remains extended and can possibly be moved mechanically) is no proof against distinctly *animal, biological* phenomena.

What a mechanist (like Descartes, for example) fails to understand is that while the animal body does remain extended and retains certain mechanical determinations and possibilities, the animal body is not *merely* determined by mechanism, because, as we said, the animal body is not simply material. The mechanist takes the animal body to be a machine, like a complicated clock. However, a machine does not reproduce itself, as an animal does when it consumes food. A clock is composed of material parts, each of which maintains its separate physical integrity throughout its operation. The living body on the other hand is a flux of "parts" (i.e., cells), though one should hesitate to call them that because the name "parts" seems to imply mechanical relations. In this flux the "parts" are constantly coming to be and passing away (as the cells making up the body are produced and perish). What maintains itself in this flux are the functions of the animal, that is, its organic *form*: respiration, circulation of blood, digestion of food, sexual reproduction.[46]

Even if a machine were programmed to mechanically replace damaged parts, this operation would have to be placed into the machine externally, by its creator. In a well-known passage of the *Physics*, Aristotle notes Antiphon's point that a wooden bed, if planted, sends up shoots of *wood* (and not small new beds):[47] thus, Antiphon argues, the nature of a thing is its matter. Aristotle on the other hand argues that the nature is the form: but not the artificial form (of a bed), but the form of the tree of which the wood was the matter. Mechanics, and the rules for artificial construction of bodies based on the concepts of mechanics (whether simple objects like a wooden bed or complex ones like physical-electrical machines) are deceptive in appearing to exhaust the reality of a body, insofar as a complete account of every extended part of a body appears to be a complete account of the body itself. Because we chop up wood and make beds of its pieces, we begin to conceive of the tree itself, though uncreated, as something to be understood along the same lines as artifacts of wooden pieces. What is more, our industrial ingenuity leads us even to think of ourselves as complex mechanical-chemical machines. But just as chopping up an oak to make it into a bed (the totality of the space of which can receive a mechanical explanation) does not destroy its nature as oak, or its ability to act teleologically (sending up an oak shoot), so the Cartesian explanation of the human or animal as a machine (and the consistency of this account by the standards of physics) does not invalidate or render absurd accounts that target the event of movement as *behavior* directed toward an end.

To recognize movement as behavior means not only seeing it as purposive, it means understanding it as something unfolding in time in a way different than the temporality of ateleological movement. The movement of billiard balls across a table can be understood physically by breaking it up into a series of discrete moments, just as the mechanical understanding of the ball itself divides the ball up into its constituent parts. In both of these cases the spatial and temporal parts are understood atomically, as isolated, self-contained units alongside other units that may be identical to them in every way except for occupying a different position in the temporal series or spatial field. But a living body involves organs that are what they are only in relation to other organs and to the whole, and if the behavior is similarly divided into units, each stage in the accomplishment of a goal would be incomprehensible without reference to the goal and the other stages. Thus while it is true that at any given moment the animal is composed of a certain number of physical parts, and that these parts are indeed "material bodies" in a sense, the mere aggregate of these parts is not the animal, and the animal simply cannot be understood by thus freezing it in one moment of time. This freezing of the animal in an instant would reduce the organized system of functions to a collection of bits of matter. Yet the animal is first and foremost the *life* that maintains itself over time by using these cells up, then taking in more matter, transforming it into new cells, and using those up, and so on. A living body is a *process*, not a mere extended *thing*, and this must be borne in mind if it is to be understood. This process and this life must be understood teleologically,[48] and mechanism is precisely the relation and causality that is not teleological. Mechanism is therefore inadequate to understand the living body, even though (as noted) there does remain something mechanical about the living body.

Mechanism is inadequate for understanding the living body because life is not a "property" of extended matter. An animal body is not "alive" in the same way that Descartes's piece of wax is "white" and "hard." To be sure, "white" and "hard" and other such qualities may be the properties of a living body insofar as it is merely extended, and related to other bodies merely mechanically, but not insofar as it is alive, and life does not belong to a body at all insofar as it is merely extended. Rather, life belongs to a higher dimension of embodiment.

If the lowliest of animals such as an amoeba thus cannot be understood as simply an extended body, determined solely by mechanism, then the human body, the body with a soul, is much more distorted by limiting it to mechanical determinations. The human body has the functions of life that are shared with animals and plants, but in addition to these it has *human* sensibilities, reason, thought, language, a will. This should shed new light on the debates that persist in some quarters about whether free will is or is not possible if mechanical causality of bodies is admitted.

When discussing the animal it was important to note that the animal as such is not that in its body which is purely material, but rather it is the organized system of vital functions that inheres in its organic matter. What then is the human being? Clearly, the human being knows itself. Yet, to call the human being a "self-knowing animal" would be inaccurate insofar as this term gives the impression that a human being is generically the same as any other animal, except with the specific difference that it knows itself, or can know itself. Self-knowledge however is not just a capacity of the human being: it is *what the human being is*. The human being is not a "self-knowing animal," because by being self-knowing the human being proves itself to be not a mere animal, not a mere part of nature, but rather to be spirit.[49] Therefore the self that the human being knows (when it knows itself truly and correctly) is not an animal: it is precisely *spirit*, the self-knowing self.

2

The Concept of Spirit

> No light, but rather darkness visible.
>
> —Milton, *Paradise Lost*

The first chapter was devoted to showing that embodiment has many "dimensions" and should not be understood univocally. Accordingly, the place of embodiment in human life, identity, and experience need not be considered reducible to extension (or even to biology). My thesis stated briefly is that human embodiment is not the body *occupied* by spirit but the corporeal existence of spirit itself. The articulation and defense of this claim will be given in chapters 3 through 8. A professional hazard of writing about Hegel is the need (or compulsion) always to give more of the context that must be understood before the main point can be grasped. This context is necessary, but I am mindful of the need to get to the point as well. The purpose of this chapter is to explain what Hegel means by "spirit" (*Geist*), and how the anthropology fits into his philosophy of spirit. This involves a brief examination of key parts of the larger *Encyclopedia of the Philosophical Sciences*. Readers already familiar with the *Encyclopedia* may decide to skim this chapter, or skip it altogether.

The "Idea" and Hegel's "Idealism"

There is no single word in English whose commonly understood definition would express all that Hegel means by *Geist*. In fact, there is no word in

German for what Hegel means either. The only advantage the German speaker has over the English speaker in discerning Hegel's meaning is that Hegel means this term to refer to the human above nature, and *Geist* does convey in German that which is distinctively human as opposed to merely natural: thus as we contrast the natural sciences to the humanities, Germans contrast the *Naturwissenschaften* to the *Geisteswissenschaften*. But *Geist* is not just what is human: it is also what is divine. Usually *Geist* is translated as "spirit" or "mind." I suspect that some prefer "mind" because they feel uncomfortable with the religious or even occult associations the term "spirit" has accreted in popular speech. However, I (along with a great many Hegel scholars) prefer the term "spirit" because it has an appropriately broader range than "mind" does. The English term "spirit" denotes: (1) an individual human being's subjectivity, or some aspect of it; (2) the subjectivity uniting a group of people (as in the common phrases "school spirit" or "team spirit," and the less common "spirit of a people" and "spirit of the time"); (3) God, especially understood as the "Holy Spirit" in Christianity. "Mind" only effectively denotes the first of these, but Hegel means to invoke all three, while articulating a concept that changes and goes beyond the way these are typically understood. Moreover, "mind" is often understood in opposition to the body—especially in philosophy—but Hegel's anthropology is devoted to showing that *Geist* is not limited by the body, so the use of "mind" to render *Geist* invites persistent misunderstandings. It is better to use a term like "spirit," the precise meaning of which the average reader is initially not quite sure about. In this way Hegel has a chance to articulate the meaning he intends, and to do so by calling on associations (like the aforementioned three) that we all have with the term.

Another problem with using "mind" to translate spirit is that the mind is often conceived as a kind of thing (e.g., the *res cogitans*) that is alongside, comparable to but different from other things.[1] Spirit on the other hand is not a thing, but an activity, namely, the activity of self-knowledge. This self-knowing cannot be understood as a property of a certain thing (such as an organism), such that what is primary is the thing and the activity of self-knowing is secondary, existing now in the thing but later perhaps may cease to exist while the thing persists. Rather, it is spirit that is primary, and all "things" (all parts of nature) are secondary to spirit.[2]

That spirit is prior to nature is a sign of Hegel's "idealism." Yet "idealism" and "idea" are terms whose meanings have been distorted as much as that of "spirit." To understand Hegel's meaning, we must straightaway remove the typical meaning of "idealism" from consideration: namely, a naïve faith in the goodness of people and the world, or a facile certainty that justice will prevail, as when people speak dismissively of "youthful idealism." Likewise, we must hold in abeyance the typical meaning given to "idea." To the average person, any mental content (whether a memory, an anticipation, a theorem, a perception, etc.) is an "idea"; and its being inaccurate, false, or impossible does not alter its claim to being a (mere) "idea." These quotidian meanings are not wholly unrelated to what Hegel means by idealism and idea: Hegel's idealism *does* involve the idea's possible, qualified distinction from empirical reality, such that we must not assent to the legitimacy of the existing state of affairs simply because it exists; and Hegel's "idea" *does* necessarily become known to itself and so is inherently "mental" in a sense.

Similarly, Hegel's idealism can be superficially compared to the other versions one finds in the history of philosophy. However, Hegel's idealism is not the same as the empirical idealism of Berkeley or the transcendental idealism of Kant. Berkeley's idealism aims to show that what he encounters in his experience ("ideas") are the only things of which he has confirmation.[3] Berkeley flatly denies that there is such a thing as matter because, as what supposedly causes ideas but never itself takes the form of an idea, matter is precisely that the existence of which can never be confirmed in experience.[4] Thus for Berkeley, "ideas" are not prior to material nature, because priority involves a relation and there is only one *relatum* here. Kant argues that attention to the conditions of possible experience allows us to conclude that true knowledge is only of representations (*Vorstellungen*) or objects of experience (what Descartes or Berkeley would call "ideas," but the term has a different meaning for Kant), and not of the extra-mental "things in themselves."[5] Thus for Kant our representations are prior to "nature" as the totality of interconnected representations governed by the forms of pure intuition and the categories[6] or the existence of things under laws,[7] insofar as the faculties of representation determine the interconnections and assign the laws—though the same cannot be said if by "nature" we mean the physical world apart from our way of experiencing it.

Yet in any case, for both Berkeley an idea and for Kant a representation is something "in our minds" and is emphatically not the same as and does not belong to the physical world of nature (whether such a thing exists or not). For Hegel, on the other hand, the "idea [*Idee*]" in some sense *is* nature, while also being our knowledge of nature and ourselves. The idea is first introduced as the most adequate way of understanding the absolute (or reality as such), while remaining on the level of (relatively abstract) onto-logic. Hegel's *Encyclopedia* has three volumes. In order, they are: *The Science of Logic* (which is an ontology or metaphysics rather than a formal logic), *The Philosophy of Nature,* and *The Philosophy of Spirit.*

Hegel's logic is a systematic study of the categories by which we may know the absolute (or "what is" in the unqualified sense). It begins with the most readily available and obvious and proceeds by analyzing each category to show its inadequacies. As the inadequacies of a certain category become explicit, a new category emerges. The new category does not come from nowhere but is simply the old category now placed in the context revealed by the emergence of its inadequacies. For example, the logic begins with "being," or that a thing simply is.[8] Examination of this category shows that the being of a thing is not any particular quality. In fact, mere "being" is so vague, abstract, and indeterminate that it is indistinguishable from nothing.[9] The "identity" of (mere) being and nothing (insofar as they are indistinguishable) is now "posited [*gesetzt*]." This positing is at once the discounting of the category of being, and the emergence of a new category: becoming.[10] Becoming (*Werden*) is the "identity" of being and nothing, insofar as that a thing is becoming means that it "is" at the same time that it "is not": that a child is becoming an adult means that adulthood is already emerging in the child (adulthood "is" to a certain extent), and adulthood remains absent and deferred (it "is not"). Becoming takes the place of being and nothing by putting them in their proper context (as moments of a more comprehensive and adequate category) rather than getting rid of them.

The logic proceeds through more categories in the doctrine of being, getting ever more concrete and adequate to the absolute, before finding that the absolute is better understood as "essence [*Wesen*]" than being: the absolute is not the particular things in their particularity but the generality that is behind, or above, or beyond the particular things: appearing in them but always transcending them.[11] Different ways of understanding essence as related to that of which it is the essence are examined, one supplanting the other due to its greater adequacy to the absolute, until it is shown that essence as such is inadequate to lay hold of the absolute because it is always an abstraction from that of which it is the essence.[12] The absolute can only be grasped (*greift*) as concept (*Begriff*).

The concept (sometimes translated as "notion") for Hegel is not comparable to Kant's "pure concepts of the understanding." For Kant, these concepts have the transcendental authority to imprint themselves on our sense data, but on their own they are empty and need to be filled by such data.[13] That is why according to Hegel Kant's theoretical philosophy remains one of the mere understanding (*Verstand*) and the doctrine of essence: it only gives rare hints of entering into the realm of reason (*Vernunft*) and the doctrine of the concept.[14] The concept for Hegel is a form that generates its own content: if it may be likened to something in Kant's philosophy, it is reason in its practical function[15] (generating laws from within itself) but not its theoretical function. Recall that the inadequacy brought to light in essence was that it was always an abstraction from existence: the positing of these two terms together (the positing of their identity insofar as each is mediated through the other) is the concept.

This does not mean that the empirical ego, or even the Kantian transcendental ego, fabricates for itself a world arbitrarily. Examination of successive categories for determining the absolute have shown that it is the indeterminate form enveloping all determinate content, but also that this form cannot be a *mere* form but must go outside of itself (which is not to say that this self-transcendence occurs at a certain moment in time), realizing or determining itself in the world and its parts.[16] This self-externalization or self-determination that the absolute is seen to have when it is grasped as concept is sometimes likened to Spinoza's argument (notwithstanding the differences between the two) that the substance is not something transcending the world (since then the world would constitute a barrier for it, rendering it not absolutely infinite and thus violating its essence) but rather immanent in it.[17]

The concept is first understood as "judgment" and "syllogism." These are not abstract representations existing only "in the mind": these are real ways in which something can exist, though these ways can still be expressed linguistically as what logicians call "judgments" and "syllogisms."[18] The key here is to see how the moment of abstract universality relates to the moment of singularity. A judgment joins an individual subject with a universal predicate *immediately*: for example, this is a rose. There is however an unresolved tension between the determinacy of *this* and the universality of *being a rose*. The subject is perishable and variable, the predicate is not, such that it is not quite right simply to assert that this *is* a rose: even as a judgment (*Urteil*) brings them together, it divides (*teilt*) them.[19] This tension is resolved in a syllogism (*Schluß*) that closes (*schließt*) the gap, by positing the inner determinacy of the universal in the particular or middle term.[20] Thus "being a rose" is posited as always already involving particular ways of existing (having these petals, living in this soil) that characterize this singular object. The syllogism displays the concept because of the universal's inner determinacy, self-effulgence, and "revelation" in particularity.

Having shown that all that belongs to the concept is immanent in objectivity, Hegel shows that the concept is now determined as "object," which has as its moments "mechanism," "chemism," and "teleology." These reappear again (with slightly different names) as the main division of the *Philosophy of Nature* (and elsewhere); and the analyses Hegel gives of them in both volumes 1 and 2 of the *Encyclopedia* have informed the account I gave of them as forms of embodiment in chapter 1. That the absolute is determined as "object" here at all means that any lingering suspicion of otherworldliness (as, e.g., in a Platonic "idea") has been removed: what is real exists, and this existence is not a shadow of the truly real, but the truly real itself. However, the precise manner in which the real exists remains to be worked out.

The object section shows first that reality cannot just be a huge number of extended objects bombarding each other (as was held by, e.g., the ancient atomists[21]), because though the concept of extension or mechanism explicitly says that each body possesses its own identity within its own boundaries, it implicitly requires that the identity of the body be mediated through *another*, outside of its boundaries.[22] Recognizing this implicit requirement means positing reality as determined chemically, such that the real things determine each other and combine to overcome their mutual abstraction.[23] But this combination and dissociation never reaches a stable, neutral state and so is never complete, such that no chemical really has its identity fixed. Implied in the concept of chemism is some overarching purpose for which the chemical exchange is carried out.[24] Positing this means understanding reality as teleological, such that the states and events of one time are not something existing in their own right, but are only moments in the development of something else, and it is the *telos*, the purpose that exists in its own right.[25] The purpose here must not be an "essence" separate from the goings-on of the world but is immanent *in* them. Understanding reality as teleological in this way means knowing it as "idea."[26]

Hegel defines the idea in §213, and it is worth going through the paragraph in detail. He says first: "The idea is the true *in and for itself, the absolute unity of concept and objectivity*." The idea is not just true "in itself," that is, it is not just a hidden truth that with mental exertion we may discover and recognize as the true, because that would mean that it would stand opposed to a world that *as such* would be untrue, a world of deceptive appearance; that would mean that this hidden truth would have its exalted status only by being raised above the untrue, through which it would thus be "mediated." That is, the truly real, the absolute, would not in fact be "absolute" because it would not be loosened (*solutus*) from (*ab*) all connection to something other than itself. The idea however, *is* absolute, and thus it is true in *and* for itself: it goes outside of itself and realizes itself in a world, overcoming the alterity between itself and what would otherwise be *not* itself and hence a limit for the idea. This revelation or manifestation of the idea thus guarantees the truth of the world and the immanence (worldliness) of the truth. This does not mean that everyone at once understands everything correctly: that is, it does not mean that no mental effort is required to attain the truth. It means only that the way the truth appears in the world and to our corporeal senses is the appearance *of the truth* itself and not the truth's contamination by its entrance into an order that is ontologically distinct from its own.

The immanence of the truth is confirmed in what Hegel says next: "Its ideal content is nothing but the concept in its determinations; its real content is only its presentation that the concept gives itself in the form of external existence and includes this form [*Gestalt*] in its ideality, in its power, such that it preserves itself in it." That is, reality (or the idea) is nothing other than the presentation of the concept itself in the form of "external existence [*äußerlichen Daseins*]." Thus the forms of the material world do not escape the concept: they are not abandoned by it, nor are they its degradation. Rather, they are the very existence of it in corporeal form (i.e., external existence). But the idea is not simply dispersed in existence such that it loses itself in this diversity: it maintains or preserves (*erhält*) its unity with itself in this dispersion. The way the idea will preserve itself is through its *self-knowledge*: the self-knowledge of the idea is *spirit*.

The Idea in Nature: Life and Death

Before examining what it means to be the idea's self-knowledge, let us turn to the idea's self-externalization in nature, which immediately follows the presentation of the idea in Hegel's account. The *Science of Logic* terminates with the exposition of the idea and the demonstration that it realizes itself in external existence. The *Encyclopedia* then proceeds to the second volume, the *Philosophy of Nature*, which is the examination of the various forms (*Gestalten*) of the idea in its self-externality. The

Philosophy of Nature is best read as the striving of the idea to return to itself:[27] not as a simple unity abstracted from difference, but a return to self that preserves the difference from itself that is a legitimate aspect of the concept and the idea. This search for unity with itself takes the idea from mechanism, through "physics" (or chemism) to organic, teleological life. The crucial truth about life that allows the transition from the *Philosophy of Nature* to the *Philosophy of Spirit* is that death does not stand outside of and opposed to life as a total opposite. Instead, death belongs to the very concept of life, and the emergence of death is part of the complete expression of the concept of life.

Death's immanence in life is expressed in three ways: sexual reproduction within a species, violent death between members of different species, and each individual animal's susceptibility to disease.[28] Briefly, in each case it is a matter of seeing that the economy of life is not able to entirely encompass nature in its vital metabolism. For instance, sexual reproduction can seem to allow life (i.e., the enduring form of assimilative processes) to triumph over the indifferent existence of nature insofar as death cannot prevent animal life from generating new sites of metabolic exchange (i.e., new lives) in perpetuity. It is true, the genus "life" survives the destruction of individual bodies. However, animal life is not able to conquer death, only to defer it by producing another individual and *equally mortal* animal.[29]

Similarly, the genus "life as such" survives as one animal kills another, but only in the same, quite literally self-destructive form: life continues only so long as it is destroyed, and always only for the sake of perpetuating what remain inherently perishable individuals. The final moment explicitly posits death as belonging to life *in principle*: Hegel's analysis of disease shows that the very processes that constitute life (the consumption and transformation of matter into energy, redirecting it toward another purpose) also bring about death. Disease is brought on by some foreign agent's presence in or influence on the living body, such that one organ begins to operate at variance with the exigencies of the whole organism. The living body is able to cure itself by ingesting medicine (another foreign agent), which spurs the whole body back into concert with itself. This involves a fever, in which the body rehearses death: weakening itself, causing itself to expel fluids and to shake violently.

In this way life is brought back into line with itself, but only by becoming indistinguishable from death: what Hegel means by "death" here is not just the cessation of the heartbeat and brain activity, but generally the ceasing of the tension or conflict that characterize both the processes of life (consumption, respiration) and disease. Life and death are in-themselves identical insofar as a state of "total health" would be one in which the living body no longer stands opposed to a desired object or irritant that stimulates its metabolic processes into action. Yet this condition is the same as death, the condition of inorganic nature. Positing that death intervenes in life not by random chance, bad luck, or even cosmic justice but that death inheres in life according to life's own concept is to make the transition from nature to spirit, that is, to posit that the idea (and the absolute) is best understood as spirit.

Even if it is clear that a transition must be made here, it may be puzzling why this transition is one from life—and in a larger sense nature—to spirit. It is clear even to the casual reader of Hegel that his dialectic proceeds by analyzing a certain concept, showing that it produces its opposition from within itself, and positing a new concept that encompasses the previous concept together with the opposition now grasped as inherent in it. A close reading of the section on life shows that life is not accidentally related to death, but that death is intrinsically related to life—even that life *as such* (a state of nature in which nothing remains outside as an irritant) is indistinguishable from death as such. But it may still be baffling even to those generally familiar with Hegel why this should be the deduction[30] of spirit, rather than of some other form of nature.

To see how spirit emerges here, consider other transitions, such as those within the philosophy of nature. A large part of understanding these transitions lies in seeing that in a sense, each transition is no transition at all (i.e., no new content is given), but only a reinterpretation of and giving of a name to what has already been deduced. Thus the "transition" from mechanism to chemism ("physics") does not introduce anything new: Hegel's method requires that everything needed for this transition to be legitimate has already been posited by the end of the section on mechanism. Thus we can call this concept "chemism," or we could call it "mechanism unrestricted by spatial separation"—because after all, that is what the phenomena in the chemism section are. Similarly, we could call life "the chemical process in which the intrinsic polarity of chemicals is not a problem (because of an overarching goal of all chemical exchange)." Along these lines, spirit can be understood as "a form of life that has integrated death into it." The only problems with this formulation of spirit are that "life" and "death" have become ambiguous in that: (1) a life that has integrated death into it is no longer a form of *natural* life (i.e., life according to its concept in the philosophy of nature); and (2) such a life involves, by this integration, a change in how "death" is understood.

To posit that life has integrated death into it is to move to spirit rather than another form of nature because life is the idea in immediate form;[31] but to posit this immediacy is at once to move beyond it. Life is the idea itself (rather than something merely presupposing the idea) because life involves determination into organs and the overcoming of this separation insofar as "separate" organs have their identity (and maintain their existence) only in relation to the other organs and the whole life of the animal, such that each part is both means and end relative to the others. This self-differentiation and return to unity is the signature of the idea. But life is the idea only in immediate form because here the concept is realized as soul in a body given by nature. Bodies in nature exist immediately, and "in-themselves" (i.e., when considered apart from their relations to anything else), they are only potentially alive:[32] they become actually alive on the condition that a life consumes them and transforms them into energy for its own vital activities. Thus an individual life must constantly appropriate given nature to transform it into itself or die—and in the end this initial separation of natural life from the conditions of its embodiment make death inevitable. The genus too can exist only by realizing itself in one perishable corporeal animal after another. But to posit that in life the natural body is only in-itself ensouled, and that the soul is thus separable from the body—in other words, to posit that life is the *immediate* idea—is at once to posit that death is immanent in life, and to bring to light a new criterion for the absolute: the idea must be a kind of life or soul that produces its own body from within itself. This is spirit: the idea knowing itself in the very externality of its external corporeity—not merely recognizing nature as in-itself the idea (but needing to be taken up and consumed in order to become actually identical with the idea), but recognizing nature as the idea even in its difference from the idea, or recognizing even death as a moment of life.

That in spirit nature is not merely "in-itself" the idea, that it does not need to be transformed in order to be recognized as the very embodiment of the idea, means that spirit's appropriation of nature will be different from the appropriation of nature in life. Rather than being a metabolic process whereby nature is chewed, digested, or inhaled, the life of spirit is a process whereby nature is *known* (though this knowing can still be embedded in practices like eating, breathing, etc.). Whereas life assimilates nature physically, spirit assimilates it cognitively (even *as* it assimilates it physically).³³ The "knowing" of nature that is spirit is not a cataloguing of facts like "when heated, water turns from liquid to gas" and "snakes lay eggs": it is not a knowledge of the details of external objects, but rather the idea's recognition of nature as its own self, its own embodiment (insofar as nature is the idea itself in self-externality). Not only that: in spirit the idea grasps the world of nature as itself (the idea) *even in nature's difference from the idea*.

While recognition of oneself in the other is present in nature (e.g., in animal life), recognition of oneself in *the otherness* of the other is nowhere to be found in mere nature. Instead, even the summit of merely natural life is the *suppression* of the otherness of the other. This suppression is seen for example in the animal's ingenuity in making nature "its own," or something responding to the animal's needs, arranged in a way that suits its mode of life: developing a taste for all manner of things lying concealed in its environment; adapting its body to changes in temperature and other inhospitable conditions to render an indifferent world convenient to its life; finding ways to survive even in the ruthless world of nature (producing offspring, becoming predator rather than prey, developing an immune system to attack certain kinds of life and introduce a state of crisis into its own body). Nature strives in all of its manifestations to stave off entropy.³⁴ In this way, nature and its most exalted form, the living animal, remains an abstraction from death and disorder. Spirit in contrast recognizes the identity of life and death. For Hegel as for Plato what from the unphilosophical and not properly human perspective—what we might call the merely natural perspective—seems to be death is in truth the life of the soul, or the life of spirit.³⁵ With this preliminary explanation of what spirit is, what the idea and nature are, and how they are all related, let us undertake a close reading of the first paragraph of the beginning of the *Philosophy of Spirit*, in which Hegel gives "the concept of spirit."³⁶

The Concept of Spirit as the Idea Knowing Itself in Its Other: A Close Reading of §381

Hegel introduces the concept of spirit by saying:

> *For us*, spirit has *nature* as its *presupposition*. It is the *truth* of nature, **and, therefore, its absolute prius**. Nature has vanished in this truth, and **spirit** has yielded itself as the Idea **which**

has attained to its being-for-self, the *object* of which, to the same extent as its *subject*, is *the concept*. This identity is *absolute negativity*, for the concept has its complete external objectivity in nature, and has become identical with itself in that this its externalization has been sublated. **At the same time** therefore, it is only as this return out of nature that the concept constitutes its identity.[37]

One can reach the best understanding of this text by going through it line by line.

"[S]pirit has *nature* as its *presupposition*": "Presupposition [*Voraussetzung*]" is a technical term in the "actuality" section of Hegel's logic (just before the transition into the doctrine of the concept) in which Hegel draws on the connotations of the German roots to express his meaning. We English-speakers are fortunate that our Latinate word "presupposition" has the same connotations.[38] *Voraussetzung* most literally means to place or posit (*setzen*) something out in front of (*voraus*) oneself. Similarly, "presupposing" connotes first of all to place or posit (*ponere*) something. To add the prefix "sub" (under) forms *suppono*, which has a range of meanings that Hegel would appreciate, including not only "placing under" but replacing, subjecting something to something else, subjugating something, or annexing something. Adding also the prefix "pre" (before) yields the meaning we are familiar with in the English "presuppose," namely, to rely on in order to reach a conclusion.

For Hegel, *Voraussetzung* means the transformation of contingency (*Zufälligkeit*), or what merely happens to exist, into a condition for or possibility of the emergence of "actuality [*Wirklichkeit*]" or what is essential into existence.[39] This is not a violent seizure of the presupposed to change it into something alien, but rather the discerning of an essential tendency that was already latent in it and initiating its unfolding.[40] That spirit has nature as its presupposition means first of all that the forms of spirit such as individual people, human institutions, and so on, must exist *in* bodies that are in some sense natural (flesh and blood, stone buildings, paper and ink, canvas and oil, etc.). Nuzzo argues that the soul-body relation that is the theme of the anthropology in fact underlies the whole of the philosophy of spirit insofar as the concept of spirit is itself articulated in reference to nature.[41] This is true insofar as nature receives its consummation only in spirit: just as mechanism gives criteria for corporeity that are only realizable in a very different (chemical) form, and the criteria for chemism are similarly only realizable in life, so the criterion of nature as such (the idea in the form of externality to itself) can exist only in spirit, that is, only in the context of the idea's recognition of itself. The consummation of nature is thus the way it is taken up, felt, and interpreted by human beings and human cultures.

This does not mean that there cannot exist mere chemicals that are not part of a living body, or that if human culture were extinguished the natural world would vanish as well. It means only that what is posterior cannot attain its immanent end except in what is prior. A helpful analogue is Aristotle's *Politics*, where he says that the state is prior to individuals and families.[42] He does not mean that the state historically predates individuals and families, which is certainly false, as Aristotle knew well. He means only that human activity implies ends that can only be satisfied in political life. In the same way, Peperzak explains that for Hegel "[s]pirit causes and reveals what nature can only realize deficiently. The formal (onto-logical) structure of the universe does not find an appropriate ontic realization unless it is expressed in spiritual phenomena."[43] The modern tendency is to see nature as intrinsically meaningless, such that any meaning attributed to it is arbitrary. By arguing that nature is spirit's "presupposition" however, and that spirit is prior to nature, Hegel wants to show that human discovery of meaning in nature may but need not be arbitrary: nature already strives to indicate meaning, though it is only we who can know and express this meaning.

"It is the *truth* of nature, **and, therefore, its absolute prius**": That nature is the presupposition of spirit is the same as to say that spirit is the truth of nature. Hegel defines truth as the agreement between concept and existence.[44] His dialectical method proceeds by showing how various forms of nature or spirit invoke certain criteria as their justification (i.e., their concepts) but fail necessarily to live up to these criteria, having their truth only in *another*. Thus the concept of chemism is that bodies can achieve neutrality and a stable identity through combination and resolution of polar opposition. But this cannot occur on the *merely* chemical level: thus the chemical has its truth in life. That spirit is the truth of nature means that even in its most sophisticated form (viz., life), nature cannot actualize its concept and thus proves to be only a moment or aspect in the development of something else (spirit).

That spirit is the *absolut Erstes* of or "absolutely prior" to nature means that for Hegel, spirit is the ἀρχή, the cause, origin, or source of nature, the search for which has animated Western philosophy from its birth in Miletus twenty-five centuries ago.[45] The connection with the Greek ἀρχή is also helpful when one considers Aristotle's treatment of its different forms. Hegel does not understand spirit to be the transitive, efficient cause of nature, as a carpenter is the cause of a table. The table needs a carpenter to bring it about, but once created, it is independent and can outlast the carpenter. In contrast, spirit is the final cause of nature, that for the sake of which nature is: nature "intends" (in a noncognitive way) certain meanings, and these only come to explicit expression in individual human minds and human cultures. In other words, it is spirit that articulates the *meaning* that lies implicit in nature.

"*For us*": By introducing this caveat ("*für uns*"), Hegel means to note that though spirit is necessarily self-knowledge, at the beginning of the philosophy of spirit (i.e., in the anthropology) spirit in the form we are examining it does not yet know that it is the truth of nature. In fact, initially spirit does not even know itself as distinct from nature (as I will show in the exposition of the anthropology in subsequent chapters). However, in the opening sections of the philosophy of spirit before the anthropology proper, where Hegel outlines the concept of spirit, he wants to make clear that though at that point we may not know all of the shapes of spirit and how it will emerge from its immersion in nature, that in principle spirit as the truth of nature is knowable *for us* who, as Peperzak says, "have seen not only how nature, in the end, destroys itself through sickness, but also how the animal's death, as the expression and effect of the *contradiction* between its living singularity and the generic or universal life of the species, is the liberation of spirit."[46]

"Nature has vanished in this truth": Hegel certainly does not mean here that nature has no enduring external existence: neither nature itself nor its meaning are the arbitrary fabrication of spirit in the way an individual mind fabricates images. Rather, as the final cause of nature, spirit expresses and brings to consciousness everything that lies in mute, unthinking existence in nature. Spirit is not discourse superadded to nature, but the idea's return to itself in thought out of the bare diversity of nature. This return renders what in nature appear to be independent objects merely "ideal" moments (i.e., aspects that may appear as independent when they are understood abstractly, but which are integrated into the unfolding of the idea when understood concretely, or in the proper context). In other words, what in nature appears to have its own identity in itself can in fact have its identity and truth only in spirit. As I will show in the next chapter, this means that the entire natural world is imbued with meaning for individual people and for cultures: this meaning is not imposed on an intrinsically meaningless nature arbitrarily by human individuals and cultures, but is rather the expression (or one possible expression) "intended" by nature itself (though not in a way involving subjective mental states on the part of mere nature), just as the blooming of a flower is the end "intended" by the bud, leaves, and roots. That is, life is for Hegel the same as teleology, and the philosophy of spirit shows that the true telos of nature is not mere life, but the reflection on nature that is spirit.

"[A]nd **spirit** has yielded itself as the idea, **which has attained to its being-for-self**, the *object* of which, to the same extent as its *subject*, is *the concept*": Spirit is thus not a dependent product, but a "product" that sublates the natural world as its presupposition, rendering the latter a condition for spirit's emergence (a step on the way to spirit, or an aspect of spirit's own self). This sublation can be clarified by explaining one of Hegel's favorite technical terms. "Being-for-itself" is scattered liberally throughout Hegel's writings (to the great vexation of graduate students in Hegel seminars[47]), so understanding this term can unlock Hegel's works in a dramatic way. By "being-for-itself" Hegel means the way the criteria that establish a separation and opposition between two terms can at once bring about their unity.

The term is a category in his logic's doctrine of being, constituting the transition between "quality"—in the form of "existence [*Dasein*]"—and "quantity." Mere existence is what we attribute to *things*:[48] each existent has its identity in its quality, its distinction from the other, because existence apart from this distinguishing mark (i.e., being-*in*-itself) would leave us with no way to distinguish one existent from another. But if this distinction or relation to another is the whole of a thing's identity, and if each thing is itself only by being similarly distinguished from the others, then implicitly, each thing is "identical" with the other insofar as it has its identity only by mediation of the other.[49] To posit that the criterion for the separate existence of things is at once what makes the overcoming of this separation necessary is to posit that being must be understood as "being-for-itself," that is, that the being of a thing, or its identity with itself, is something it has only by *returning* to itself from its relation to another.

This externalization (having one's identity in another) and return (possessing one's identity by making the other a moment of one's return to oneself) do not take place in time: the moments are separate only *for us* in our philosophical analysis. In the same way, spirit is the idea "returning to itself" from its externalization in nature—none of which occurs temporally. The proof that spirit is the final cause of nature, which is the proof of Hegel's own brand of "idealism," is just the deduction of being-for-itself in the logic's doctrine of being, and the deduction of the articulated structure and self-mediation of the concept as idea in the logic's culmination. Recall, the concept has a "syllogistic" structure, such that it is a self-particularizing or self-determining universal. The immanence of the particular term (i.e., middle term) in the universal guarantees that the difference between the universal and singular terms is no sooner made explicit than it is overcome. The natural world is the idea, the self-determination of the concept: in other words, what is ultimately real is not something hiding behind nature, but realizes itself in nature, and so *is* nature (i.e., nature *is* the idea); but nature's truth is in spirit, which is nothing other than the idea returning to itself in thought, from nature. In this way spirit is the idea, a form of (self-)knowledge whose object, just as much as its subject, is the concept.[50]

"This identity is *absolute negativity*, for the concept has its complete external objectivity in nature, and has become identical with itself in that this its externalization has been sublated. **At the same time** therefore, it is only as this return out of nature that the concept constitutes this identity": Hegel means by "absolute negativity" in §381 the same thing he means by "infinite pain" in §382: the idea's complete self-externalization in nature, its submission to total dismemberment as it spreads itself throughout the material universe. It is hard to speak of this without using language evoking action and events, but this realization of the idea is not a divine act of creation, as in a religious narrative, but rather a feature always already present in the idea and always already accomplished. The point here in referring to this negativity (the externalization of the idea in and as nature) as "absolute" is that the idea's identity with its other is not achieved by the qualification or attenuation of its negativity (the idea's difference from its other): the identity is achieved through the negativity itself, or difference itself, such that the idea reunites with itself through *absolute* (unlimited) negativity. Put differently, the idea submits to infinite pain (*unendliche Schmerz*), "the negation of its individual immediacy,"[51] insofar as it loses its identity in the other (its own individual existence and determinacy are nothing but a relation to another) "and has become identical with itself in that this its externalization has been sublated." That is, in alienating the very principle of its identity, the idea has overcome any distinction between itself and another, has returned to itself from nature, and become genuinely absolute (freed from any relation to something external).

Spirit is thus able to "take possession" of the world in a way that is infinitely more powerful than mere life can. The animal physically consumes parts of nature, but always only for the sake of reproducing its own natural body. Spirit in contrast permeates nature entirely, such that in its knowledge it at once leaves nature untouched (not needing to assimilate it physically) and draws it into its very self, insofar as nothing in nature constitutes a barrier for spirit. The whole of the natural world is rather the elaboration of the idea that is at once spirit.

De Boer has argued that the absolute negativity that permeates all of Hegel's work after 1806 (beginning with the *Phenomenology*, and including the *Science of Logic* and all three volumes of the *Encyclopedia*) obscures the true form of negativity, which she calls tragic negativity, and that by taking this path Hegel ends up depriving himself of the theoretical resources to explain the deficiencies of modernity that he nonetheless recognized (the enduring contingency in our attempts to resolve the problems of income disparity and alienation in civil society, the absence of a mechanism to ensure stability in political succession, and the unabated potential for intercultural conflict).[52] According to De Boer, Hegel compares abstract negativity (the determination of one thing by its differences from another, as when we say "this is red, that is not red") and contradictory negativity (the determination of one moment by its explicit differences from its other, as in what is essential from what is accidental) to absolute negativity. This sequence makes it appear that absolute negativity must be primary since unlike the other two, absolute negativity is syllogistic and self-determining, differentiating itself from its other and encompassing this other as a moment in its return to itself.

Tragic negativity, she says, is the "common root" of the other modes of negativity, and is characterized by not disentangling the various moments implicit in it and not reducing them to moments of itself.[53] A helpful example she uses and returns to is Hegel's distinction between the true infinite and the "bad" or spurious infinite: the latter is set apart from the finite as its opposite, but this very separation thus constitutes a limit for it, rendering it finite, not truly infinite. The true infinite is a universal that displays absolute negativity, determining and realizing itself in the finite. According to De Boer, Hegel stacks the deck by having one side of the opposition finite-infinite swallow up the other.[54] Tragic negativity, in contrast, would recognize the mutual implication of finite and infinite, refusing to disentangle them since: first, that would mar and distort what they are; and second, such disentangling is the prelude to one moment subordinating the other to itself as the material in which it was always destined to realize itself—De Boer objects less to this subordination than to what she considers the pretense that this subordination was always implicit in what ends up as the *mere* moment and is labeled "the poorest possible determination."[55]

De Boer's is a penetrating and subtle reading of works spanning Hegel's career, and our knowledge of Hegel is certainly enriched by changes she highlights in Hegel's presentation before and beginning with the *Phenomenology*. I agree that in some cases Hegel's presentation can unduly privilege one moment.[56] Furthermore, I agree that in cases where the way an opposition is to be resolved is unclear, the way of treating it that De Boer suggests is appropriate: in the case of civil society and its deeply flawed way of meeting people's needs, we should treat individuals in civil society as people who both are able to do some kind of work that meets the needs of others (able to be integrated into the universal network Hegel describes) and as having needs themselves; we should not too quickly take the matter to be resolved, holding the right of association-formation to eventually, somehow, make sure everyone's needs are met. We should refuse in this case to disentangle universality and particularity and take them to be properly, syllogistically ordered: the needs of the laid-off worker are not recognized as economically significant by bankers and bosses, but we should recognize them (as Hegel does, with some ambivalence) as not an individual misfortune but as socially valid and demanding social action.[57]

Moreover, I will argue that the precise way in which nature must be taken up by spirit cannot be prescribed once and for all:[58] there is a great deal of malleability in the ways we can interpret nature, and this is not because of some lack of knowledge on our part that might be corrected in the future, but because while nature is permeated by spirit, its meaning for spirit is necessarily ambiguous. This is not exactly what De Boer argues (I make this claim only about anthropological phenomena), but I think it resembles the case she makes.

However, I disagree with De Boer that Hegel's method itself is illegitimate. The method does not require that one moment (such as the infinite) absorb the other (the finite): the third, the true infinite in this case, is not the first moment, nor even the first moment altered to incorporate certain changes, but is no more the first than the second; it is both and neither (if we take strictly the way they were initially presented). Becoming, for instance, is neither more nor less being than nothing. Since what is becoming *is*, and because it is, it can go through things like developmental processes, it can appear that becoming is "mostly" being, with a bit of nothing mixed in. But that is only because we are used to thinking of nothing in an absolute sense and being as a minimal criterion, satisfied by what is eternal and substantial as well as what is transient and dependent. Accordingly, it can seem that in the transition to what is becoming, being has been privileged. But we could just as easily hold to the strictest, Parmenidean definition of being, and a minimal definition of nothing (as being introduced by any determination): then becoming would seem to be more nothing than being—just enough being to let the nothing, the determinacy, appear. The proper understanding, I would argue, is that in any such resolution (including the true infinite), neither moment is given a privileged place.

In this way, spirit is the resolution of the concept (the principle of internal differentiation and movement toward unity) and nature (real existence in externality), but neither more one than the other. The order of Hegel's presentation can make it appear that nature must be present just enough for the self-determination and return to unity characterizing the concept to appear as spirit, but it could be viewed equally well from another angle, in the manner of a gestalt image: spirit requires ontological categories just sophisticated enough for nature to fully actualize itself (in spirit). Indeed, to read the *Philosophy of Nature* on its own, apart from the logic, it appears as a series of parts of nature, the progression of which is in each case determined by the incorporation of an ontological category just sophisticated enough to allow for the concrete existence of that shape of nature.

Revelation

Spirit is thus not the naturalization of the concept, any more than it is the "logification" of nature: both the (mere) concept and nature are subordinate moments. In spirit there is no true identity hidden in an alien guise: thus Hegel says that the determinacy (*Bestimmtheit*) of spirit, the particular way in which it exists in this or that case, is "*manifestation* [Manifestation]"[59] and "*revelation* [Offenbaren]"[60]—not the revelation *of* something else (*er nicht Etwas offenbart*), but its determinacy and content is this revelation itself (*sondern seine Bestimmtheit und Inhalt ist dieses Offenbaren selbst*).[61] Peperzak notes that Hegel explains spirit's self-actualization from three perspectives, which correspond to the three parts of the logic (being, essence, and concept): the transition from logic to nature, the manifestation of nature, displays this self-determination in the immediate manner of the logic of being; spirit's withdrawal of itself from all determinacy (its "infinite pain") reveals it according to the logic of essence; but spirit is perfectly revealed only by the logic of the concept, as it makes immediate determinacy a presupposition for its return to itself.[62] The self-determining structure of spirit guarantees that its determinacy is only not an image or shadow of the universal, but the universal itself (which was always inwardly determinate).

The use of the word "revelation" is not accidental: Hegel means to invoke the Christian understanding of the incarnation of God as the revelation of God. In Catholicism it is taken as a "pure dogma" (a truth that can be known only through revelation, and one that reason alone cannot establish) that God is a trinity, three persons of one substance, such that Jesus of Nazareth, a man who walked the earth in Palestine two thousand years ago, was at once God, and thus that Jesus's apostles could see God with their own eyes and touch God with their own hands. The same miracle is reproduced in the Eucharist, which is God again become flesh. Pure dogmas are held to be insusceptible of rational proof (but also insusceptible of disproof), and known only through revelation.

For Hegel as well spirit is known by a sort of revelation. To be sure, the entire content of his logic could be the product of reason alone: thus apart from any experience we could know the concept as self-differentiating, realizing itself as self-conscious idea. Yet Hegel's *Realphilosophie*, his philosophy of nature and philosophy of spirit, presuppose a sort of "revelation" that comes through the acquaintance with nature and spirit that each of us has simply because we are embodied thinkers and agents, as well as what we get from specialized natural sciences and disciplines in the humanities such as history.[63] Hegel is thus not promoting an "idealism" according to which all of the natural world and human history could be deduced from our faculty of thinking in isolation from experience. We know which chemical elements can combine and in what form, and that Caesar crossed the Rubicon only by revelation, a posteriori, though we can then understand these natural and historical facts and see them in their necessity. In other words, although this revelation is necessary for knowing nature and spirit, the latter do not remain for us something merely "given" as the content of a revelation might seem to be. Rather, we may know nature and spirit in a genuinely rational way, *as if* they were not received externally: and in a sense they were not, since we are the idea, and nature and spirit are likewise nothing but the idea. Thus though these are revealed, they do not remain for us mere immediacies. This revelation is not opposed to reason because nature and spirit are not the content that arrives to fill the empty, abstract categories we know from the logic: the revelation of nature and spirit is not the uncovering of some given, immediate truth. Rather, the summit of Hegel's logic shows that the idea goes outside of itself and determines itself in a natural world. This self-determination is the articulation of the *self-conscious* idea in its self-externality (in nature) and its self-recognition (in spirit); and by thinking philosophically we can participate in this, the idea's awareness of itself.

"Spirit" is thus the best translation of *Geist* because Hegel in his understanding of spirit clearly means to invoke the Holy Spirit or Holy Ghost (*heilige Geist*). In the Christian tradition the Holy Spirit is the third person of the trinity, and it is associated with truth and with the presence of God in any gathering of those devoted to God. The Holy Spirit makes its appearance after the incarnation of God in Jesus of Nazareth and his subsequent death. This incarnation and death are the "infinite pain," spirit's negation of *its own* immediacy: but this is also the return to self in knowledge that characterizes spirit in its full expression. In its total alienation in individuality spirit overcomes the opposition between individuality and the universal, and all individuals are henceforth "saved," or brought into unity with the universal, which is understood as always already present among the individuals themselves, just as the Holy Spirit appears as tongues of fire above each of the apostles as they gather together to mourn Jesus's death. If the incarnation is what allows the transition from volume 1 of the *Encyclopedia* to volume 2, Pentecost—the immanence of the Holy Spirit not just in life but even *or especially* in the death of the flesh and blood, natural body—is what allows the transition to volume 3, the philosophy of spirit. These parallels with Christian doctrine notwithstanding, it should go without saying that the success of Hegel's argument does not hang on the veracity or legitimacy of Christianity taken as most people mean it, namely, as a system of beliefs (as opposed to the emblem of speculative philosophy that Hegel takes it to be).

The Soul as Natural Spirit

Its concept shows that spirit is defined by its relation to nature. However, the anthropology's place at the beginning of the philosophy of spirit, such that it serves as a kind of bridge between nature and spirit, can make the soul appear ambiguous: there is some disagreement about whether it should be admitted as a legitimate part of spirit, of the distinctively human. The first two parts of the philosophy of spirit (subjective and objective spirit) are "finite spirit," in contrast to infinite, absolute spirit. Subjective spirit is spirit's finding of a world before itself as its presupposition; objective spirit is the production of a world as something posited by it; and absolute spirit is spirit's liberation of itself in and from this world.[64] The finitude of subjective and objective spirit lies in an incongruity (*Unangemessenheit*) between the concept of spirit and its reality.[65] The "world" subjective spirit finds before it is the world of nature, including the individual human being's own body and her own empirical, adventitious experiences, both of the theoretical and practical kind. Hegel therefore calls the soul "*natural spirit* [Naturgeist],"[66] spirit recognizing itself in nature. Yet we should not take this to mean that the soul is a form of nature, to be known in the ways nature is known.

That the question of the relative priority of these explanatory schemes comes up at all however indicates something deeply enigmatic about natural spirit. Nature and spirit are, after all, opposites in a sense, and this makes it unclear how to take the phenomena belonging to natural spirit. Some expert commentators deny that the anthropology at least (and perhaps also the phenomenology and parts of the psychology) belongs to humanity proper.[67] Wolff for instance argues that the anthropology is limited to "psychical and mental dispositions and activities in their dependence on material and physical conditions," which are shared with (nonhuman) animals.[68] Nuzzo says that the topic there is "the *animal* soul or spirit, and not the human soul or spirit,"[69] and that "in the soul's relation to corporeality spirit is not yet spirit, is not yet in relation to itself, hence is not free," that though "the body is the soul's body, *Leiblichkeit* is still spirit's natural 'other.'"[70] The *conditio sine qua non* for human life, according to Wolff, is genuinely social life, but this is absent in the anthropology.[71] Similarly, Nuzzo argues that "in the proper sense one can speak [of humans] only at the level of objective spirit, for only within social structures and institutions does the human being satisfy its natural needs differently than do mere animals."[72] The two questions that must be answered are therefore: (1) whether that which is distinctively human (social life) is absent in the anthropology, so that it concerns either animal life, or the animal side of human life; (2) whether the grade of corporeity involved in the anthropology is of the rude, natural, unassimilated, inhuman sort.

I agree with Nuzzo and Wolff that there is no full-fledged humanity on display in the anthropology. Subjective (and objective) spirit are finite spirit because of an incongruity between the concept of spirit and its reality.[73] Since truth is the agreement between concept and reality,[74] Wolff and Nuzzo are completely correct that subjective spirit is by definition not true spirit. However, I would not interpret the finitude of spirit here to mean that the soul is mere nature: according to its concept, nature is externality[75] in such a way that it returns to itself out of its immediacy and externality, which are its death, until it ultimately realizes itself adequately as spirit.[76] The line between nature and what minimally counts as spirit is thus between animal and human life, insofar as in animal life the universal (the genus) realizes itself immediately in perishable lives that persist by consuming the world around them: as the genus stands separate from the individual members, so each animal stands separate from the conditions of its life; and as the animal must then violently assimilate nature to maintain its life, so the genus only realizes itself fully by destroying the individual life in which it was realized, returning to itself in this death.[77]

To be sure, taken biologically (and the human being does of course have biological determinations) human life *is* animal life. Accordingly, human life (taken biologically) shows all of the same features essential to animal life, including the need to maintain life by consuming nature and the fact that the genus realizes itself fully only in the destruction of the individual. Yet, these biological determinations neither exhaust nor adequately define human life (even in its anthropological side), which has the added dimension of spirit. As I will show in chapter 4, this means that for us the "genus [*Gattung*]" to which we most properly belong is *reason* rather than a biological class[78] (of which we nonetheless continue to partake). Because our genus is reason, it does not share the defects of a natural biological class and can determine itself concretely in the life of an individual human being's development.

I will also show (in chapter 3) that though there is no ethical life proper in the anthropology, the foundation for human social life belongs there. The most primitive sorts of communities (races and nations, cultures not yet articulated into states) have their origin in the human experience of nature as meaningful in a certain way—an experience that is impossible for animals who experience nature only through vital drives. The exhaustive account of this is given in the lectures on the philosophy of history rather than the anthropology itself (which offers a more scant version),[79] but though Hegel discusses it at greater length in the former, he restricts to the introduction his discussion of the geographical basis of social life (which is clearly an *anthropological* basis for history) and later explicitly denies that the formation of the most primitive social groups belongs to world history as such.[80] So even if much of the textual material comes in fact from another source, the topic of the human meaning of nature and the way it lies at the heart of social life belongs squarely in the anthropology.

Furthermore, I will show in chapter 4 that the theory of gender he gives in the anthropology underpins the account he gives later in the *Encyclopedia*'s objective spirit section and in the *Philosophy of Right*. In both the latter accounts and in the anthropology it is explicit that genders are roles taken on in the context of a family and are not just physiological features of the body, or other phenomena following from physiology, like dispositions reducible to biological factors. The case of the family is a helpful analogy, since just as the anthropology is not *true* spirit, the family is not *true* ethical life—yet it is still a form of ethical life, however impoverished. The family is ethical life in its immediacy, which prevents it from displaying fully the essential features of ethical life, such as full development of the individual personality. Hegel even calls the family "*natural* spirit [natürlicher *Geist*]."[81] Indeed, the family could be called the anthropological basis for the ethical life of civil society and the state: in the family natural ties (parenthood, relations between siblings) are invested with spiritual significance: here we receive our first experience of things like fairness, obligation, compassion, loyalty, and so on. In the family children (and most of the time parents as well) experience these virtues "naturally," that is, immediately as *feelings*; and the objects of these feelings are those with whom a biological bond is shared. But love among family members is not an instinct in the service of evolution: parental love for children involves inculcating in them values that transcend mere survival and procreation. In the family, as in anthropological phenomena generally, the spiritual exists immediately, but in this immediacy it shines through what can otherwise appear to be mere nature.

Even in its perversions, anthropological phenomena show spirit revealing itself through its natural guise: in chapters 6 and 7 I will show how Hegel contrasts the anthropological, specifically human sickness (mental illness), with the purely natural, animal illness, showing how they are similar, while one belongs strictly to nature and the other just as clearly escapes it.[84] If the anthropology concerns the first stirrings of familial life as well as the bonds of a larger culture, if growth and maturation take on a distinctively human meaning, and if mental illness is a sickness of the soul that stands in stark contrast to the animalistic diseases of the body (insofar as the former has nothing to do with natural factors and is curable—and this by nonphysiological means), then the anthropology must concern what is distinctively human, and the sort of corporeity at issue there, the way objects are mediated and experienced, is not just the animal body, but the body of spirit.[83]

Nuzzo puts her finger on the crucial point when she says: "one should not forget that the 'social anthropology' developed at the level of 'ethical life' presupposes and is grounded in the 'animal' anthropology of subjective spirit."[84] Similarly, De Laurentiis says "soul relates to nature as a formal principle but to spirit as a material ground."[85] The anthropological cannot be extricated from forms of spirit such as ethical life, of which it is the preliminary stage. Yet spirit is characterized by self-differentiation, objectification of itself, and return to itself. If this cycle is not fully explicit, as in the case of the soul, should we call it spirit?[86]

To a certain extent the argument is semantic and depends on whether by "spirit" we mean what at least minimally qualifies as spirit or what is spirit in the full sense. Ferrarin notes:

> Spirit *is* as an *ought*; spirit is the movement of adequating itself to its essence, its concept to reality. Spirit's life is this movement. This in turn means that finitude is part and parcel of spirit, and that absolute spirit alone is this self-knowledge. But no less important than the result is the path that takes us there. The philosophy of finite spirit is this path.[87]

Certainly the anthropology does not show spirit in the full sense—true spirit—but I believe it does show what minimally qualifies as spirit. There are many forms of spirit accepted by all, such as ethical life, which are not spirit in the highest sense, so we should not refuse to accept a shape of spirit unless it is the full unfolding of self-knowledge. On the other hand, nature has its own scale, and things on the higher end can appear in some ways more like spirit than the simplest parts of nature, though it would be too much to admit all of life to spirit. The red line separating nature from spirit is what separates what strives to overcome its self-externality by physically assimilating its other, trying to halt the natural flux (what is merely natural), and what is spirit, which instead returns to itself out of the *sich auseinander sein* of nature in self-knowledge, by recognizing meaning in disparate, shifting nature. The anthropology is *Naturgeist* not because it is the merely natural aspect of spirit, but rather because it is the form in which spirit recognizes nature *almost* transcending itself by indicating meaning without being able to think or express it, and anthropological spirit grasps this meaning. This is the minimal way (minimal because already existing nature is simply taken up by spirit) that spirit can show nature to be its "presupposition," showing itself to be nature's truth, and thus to be spirit.

Whether the Anthropology Is Normative

I must return to one final question (touched on in chapter 1) before turning to the anthropology itself: whether we are to take what Hegel says about human embodiment to be merely descriptive or prescriptive, that is, arguing for norms that *ought* to be the case. How this question is answered radically alters how the anthropology would be read. For instance, Hegel talks about racial characteristics (§393), and attributes different attitudes, abilities and roles to male and female (§397). Should we take him to mean that, historically, people living in different parts of the world have different physiological characteristics, and also show different typical behaviors and abilities, or that differences in physical appearance and ability are written into human nature, and that we should act accordingly? Should we take Hegel to mean that historically women have been more confined to the home while men have been more free to engage in politics, the sciences, and the arts, or that the female as such is better suited to a life of domesticity, and women are out of place in government and academia? How we answer these questions can determine whether we classify Hegel as a bigot, or perhaps only the degree of circumspection his bigotry involves.

There is not a simple answer to this question. If asked whether the anthropology is descriptive or prescriptive, the only correct answer is "both, in a way." The anthropology gives an outline of the basic framework of what it is to be human, what must be involved, at least at the most basic level, in human life and culture. This outline is not conceived in abstraction from real humanity existing in nature and history, but nor is it the kind that we could expect to be always confirmed by direct observation in concrete human beings and cultures. In any actual human being or society, what could be observed is much more complex and what the anthropology concerns is to a great extent overlaid, obscured, and qualified by these more sophisticated developments of humanity. If the reader does not bear in mind that much of what is argued in the anthropology will be qualified and limited in certain ways by what comes later in the philosophy of spirit, reading Hegel's anthropology can easily give the impression that Hegel is making much bolder claims than he really is. A good commentary on the anthropology should make clear the extent to which a certain point seems to be limited by what comes later, as I have tried to do.

The anthropology is prescriptive insofar as it does give norms, but only in a rough outline. When Hegel's whole presentation has been given, it becomes clear that the norms he defends in the anthropology are reasonable, though if what he says were to be taken as his position without qualification, they could be easily dismissed. Yet these norms draw their justification in part from our factual experience of our own humanity. An example from the discipline of anthropology might help. A perennial dispute among anthropologists concerns where exactly to draw the line between what is human and what belongs rather to nonhuman animality. It seems that the flexibility of the human mind, its almost unlimited potential for learning and adapting, sets humans apart from other animals. However, many animals show some ability to learn, and some, like other primates, show a very highly developed ability to learn and teach that can appear to rival human capacities.

In response, anthropologists have distinguished higher and lower forms of instruction and learning: the lowest level involves exchange of information without intention on the part of giver or of the receiver (as when a rat eats its first solid food based on odors first encountered in its mother's milk); the intermediate level involves the learner (the "novice") but not the teacher ("the model") acting intentionally (as when an ape learns to use a tool by watching another ape use it); the highest level, "pedagogy," involves the novice intending to learn and the model intending to instruct, observing the novice in his or her learning, and changing the mode of instruction to suit the needs of the novice.[88] The intermediate grade ("imitation") is arguably distinctly human insofar as it is exceedingly rare in any nonhuman, not occurring among nonhumans under natural conditions at all but only in some cases in captivity (whereas humans begin to imitate without prompting at eleven months).[89] Pedagogy however is more clearly a distinctly human possibility. Some animals instill certain behaviors in their young deliberately, but apparently only as a form of social control for the benefit of the parent: for example, a monkey mother will hold away an infant who has just defecated on her. While this may end up training the infant to better control its bowels, for the mother's part it is a matter of avoiding an unpleasant stimulus. Other cases of apparent pedagogy may be delayed imitation, as when a human tickles a chimpanzee, then later the chimpanzee tickles another in the same way. Pedagogy requires that the model do more than execute the act that others may happen to witness: the model must intervene and correct the novice, thereby executing a pedagogical act different from the act to be taught; but anything resembling this in animals is observed so rarely that it can be dismissed as chance.[90]

In identifying pedagogy as something anthropological, Premack and Premack are arguing only that pedagogy will always be involved, at some level, in an organized community of human beings. They are neither arguing that every case of behavior enforcement among humans will rise to the level of pedagogy, nor are they denying that in many concrete cases pedagogy will also involve or occur in a context of much more complex social activities and processes. For instance, in teaching students philosophy, the professor is carrying out pedagogy, but this pedagogy is perhaps subordinated to the larger aim of shaping critical thinkers capable of discriminating the well founded from the groundless, or good citizens capable of distinguishing the revolutionary from the ideological in the political sphere. The pedagogy is also carried out as part of an economic exchange between the (academic) worker and the tuition-paying student, and involves the professor's integration into a historical tradition of those devoting themselves to philosophy.

Identifying pedagogy as something anthropological is thus descriptive, but not in the naïve way Bacon would observe and record what is observed simply and plainly: the descriptions are built upon a good deal of reflection and prior knowledge of what is merely natural, and what ways culture differs from nature. It is also prescriptive insofar as it allows us to withhold the designation of pedagogy from mere imitation when it is observed in humans. And while normative identification of pedagogy as "anthropological" does involve the claim that pedagogy is more sophisticated, and a better expression of human culture than imitation is, it need not claim that in practice all cases of imitation can or should be transformed into cases of pedagogy. Nor does it mean that all human learning must involve the one-way transmission of knowledge from teacher to student, and the hierarchy that goes along with it. Peers can learn from each other in conversation in nonhierarchical instruction, and one who is superior to another by many different social criteria can still learn from the latter in a kind of instruction that disrupts existing hierarchies.

In the end, the reason Hegel's anthropology (and indeed, the discipline going by that name today) cannot be straightforwardly pinned down as either descriptive or normative is that these designations are designed to be applied to what can easily and clearly be treated as a separate and external object. Chemistry is descriptive because chemicals are the way they are apart from the chemist's thoughts; and any shaping of the former by the latter would be a distortion. Medicine on the other hand is prescriptive because the patient may or may not exhibit health, but as a technical discipline, medicine is designed to bring about or preserve a state of health in whatever body comes before it. In chemistry the chemist's thoughts are not authoritative in the face of the chemical events, and in medicine the way the patient's body functions in fact is not authoritative in the face of medical knowledge. In contrast, human behavior, experience, culture, and institutions are never external to the discipline of philosophical anthropology. Such "objects" are known from the inside as well as observed from the outside, and the observation is always conditioned by this firsthand experience. We must not remain in a state of unreflective familiarity if we are to understand them deeply, but nor should we artificially separate ourselves from these "objects," as if they were external and independent—"natural" as chemicals are.

In what follows I will go through Hegel's anthropology in detail, showing where appropriate how what he says can be better understood by pointing out the larger context his work establishes, but many misunderstandings can be avoided if the aim and method of the anthropology is borne in mind. Nothing in the anthropology is without justification, but nothing in it is meant to stand on its own and hold without qualification.

3

Immersion in Nature

In looking at objects of Nature while I am thinking, as at yonder moon dim-glimmering thro' the dewy window-pane, I seem rather to be seeking, as it were *asking* a symbolical language within me that already and forever exists, than observing any thing new. Even when the latter is the case, yet still I have an obscure feeling as if that new phaenomenon were the dim Awakening of a forgotten or hidden Truth of my inner Nature. It is still interesting as a Word, a Symbol! It is Λόγος, the Creator!

—Coleridge, *The Notebooks of Samuel Taylor Coleridge*

For to define nature and its complement, spirit, is inevitably to pose either their dualism or their unity, and to pose one or the other as an ultimate, a "fact," while in truth these two fundamental philosophical categories are inextricably interconnected. A concept such as that of "fact" can itself be understood only as a consequence of the alienation of humanity from extra human and human nature, which is in turn a consequence of civilization.

—Horkheimer, *The Eclipse of Reason*

Chapters 1 and 2 have given general sketches of the ways different dimensions of embodiment relate to each other, what "spirit" is and how it relates to nature. Chapter 3 covers the beginning sections of Hegel's anthropology (what he calls "natural qualities"), where he shows that human subjectivity is always already absorbed in the world around it, undistinguished from its natural determinacy (as "quality" is in the logic[1]). Beginning this way allows Hegel to avoid the early modern impasse of skepticism regarding the relation between mind and body, or mind and the "outer" world generally.[2] By beginning with a soul that is already prereflectively immersed in its own body and the world around it, Hegel also anticipates the approach of Husserlian and Heideggerian phenomenology by nearly a century.

Drawing inspiration both from ancient works like Plato's *Timaeus* and Aristotle's *De Anima*, as well as from Rousseau and the romantic spirit of his own age, Hegel argues that human embodiment involves at its most basic level an unreflective, emotional, and spontaneous identification with nature. Nature in human experience, even in its most primitive state, is thus not something of only biological-evolutionary significance for us. Animal experience on the other hand is thoroughly determined by biological drives and imperatives, such that nature is experienced according to how it is conducive or harmful to survival and perpetuation of the species.[3] The animal cannot see a meaning in nature that transcends nature, because the animal itself does not transcend nature. Human life on the other hand is characterized by the ability to hold biological imperatives in check and experience nature independent of this mediation. This makes possible both nihilism, the appearance of nature as the meaningless, purposeless movement of bodies, and the experience of nature as an "anthropological" phenomenon, something having human, cultural significance—an experience peculiar to the ensouled body. Controversially, Hegel also considered "racial difference" to be real and to indicate differences in outlook and ability. I will explain in this chapter why he made such mistakes and begin to show the extent to which his underlying philosophical approach allows a different direction on race. I will return to the issue of race in chapter 8, after the survey of the anthropology is complete and the issue can be treated more adequately. Here in this chapter I will also cover how Hegel develops the soul's individuality organically out of its prepersonal absorption in its environment, in which it fails to distinguish itself from other objects and other individual souls.

What Hegel Means by "Soul [*Seele*]"

In common speech, no less than in academic contexts, the word "soul" is used in diverse and apparently contradictory ways. The word refers often to the invisible part of human beings that many religions maintain makes decisions to act morally or immorally and is susceptible to eternal punishment or salvation. Because of this association with religion, many atheist or otherwise secular people would quickly deny that there is "such a thing" as the soul. Students of philosophy will know that "soul" is often a translation for the Greek ψυχή (*psuchē*), though recently some translators, perhaps embarrassed by the religious connotations, render this term "mind." In everyday speech we also talk about "the soul of the movie" or "the soul of the country." There is even soul music and soul food.

In all of these uses however, the word "soul" denotes that deepest part of something in which its true identity lies. For the devout, such as Plato, moral action that cares for the soul is prudent as well as pious because one's body is transient, whereas one's soul is who one *truly* is and will survive the body. An atheist who denies a soul really only disputes some of the religious trappings the word "soul" has accumulated and still probably admits some central principle of her identity. For Aristotle the soul (at least most of it) does not survive the body, but it is still real as precisely this kind of principle of a thing's identity: thus he even speaks of the "souls" of inanimate objects being their uses, without which they would not be what they are. In the same vein, today one might speak of the soul of a movie as what the audience must grasp if they are to have understood it. The soul of a nation is what animates the body politic and cannot be sacrificed without destroying it. The word "soul" is attached to food and music to express their authenticity to African American experience, as opposed to externally introduced parts of American culture that may reflect African American identity only superficially, or not at all.

In all of these cases the soul is: (1) what makes a thing what it is; (2) not a physically separable part of the thing, nor the totality of parts, but rather a common theme running through the whole, present in each part but isolable only in thought. To put it simply, we might say that a thing's soul is its *meaning*. The meaning of a thing (if it has one) is distinct from its immediate existence, or its appearance, but in such a way that the meaning is the true identity of the thing; and the parts or the appearance of the thing must be understood as pointing to the meaning if they are to be properly understood. In the case of the soul it is at once the meaning of the body and, in the case of humans, the faculty by which they grasp the meaning of other bodies, such as those in nature. Accordingly, when Hegel presents spirit (thinking subjectivity) at its most basic level as "soul," he means that it is an attunement humans have to the meaning present throughout the whole of nature, or the corporeal world, without regard to distinction of parts.

The "soul" in nature can thus be seen in two ways, similar to the way Aristotle earlier described it:[4] it can be present passively, as a latent meaning present in nature, or it can be present as active knowing is, as when the human soul recognizes meaning in nature. Since for Hegel "the soul" refers to the most simple form of human subjectivity, this recognition of meaning in nature need not be an explicit affirmation but may instead take the form of an unthematized awareness of meaning. Since any actual human being has a fully developed subjectivity, and a mental life characterized by comparatively much more sophisticated ways of knowing (e.g., intellect, calculation, will), the inchoate moods of the soul can be hard to discern. Yet the activity of the soul is never extinguished in human life but rather always subtends and shapes our experience. It is precisely because of its obscurity that an investigation into the soul in its own right is called for.

Because of its obscurity, Hegel also calls the soul "the sleep of spirit,"[5] likening it to what Aristotle calls "passive *nous*,"[6] which is not one particular, isolable part of nature but potentially all things. Hegel warns against reifying the soul: removing it from the material world but still imagining it as an immaterial sort of *thing*, a *res cogitans* or resident of a distant world of forms, separate from corporeal nature.[7] The soul belongs to this world but cannot be grasped through concepts of nature, like extension. Hence also we should not immediately think of the soul as an individual soul, bound and limited to a *particular* body: its individuation must be deduced over the course of the anthropology.

A simple way of describing the soul in its most basic state is to say that it is "immersed" in nature, but this is already to fall back on a *natural* metaphor: the soul is not immersed in nature as a body can be immersed in water. The soul is not simply *surrounded* by nature, touching it but still occupying different a space, because the soul is not itself an extended thing. Rather, the soul is a symbiotic feeling or dim awareness that is projected into and pervades the natural world, rather like the way phenomenologists understand the "intentionality" of consciousness and Heidegger in particular understands the "thrownness" of Dasein as a result of Dasein's being as care.[8] Because the soul here fails to distinguish itself from nature, much of the initial paragraphs of the anthropology retrieve material from Hegel's philosophy of nature, reinterpreting it to show its "spiritual" or human significance.[9] Thus in studying the soul we are not turning our attention away from nature, but rather attending to the fact that nature itself already has an "anthropological" dimension, in which it first attains its truth. Hegel wants to show that what some would consider "merely natural" things (such as space, time, sound, light, shape, heat, the physical geography of a region) are genuinely meaningful, even if this meaning seems to vanish when we approach nature with the more abstract and restrictive concepts belonging to the philosophy of nature.

Hegel's remarks about recognizing meaning in the natural world can appear uninteresting. In §392 Hegel simply draws a connection between on the one hand climates, seasons, and times of day and "vague moods [*trüben Stimmungen*]" on the other. In the *Anmerkung* and *Zusatz* he is primarily concerned with confronting and rejecting superstitious claims of such an influence, as promoted by astrology and arguing that a sympathetic relation to nature better characterizes nonhuman life than properly spiritual life (for which it is abnormal). Yet he goes on (in §§393–394) to show how geographical differences align with cultural divisions. When this is read together with the introduction to the lectures on the philosophy of history where the geographical basis of history[10] (i.e., its anthropological foundation) is discussed, and his lectures on determinate religions,[11] it becomes clear that he is committed to anything and everything in the natural world being a possible expression of meaning. Before getting into separate cultures I want first to say a bit about the meaningfulness of nature generally.

The Soul of the World; or, That Meaning in Nature Is Not Fabricated Arbitrarily

That nature is meaningful may initially strike some as very bizarre, but really it is a commonplace observation, likely confirmed by most people's immediate experience. Though not everyone dwells on this fact, people typically have experiences of, say, a powerful thunderstorm as sublime, freshly fallen snow as peaceful, a blooming flower as wonderful, and so forth. And yet, it is fair to be suspicious of Hegel's claim, because it is always possible to superimpose human meaning on nature in an arbitrary way: any individual may or may not have a soft spot for the tree at her childhood home, or the sound of crickets chirping in the summer. There need be nothing intrinsically comforting or nostalgic about such experiences of nature. A skeptic could point to the distinction between primary qualities (which belong to the object itself, e.g., extension) and secondary qualities (which arise only because of the object's relation to the perceiver, e.g., color), claiming in fact that "anthropological meaning" is even further removed from reality, perhaps a tertiary, or even quaternary quality, depending not only on a perceiver with very precise kinds of sense organs, but also individual idiosyncrasies and cultural biases.

Indeed, one of the pillars of the modern outlook is the disenchantment of nature in philosophy following Descartes and natural science following Galileo. In their zeal to end the influence of Aristotle, many early moderns presented nature as intrinsically purposeless and meaningless: bodies were conceived as composites of bits of inert matter moved only externally. Hegel of course was intimately familiar with Descartes and Galileo, and with their epigones closer to his own time: thus he criticized the "one-sidedness" of Enlightenment thinkers like d'Holbach and Robinet that led them to a crude and abstract materialism.[12] He would have said the same of the presentation given later by J. S. Mill,[13] who argued that the world of existence (i.e., what is) and the world of values or meaning (what ought to be) are separate and are brought into relation only arbitrarily, that is, that the natural world acquires meaning only by having meaning externally imposed it, for instance by being made the vehicle of an abstract will, which is itself independent of nature. For Mill, nature operates according to necessary laws, and nothing in nature is either good or bad except in relation to the pleasure or pain it causes.

Hegel is not trying to resurrect the superstitions targeted by the Enlightenment: for example, that diseases or natural disasters are divine retribution for our immoral behavior. He does not deny that it is possible to superimpose human meaning on nature in an arbitrary way. The Enlightenment and the natural sciences are right to separate "facts" (even in the narrow way they use this term) from the values that may be arbitrarily attributed to them. Moreover, the sciences perform a useful service in progressively refining our concepts of natural phenomena, making them more and more abstract to isolate more and more minute aspects of natural bodies, even though this moves these parts of nature further and further from any perceivable connection to human meaning. In this way our ideas of an electron cloud, or the element xenon, may seem to be simply ideas of brute facts, very far indeed from having any human significance.

However, the procedure of the natural sciences, while certainly *useful* and legitimate within certain limits, commits the Cartesian error of assuming that nature is best understood by separating it into its most simple parts, then reassembling them, explaining complex properties by sums of simple properties. This method is appropriate only for machines. Besides, Hegel's argument does not depend on defending whatever random meanings anyone at all may attribute to nature. His concern is rather to undermine the contention of some that the world of existence and the world of values or meaning are separate and are only ever brought into relation arbitrarily.

Hegel argues that there are not two worlds, one of meaningless facts and one of arbitrary values: there is one world, and in this world the soul is neither an alien nor a visitor, but at home. The soul is first determined as the soul of the world (*Weltseele*)[14] not because it is a superhuman ghost over and above human souls, but because according to its concept the soul makes no distinction between itself and another. This "world soul" only actually exists in the individual, ensouled human beings, but refers to the unreflective way the soul can know itself throughout the natural world, feeling the significance of all parts of nature. We do not need to interpret or arbitrarily impose meaning on the natural world because from the very beginning, before any reflection takes place, we are immersed in a world where a sunrise itself is joyous, a loon's call is itself lonely, and autumn is itself melancholy.[15] The "before" here may but need not be understood as strictly one of temporal sequence: even if due to cultural peculiarities (e.g., living in a modern, industrial society) we have *always* experienced nature overlaid with certain presuppositions inherited from Galileo and Descartes (e.g., that nature is inert, meaningless, and purposeless),[16] our factual experience of nature can still be patiently analyzed to dig out the original, primordial experience that shows meaning as always already present in it.[17] The human embodiment that is the subject of the anthropology includes not just the human face, hands, and so on, but any phenomena that straddle the hard and fast division some would impose between nature and spirit. When Hegel talks about spirit being "revealed," and incarnated, he means not just in human beings, but in the whole human (natural) world.

Reconciling Different Explanations of the Same Phenomenon

Of course, to claim that falling leaves in autumn has an objective anthropological significance does not mean the botanist errs in understanding trees as plants and the falling of leaves as a natural phenomenon. The event of a leaf falling from a tree certainly follows previous events as their effect and obeys all manner of natural laws. And it would be facetious to question whether this event occurs even in unpopulated areas where no humans witness it. What Hegel calls the "anthropological" account does not come into conflict with the biological one any more than the biological one does with the physical explanation. The physicist would explain the falling leaf by reference to the force of wind, the tensile strength of the stem, the shape of the leaf, and the force of gravity, without any mention of the fact that the tree is passing from a state of life to one of temporary hibernal death. The botanist's biological explanation that refers to internal changes in the life of the tree, its cycles, and so on, does not compete with the physicist's explanation, but rather augments it by conceiving of the tree and its leaves as a living thing and its members, rather than mere extended bodies with precise masses subject to precise forces—though the tree and its leaves are not any less extended or subject to forces for being alive. Similarly, the anthropological account of the human significance of autumn does not negate or undermine the physical or biological explanations but only augments them by conceiving of the tree and its leaves as belonging to a human world.

While the abstract intellect used in physics is more precise and fine-tuned in a certain sense, this greater precision does not destroy the legitimacy of a more direct experience of nature. The anthropological familiarity with nature always subtends our experience of it, even if it is more or less covered over by more complex forms of knowing that turn back to isolate the abstract, less clearly meaningful, and more "purely natural" aspects of nature. One and the same thing, falling leaves, can be understood physically as extended bodies moving in space through being acted on by forces, biologically as an organism's conservation of vital resources by expelling excess members during seasons inhospitable to life, and anthropologically as an incarnation of the soul's somber mood.

Someone who is reluctant to admit of this anthropological character may still object: "Yes, but the physicist and botanist are still describing the same object (the falling leaves), whereas the philosophical 'anthropologist' is describing an unrelated object (the observer) and her arbitrary, internal reactions to the first object." This objection begs the question by assuming that what nature is has nothing to do with the human experience of it (in other words, in assuming that nature is a collection of "facts" divorced from all meaning). Hegel could have turned to the epistemological principle Merleau-Ponty later did to defend the presence of meaning in nature, namely, that nature is only ever encountered in human experience, such that there is no objectivity utterly unrelated to a subjectivity, and that it is mere sophistry to try to dissociate them.[18] Hegel's argument is instead based on showing that nature sets for itself goals that can only be accomplished in spirit. That is, the concept of nature (and of various particular forms of natural embodiment) cannot be realized on their own terms, but only in "higher" forms of embodiment: mechanism in chemism, chemism in natural life, and natural life in spirit. Biological or natural life is not able to adequately determine itself insofar as instinct-motivated consumption and physical assimilation of nature is at once the maintenance and the destruction of life. Life can realize itself concretely only in one who assimilates nature cognitively, experiencing it independent of biological exigencies; and nature itself only ever attains a state of wholeness and a stable identity for its various parts in human experience.

The preceding objection is thus no more valid than if the physicist objected to the botanical explanation, responding, "Yes, but I can explain the entire event using only physics, and talking only about the leaves, the wind that moves them, the ground on which they fall, and its force of attraction. The biological explanation, with its dubious concept of 'life' would render the tree explicable only by reference to" what are from the standpoint of physics "unrelated objects like the sun, rain, and passing animals—and it would be explicable only over the course of decades rather than seconds." Though the concept of life is useless and meaningless from the standpoint of physics, it is not only helpful but necessary for understanding something like a tree and its leaves. This point seems more obvious than the one justifying anthropological description because we already call these objects "a tree" and "leaves," that is, we already understand them biologically, though to give them physical names that classify them as extended objects of certain densities would not be inaccurate, just more abstract. Similarly, though human emotions like melancholy are useless and meaningless from the standpoint of botany, they are helpful and necessary for understanding objects of human subjectivity, such that we must not reject the claim out of hand that gloomy anthropological phenomena like leaves falling "are" in some sense melancholy. Indeed, our language preserves for us what the sophistication of our knowledge of nature has caused us to lose sight of. The words "gloom" and "gloomy" that describe equally a dark autumn day and a downhearted mood, bear witness to the deep, anthropological encounter with nature. Hegel's reference to "vague moods [*trüben Stimmungen*]"[19] is the same: *trüben* refers at once to an overcast sky and a troubled mood. One does not need to *understand* the causal effect that the change of seasons has on one's mood. It is not a matter of sloppy language: the word only preserves the *real* ambiguity in nature, whose apparent physical shape is no more real than its evocation of human meaning. Spiritual refinement can lead away from this naïve immersion in nature, by applying the understanding to systematically distinguish natural "facts" from significance, which are originally joined and should not be totally dissociated.[20]

Another reason for confusion on this point is in the different purposes an "explanation" can have. The natural sciences are often subordinated to the technical demands of this or that industry, and so can be interested in "explaining" a phenomenon only in the sense of identifying which conditions will produce the phenomenon and which will prevent it, so that the phenomenon can be brought into being or suppressed at the will of the industry for which the science is only a tool. Accordingly, the scientific "explanation" is not meant as an exhaustive description, but rather a truncated list only of the thing's sufficient causes. Failure to recognize this common practice in the sciences, along with the persistence of the heroic mythology of natural science as a disinterested way of uncovering the final truth of nature, can lead people to think that the explanations offered by the sciences for a part of nature are the complete account of the truth of the thing, and anything else must be only "opinion." The technical findings of the sciences can all be accepted, however, without giving up the possibility that there is more to nature. Analogously, a pediatrician understands in a certain sense what the life of a child is and understands the death of a child as the cessation of activity in certain organ systems. That knowledge is accurate, but the claim that a child's death is horrible and unjust is certainly not an arbitrary opinion, though "horribleness" and "injustice" are not physiological phenomena and cannot be measured by any medical instruments.

Anthropological Description Is Interpretation, Not Classification

Someone might object at this point: "Suppose I grant that subjectivity and objectivity are inseparable. It is still a wildly bold claim that a precise objective event like falling leaves bears some legitimate relation to a precise subjective mood like melancholy. What can be said to establish the necessity of this connection?" I would respond that this connection is not at all necessary. Hegel does not provide much in the way of a rule or schema for deciding these questions. And I do not think one can be given. To give an anthropological description of meaning in nature one must first begin from the appropriate standpoint (recognizing that the notion of "pure nature" unrelated to human subjectivity is an absurdity), then patiently reflect on the experience of nature in such a way that the more sophisticated parts of human cognition are held in abeyance so that the experience belonging to the bare soul can stand out clearly. We can then invite others to appeal to their own experience and see if our descriptions are not accurate. Such descriptions are meant to uncover a latent rationality in the phenomena discussed, but the anthropological meaning is never attributed to any part of nature according to a rule that we could hope to discern and articulate before, or independent of our encounter with nature.

The account I am giving here can include the properly aesthetic experience of nature, but I consider the anthropological experience of meaning in nature to be broader than just the experience of nature as beautiful, so I do not want to draw too close a connection with aesthetics. However, sometimes Hegel talks about the experience of beauty in nature in a way that could have been in the anthropology:

> [T]he beauty of nature gains a special relation to us because it arouses emotional moods and because of its harmony with them. A relationship like this is produced, for example, by the stillness of the moonlit night, the peace of a glen through which a burn meanders, the sublimity of the immeasurable and troubled sea, the restful immensity of the starry heaven. Here significance does not belong to the object as such [as I interpret Hegel I would say, not to the object determined by concepts from the philosophy of nature], but must be sought in the emotional mood which they arouse. Similarly we call animals beautiful if they betray an expression of soul which chimes in with the human qualities such as courage, strength, cunning, good nature, etc. This is an expression which, on the one hand, does of course belong to the animals as we see them and displays one aspect of their life, but, on the other hand, it belongs to our ideas and our own emotions.[21]

In describing the anthropological dimension of nature we are not searching for discrete causes as one does in physics. Seeing the human meaning in nature is much more akin to the interpretation of poetry than to the methodical labor of the natural sciences. On hearing this, the natural scientist—at least the stereotypical one—would turn up her nose at the whole project, sneering, "I knew it was nonsense, *mere opinion*." But any halfway decent student of the humanities (and no doubt many scientists are at least that) knows that while mathematical precision is not to be found there (except perhaps in formal logic, which, like mathematics, is artificially abstract), not all positions given in matters of interpretation are of equal accuracy and value: a careful, sensitive, and scholarly interpretation of a poem is certainly superior to a ham-fisted, trite, hurried one. What Aristotle says of ethics (that if we use the method belonging to another body of knowledge, demanding precision in the wrong context, then we risk losing what we are after) is likewise true of interpreting both poetry and nature. It is one of the most embarrassing excesses of modern scientism to allege that there is nothing in nature that transcends the concepts, methods, and instruments used by physicists, chemists, and biologists, and that poets who rhapsodize about nature say nothing *true* about it. Scientists perform a valuable service, and they are not obligated to refer to the anthropological significance of their objects of study. However, they are obligated not to positively affirm the false *metaphysical* claim that nature is merely a collection of brute facts signifying nothing.

The German Idealists recoiled when they saw how in modernity the human mind had been fragmented into various pieces, the aggregate of which can never add up to a real or complete human being. It is perverse that an economist wakes up, greeting her family by recognizing their intrinsic value before heading to work and spending all day calculating human lives as so many dollars and cents; or that a physician might go to the theater or symphony and be transported by an aesthetic experience but would notice no contradiction the next day in taking the human being to be a complicated machine, with the proper and improper human conditions involving perhaps only a slight difference in chemical exchange or electrical activity. We today are stunned that people in antiquity could in some ways be so wise and gentle, but in other ways so gullible and barbaric. We can only hope that future generations will have the perspective to see the gullibility and barbarism of us today, who delight in gazing at the stars or exult in a walk in the forest, though, when asked, affirm that the natural world is simply matter in motion, with no meaning. Not all human experience is equally perspicuous, but if we are honest with ourselves, few would claim to experience the natural world as meaningless, stacked matter.

To understand how anthropological significance can be recognized for Hegel it is helpful to recall how Kant understands recognizing beauty.[22] Just as for Kant one must see the beautiful object neither as the illustration or exemplification of a preexisting concept, nor as a causal source of impure, empirically pleasant sensation, so for Hegel one must see the anthropological significance neither as an abstract principle knowable apart from its natural incarnation and our experience of it, nor as a statistical likelihood based on the mechanical effect of nature on the brain. "Autumn is melancholy" is thus a bit like a reflective judgment. Melancholy does not hold of autumn qua natural (physical, chemical, or biological) phenomenon, but only of autumn as experienced by the human soul. Yet this melancholy is not an impression confined to the soul and having no external, natural reality, as "painful" can be an internal impression that is nowhere in the knife that causes it. Nor is this melancholy an abstract concept constructed by the intellect and attributed to a part of nature that never really possesses it, as when we say that the rain "has utility" insofar as it irrigates our crops. We do not—consciously *or* unconsciously—import melancholy into autumn as a foreign addition. Instead, we originally *find* melancholy in autumn, even though upon reflection we know that *as a biological phenomenon*, it makes no sense to predicate "melancholy" of "autumn." What Hegel would have us understand here is that though autumn can and, for certain purposes, should be understood biologically, it is neither solely *nor principally* biological—just as Aristotle famously remarked that what it is to be a lintel cannot be accounted for merely by its material parts.[23] The anthropological determinations of an object that is commonly understood as biological are no less legitimate than the biological determinations of an object commonly understood chemically, or the chemical determinations of an object commonly understood mechanically. In other words, to say "autumn *is* melancholy" is no less true than to say "oxygen *is* conducive to animal life" or "those eight cubic feet of space *are* flammable."[24]

Of course, "autumn is melancholy" can also have a biological meaning: it is well known and recognized in the natural sciences that climate and weather can have a causal effect on human moods. Many studies have shown that exposure to sunlight improves people's moods such that in the winter, when there is less sunlight, some people who were happy in the summer become depressed. Indeed, rates of depression are consistently higher in places with less sunshine (which are comparable in other relevant respects).[25] However, the relation between sunlight and the human nervous system as an organic, biological interaction (if, as seems to be the case, that is indeed what is happening in seasonal affective disorder) is not properly anthropological. Hegel is not giving a materialist account, in which nature determines human moods, as one biological object determines the vital activities or states of another. That is not at all to say that such a biological interaction does not occur. Moreover, it is not to say that there could not be both a *biological* relation between sunlight and the human nervous system (considering *both* as merely natural phenomena) and an *anthropological* relation between sunlight and the human soul. The correlation between sunlight and happy moods could be taken as genuinely anthropological only insofar as the soul unreflective finds itself reflected back to it in nature, such that sunlight is seen to bear human significance that is its meaning, or its "truth."

Truth, for Hegel, is the agreement between concept and objectivity, agreement between what something should be (what it is according to its concept) and what it is in fact.[26] That spirit is the truth of nature[27] means therefore not that the earth acts as efficient cause on the human being such that a mood is produced in the latter as an image of the terrestrial cause. Instead, it means the soul actually is what nature in its highest form (animal life) should be according to its concept but fails to be: something whose experience of nature is not necessarily guided or limited by its vital drives. The human life of the soul is the truth not just of animal life (by surpassing its limits), but of all of nature, by revealing its not-merely-biological meaning. In this way, the soul recognizes the shining sun, the crashing waves, and overpowering heat as carrying human significance, revealing something human, such that experience of nature is a form of self-knowledge.

To say that the recognition of human meaning in nature is not arbitrary is not to say that each part of nature has a single meaning that can be discovered and fixed to it once and for all. On this point I depart from the way Hegel sometimes seems to treat this experience of nature,[28] but I do so in fidelity to the deduction of spirit from nature (and I want to underline this departure, because it leads me to take Hegel in a different direction in chapter 8). The highest form of nature, animal life, is characterized by a relation to nature that is abstract and rigidly determined: abstract because animal life cannot concretely determine itself (producing rather only life that sustains itself by constantly transforming certain parts of nature into itself, and its own body parts are in-themselves only potentially alive); rigidly determined because insofar as the animal lives in a body that must be gathered up in its vital processes and *made* to be alive, the animal's experience of nature is always mediated by the demands of its biological urges.[29] This is true of us as well (our material organs are likewise in-themselves only potentially living), but not insofar as we are human: our humanity allows us to experience nature independent of our vital drives. Thus for us there is no schema given by which a certain part of nature must have this or that meaning. It is not only that nature can have not-merely-biological meaning (being beautiful, for example, or illustrating a moral lesson), but that we must generate (in culture) our own way of mediating our relation to nature and interpreting it as meaningful, allowing unlimited variety in how this interpretation may be carried out.

Indeed, the recognition of meaning in nature is notable for the fact that the understanding (which would recognize an abstract essence hidden in the appearance) is *not* involved. The comparison with art is so helpful because, like art, nature cannot be encountered as insignificant (if one is sincere and open-minded in the encounter), but nor can it be "solved" like a puzzle, so that it no longer captivates us and excites our wonder. This does not mean that any interpretation is as good as any other (as an art critic is probably better at interpretation than is a high school student), but it does mean that the opacity of nature and art make a deeper intimacy always possible. Another comparison might be a human personality: I know my brother better than almost anyone, but that does not mean I understand him completely, nor that I cannot grow in my understanding of him.

Examples of Finding Meaning in Nature

Let me attempt here for illustration's sake to describe such an encounter with nature. This illustration cannot simply begin as a description of how nature would be encountered on the level of the soul, since human subjectivity is much more complex; but the anthropological encounter with nature can be uncovered if the analysis of experience is carried out with a sensitivity sufficient to peel away the more complex forms of experience. I often walk in a botanical garden near where I live, which features mostly cactus and other succulents of the Sonoran Desert. I say it is near where I live, but in fact it is ten miles from me, too far to walk. A trip there thus usually involves a car and some planning to fit it in with other obligations. Already, this means I am significantly separated from nature, having to plan ahead, scheduling time to make a special trip to encounter nature in this way. After parking on these visits, I must show my membership card to gain entrance to the garden, to nature. My encounter with nature is now overlaid with my consciousness of the expense of the annual membership and the compulsion to "get a lot out of" this encounter, to make it "worth" the money: in other words, my experience of nature is now mediated through commercial considerations and is expressed, even to myself, in monetary terms.

A properly anthropological experience is never *sought out* since the discrimination of ends and means and the desire for the end are not involved in this primitive experience. Thus the commercial transaction involved here, and my initial separation necessitating this minor pilgrimage, as well as the worry and guilt that I am too unsophisticated to have a sufficiently deep experience with nature, are impediments to the kind of encounter I hope to have, but they are nonetheless constitutive of the way nature is approached and experienced by me, and I expect by many others in the twenty-first-century United States. Yet because I am a reflective person I am aware of these obstacles, and such awareness is the beginning of liberation from them. As I walk I try to minimize the disturbing effect of these circumstances, so that I may turn myself over to nature in its purity.

I tell myself that these plants—the senita, the Mexican fence-post cactus, teddy bear cholla, bunny ears prickly pear—are the native plants, and though they have been carefully cultivated and displayed in this garden, still I am in a certain sense in the authentic natural environment of my region. I reflect on the fact that the Sonoran Desert spans the northern Mexican state of Sonora and the US state of Arizona, and that, as far as nature is concerned, the national border is arbitrary and based on force. It dawns on me that I am turning to nature as a kind of refuge, insofar as nature is free of the foolishness, shortsightedness, and pigheadedness of our politics, and that this is still defining nature by its relation to the unnatural world of contemporary American life. I become frustrated and walk on.

My mind wanders as I pass more of the gardens, such that I cease trying to have the right experience of nature, and this naïve openness first puts me in a position to have the kind of experience I sought. Unreflectively, I kneel next to a long "creeping devil" cactus to examine it closely. I marvel at how plant life adapts to harsh conditions: this plant moves almost like an animal, but very, very slowly. The tip rises from the ground, then falls, rooting itself as its already-rooted end dies of starvation and thirst. The cactus repeats this desperate, undulating flight again and again. It looks like a snake frantically stretching out past the parts of itself that are already dying. It seems that the roots *should* be its secure foundation, but in this treacherous environment the ground provides little security for life. I notice how many cacti are green, that they absorb and consume light through their trunks rather than through leaves (which would burn and shrivel in the extreme heat): this renders the trunks soft and vulnerable, necessitating needles. The aggressive, tough appearance of these plants belies a deeper, awful defenselessness. I see one barrel cactus that has been kicked over: though it was as large as a basketball, its roots are startlingly small. With negligible groundwater to rely on, the cactus spreads its roots out wide rather than deep to catch maximal rainfall during the few storms each year.

The plant's life is so precarious it can do nothing to secure on its own the means of its life: all it can do is sit and wait patiently, helplessly, for rain that may or may not come. I feel a sense of forlornness for these wretched plants living in such an unforgiving world. The dominant feeling is one of the mercilessness of nature and the powerlessness of life. This sorrow here is tempered by an uplifting feeling of the sublime insofar as life is here utterly dependent on natural conditions that are completely indifferent to its needs, but this very drama and the attendant suffering endow life with a dignity and majesty that is absent in the adversarial inorganic environment.

It hardly needs to be said that there are much better examples of this encounter with nature than the attempt I've given here. As poetry can be the best example of direct perception and its frank and precise rendering in language, we can expect to find a great deal of what we might call accounts of an anthropological encounter with nature there. A well-known example is the opening lines of Eliot's *The Waste Land*:

> April is the cruelest month, breeding
> Lilacs out of the dead land, mixing
> Memory and desire, stirring
> Dull roots with spring rain.[30]

What for the understanding is nonsensical, the metaphorical ascription of cruelty to a month, bespeaks the melancholy that can be the meaning of spring rains that make promises of flourishing that will not be kept. Or, consider Blake's "The Tyger," which presents a part of the animal kingdom as not merely fearsome and dangerous but as total malignancy, pure evil whose presence makes the whole world lose its appearance of moral groundedness, of being guided by a loving God:

> Tyger! Tyger! burning bright
> In the forests of the night;
> What immortal hand or eye
> Could frame thy fearful symmetry?
> [. . .] When the stars threw down their spears,
> And water'd heaven with their tears,
> Did he smile his work to see?
> Did he who made the Lamb make thee?[31]

Another poem of Blake's, "The Sick Rose," displays how the experience of a part of vegetal nature can be charged with the human emotional meaning of love lost:

> O Rose, thou art sick!
> The invisible worm,
> That flies in the night,
> In the howling storm,
> Has found out thy bed
> Of crimson joy;
> And his dark secret love
> Does thy life destroy.[32]

Francis Ponge provides an especially helpful example in how he likens parts of nature to words as treated by poetry (as retaining an opacity and resisting domination by what Hegel would call the understanding). Thus Ponge at once identifies meaning in nature and pays homage to its opacity, reproducing it in his poetry, like when he speaks of the oyster as "a world that is obstinately closed-off. Yet we can open it [. . .] using a blade that is serrated and dull [*peu franc*, which also means not clearly expressing its meaning], taking it up again and again. Curious fingers get cut on it, nails break: it's rough work."[33]

In fact, the way nature is revealed to us as meaningful not only draws us toward nature, making possible an identification with, say, plant or animal life, it binds us to each other as well: at its most basic level the soul is intersubjective, such that for Hegel social bonds do not come into play only at comparatively high levels of thinking where people make contracts with each other and form political communities. Rather, we are preconsciously rooted in the social,[34] which Hegel understands as being rooted in communities that can in some sense be interpreted as natural: races (*Rassen*) and nations (*Volkern*).

What "Race" Is Not, and What It Means for Hegel

It is in discussing races and nations that Hegel gives the closest thing to a guide for how exactly anthropological significance can be discerned in natural phenomena. Unfortunately, this guide is bound to a social philosophy that seems to be an apology for racist systems of colonization and exploitation: the preconscious rooting in the social that is given in the anthropology is not a deep, unquestioned sentiment of human identity across cultures but rather an emphatically distinctive, cultural identity, one's feeling of belonging with some people and not with others. Hegel's remarks on race are incendiary and have occasioned much recent commentary.[35] The implicit Hegelian position on race and nationality is much more complicated than it seems at first glance. In the last chapter of the book, when a survey of the entire anthropology is possible, I will give an account of a critical theory of race and ethnic identity that is implicit in Hegel's account but runs contrary to much of the surface meaning. Here too I will show that Hegel's doctrine of race and nationality is not as it is commonly represented by relying not on later parts of the anthropology, but on the social philosophy expressed in the sections on "objective spirit."

To begin with, one must see why race and nationality emerge at precisely this point in the anthropology. Having argued that on the level of the soul the human being can sink into a state of attunement with nature, Hegel turns to the structure of that natural world in which the soul is absorbed, saying that "the universal planetary life [. . .] **particularizes itself into the concrete** differences of the earth, and separates into particular *natural spirits* [besonderen Naturgeister]. On the whole, these express [*ausdrücken*] the nature [*Natur*] of the geographical continents and constitute *racial variety* [Rassenverschiedenheit]."[36]

In his *Philosophy of Nature* (§339) Hegel distinguishes the "new world" (North America and South America) from the "old world," which is itself divided into its three continents[37] (Africa, Asia, and Europe), each with their physical, organic, and anthropological character (*physikalischen, organischen und anthropologischen Charakter*). In the *Zusatz* to §393 Hegel explains what he considers to be the relevant geographical features of these continents: Africa is an undisturbed, simple unity surrounded by mountains; Asia presents a contrast of inlands and great rivers (without the two terms reaching a unity); and Europe contains the diversity that Africa excludes and the unity Asia fails to achieve.[38] The anthropological character of the races belonging to these continents "expresses" the geography of each of these continents. The division into nations is but a further differentiation according to the same principle.[39]

Hegel's apparent meaning here, for which commentators today have lambasted him, is that the intellectual and moral characters of people vary depending on their natural environment, and that there is a geographical hierarchy (descending from Europe to Asia to Africa to the Americas) underlying and "expressed" in a hierarchy of people's moral and intellectual capacities. Let me state clearly at this point that I have no intention of exonerating the man G. W. F. Hegel: by our standards he easily meets the criteria for being shockingly racist and wildly misinformed. I am interested rather in the more relevant question of whether the substance of the philosophy he articulated is racist. Answering this question involves deciding whether the racist conclusions he articulates in his lectures are legitimately derived from the fundamentals of speculative philosophy or, as I will argue, he was so swayed by his own prejudices and those of his time that he mistook the implications of his own philosophy.

Some may balk at my allegation that in some respects Hegel himself was a poor Hegelian: it is not my intention to defend "the teaching of the good father,"[40] as Seyla Benhabib calls accounts that paint rosy pictures of Enlightenment philosophers, interpreting away any uncomfortable conclusions they draw. Admittedly, it is easy to see how the Hegelian concept of the anthropological led Hegel to racist conclusions: if the soul can experience natural phenomena (e.g., autumn) as having a certain, not arbitrary, anthropological significance, why should not the same be true of natural differences among humans, such as skin color?[41] The difficulty for one sympathetic to Hegel's approach is to explain why some aspects of nature have anthropological significance while others do not without relying only on a general consensus. For, even if most people agree that autumn suggests melancholy to the experiencing soul, there was certainly a time when many or most Europeans accepted that darker skin indicated moral and intellectual deficiency. Indeed, it is not at all clear that these opinions are uncommon today in Europe or the United States.

I have noted the parallels between Hegel's anthropology and Kant's aesthetics and teleology, and that just as one cannot give rules for taste, or what counts as art, there are no guidelines to cite for what in nature counts as having anthropological significance. But, just as experience, attention, and sensitivity can help to cultivate and improve one's sense of taste, so can it improve one's discernment of anthropological significance. Despite being relatively well traveled compared to his contemporaries (having been throughout the German states as well as Switzerland, France, Italy, the Netherlands, Belgium, and Austria), Hegel never left Europe and probably never spoke with a single non-European. Hegel thus certainly had a dire lack of experience in racial diversity, and this naïveté as well as the almost unquestioned currency of racist ideas in his time corrupted his understanding of race, leading him to mistakenly take it as something anthropological.[42] Though I am not and my contemporaries generally are not immune to the distorting influences to which Hegel was clearly subject, I feel confident in affirming that Hegel erred tremendously in his account of race's anthropological significance and in condemning his error.

But we must be clear on what we mean by "race" here. It was previously thought that geographical variety had, over hundreds of generations, produced differences between humans serious enough to justify genuine biological divisions into human subspecies, which is how races were conceived.[43] This is not at all the way that Hegel thought geographical variation was significant but is rather a strictly biological account. Yet this account itself is severely flawed on biological grounds. Progress in biology and genetics has established that as a physiological category race is simply unreal. While there is certainly much variety in physical appearance among people, the divisions established in the early modern period between one ostensible race and another are arbitrary: there are no clear demarcations in skin color for example, but only a continuous spectrum; and there is often more genetic variation among people supposedly of the same race than between people held to be of different races.[44]

Moreover, the supposed rootedness of race in geography refers not to any individual's current location, but to a primordial origin of a race, before migration (which may have been hundreds of thousands of years ago). But what people think of as racial traits (e.g., skin color, hair texture, the shapes of the eyes, nose, and lips) are mostly present in soft tissue, which are not easily reconstructed from skeletal remains and so are extremely difficult or impossible to establish. In addition, populations are best tracked by mutations that mostly produce no protein and so have no adaptive function (and are thus unrelated to geographical variety).[45] Besides, contrary to popular belief, variation in skin color cannot be explained as adaptation anyway.[46]

Phenotypical explanations fail because of the indefinite and unscientific nature of observable traits:[47] migration groups can be tracked, but the genetic material used in this is not the same as that determining phenotypes.⁴⁸ Thus some "white" people are actually darker than some "black" people.⁴⁹ There are also insurmountable problems in using heredity to define race: all humans share the same genes, though they have different alleles. Of the thirty thousand to forty thousand genes believed to be in the human genome, individual humans vary only in about 0.2 percent of their genetic material. Of this 0.2 percent of varying genetic material, 90 to 94 percent falls *within* what is considered to be a certain race. That is, "most human genetic variation—no less than 90%—occurs locally, between any two people who happen to be neighbors."⁵⁰ In cases of "race-mixing" the mythology of race distorts what actually happens in reproduction: each allele is discrete and does not combine with others during meiosis, so there is no "mixing" of genes or splitting of the difference. In cases where such mixing appears to occur (e.g., skin color), the trait is "polygenetic," or depends on more than one gene. Moreover, there are *over seventy trillion* genetically unique offspring possible between any two parents.⁵¹ And while it is true that half of one's genetic material comes from one's mother and half from one's father, there is no way to determine *which genes* (nearly all of which are common among all human beings) will be passed down as *that* parent's contribution.

Despite the continued widespread acceptance on the part of the general public of race as a biological category, its status among experts began to erode quite a while ago. In the early twentieth century the pioneer of modern anthropology, Franz Boas, argued that race is biologically unreal insofar as what are considered racial characteristics are separable in heredity and are not united genetically.⁵² More recently, Appiah has made the similar point that what people mean by race (a biological trait or group of traits that causes or is regularly correlated with certain moral and intellectual qualities) is incoherent since the biological basis for the traits usually identified as racial have no relation to behavior or talents.⁵³

All of this is more than enough to establish that, biologically speaking, the commonsense idea of race is nonsense. To Hegel's credit, the mere fact that he included race in his anthropology means Hegel did not make the mistake of treating it as something merely natural, that is, "biological" (as Harris claims he did).⁵⁴ But if Hegel did not treat race as a biological category, and if race is inadmissible by the very standards of biology, then what is race, and how does Hegel understand it? In other words, if race has no natural basis, it would seem that it can have no anthropological significance, any more than can fictions like phlogiston, ichor, or ether.

Racial distinction does rest on a natural basis for Hegel, though this basis is not the physical differences between human bodies (whether these are the result of environmental factors in the distant past or not). Physical differences in human bodies do come up in his lectures, but the only source of racial distinction he identifies in the main text is geographical variation itself, not as a remote cause of different biological traits but as that in which the soul recognizes itself in experience.[55] The idea was that since the soul identified immediately with the natural world, and different parts of the natural world showed different levels of sophistication (the most sophisticated being Europe's unity in diversity), people in these regions have different anthropological characters and are disposed to think and behave in certain more or less sophisticated ways. But since the "natural basis" for race is the experience of geography rather than indelible characteristics of one's own body, one never "has" a race as an inborn, unalterable trait: the relevance of geography is not as the distant origin of one's inherited biological traits, but as the environment in which one has lived one's own individual life. This is no doubt part of the reason why Hegel refused to accept the idea of using descent (*Abstammung*) as a reason to grant or withhold rights to people[56] and why he vociferously condemned slavery.[57]

The anthropology itself contains few descriptions of this correspondence between natural geography and social culture, but his lectures on the philosophy of history and philosophy of religion give a more thorough account. The key to understanding race and nationality in Hegel's view is to familiarize oneself both with the natural features of the land and climate of the different regions of the world and with all cultures in all of their varied manifestations (art, language, politics, manners, dress, and most importantly religion). With this encyclopedic knowledge, one must then discern the centrally operating ontological principle that governs both its natural environment and the forms of its culture.

Recognizing an isomorphism between the shape of cultural practices and institutions, on the one hand, and features of the natural environment inhabited by a culture on the other is an enduring and accepted hermeneutical tool within anthropology. For instance, caste divisions in parts of South Asia reflect and are reflected by natural distinctions in the environment: aluminum is thought to be a metal of the lower castes, while brass is an upper-caste metal; the same distinctions are made in different kinds of wood.[58] The features of the natural environment have natural, biological, or physical differences that are not the same as the anthropological meaning the culture reads into them, but which mutely point toward this meaning.[59] For people in the culture, seeing the same principles embodied in uncreated nature and in their social institutions gives the latter a legitimacy, while also reifying those institutions.

In my description of an anthropological meaning in the Sonoran Desert the meaning was the cheapness of life and the ruthlessness of the agency that holds the power over life and death, its indifference to the suffering of what lies within its power. Social and political institutions that embody this principle might be rigidly hierarchical, with the ruling clique identified with the all-important but frivolous and inscrutable rain clouds; the social morality of the people might encourage resourcefulness and tenacity in the face of unending adversity as well as humility in light of their ultimate impotence to establish their own security.

If this isomorphism seems far-fetched, consider also how other "natural" features of humanity are deeply invested with anthropological significance. Like all life, humans follow a path of development from infancy to maturity. Since for us the passage of time is always also the passage through these developmental stages (gaining throughout childhood strength, ability, experience, prudence, etc.), we see in ourselves and others that age brings an increase of power and knowledge, and we are disposed to defer to age and recognize this deference as an obligatory rule. The very difference in stature between a child and an adult expresses in stark physical terms what filial piety makes into an institution: the initial esteem parents have in the eyes of their children, the fact that children respect them, model themselves on their parents, is originally bound up with the *physical* need to "look up to" one's parents due to their greater size.

Here the physical conditions of human embodiment lead straight to certain moral attitudes: the human relation to the larger natural environment should be understood along similar lines. As a child is initially in a state of total physical and emotional dependence on his or her parents, this dependence is grasped in such a way that the parents' size and ability to physically protect (and overpower) the child is not separated in the mind of the child from the parents' ability to discriminate truth from falsity, real from unreal, good from evil, so it is with people and their natural environment. In a preindustrial society, where the total human dependence on the natural world for survival remains at the forefront of the cultural consciousness, events like the changing of seasons, the death and rebirth of natural life cannot fail to be central to the culture's self-understanding and its conception of how the world is organized, and for what ends (see, e.g., the "Hymn to Demeter"[60]).

But more than that, precise environmental situations and challenges will similarly be expressed in cultural forms. Those who live in a lush rainforest will likely not produce indigenous conceptions of God or the gods as fickle in bestowing the means for life, whereas those in a desert may very well. Those in a rainforest will likely conceive of the ordering principle of the universe as one of curbing ever-encroaching chaos as the people must constantly pare back overabundant vegetation; those in a desert may rather conceive of gods as guides, leading people across vast stretches of barren desert to hidden oases, or as generous deities, giving unanticipated boons, as one might stumble upon such a life-preserving pool.

The philologist Walter Otto argued that the Greeks saw gods in those obscure regions of the world and human consciousness, where modern people are more likely to see chance or arbitrary fancy. Those forces that are dimly understood and cannot be controlled are the interventions of the gods in human affairs. Wars break out despite the best efforts of diplomats on each side, and they destroy both nations because Ares, "destroyer of men, reeking blood [. . .] has no sense of justice,"[61] and yet for all that is no less a god, an ineradicable part of reality.[62] Similarly, people who are otherwise prudent may behave foolishly, unable to resist an overpowering sexual desire, since Aphrodite is a goddess and cannot be denied. And, some people do not plan carefully or work diligently but succeed by luck because they are favored by Hermes, who can bestow a *hermaion*, or windfall, according to his fancy.[63] We who live in an industrial society are not well prepared by our cultures to experience nature along these lines, as nature is presented to us as something not only well understood but totally subordinated to the demands of our industries and individual desires: nature has lost its mystery and power for us, such that we must undergo the proper rituals, mentally conditioning ourselves to mitigate this disenchantment in order to experience nature properly, as something anthropological.

It is a pity that Hegel's position on the changes in the human relation to nature across epochs is mostly implicit: his account of national cultures is nearly always of those in the ancient world. For example, he argued that geographically Italy was a union of parts that did not in-themselves belong together, that the various parts of the Italian peninsula did not resemble each other yet were still brought together in one land mass. This principle, of a union of intrinsically disparate parts, also governed Italian cultural, political, and religious life in the Roman republic and empire.[64] The ontological principle governing both Italian geography and Roman culture was thus "the unification of seemingly unrelated parts."

Other nations and races, Hegel thought, are governed by different principles, just as surely as they inhabit different parts of the natural world. Moreover, in his view these ontological principles could be contrasted with each other, and some are more rational (i.e., more adequate to the absolute) than others. For example, he understood the central animating principle of ancient Chinese cultural life to be universality failing to distinguish itself from difference.[65] Thus, he says, the individual in ancient China had no identity separate from the family; and the individual emperor was immediately identified with the entire nation (such that his fate was understood as the fate of the nation).[66] In contrast, the fundamental determining principle of ancient India was universality that distinguishes itself from difference, but in such a way that the two seem unrelated. Thus in ancient India the belief that all were one in Brahman persisted alongside rigid caste distinctions, and a kind of monotheism of Brahman alongside a vast proliferation of gods into the thousands.[67] Hegel understood the central principle of ancient Persia on the other hand as being a unity that is reflected *in* differences. Thus the Persian God was one of light, which pervades everything, but far from obscuring or smothering differences it illuminates and clarifies them. By the same principle, the Persian empire spreads swiftly throughout Asia without suppressing the distinctiveness of its constituent nations.[68]

In Hegel's view, the course of history shows ancient China giving way to ancient India, which subsequently gives way to ancient Persia. The same sequence can be understood by the modern philosopher, whose knowledge of the geography and cultural forms of these nations allows her to discern the guiding principles of each. The philosopher can then contemplate these principles and see how one is progressively more rational than the one before. Greater rationality lies in what was merely implicit becoming explicit. So, for example, unity and difference are in truth distinct, even if this difference is only implicit, as when one identifies oneself with one's family *simpliciter*. It is more rational to distinguish universality and diversity explicitly, as in India. Yet this is still less rational than Persia's culture, since if universality is completely external to diversity rather than encompassing it, it will be limited, and hence not truly universal. In this way Hegel thought the course of history was neither amorally random nor immorally determined by the so-called right of the stronger. To be sure, in the short term (which may still last centuries), progress may fail and good people may suffer unjustly.[69] But on the very large scale and in the very long run, history follows a persistently moral course, even, Hegel thought, as this course involves the conquering of one race or nation by another.

What Can Be Salvaged in Hegel's Philosophy of Race?

One might interject at this point: "What does it matter if race is rooted in physiological traits or the experience of geography? Either one involves a racial hierarchy. Affirmation of racial hierarchy is racist and flies in the face of our best knowledge and most just tendencies." However, the claim that one culture is superior to another need not be racist or chauvinistic. Any major social or political change replaces a prevalent culture with what is thought to be a superior, emergent one. We often criticize past *or present* societies, including our own, for practicing or having practiced slavery, torture, patriarchy, killing civilians or prisoners in war, determining criminal guilt by "ordeal" rather than accounts of witnesses and presentation of material evidence, restraints on free inquiry in the sciences or free speech in civil society, religious persecution, lack of control by workers over their workplace, disregard for environmental degradation, and so on. In those cases where we notice that these abuses are not random legislative errors (as they rarely are) but represent a flaw more deeply embedded in the way a culture understands itself, what it is to be human, and in what justice consists, we are contrasting what we hold to be an inferior culture to a superior one.

I beg the reader not to rush to attribute the most incendiary implications of the terms "superiority" and "inferiority" to the account I am giving here. Criticism of cultural shortcomings need not mean that we hold people from those societies in contempt, that we would treat them badly given the opportunity, nor that we hold ourselves as individuals superior to people in those societies as individuals. We can adore the achievements of the fourth-century Athenians while abhorring their cultural shortcomings; and there is certainly something absurd in suggesting that the most dim-witted and backward of our contemporaries, who yet opposes slavery and supports women's suffrage, has a more sophisticated understanding of justice than either Plato or Aristotle did.

In his account of historical progress it can sound like Hegel offers a blanket justification for war and imperialism, but the course of history for Hegel is not about cultures uprooting and destroying rival cultures. It is crucial to Hegel's account that the more rational a culture is, the more it expresses and embodies the fundamental truths aimed at by other cultures, even the ones it conquers. For Hegel, in any case of a truly more rational culture rising to prominence, the "conquered" should be able to embrace the new culture wholeheartedly. This smacks of disingenuous white paternalism only if we take it uncritically to be the triumph of the more rational culture whenever one culture conquers another, even when the victor is clearly barbaric (such as the Christian invasion of the Middle East in the Crusades, early modern Europeans capturing slaves from West Africa, or the recent American invasion of Iraq).[70]

For an example of one culture legitimately overcoming another, less rational culture, we would do better to look at Hegel's own support of the French Revolution's *Grande Armée* conquering Italian, Spanish, Austro-Hungarian, and German feudal states (including his own) and transforming them into republics or at least constitutional monarchies.[71] In this case many of the "conquered" (including Hegel himself) supported the invading French because they saw it as a way to advance the cause of justice in their own countries. Moreover, that the so-called "Wars of Liberation" that subsequently drove out the French resulted in the restoration of the most repugnant, reactionary regimes gives further credit to those like Hegel who discerned that national (or racial) separateness and autonomy are not sacred, inviolable values. Thus any justified case of "conquest" will not involve one culture simply smothering or destroying another culture, nor would it involve hollowing out the other culture to colonize it with alien values.

We are right to be wary of Hegel's account, if only because historically whites have tried to justify brutal colonial regimes with paternalistic speeches that bear a strong resemblance to what Hegel seems to be saying. However, it is one thing to argue that in a certain case what is being presented by one culture as being in the common interest of both is not truly in the common interest. It is quite another to claim that each culture is an atom, wholly unrelated to others such that there is no common interest between cultures (except perhaps that each should leave the others to settle their own internal affairs), and that any intercultural conflict would be imperial. This notion of totally separate cultures, each of which ought to have absolute control over its members with no outside interference, is not a timeless truth of human relations but a creation of the Peace of Westphalia after the Wars of Religion in the seventeenth century. It is to Hegel's credit that he dismantled in thought this notion of absolute national sovereignty one hundred years before it imploded in reality.

Intercultural conflict, when justified, thus involves the victor asserting itself and the institutions and practices (e.g., the abolition of feudal privilege), which have freed it from the problems (e.g., feudalism), that the "defeated" culture still struggles with. When this happens, the "defeated" (or liberated) people are not stripped of their culture so much as their cultural life reaches its culmination and surpasses itself into the new culture. From the standpoint of this new culture, such people can look back at the way their culture was formerly articulated and see just how inadequate it is.

Yet if it is Hegel's position that the culture of a race or nation involuntarily reflects its natural environment, then he would be committed to a hierarchy of continents and a corresponding hierarchy of races whose divisions cut along precisely those lines established by modern racism; and this would make Hegel's position both racist and downright weird. The contention that Europe is geographically superior to Africa or Asia because of the relationship between its mountains and rivers is certainly bizarre and one I feel confident in rejecting. However, the position that there can be a social consciousness rooted in the experience of a particular environment need involve neither a hierarchy of environments (not even an *evaluation* of the environment at all) nor a racial hierarchy. Strange though Hegel's position may seem to some, he was neither the first nor the last to take it, and these others usually do not understand this position to imply any hierarchy.

Herder for instance held that each people has its own standards for social organization, that these standards are rooted in and reflect the people's relation to its climate and geography, and that each people's standard is incomparable to the standards of other nations just as environments are unique and irreducible to each other.[72] Similarly, the twentieth-century intellectual and environmentalist movement known as "bioregionalism" calls for social culture to root itself in the land, willingly reflecting the particular character of its natural region.[73]

However, Hegel cannot be identified as either a faithful disciple of Herder on this question or a forerunner of bioregionalism.[74] Even if we stretch our interpretation of Hegel to downplay the hierarchical relationships between cultures, we cannot get rid of intercultural relations altogether, as is implied in both Herder's account and in contemporary bioregionalism. These would both present natural regions as simply differing insofar as each is completely external to the others. This approach would imply that each culture comes with its own standards for what is just, such that any claim about justice is strictly relative to the culture in which it is articulated and is inapplicable to any others. Yet Hegel's social philosophy is nothing if not a rejection of this kind of self-righteous particularism and glorification of idiosyncrasy.

I am not arguing that cultural distinctions are meaningless or easily traversed: quite the contrary. It can be exceedingly difficult for a member of one culture to understand properly what exactly another culture understands by something like "justice." But this does not mean that intercultural understanding is impossible. Moreover, a careful and sensitive account of what it is to find meaning in nature can preserve the basic idea of what the anthropology is about while rejecting the claim that a certain part of the world only displays a higher or lower expression of the idea. I propose the very modest claim that higher and lower degrees of sophistication in culture can likely be reflected in any environment insofar as any part of the world displays a wealth of natural phenomena, and all natural phenomena have a kind of opacity that make it impossible to settle once and for all what meaning can be found in them. So for example sublimity can be found in the Sahara, the Himalayas, and the Grand Canyon (and there is no reason to claim that one must even be more sublime than the others), while solemnity can be found in Scottish lochs, Iranian mountain ranges, and Japanese forests, among others. And, a Japanese forest's solemnity does not prevent it from permitting other ways of experiencing it, for example, as cheerful.

After all, the isolation of one feature, like mountain ranges in Africa to dismiss the entire continent as closed in on itself, is not only arbitrary to the point of absurdity, it is not even geographically accurate.[75] Even if we suppose that Africa were geographically as Hegel said it is, it would still be true that while mountain ranges *can* have the effect of isolating people, it makes little sense to call people "isolated" if they are confined to an area over 11.7 million square miles.[76] But even when people have been isolated by mountain ranges (as occurred in Appalachia for instance), that would still have nothing to do with what *anthropological meaning* can be drawn from the *experience* of a mountain range: more likely the experience would involve majesty, humility (for oneself), sublimity, and so forth.

The Indian philosopher Madhva uses the image of a mountain to convey something about Brahman, the god of gods (or the one God) in the Hindu tradition, which in the Indian intellectual tradition serves the same role as God does in the European and Middle Eastern traditions, namely, as a principle for everything that is. Madhva says that Brahman is not accessible to our knowledge and defies our attempts to know it, such that even as one is able to wrest from Brahman some knowledge of it, this is at the same time to be ignorant of Brahman; the seeing of Brahman is at once the obscuring of Brahman. He likens Brahman to a mountain that can be seen, but not in all of its dimensions,[77] such that not only is our knowledge also at the same time ignorance, but it is the limited knowledge itself that we have of Brahman that obscures the true nature of Brahman (just as the very side of the mountain that we see is what stands in the way, obscuring for us the other side, and a view of the whole). Madhva's metaphor is helpful not only because it shows one way a part of nature can be imbued with meaning, but because the meaning found in this case highlights the fundamental ambiguity and provisional nature of any meaning found in the natural world.

A cursory look elsewhere yields a wealth of other natural metaphors. The experience of light and the sun have provided a treasure trove of meaning in the Indian intellectual tradition (in the Upanishads, as well as the commentaries of Śaṅkara, Rāmānuja, and Madhva, to name a few), the Islamic intellectual tradition (it is the dominant image for Suhrawardi), and in the West (Plato being the obvious example). But the meaning drawn from light, or from a mountain, is not the same in all of these cases, because nature (again, like poetry) has a solidity and opacity that resists total domination by the intellect. Robert Frost once defined poetry as what "gets lost in translation." That is, a poem cannot be removed from the shape in which it is originally embodied because a poem does not have a prosaic meaning that is then clothed in fine images, which may then be removed and discarded: the shape in which the poem is encountered is an indispensable part of its meaning, such that it remains ambiguous as an inexhaustible source of meaning. Nature is the same way. Consider the way Matthew Arnold presents the sea in "Dover Beach," first as tranquil and beautiful:

> The sea air is calm tonight.
> The tide is full, the moon lies fair
> Upon the straits—on the French coast the light
> Gleams and is gone; the cliffs of England stand
> Glimmering and vast, out in the tranquil bay.
> Come to the window, sweet is the night air!

But the mood then shifts as the sea's monstrous inhumanity and meaninglessness come into relief:

> Only, from the long line of spray
> Where the sea meets the moon-blanched land,
> Listen! You hear the grating roar
> Of pebbles which the waves draw back and fling,

> At their return, up the high strand.
> Begin, and cease, and then again begin,
> With tremulous cadence slow, and bring
> The eternal sadness in.
> Sophocles long ago
> Heard it in the Aegean, and it brought
> Into his mind the turbid ebb and flow
> Of human misery.[78]

Or, consider the way Aimé Césaire contrasts the disparaging meaning colonialism and racism have attached to his black body to the glory that he attributes to it. In doing this Césaire uses as images disruptive natural phenomena to which his native Martinique is susceptible, like hurricanes and volcanic eruptions, but he subverts the anthropological meaning that seems to suggest itself most readily, namely, horror, fear, disaster. Rather, Césaire presents these geographical events as conditions for, or the announcement of, triumphant rebirth:

> At the brink of dawn, lost puddles, wandering fragrances, stranded hurricanes, unmasted hulls, old sores, rotten bones, mists, chained volcanoes, badly rooted dead, bitter screaming. I accept!
> [. . .]
> And suddenly, strength and life charge me like a bull and the tide of life surrounds the taste bud of the morne, and all the veins and veinlets busy themselves with new blood, and enormous lung of the cyclones breathes and the hoarded fire of the volcanoes and the gigantic seismic pulse now beats the measure of my body alive in my firm blazing.[79]

The surprise we feel in seeing what we typically call natural "disasters" presented in this way prompts us to reflect on the unnatural way we uncritically attribute univocal meaning to other natural phenomena like skin color.

If we understand our encounter with nature in this way, then while there are more or less sophisticated ways of being attuned to nature, there is no reason to distribute these higher and lower degrees of sophistication to different continents, or to the people in these lands. In every land it will be possible to have a superficial encounter with nature, or a deeper one.

While intercultural exchange (whether peaceful or violent) can still be a catalyst for advancement, it is not the only one. Culture, with its varying degrees of sophistication, can still reflect the encounter with nature, without a hierarchy in the pernicious sense: each culture would be able to ascend on its own, or by influence from another, within its own environment.[80] Progress would then not necessarily be a matter of receiving a lesson from outside. After all, many cultural conflicts (whether ending up progressive or regressive) take place among people under the same political authority, or living in the same area and intermarrying (thus within the same "race" or "nation"): for example, the democratic reforms in Athens, the Christianization of Rome, the Islamization of the Arab world, the Italian Renaissance, the Protestant Reformation, the French Revolution, the Russian and Chinese revolutions, and so on.

The Extent to Which Race Can Be Transcended

This sort of growth, as one passes from a less to a more rational culture (whether by conquest or indigenous development), protects Hegel's notion of race and nationality (or at least my version of it) from the kind of criticism we can imagine Foucault or Butler giving: namely, that for Hegel race is constitutive of human subjectivity itself, in such a way that the latter is never able to turn back and subject racial identity to criticism. Not only is it possible to establish a critical distance between oneself and one's erstwhile culture, history for Hegel is precisely the story of this distancing—not only from the culture in which one previously lived unreflectively but also from an immersion in nature.

Of course, history is also the story of people failing to establish this kind of distance, even as they claim, and convince themselves, that they have succeeded. Thus Alcoff has recently underlined how disingenuous it is for white liberals to glibly claim that they are colorblind and have transcended race (while continuing to enjoy their privileged position).[81] This raises the question of whether, even if the defeated/liberated people can establish a critical distance to their former culture, they (or the victorious culture for that matter) are in a position to examine critically the newly dominant culture, the culture they currently inhabit. Such critical analysis would seem to be possible only from the perspective of still another culture, built on a more rational foundation, and the first culture would not be able to adopt this more rational perspective until that more rational culture brings over its ideas and institutions, whether through immigration, peaceful cultural exchange, or warfare. Thus it would seem that for Hegel our subjectivity is inherently social in such a way that we always think through the concepts of whatever culture we currently have; and with these concepts we can only examine critically the shortcomings of other, less rational cultures, but the individual can never hold his or her own culture at arm's length to critically examine it. Critique seems to be further hamstrung by the effect of the environment on culture. Recall, a culture can appear justified in its social forms because these bear the same form as the natural environment, whose permanence and naturalness make these forms appear legitimate.

Hegel thus easily gives the impression that internal critique is impossible, but this is not in fact his position.[82] To see this one need only note that the summit of Hegel's racial/national hierarchy is a quasi-"nation" that defies the conditions of national and racial identity: the Germans. The term "Germans [*Germanische*]" is misleading not only because it does not refer to what we English-speakers call the country of Germany (which is rather Deutschland), but principally because Hegel's notion of "the Germans" makes clear they cannot be understood as a race or nation at all. To be sure, Hegel uses the term "Germans" because he thought the Germanic peoples of late antiquity were in an ideal position to usher in a genuinely free and inclusive political culture. Yet he thought this not because of some peculiar feature of Germanness, but rather because there was no Germanness to speak of: Germans were according to Hegel devoid of any national character.[83]

Recall, the criterion for being a race or nation is that a social culture is produced through immediate identification with a particular part of the natural world, and this culture given objective existence in a nation-state.[84] Yet the central feature of "the Germans" is that they do not belong only to a particular part of the world,[85] and thus lack any determinate national character, and do not strive to give their national particularity positive legal expression in a nation-state. Instead, "the Germans" see the objective existence of justice only in the unfolding of freedom in the history of the entire world, and thus of all nations. And since the course of history is the course by which spirit frees itself of national particularity,[86] the proper social and political community for Hegel is one that is not nationally particular, one in which the individual's identification with *any* particular culture is qualified, and one that is in principle inclusive of all races and nations.[87] Thus whether Hegel the man understood it this way or not, his own analysis of race and nationality concludes that the highest point of social culture is the abandonment of any particular racial or national identity in favor of an identity as human that embraces the whole panoply of cultures in history. To be "German" in Hegel's sense thus really means simply to be modern (as Hegel means modernity to be understood), not to be bereft of culture but to be liberated from an unreflective identification with a particular, limited culture, identifying instead with humanity in all of its various guises. Thus people from the country we call Germany—like whites generally—are not necessarily more "German" (in Hegel's special sense) than anyone else. It is possible for one of any color, from any corner of the world, to be "German" in Hegel's sense.[88]

Yet not all ways of "transcending" race are equally appropriate, and some are in fact pernicious. Alcoff for instance argues that while race is not biologically real, it is a social fact insofar as the treatment of everyone as belonging to a certain race has such a pervasive effect that people designated as being of different races end up with radically differing experiences of what would otherwise be the same world.[89] It is thus not possible simply to transcend one's race by an individual act of will. Moreover, Alcoff argues, it is not desirable. For the oppressed, their racialization is not purely a matter of subordination or shaming: it is also a source of identity that provides a sense of solidarity and pride.[90] And the exercise of supposedly impersonal capacities like reason always involves recourse to individual experiences, with which racial identity is inextricably linked: thus racial identity can actually make positive contributions to philosophical discourse.[92]

However, it is not only the oppressed who should refrain from suppressing their racial identity. Whites are every bit as incapable as everyone else of genuinely transcending their racial identity, Alcoff argues. And the well-meaning attempts by some whites to renounce whiteness and even adopt significant parts of the cultures of other races (what she calls "crossover culture") functions not only as a kind of cultural imperialism but also deceives whites into thinking that, even as they continue to enjoy significant privileges for being white, their role in overcoming entrenched racial disparities has already been accomplished.[92]

These are valid concerns. When Hegel calls on us moderns to distance ourselves from the race or nation in which we were born and identify instead with the unfolding of human spirit across all nations and all times, is he calling for precisely the pseudo-egalitarian "crossover culture" that Alcoff so incisively condemns? I think not. When Alcoff says that whites need to acknowledge and attend to their whiteness, she means that whites must take note of how their experience of the world is shaped by their privileged place in the social order: for instance, the United States presents itself as a rather friendly place to white faces, who are not singled out by the police for arbitrary searches and unprovoked violence to the astonishing degree that black and brown people are. Alcoff also means that taking a stand against racism means more than checking the antiracism box in one's mind: it requires seeing that one's material wealth and available opportunities result in part *or in full* from one's place in a racist system and being prepared to do what is necessary to change this system. Alcoff is not saying however that it is always hypocritical or imperialistic for whites to make an effort to see things from the perspective of other races. Nor is she saying that an overarching human identity is impossible given the division into races. Her insistence that whites acknowledge their whiteness is meant rather to put them in the best position possible to distance themselves from their privileged status in an *honest* way, such that they admit that renouncing racism does not change their color, and that this color will continue to bestow on them unjust privileges. In this way, it is impossible for whites—even despite the best efforts of some—ever to be completely on the side of the oppressed: but the most honest attempt involves acknowledging precisely these difficulties.[93]

Alcoff's account differs from Hegel's by approaching race as a bodily appearance for others that is internalized through the other's treatment of oneself, rather than as a mental attitude and disposition rooted in an intimate sympathetic relation to a certain part of the natural world. Yet the two accounts are more compatible than they may appear, and in the last chapter I will be in a position to treat this issue more thoroughly. Only after going through the whole of the anthropology will we be in a position to give a truly critical theory of race, because so much of social life presupposes habit, which is the culmination of the anthropology. Here let me say however that both Hegel and Alcoff offer a criticism of what is perhaps the central idea of racist ideology: the assumption that the white race is unmarked in contrast to all others, and that the white gaze is therefore normative.[94] That the white race is "unmarked" means that it is taken as the default race and so not really a race at all: thus not only whites but many nonwhites will call a white man simply "a man," whereas a black man is called "a *black* man." In other words, nonwhites carry their race as something setting them off against the norm, whereas whiteness enjoys authoritative status precisely because it is identified with the norm and so not seen as something particular. Thus white experience is presented as experience *simpliciter*: this is true not only in the workplace and mass media but also in academia, and the history of philosophy, whereas the experience of an Arab or a Latino is "a particular perspective."[95]

It may seem that Hegel renders the white gaze normative in presenting "the Germans" as transcending race and nationality altogether. But remember that being white is not being "German" in Hegel's special sense. Europe is a particular region of the world like any other, and a white, European identity is every bit as subject as any other to insularity (which disqualifies it from "Germanness"). It is no exaggeration to say that Hegel's philosophy of race culminates in the marking of the white race, so that its experience is stripped of its normative status. To see how Hegel "marks" whites, see how he highlights the peculiarities of Europeans (including the *Deutschen*), and how these peculiarities distorted the outlook of the typical European and Europe's intellectual luminaries alike.[96] The only normative gaze for Hegel is one that at once includes and qualifies the experiences of every culture. This qualification does not mean an alienation from one's own culture. Indeed, by placing one's culture in perspective, one can identify with and affirm the threads running through it that best exemplify the self-knowledge that is spirit with a depth and gusto that would be impossible from within the confines of narrow ethnic identity. Hegel does not mean modernity to strip people of their rootedness and particularity, but only to orient these explicitly toward what was always their immanent end.

This "normative gaze," which looks back on the history of all races and nations affirming each with qualification, necessarily involves establishing a certain distance between oneself and the "race" and nation into which one was born. Ironically, it is by examining Hegel's philosophy of race and nationality (the only place where he explains concretely how a certain part of the natural world has anthropological significance) that one can see how important Hegel thought it was for human subjectivity to step back from the immediate absorption in nature characterizing the soul. Because this distancing is possible, we can examine the individual soul and its individual experiences as such, and not as instances of a cultural type of experience. However, although it is necessary to subject one's own cultural background to as much criticism as possible, this kind of criticism need not involve a disenchantment of nature.

In summary, there are many reasons why Hegel need not have drawn the racist conclusions he drew from his notion of philosophical anthropology. That is, even if we accept that the natural world is always already imbued with meaning, and that though this meaning is obscure to the more sophisticated mental faculties, it is revealed to the soul, we can reject the terrible remarks on race found in Hegel's lectures. These reasons are: geographical variation need not involve a *hierarchy* of continents, nor a corresponding hierarchy of peoples; Hegel's social philosophy is a philosophy of history more than a philosophy of geography, such that the cultural hierarchy is necessarily distributed temporally, but only incidentally distributed spatially, and could be refashioned to be the story of particular cultures developing contradictions from within themselves and transcending them; the apex of this social philosophy is the emergence of a culture of cultures, with open membership and embracing all cultures.

Yet one can retain a receptivity for the meaningfulness of nature even as one subjects her social culture to critique. Nature is the body of the soul. Human subjectivity at its most primitive, prereflective level feels itself embodied not just in a particular set of arms and legs but in the whole natural world. As the soul's body, nature is inseparable from the soul, or at least not absolutely separable. Critical distance between oneself and one's native environment and native culture does not render either foreign or meaningless. Human subjectivity knows itself as originally projected into a natural world. Hegel's philosophy of spirit is a running proof not only that nature is itself only a moment of thinking subjectivity's return to itself in contemplation, but also that subjectivity knows *itself* as something external and corporeal, that nature is spirit's incarnation. The tempering or mediation of this original identification with nature cannot and should not eradicate it. After all, we can remove ourselves from immediate, unreflective absorption in the feelings of our own bodies without becoming irrevocably alienated from them and considering them to be meaningless matter.

The Individual Soul

As I mentioned at the beginning of this chapter, Hegel calls the paragraphs under examination here "natural qualities" because in his logic "quality" refers to being that is inseparable from its determinacy. The individual soul comes up here because of the intersection of two threads Hegel's argument has been pursuing. First, for the whole natural qualities section, even as we have discussed the "world soul" and the various particular racial and national forms the world soul takes, the reality of the soul, its concrete foothold, is this or that individual soul. Whatever claims are made about climactic influence and unreflective sympathy with nature, or prereflective tribal identity, must ultimately be cashed out in the experiences of flesh-and-blood individual human beings.

Second, as we have examined the foregoing moments of natural qualities, we have been focused on the soul as it is completely absorbed in the world around it but laying the groundwork for the qualification of this otherwise total identification in the individual's experience. The world soul is the unity of nature, which is defined by multiplicity: analysis of this concept would have to pinpoint some principle for qualifying the identification of the soul with nature, since nature is many diverse parts. The positing of diversity within the soul (as various particular national communities) maintains the soul's identity with nature in the case of each community, which brings the tension within the concept of the soul into open, *real* conflict with itself (in war). The final moment of natural qualities is at once the resolution of this conflict and its most extreme exacerbation, as the soul's identification with nature—and thus its failure to distinguish itself from its determinacy—emerges at the very point of the reality of spirit, in the individual soul.

To say that the individual can—at least through the historical emergence of a culture of cultures—distance herself from her native culture and native environment is the same as to say that the individual soul is already able to mediate its relation to itself: that is, it is to say that the human being is spirit. Though a certain degree of historical development is required for the explicit articulation of the principle that all people are in principle free (Hegel understands the emergence of Christianity to be this sea change), the individual soul as such already possesses what is needed for this self-mediation in the "natural" aspects of one's personality:[97] (1) inborn talents and idiosyncrasies in an individual or family, (2) the susceptibility to this or that temperament, and (3) the inborn tendency to develop a character. That these traits are "natural" can mean only that they are given from the beginning of life rather than chosen and deliberately cultivated, not that they can be reduced to merely mechanical, chemical, or biological causes. Talent, temperament, and character exhibit the familiar Hegelian triad of immediacy, mediation, and mediated immediacy, respectively.

A talent is "immediate" insofar as: (1) the individual finds herself with this or that talent, without mediation of education or training; (2) the talent presents the world to the soul to be experienced in a certain way but does not present the soul to itself in experience. A talent may lie dormant in the soul years or decades until the person finds herself in the right situation to activate it and bring it out. Because talents have this immediacy, they seem more like animal instincts than something properly human: both talents and instincts are a disposition to experience and act in a certain way; and both respond to the presence of a certain object outside of the soul at which point the talent or instinct makes itself known. Yet in contrast to animal instinct, human talent need have nothing at all to do with the promotion of the survival of the individual or species.[98] A talent in fact may be completely useless, having nothing at all to do with the concrete circumstances of one's life, nor with other talents one may possess.[99] A person thus inhabits her talents unreflectively: for instance, a person who is very dexterous and graceful passes quickly and effortlessly over a rocky mountain path without notice, whereas someone without that talent experiences the same path as forbidding and dangerous. Each person's talent determines the way she experiences the world, but the soul does not reflect on the talent itself since (unless we suppose the aid of more sophisticated forms of cognition) it does not know what it would be like to be embodied any other way.

A temperament on the other hand is a mediated determinacy for the individual, insofar as: (1) it arises and fades in the soul's experience and is experienced *as* coming to be and passing away; (2) the soul is occupied with itself in its temperament, especially in melancholy. Hegel uses the Hippocratic tetrad of temperaments (sanguine, phlegmatic, choleric, and melancholic), though there is no reason to believe he accepted the contention that these were caused by the preponderance in the body of one fluid or another. People of the sanguine temperament are extroverted, cheerful, and actively sociable. The phlegmatic are not easily moved or excited and are personable in a passive, unoffending way. The choleric are quick to anger and tend toward aggressiveness. The melancholic are withdrawn, thoughtful, and often also sad. Each temperament is mediated through the others insofar as what it is to have a certain temperament is only to have the *contrary* disposition of another temperament, as for instance the sanguine is the most extreme opposite of the melancholic.[100]

Character unites the fixity of talent with the inward reflection of temperament[101] insofar as character is inwardly reflected (related to its opposite like temperament, and also cultivated) yet, if not impossible to change, at least resistant to change (i.e., "fixed" like talent). Character (*Charakter*), as Hegel understands it, is the acquisition of a certain pattern by virtue of which one seeks out and accepts certain feelings and experiences rejecting and being able to resist others.[102] The fixity of character differs from that in talent insofar as character is acquired (not given by nature), but also because character must be maintained: a talent for diligence needs no cultivation, but diligence acquired by effort requires maintenance and is always subject to waning. A characteristic is thus always possibly on its way to becoming its opposite, whereas a talent has no proper opposite. Yet character differs from temperament insofar as character is able to resist its contrary. A person's diligent character allows her to resist impulses to laziness, while temperaments pass into one another freely.

Because character involves the soul creating for itself its own form of mediation with the world—its own "body" in a sense—it prefigures the culmination of the anthropology in habit. Character in fact really is nothing but a system of habits. Yet at this stage in the anthropology Hegel is not concerned with character as such but rather only with the "*natural* foundation [natürliche *Grundlage*]"[103] of character, that is, that *natural* (unchosen, uncreated) determination by virtue of which some are more disposed to develop strong characters than others. This "*natural* foundation" of character seems however to be only an inborn *talent* (an immediate, given determination of the soul) that one may have for developing a strong character. Yet this natural disposition to character development is still the unity of talent and temperament at least *implicitly*, insofar as it amounts to being "naturally" determined to supersede mere natural determination by the development of character, in which one wrests oneself from being the mere plaything of whatever impulses nature chances to send one's way, thereby subordinating what is naturally given to what is the product of the will.[104]

Because talent, temperament, and character are structurally similar to the "races" Hegel discusses in his lectures on anthropology[105] and because all of these moments are present in the *individual* soul as such (whatever "race" or geographical origin) casts further doubt on the relationship between racism and the Hegelian, speculative approach to embodiment (whatever the illusions of Hegel the man). In line with this, the true trend in his thought, Hegel himself says that "genius, talent, moral virtues and sentiments, piety, can be found in all zones, constitutions, and political states."[106]

Therefore the course of the section on natural qualities can be seen as a demonstration that what belong to the soul generally is present also in the *individual* soul, which is thus a sort of microcosm of the universal soul. In some sense, all of nature is contained in the individual soul as its *inner* world.[107] It is not that the universal soul and the individual soul are both souls, but the one is bigger than the other, so that the one is present throughout all of nature whereas an individual soul is only present throughout its own body. The universal or "world soul" was only ever something actual to the extent that individual souls sink into an unreflective sympathy with nature generally. The individual soul does not do what the universal soul does but on a smaller scale: the individual soul *is* the universal soul, though without excluding other individual souls from likewise being the universal soul. When Hegel says that the individual soul has its own inner *world*, he is not being hyperbolic: the individual soul does in a sense encompass the whole of nature. Of course, everything turns on what "in a sense" means in the last sentence: Hegel's method is to state a principle like "the soul encompasses all of nature" or "the human being as such is free" before patiently teasing out the various apparently contradictory implications, examining each in turn and showing how each must be interpreted so as to be incorporated into what has then become an amplified, more concrete conception of the soul, the human being, and so forth. Beginning in chapter 4, I will turn to what it means to consider the soul to have its own *inner world*.

4

The Inner World of the Soul

> Sleep, the all-ensnaring.
>
> —Sophocles, *Antigone*

The last chapter concluded with talent, temperament, and character, the natural determinacies of the human individual: those qualities all humans have, but which in their particularity contribute to the distinctive identities of individuals. There are various ways to explain how a number of different things have a common essence, but in the cases of the seven billion individuals who are all human, Hegel is careful to avoid treating your and my shared humanity as comparable to the way one yardstick and another yardstick share a common length. With yardsticks, the length "thirty-six inches" is completely identical in the two cases; indeed, this length can be reproduced indefinitely in a wide variety of materials. In contrast, while it is meaningful to say that you and I are both human (this concept does identify a genuine commonality between us), my humanity is not exactly the same as yours: I have a talent for drawing, you may have one for dancing; I am temperamentally reserved, you may be exuberant. These differences form the foundation for the differences between your character and mine. I do not have a *greater measure* of humanity than you, nor a lesser one. While there are certainly innumerable accidental (and meaningless) differences between you and me, some, like those of talents, temperament, and others to be covered later are constitutive of our humanity. Thus while we must not be misled by superficial peculiarities, nor should we abstract from *all* differences to arrive at a common humanity that is identical in you and me (as we can for example when we abstract from the different types of material in which "thirty-six inches" may inhere). Being human involves, not merely in fact but in principle, being *this particular* type of person, a person for whom the world appears in a *particular* way.

The course of the "natural changes" paragraphs (§§396–398), the ones I am concerned with in this chapter, shows an intricate dialectic between *being* nature (having a body) and *knowing* nature. This dialectic emerges here through the exploration of the inevitable determinacy of human existence (which was only briefly introduced in the paragraphs on natural qualities). This determinacy is not a mere brute fact but is rather intimately related to the concept of spirit as the self-knowing idea, and unfolding the way human determinacy at once makes possible and obstructs self-knowledge constitutes the drama of the rest of the anthropology—and much of Hegel's work generally. Russon has identified this tension in the sense-certainty section of the Jena *Phenomenology*, where knowing is examined first in its simplest form, as merely a knower knowing something, only to reveal that such knowing involves positing determinacy in space and time. Russon says the "transcendental conditions of the experience of the present are, as Marx might say, material. [. . .] I can *experience* the present only by *being* present, which means I must *be* some *where* and some *when*: I must be *in* the world, determinately situated."[1]

The possession of an interiority based on which one and the same world presents itself with one aspect predominant for me, and one very or only slightly different for you is, at bottom, what we are left with if we persist in searching for an identical human essence in all people.[2] But this interiority—at least the part under consideration here—is not a full-fledged intellect in the manner of a Cartesian *res cogitans*: it is not a faculty for grasping the same universal truths graspable by any similar soul. These truths are genuine, and the intellect that grasps them is real and identical in all of us, but the *personality* that wields the intellect, and provides the unique vantage point from which the intellect begins, is not the same; and that is what Hegel is concerned with here. The soul, in its most basic definition, is self-knowledge for which the self-externality of matter is nothing. Directed outward, when the person is absorbed in her experience of nature, the soul is the "universal soul" examined in the last chapter. But despite the soul's intentionality, projecting itself into nature and finding meaning in it, the natural world for its part remains fundamentally self-external, *partes extra partes*. It is only in the experience of nature (which belongs to the soul rather than to nature as such) that nature ever really attains unity.[3] In other words, considered as mere nature, the external world remains always separated from itself, never truly attaining the condition it should have according to its concept: only in spirit's self-knowledge, recognizing itself in nature (i.e., in the soul's own *inner* world), is nature one.

The inner world of each human soul is intact and complete: new experiences never cease to flow into the soul, but this inner world provides the terms according to which what is experienced will be admitted and how it will be felt and ordered. And a person is at home in this inner world: absorption in external nature is fascinating and stimulating, but drawing back a bit, which can be as simple as attending to the fact that one is experiencing something rather than simply experiencing it, is a source of comfort and rejuvenation for the soul. Some people are familiar with the mental trick of attending to the *fact* that something unpleasant is happening (e.g., itching from a mosquito bite or having dental work done) rather than losing oneself in the suffering of it. In this way, the pain or discomfort is markedly mitigated by bringing it within, attending to it as a content over which the soul has some control. This sort of thing would be impossible if we lacked the interiority at issue here, if we did not have an inner world to which we may always retire.

I've been referring to it as if each were the same, but this inner world is always of one particular sort or another. For example, a baby, a child, a youth, an adult, or an old person organize and understand their experience of the world in very different ways. To be sure, what is involved in the concept of spirit, the basic notion of what it is to be human, is not displayed equally well by people in different ages, but none are only partially human. Similarly, one may be male or female, but the case of gender is more complicated.[4] Though Hegel seems to think the male is truly superior to the female, the circumstantial evidence that made that conviction a common one in Hegel's time (such as the near-total dearth of women in the fine arts, academia, politics, etc.) has changed dramatically today; and in those spheres where women are still a minority we can account for their minority status with explanations that are at once much more plausible and that easily support the principle of equal ability across genders. Moreover, the very notion of gender and its relation to sex has come under increased scrutiny, especially in the past half century. I will do my best to sort out what is living and what is dead in Hegel on this issue. The final form of "natural change" to consider in this chapter is the alternation between states of consciousness, passage from waking life to sleep and back again. The focus on these states will be especially relevant for subsequent chapters that concern Hegel's treatment of mental illness, which has often been considered a form of sleeping while awake. A constant theme throughout this chapter (as in previous and subsequent ones) will be the recognition of death in life, the allowance of it to appear, and its suppression, as well as the increasing focus on the embodiment of individual human beings.

The Ages of Life

Spirit is the truth of nature: that is, it is only in the self-knowledge of human life and culture that the natural world attains what it should according to its concept. The final form of mere nature is animal life, which succeeds at maintaining its identity throughout the innumerable chemical exchanges characterizing its relation to the natural world. Yet animal life never succeeds at realizing itself in the manner of a "concrete universal." Each animal life is a complex of assimilative processes (consumption, respiration) that seize the needed parts of the natural environment and transform them into the animal life itself, that is, into energy for the continuation of these same assimilative processes. But animal life (the universal) always initially stands external to the (individual) parts of nature it will consume: though the former requires the latter, and is nothing else than the transformation of the latter, animal life does not produce its own content from within itself. The "universal" that is animal life is an *abstraction* from its needed content.[5] If we attend not to individual animals but to animal life as such, we see comparable deficiencies: the genus is able to maintain itself through the reproductive activities of individual, perishable animals, but this self-maintenance only accomplishes the continued production of equally perishable individuals. Even as a genus, animal life cannot realize itself adequately in individual form.[6]

The kind of mortality belonging to animal life is intimately related to the fact that animal life is an abstraction from nature. It is in fact only in death that the truth of animal life is revealed: animal life only succeeds at coming close to what it should be according to its concept (total assimilation of nature) in death, as the animal's body itself succumbs to dissolution, whether through predation or disease.[7] But this only means that animal life successfully realizes itself by destroying itself. It is thus only in spirit, or *human* life, that the concept of life is realized in a stable, enduring form, where the universal determines itself concretely, and all of nature is assimilated to life as each individual human being is the site of an entire inner world. Indeed, only in human life is nature apprehended in its totality: not through the restrictive lens of what is helpful or harmful to life alone but rather in a way that is open to finding nonbiological meaning in nature, humans are able to experience death (transcendence of the vital drives) in a way unavailable to animals. Yet insofar as the soul is the most primitive form of spirit, it is characterized by the strange coincidence of being the truth of nature generally and—due to the vagaries of spatial location, temporality, or inheritance—only actually exhibiting a more or less distorted form of spirit.

But we must not let this "strange coincidence" obscure for us the decisive break involved in passing from nature to spirit. Though no human concretizes humanity in the simple way that any thirty-six-inch object concretizes that measure, a close and sustained look at any human life will show spirit in all of its complexity—or at least enough complexity to guarantee that human life is of a different order than animal life. This difference is clear if we look to the way humans and animals relate to their respective genera. Hegel makes a very revealing remark in the *Zusätze* that what the genus (*Gattung*) is for the animal, rationality (*Vernünftigkeit*) is for the human being.[8] As a rule, it is important not to give undue weight to what appears in the *Zusätze*, but the position expressed here can be authenticated: the same position is supported in the Erdmann/Walter transcripts[9] and in the *Phenomenology*.[10] To grasp this comparison, recall that the genus is what the singular animal *ought* to be, namely, life's perpetual assimilation of nature and reproduction of itself. Yet, the singular animal always falls short of this standard, for its own part collapsing into death and succeeding at delaying the annihilation of the genus only by producing still more perishable animals.[11] Consequently, not only does the singular animal fail to be adequate to its genus, but the genus fails to realize itself, to give itself determinate existence in a way that is adequate to what it is essentially. But the human being's relation to its "genus" (rationality) does not have this defect because the relation is one of *thought* (*Denken*).[12]

Denken for Hegel does not refer to just any mental activity but to a form of spirit that is syllogistic and thus self-determining—that is, in fact, identical to the will.[13] A syllogism is self-determining because its universal is inwardly determined, such that its existence in singular form does not violate its universality. The animal genus is not self-determining in this way, being rather only as Hegel puts it a *judgment*:[14] an immediate union of universal and singular (affirming that this singular thing "is" this universal without sorting out the incompatibility between universality and concrete, individual existence). The animal is impelled by the drives and forms of experience it has by virtue of its genus: none of its behaviors gives any indication of an awareness of its own individuality in contrast with its species identity. Yet despite this seamlessness between individual and universal (the affirmation that the individual "is" the universal that characterizes judgment), the individual is unable to fulfill the genus's demand of total assimilation of nature. The animal dies, revealing the vast gulf that remains between the (universal) genus, which persists and retains its identity with itself, and the individual animal, which loses its identity in its destruction: this is the other aspect of judgment (*Urteil*), the *Teilung*, or division of what is affirmed as one.

In contrast, the human relation to its genus is syllogistic insofar as the (universal) genus is inwardly determined: the very concept of humanity involves being a human at this or that stage of life and passing through these ages in succession. The particularity of human existence (being a youth or an elderly person, for example) does not violate its universality because this particularity itself is an expression of the universality: what it is to be human becomes articulated and attains full expression over the course of a changing, developing life. The difference between animal and human life can be seen by observing how in the latter the genus is "self-determining," or in looking at the completeness belonging to the individual human but lacking in the animal. The human being can say "I," knowing itself as in some sense the center of an inner world, whereas the animal is always only a token for the genus, possessing in its subjectivity only the common property of the entire genus.

Life and Death

The ages of life are the various stages through which a human being passes, from birth (or perhaps conception) to death. Of course, there are stages of life that most or all organisms pass through: if not all organisms have a complex series of well-defined stages, at the very least all must have some sort of growth toward a state of maturity at which point reproduction becomes possible. But this course of development does not succeed in giving the concept of animal life concrete existence. The growth of a human being can similarly be understood biologically, though such an understanding taken by itself would obscure the specifically anthropological dimension of human development over time (which is Hegel's concern here). Hegel mentions physiological changes here but only to show that in the human being, there is a *corresponding* ("entsprechen[d]") series of "spiritual appearances":[15] that is, in tandem and in agreement with the physiological changes the body undergoes (e.g., growth, puberty, maturation), there are spiritual stages (forms of cognitive relation to the world) that more properly belong to and define the human being and anthropological life.[16]

It will help to briefly introduce these stages before examining them in detail. There are three major divisions: childhood, adulthood,[17] and old age. Childhood however can be further divided into three (or perhaps four) substages: infancy (what Hegel simply calls the life of the *Kind*, using the general term for "child"), what we may call childhood (what Hegel calls the life of the *Knabe*), and youth (the life of the *Jüngling*). Hegel mentions the unborn child (*ungeborene Kind*) as a possible stage of childhood preceding infancy, but he leaves it unclear whether it is ultimately to be accepted as a stage of life.[18]

The life of the unborn child is life in a "vegetative state [*vegetativen Zustand*],"[19] the "life of a plant [*Leben der Pflanze*]"[20] insofar as the fetus has no notion of particular objects, or indeed of anything objective at all, anything standing against it. The fetus is in uninterrupted commerce with its environment, aware neither of subject nor of object. This is a "vegetative state" because according to Hegel's account in the philosophy of nature, plants draw their nourishment from nature in an unbroken flow, never relating to inorganic nature in its individuality.[21]

Birth is the *physiological* "natural change" that is "correlated" with the transition to a new stage: infancy.[22] The life of the infant consists in growth: not in the production of new members but in the quantitative increase in size and strength.[23] The former sort of growth would be typical of plants (and unborn children), which produce new "parts" (as, e.g., the plant produces new leaves and buds, though each of these parts is simply the plant itself immediately existing and when severed can become a new and complete plant): these "parts" are not members that are reduced to moments for a *subject* that has *being-for-itself*.[24]

The infant in contrast does have a center for which its members are only moments. That is, the infant is in some sense a *subject* of a single life, which lives in and through its parts. The infant's growth is not the proliferation of new immediacies (each of which would be itself a potential infant) but rather an enlarging of what are only moments of the one infant. In its respiration and consumption the infant has dealings with singular objects, but insofar as it is only an infant, it has no appreciation of the fact that objects are separate and independent of it. Its cries (which, as every parent knows, ring out whenever the infant is in anything but total comfort) are the expression of its immediate certainty that the objects before it *ought* to be reduced to moments for it, though also an implicit acknowledgment that they are not.[25]

When the infant begins to sense these objects in their determinacy, then it begins to pass over into the next stage, childhood.[26] By sensing and perceiving objects, the infant comes to see that objects are out of its reach—and thus begins to see that it is *itself* an object, occupying only a determinate space. The child knows the resistance of the world to his or her subjectivity and can thus be thought of as a humbled infant. But it is by accepting that she or he is a limited being alongside others that the child is able to exert the kind of real control over objects that the infant merely demanded. By walking, for instance, the child—while remaining of a determinate size—still manages to conquer space.[27] It is worth noting that while the infant extended itself through space only by unconscious growth (and felt itself entitled to *all* of space), the child occupies determinate positions in space *willfully*—as a directive from his or her own determinate self of which the child, unlike the infant, is aware. Indeed, by speech, the child is acquainted with universals and begins in other ways to look beyond what is immediately present, for example, by enjoying stories.[28] Since stories present a series of events leading up to a climax, it is crucial, if one is to understand it *as* a story, that one be able to adopt an idealistic attitude toward the events recounted: seeing an event not as something with validity or reality in itself but rather as moments in the development of something else, which may not at that point be fully clear. The child likewise begins to take an idealistic view of him- or herself, seeing that the child is not what he or she ought to be (viz., an adult).[29] In contrast, the infant only has a dim awareness that *other* things are not as *they* ought to be (viz., at its disposal), but it does not succeed even at beginning to differentiate itself from its immediacy. Yet though the child does make this distinction, he or she still only knows what he or she ought to be in the form of an immediacy: namely, another existing individual, such as his or her mother or father.[30]

But parents do not retain this godlike status in their children's eyes forever. With the physical change of puberty, there is a corresponding spiritual change, as the child enters the final stage of childhood, namely, youth.[31] Of the youth, Hegel says, "[T]he life of the genus begins to work and seek satisfaction within him."[32] To be sure, as a physiological change, puberty involves the emergence of the sex drive, which is in some respects a merely animal phenomenon in which the individual is driven to reproduce the genus. Yet this is not what Hegel means here by the stirring of the "genus [*Gattung*]" in the individual. Recall, "the *genus* [Gattung] is to [the] living being [*Lebendignen*, i.e., the *animal*, whether human or beast] what *rationality* [Vernünftigkeit] is to that which is spiritual [*Geistigen*],"[33] that is, to the human being as such.

Here emerges still another reason to oppose Wolff in his judgment that all of the phenomena of the anthropology are of what is shared between humans and animals. In defense of this position, Wolff points to the distinction Hegel makes in §396 between vegetable or "external" growth (in which the plant is simply duplicated again and again in what are essentially new plants) and animal or "internal" growth (in which the one life differentiates itself into different members whose independence is canceled in the activity and self-maintenance of the single life).[34] As noted earlier however, the difference between vegetable growth and "animal" growth is limited to the difference between the life of the fetus and the life of the infant. The ages of life continue beyond infancy, however, and the distinctively human aspect emerges unambiguously in adolescence, where the life of the genus (which is *reason*, not a biological classification) awakens in the individual.

Hegel discusses reason at the conclusion of the *Encyclopedia*'s phenomenology of spirit, the section following the anthropology, defining it there as the identity that ought to obtain between subjectivity and objectivity.[35] This means that the rational subject can be assured that its subjective representations ought to be of the same order and connection as the materially existing objects in nature. Here, in the ages of life, the stirring of "reason" in the adolescent means that once the child has become acquainted with universality in language no immediately existing individual, not even the child's parent, will suffice as the image of what the child ought to be. This universality is the "genus" within the youth, which now "begins to seek satisfaction" by rejecting everything immediately existing in favor of the universality in the youth's heart (as "an ideal of love and friendship, or a universal state [*Weltzustand*] of the world"[36]), a (subjective) universality with which the youth knows that the (objective) world *ought* to agree and must be *made* to agree. However, just as Hegel defines reason as the identity of subject and object that only *ought* to be actual,[37] so the reason that stirs in the youth's breast is essentially "in opposition to the extant [*vorhandene*] world"[38] and hence is an ideal that only *ought* to be.³⁹ The abstractness of this ideal is what renders the youth *only* a youth, and not an adult.

Adulthood for Hegel involves one abandoning not youthful idealism but only its abstract character: accepting to a certain extent the reality of the world that resisted those ideals and setting oneself to work, thus gradually bringing about in reality something resembling the abstraction that enthralls the youth. As the child is an infant who has been humbled by the reality of the world outside, so the adult is a youth who has been so humbled. Along with the revolutionary fervor of the youth, the adult has lost the youth's carefree *joie de vivre* and feels the hard life of work imposed by necessity.⁴⁰

However, by turning toward the concrete reality of the world, the adult in time transforms it to a certain extent and transforms him- or herself, such that by old age (the last stage) he or she is habituated to the world, which he or she henceforth no longer experiences as offering any resistance. The old person can look back on his or her life and see not merely a series of particular, contingent activities; rather, the old person can see his or her activity as part of the realization of ends larger than the individual, ends that are legitimate and that come to be in their own right. Just as the child takes an interest in stories that for an infant would be a series of disconnected, immediate events, the old person can take satisfaction and find meaning in the narrative structure of his or her own life, the story of actuality, a personal history that in adulthood proper can at times seem burdensome and aimless. The old person is thus freed from grief over the destruction of youthful ideals (the grief characteristic of adulthood). As the world is no longer felt as something distinct, the vitality (*Lebendigkeit*) of the person is extinguished.⁴¹

This last stage does not end in death but rather *is* death throughout, the extinction of the person's vitality. "Death" is an equivocal term for Hegel, referring possibly to a physical event terminating the life of the organism or to the final stage of a *human* life. Similarly, "life" is an equivocal term insofar as it can refer to animal life or to human life. Yet both life and death can be given general descriptions that, because they abstract from the very different particularities of biology and spirit, apply to both animal life and human life. Life can be thus abstractly defined as the process whereby a form, stimulated by the presence of alien contents, acts on these contents, assimilating them to itself.⁴² Death can similarly be abstractly defined as the end of life, when no foreign content still stands against the assimilating form.

Now, for the animal, the "form" characteristic of life is the system of biological processes, and its assimilation of its contents is its consumption, respiration, and reproduction. For the human being on the other hand, the "form" is the soul, the self-knowing idea, and its assimilation of its contents is its knowing of the world in which it finds itself, its transformation of its outer world into an inner, spiritual world such that the jumble of nature receives a *meaningful* order. Death for the animal arrives when it no longer feels inorganic nature as something opposed to itself, at which point the vital processes cease and the animal is annihilated.[43] Human death on the other hand arrives when the human being no longer feels its world standing against it as something foreign but rather knows it as its own product, and something meaningful. At that point the work characteristic of adulthood ceases, but in its "death" the human being is *perfected* rather than annihilated. In this "death" the opposition between the "genus" (i.e., reason) and its own singular existence has been overcome. The particular term mediating between these two extremes are the ages of life themselves.[44] As a human being with these successive determinations (the ages of life), the individual has realized the genus, that is, given reason real existence in the world (insofar as by old age the opposition between subjectivity and objectivity is overcome).

Like many others, Hegel considers the knowledge of death to be a uniquely human possibility. The animal does not know death because in death it is annihilated and hence does not feel or know anything. The animal's identity is constituted by its organic life, which is present only so long as death is absent. Yet the human's identity is constituted by her soul, not "life," in the biological sense and so human life does not have death as its opposite. Consequently, the human can actually *experience* a sort of "death," an extinction of vitality, an identity of subject and object, when the "life has become processless *habit*."[45] This death is the extinguishing of the opposition between reason (the "genus") and particularity through a lifetime of labor and the consequent reconciliation to the course of the world and satisfaction with one's place in it.[46] In other words, the old person is able to see that the results of his or her work are the existence of what is essential—that is, that they are *actuality*.[47] This retrospective cognition of actuality is of course wisdom, philosophy.[48] Hegel's famous "owl of Minerva" dictum (viz., that philosophy emerges only when a way of life has grown *old*[49]) should be understood in this context.[50]

Indeed, this identity of subject and object is the "end" of human life in both senses: it is the point to which one's life leads (with any luck), but also it is the goal and vocation proper to the human being. Thus what for the animal is death is the only kind of life that deserves to be called a *human life*, or the life of spirit.[51] It goes without saying that if this is the way that what seems to be death is actually the life of the soul, then we have little reason to hope for a continuation of consciousness and personal identity in heaven (or hell), as is typically represented in Christianity and Islam. Hegel seems to have considered the traditional notion of the immortality of the soul to be an ideal of the imagination, not of reason. Though there is very good reason to believe Hegel's sincerity when he called himself a Christian, his understanding of what that involves departs widely from the common conception, here and on certain other questions.

Additionally, one might say that one of the phenomena that make the difference between human beings and animals most clear is old age. The animal spends its life as an individual in a state of tension with its genus, which is resolved only in the animal's death. The genus returns to itself through this death of the individual animal, but not in the feeling or activity of the individual animal while it is alive. All of the vital processes of the animal *stand in opposition to* dead, inorganic matter, which they try to assimilate. Thus animal *life* itself stands opposed to *death*. The life of spirit on the other hand does not have death as its opposite, because it has no opposite at all: spirit is the suffering of "infinite *pain*,"[52] the complete emptying of subjectivity and its identification with or "manifestation" in its "opposite" (see chapter 2).

Therefore insofar as the human being is an animal (i.e., a living organism), "old age" is only the decaying of the body, the phenomenal "manifestation" of the individual animal's inadequacy to its genus. This is only a *negative* manifestation insofar as the genus itself is only ever actualized in imperfect individual animals, whose inadequacy becomes apparent not with the revelation of anything positive but only with the death and disappearance of this individual creature (a process that is senselessly repeated ad infinitum). In spirit, however, the genus (reason) attains a *positive* manifestation as the individual human being knows himself and his life to be the reality of this genus. Thus, for the human being, old age is a time in which the *human* genus (rationality) attains singular existence, but the inadequacy of this singular *insofar as it is an animal* to its genus has not yet appeared (i.e., death has not yet destroyed the old person's body). In the light of the difference between the life of spirit and the life of organic nature, the fact that human life is a march toward death (in the biological sense) does not render it absurd or meaningless. Insofar as the human being is *human*, she is *not* necessarily inadequate to her "genus" (i.e., reason), and thus human life is not (as that "profound" observation would imply) the meaningless cycle of birth, procreation, and death that animal life is.

Yet I do not want to give the impression that for Hegel the ages of life allow for all of the diversity and conflict in the natural world can be corralled into the individual soul over the course of its development. It is true that this development does allow for the true concretion of spirit itself, the truth of nature, in individual form. However, this possibility relies on the individual's integration into a larger social world: a family, a culture, a profession, and so on. The description of childhood makes clear that the institution of the family is presupposed, just as the activities of adulthood depend on the presence of a complex network of social relations within which people perform work that contributes to goals larger than any individual can accomplish alone, and which make sense only in the context of the actions of many who are absent: those who worked toward the same goals in the past (and have since died), and those in the future who will see what those today labor to bring about. The tranquility Hegel describes as being possible in old age comes not from the individual as such being sufficient to concretize spirit adequately all on her own, but on the way aging allows one not just to actually coordinate with others in work but to imaginatively identify with others, and their aspirations. An individual qua individual can only ever be a fragment of this overarching unity, and that is why an examination of gender follows the paragraph on the ages of life: gender, as Hegel understands it, is an original limitation in the individual human, whose presence is ineradicable, and whose influence is powerful.

What Lies on the Surface of Hegel's Theory of Gender

Hegel's analysis of gender invites similar objections to those aroused by his analysis of race: so much of his presentation uncritically reflects prejudices of his time and place that have been thoroughly discredited in more recent decades. In Hegel's view, it is the business of men to leave the home and enter society, such that not only paid work but also politics, science, and the arts—all "universal" matters, that is, justice, nature, truth, and beauty as such—are the exclusive province of men. Women on the other hand are relegated to the home and may concern themselves with lofty matters like justice only through their emotional attachment to their family members.[53] Hegel adds insult to injury by presenting the domesticity of women (and the inferior intellectual and moral state he takes their domesticity to involve) as something anthropological rather than something contingently historical. That he was firmly convinced of the inferiority of women is beyond doubt: the difference between the sexes and the status of women come up repeatedly, and from his earliest to his latest work he echoes the same patriarchal theme.[54]

Moreover, his own dealings with women bear witness to his sexism: when his wife voiced her position that moral guidance comes from the heart and sentiments, Hegel not only launched into a lecture (which is perhaps forgivable for a philosopher) but condescendingly explained to her that what she expressed could certainly not be her *real* position.[55] Women, Hegel further explained, act only based on character and cannot act on principle as a man can.[56] When confronted with an understandable reaction to living in these suffocating circumstances, Hegel took it as a sign of female inferiority rather than of the perverse living conditions in a patriarchal world, as when Hegel's sister suffered from mental illness and Hegel wondered whether her affliction was not due to the hysteria natural to her gender.[57] Even when Hegel seems to redeem himself, we must not be too quick to credit his acumen, as when during his time as a headmaster he authorized the building of a girls' school, but only because he felt girls needed education solely for the purpose of making good wives for cultured men, not to excel in their own right.[58] Even late into his middle age, as it was becoming more and more common to encounter an educated woman in academic circles, Hegel was known for resisting discussing his ideas with women.[59]

There is therefore no question that Hegel's personal views on women are retrograde, arbitrary, and demonstrably false: that question is settled and uninteresting. What remains to be settled however is what can be salvaged in Hegel's theory of gender. Though if we restrict ourselves to the ninety-eight words composing *Encyclopedia* §397 there is nothing to fix upon to rehabilitate this theory, we are aided by the fact that Hegel's mature theory on most things is remarkably consistent, and gender is no exception: from 1802 to 1830 he presents a single theory of gender in versions that are more or less detailed, and shifting in their precise focus, but that are all consistent with each other. Yet a consistency across articulations of his theory does not mean they were all of equal depth: a close study of the version presented at the opening of the "Spirit" section of the Jena

Phenomenology allows for a richer and more nuanced understanding of what I will call the standard presentation of Hegel's theory of gender (the one given in the anthropology's §397 as well as later in §519 on family life in objective spirit and §§165–166 of the *Grundlinien*), one that allows for a reinterpretation and partial rehabilitation of the theory as a whole. Before seeing how the account in the *Phenomenology* can deepen one's reading of the standard version, allow me to briefly present this standard version in its own right.

The most commonly presented version of Hegel's theory of gender makes three principal points: (1) the social and cultural distinction between genders is legitimately based on the natural (biological) distinction of the sexes; (2) one's gender determines the way one experiences the feeling of love and relations to others, as well as one's social identity generally; (3) the gender distinction establishes legitimate norms governing the behavior, responsibilities, and delimitation of the sphere of activity of a person.

There is a natural distinction of genders and unification of them in reproduction found toward the end of the *Philosophy of Nature*, but in the *Haupttext* (published by Hegel himself) there is nothing about assigning characters to male and female. In the lecture material there are remarks about a mirroring of the male and female genitalia (*Geschlechtsteilen*) and the opposite characters of feminine indifference and masculine division or duality,[60] but it does not appear that the gender character here should be understood as anything like the phenomena belonging to the anthropology: in the examples Hegel is mainly concerned to show that in reproductive sex one gender gives while the other receives, though as he notes male and female genitalia have many morphological similarities.

In the anthropology and the philosophy of objective spirit on the other hand, Hegel consistently argues that the *natural* sex distinction underlies differing gender identities.[61] Hegel's apparent meaning here is that as reproductive sex involves a man penetrating a woman, and to this extent, two sexes corporeally enacting roles of passivity and activity, so men and women are disposed to experience things differently: women are passive, absorbed in sentiments, confined to a state of undifferentiated unity with their objects whereas men are active, involved in serious matters outside the home and thus able to separate what is valid in its own right from what is merely of private or personal (i.e., domestic) significance.

The gender difference shows up in their feelings as well, with implications for gendered roles and responsibilities. A husband and wife love each other: each seeks itself, that is, the principle of its identity, in the other,[62] but love and family life have different meanings for men and women. For men, a loving marriage is a repose from the larger social world: masculinity requires occupation outside the home, entering into relationships freely and competing with other men in civil society. Taking part in the hearty give-and-take of society is a necessary part of what appears to be the fuller selfhood available to men, but it involves implicit or explicit hostility between man and man, engendering a feeling of alienation. A happy home where his position is secure and acknowledged by others is a welcome repose for men. For women on the other hand family and marriage are not a way to withdraw from obligations and the seriousness of life, but rather they comprise the sphere of their most serious obligations—which of course places women in the position of servants, ministering to the needs of their fathers, and later husbands and sons, so that the latter may experience peaceful domesticity as well as the bustle of civic life.

At this point I must reiterate the statement I made at the end of chapter 2 on whether the anthropology should be taken as normative: Hegel aims to articulate what belongs to human nature at the most basic and primitive level, without maintaining that what he identifies will be equally apparent in all human behavior, or that the way he describes an anthropological phenomenon is not misleading if taken out of the context of the entire philosophy of spirit, the later parts of which frequently clarify and qualify how we should understand what was stated in the earlier parts. This is not to exonerate Hegel, but only to let him speak for himself, in the way that he can best be understood, before we evaluate what he has said.

As in the case of race, I believe Hegel's theory of gender is more complicated than is commonly appreciated. Though I have no doubt that Hegel personally felt men to be superior to women, it often happens even to the best philosophers—or perhaps *especially* to the best philosophers—that they do not exercise complete command over their arguments, which instead are so extraordinarily incisive that they cut deeper into the matter at issue than the philosopher or any contemporaries realize. The more radical implications of a great philosopher's work remain after the philosopher's death to be explored and brought to light by lesser students of philosophy, who yet benefit by having access from the beginning to the complete work of a great thinker. In this way I intend to bring to light certain threads in his theory that allow for a more complex and—I do not think it is too bold to say—feminist understanding of gender.

The Law of the Netherworld and Radical Guilt

In the midst of presenting the standard version of his theory of gender,[63] Hegel refers to Sophocles's *Antigone* as "one of the most sublime presentations of piety," which in the previous paragraph he identified as the "ethical disposition" of womanhood, and even refers (in the *Anmerkung*) explicitly to his treatment of the play in the Jena *Phenomenology*, where we find Hegel's richest treatment of gender. The reader will know that Antigone belonged to the cursed house of Oedipus, who on his journey to Thebes both saved it (ridding it of the Sphinx by answering her riddle, recognizing one and the same humanity in the various ages of life) and brought a plague on the city (which was sheltering a parricide, viz., Oedipus himself). After Oedipus's shame was revealed, he left Thebes to wander in the company of his daughters Antigone and Ismene, while his sons Eteocles and Polyneices fought for control of the city and ended by killing each other. Eteocles usurped power from Polyneices so that the former defended Thebes while the latter gathered an army to attack it. For this outrage, Eteocles's uncle and successor Creon forbade anyone to honor Polyneices with a burial.

In tragic fashion the law of the city thus comes into conflict with the demands of familial piety, which requires burial of one's deceased relatives. Hegel notes that the burial ritual saves the dead human being from being carried away by a meaningless current of natural causes and effects by making the death something *willed* and made to be—something meaningful—rather than the annihilation of a human individual being something that simply happens, as if for no reason. Death is thus incorporated into human culture and explanation through this ritual act.[64] The command to carry out this ritual is part of the divine law, rooted in the institution of the family, its household gods, and cult of dead ancestors. This law of the netherworld, the province of women, sometimes comes into opposition with the civic law, the human law of the masculine state (the state that admits as citizens only men), whose origin is historical and clear, as opposed to the divine law, obscurely originating in a time as distant and inaccessible as the very underworld where the dead reside. In obedience to the divine law, Antigone flagrantly defies the human law, casting a handful of dirt on Polyneices's corpse. Running afoul of the civic law, Antigone clashes with Creon and is sentenced to be shut up in a tomb while still alive. But Creon is no more successful in escaping his fate: his son Haemon was betrothed to Antigone, and Haemon kills himself (in front of his father) with his sword once he enters the tomb to discover that Antigone has hanged herself.

The account in the *Phenomenology* is superior to the others because it makes clear that the feminine is not a defective version of the masculine.[65] Spirit dirempts itself into two genders, each of which display humanity in its own right. Admittedly, Hegel does in the anthropology and the philosophy of objective spirit give the impression that the masculine is finer and of greater value than the feminine: there the masculine "activity [*Tätigkeit*]" is contrasted with the feminine "subjectivity [*Subjektivität*]." That the masculine bears within it a tension between what is universal and its own individual existence, and struggles to bring about a unity of the two (a point mentioned both in *Encyclopedia* §397 and *Grundlinien* §166), is the only indication that the male is somehow higher than the female. But the much richer treatment given in the *Phenomenology* casts doubt on this simple hierarchy by identifying masculinity and femininity with two distinct institutions (the household and the state), each of which has its own utterly valid and binding law.

Antigone is a tragedy and Hegel's understanding of it faithfully preserves its tragic character: it is not a conflict between the good hero and the evil villain, but rather a conflict of right against right.[66] The law of the household (the divine law of religion, the netherworld, and the feminine) is no less valid than the law of the city.[67] While the political law can seem to be the stable reconciliation of the family with other families and with the state, the apparent harmony of the two in theory is disrupted in the *deed*, the entrance of either into actuality insofar as the deed must follow one law or the other, but not both. To be *actual*, spirit must take *determinate* form, which sets it off from other such actualities. This means existing temporally as a person at the one particular stage of one's life, as well as existing as one determinate gender with a particular character (*Charakter*)[68] or way of experiencing the world, different from and in apparent opposition to another gender.[69]

Sophocles presents the gendered characters as not only distinct ways of experiencing the world but as on a par with each other, each legitimately expressing one law of human life while being limited by its unconsciousness of the other law. Thus in *Antigone* the eponymous heroine says to Creon, "[I]f my present deeds are foolish in your sight, it may be that a foolish judge arraigns my folly."[70] In other words, it is granted that Antigone's act is criminal and mad from the masculine, political perspective; but Creon's dictates and inflexibility are equally criminal and mad from the feminine, familial-religious perspective. The blindness of each to the law of the other (which indicates both a certain completeness and sufficiency of each law on its own, as the principle of an entire inner world, and its ultimate limitation as the law of only *one particular* inner world) is further on display in Haemon's warning to Creon: "Do not think that your word and yours alone must be right";[71] and the chorus of Theban elders' judgment of Antigone, that "she does not know how to bend before troubles,"[72] that is, that she cannot see a law other than her own.

The way the genders are distinguished here thus does not serve to justify the authority of men over women (even if this was Hegel's intention, following many philosophers before him). The deeper point, the one that plays a larger role in the development of the philosophy of spirit as a whole, is the one that highlights the determinacy of human embodiment and shows the radical guilt imprinted on the human soul. This guilt is radical in the way original sin belongs to the very origin of human beings: you are guilty not because of something you did (and thus might not have done), but because the conditions of your actual existence, your particularity, present only one aspect of what you are according to your concept.

To be human, in other words, always means to have an excess of particularity that sets one off from the concept of humanity understood abstractly. In the tragedy this means that entrance into actuality means carrying out one law and violating another. The guilt here is unavoidable: "to be innocent is to have the non-action typical of a stone's way of existing: not even children are innocent."[73] For us humans, there is thus no state of innocence "before" the act, but dramatic form allows the aesthetic exploration of such a state of quasi-innocence, before one's guilt is revealed to oneself and others. In such a state, one's identity is secured at the price of ignorance of the conditions that establish a contrary identity: consciousness of one law means unconsciousness of another law.[74] One becomes conscious of the contrary law only by the catastrophe ensuing when one acts in accordance with one's gendered identity.

Tragedians represent this as the exaction of revenge in response to an outrage, and indeed, the guilt is expiated only by the destruction of the guilty person. This destruction might mean killing the person (as Clytemnestra killed Agamemnon and was in turn killed by Orestes, for example), or the destruction of the character (but not extinguishing the life) of the offender, as in Oedipus's torment as his crimes are revealed to him, or Creon's in witnessing his son's suicide, or the madness that descends on Orestes after killing his mother—the "pathos" that Hegel mentions.[75]

This destruction of one's character does not just mean something very bad or sad happening but the unraveling of a person's identity. Oedipus was a hero because he had self-knowledge (recognizing humanity in the diverse appearances the Sphinx presented in her riddle), but his knowledge of humanity in its generality was equally ignorance of humanity in its particularity: he did not know his own family and so killed his father and wed his mother. Oedipus's very identity, as the hero who conquers through self-knowledge, was undone—not despite but *because of* his actions. Oedipus then wanders, blind, with his daughters (reminders of his unnatural union with his mother) just as Orestes was pursued by the Furies after murdering his mother. The inevitability of tragic actions like this (due to the clash of distinct laws) belongs to the way spirit determines itself in distinct genders, but to explain the emergence of madness after the crime has been committed will require a brief exposition of the subsequent parts of the anthropology, beginning with the next paragraph, §398, on sleeping and waking.

Waking from Sleep and the Masculine Pathos

After the paragraph on the sex relation is one on sleeping and waking, which Hegel treats similarly to femininity and masculinity, respectively. Like femininity, sleep is a condition of "subjectivity" such that the soul is in immediate contact with its object (in such a way that reality and fantasy lose their distinction). Being awake resembles the "activity" of masculinity insofar as in it the soul begins to grasp the existence of objects as something distinct from itself, existing in its own right and having nothing to do with one's subjective condition.

The paragraph on sleep and waking is followed by the last section of the "natural soul," sensibility, which concerns the way the soul knows objects through corporeal sense organs in such a way that only objects distinct from the body are known, but, because the soul is completely absorbed in its body, it does not manage to experience its own body (or at least not the sense organ presently doing the sensing) as an object, remaining "asleep," at least regarding its own corporeity. That the soul in sensibility only achieves a "waking" state toward external objects by remaining "asleep" toward its own body means that both states of consciousness, waking and sleep (the one "active" and the other "subjective") are one-sided, without true selfhood (*selbstlose Sein*, as he calls them elsewhere[76]). Yet the soul in its awoken state does not acknowledge its one-sidedness but rather takes waking experience to be the whole truth, and any passage into sleep to be a lapse into nonsense.

It is because of how deeply the awoken soul depends on the sleeping condition that it remains completely unaware of this dependence. In sensibility it is always the body itself that grants access to the external world, but precisely because the soul is absorbed in this body, "asleep" to it, the awoken soul may take itself to know objects directly, without mediation of the body, or "sleep." In this way, in its waking state the soul denies its own substantial foundation and thus brings on itself the danger of disordered experience characterizing "feeling in its immediacy" and "self-feeling" or *madness* (the sections of the anthropology after sensation). The soul here repudiates the stage of sleepy absorption in objects altogether, even the absorption in its own body that enables sensibility: this demand to know objects without mediation of the body means the most extreme form of waking life becomes indistinguishable from the disordered experience of dreams. Order is reestablished only when the soul makes madness (the condition of knowing apart from the natural body's mediation) into something that does not just *happen* to the soul but that the soul imposes on itself. This ritual conquering of madness occurs in habit (the culmination of the anthropology), as the soul creates its own mediation with the world, fashioning its own body for itself.

Returning to §397 but placing it in this broader context, it is clear that the point is to show that being human in actuality means having a *determinate* character according to which the world is experienced rather than entering existence as a blank slate—identical to all others—that then passively receives whatever imprints the world offers it. Hegel associates these characters with masculinity and femininity, though for us today, it would be more accurate to understand these as domesticity on the one hand and a life of civic participation on the other, which can but need not have anything to do with the physiological constitution of the person. Despite the extent to which our world differs from that of Antigone and Creon,[77] to a considerable extent for us today women around the world are less likely than men to work outside the home. Thus even if we no longer have hearths devoted to the penates, domesticity still involves a blending of "high ideals" like love and justice with the personal, familial attachments of one's household. To this extent the "law" of femininity can still come into conflict with the "law" of masculinity. That the "subjectivity" belonging to the domestic attitude arises naturally from bodies possessing female genitals, or bodies penetrated during sex, is of course absurd.

What is of deeper and more enduring significance is Hegel's development of what he associates with femininity and masculinity over the course of the anthropology, and how this shows that the ever-present danger in gender identity is that the feminine is devalued, ignored, and taken for granted. Thus according to Hegel the social delusion of male chauvinism has as its parallel in the individual psyche the actual condition of madness. The masculine tendency is to separate itself from the conditions of its corporeity and to associate the body with womanhood: this tendency is well documented in the history of philosophy, both in those who advance it and those who criticize it.[78] From the traditionally masculine perspective, the man is only incidentally embodied. Much like Caucasians enjoy an "unmarked" status in the white supremacism that is the norm in Western culture, such that one is "ethnic" or particular precisely to the extent that one is not white, whereas white characteristics are identified with humanity as such, so are men "unmarked" with respect to gender. But just as a comprehensive and sympathetic reading of Hegel's philosophy of race shows that it aims at a *marking* of whites (whatever Hegel's personal feelings and motives may have been), so his theory of gender aims at marking men.

This "marking" is nowhere to be found in §397, but the "ethical world" and "ethical action" sections of the *Phenomenology*, read together with the course of the anthropology, show that the sinking into madness is due to the conceit of the masculine principle. Moreover, in critiquing masculinity Hegel does not cede to it all agency, making it the protagonist of the story. It is true that abstract masculinity brings about madness, but the drama is resolved by the soul paying respect to the feminine law and mirroring the act of Antigone in ritually affirming[79] that the catastrophe that has befallen the soul will not be merely something that has happened but rather will be something *willed* and made to happen. The independence asserted by the awoken soul from the natural body (insofar as all of nature, including its own body, becomes an *object* for the awoken soul) is an outrage, an act of hubris that brings on madness as a kind of death (a radical disturbance in which the soul separates itself from the body). But this independence of the soul from its natural body is ritually affirmed in *habit*, the creation of a new form of mediation between the soul and its world (viz., the habits that the soul does not have by nature), effectively curtailing the dependence on the given corporeal conditions for experience. The feminine principle of "subjectivity" or "sleep" is thus not the incapacitation of the male principle but rather what first makes the male principle possible and is needed to provide a check on the tendency of masculinity to get carried away with itself. Moreover, Antigone, the feminine heroine, demonstrates not only the commitment to the law of the household that makes the political (masculine) world possible but, in her burial of Polyneices (ritually affirming yet qualifying the masculine break with its natural foundation), also surpasses even the tragic division of genders and gendered norms.

The criticism Hegel gives of the masculine perspective, or the awoken soul, has gone largely unnoticed by commentators. Butler presents Antigone and the feminine in Hegel's account as something to be "transformed and surpassed"[80] into the masculine, as (she argues) the household is absorbed into the state. Not only does this miss the hubris of the male separation of itself from its natural foundation, it also undermines the tragic character of the household-state relation that both Sophocles and Hegel preserve. Butler says that for Hegel womankind perverts the universal,[81] making the state something of merely private significance, and that the feminine association with the unwritten divine law in opposition to the public, articulated law of the state amounts to the a priori exclusion of women from speech and the sphere of universality.[82] It is true that Hegel wants to show what is in some respects the one-sidedness of the feminine perspective, but we would misunderstand his point if we fail to also note: first, that the "universal" at the stage (exemplified by the masculine law) under examination is itself already false and perverse; and second, that Antigone can represent the law of the household in its simplicity, tragically clashing with the law of the state, but she also represents the level of culture or spirit that encompasses and reintegrates its opposite.[83] The same oversight found in Butler's treatment is present in that of Mills.[84]

De Boer argues that Hegel imperfectly represents the authentically tragic situation. She acknowledges that Antigone and Creon each occupy a one-sided position, and that the two laws are presented in the *Phenomenology* as largely symmetrical.[85] However, this faithfulness is undermined by the fact that the two are equally valid only for the understanding,[86] while reason knows the state to have the family as one of its moments, without the reverse being the case.[87] The resolution of the opposition thus ends up introducing an asymmetry between the two moments.[88] This way of representing the conflict is symptomatic of what De Boer sees as Hegel's failure to properly identify the "tragic negativity" that should be his principle for everything (instead of absolute negativity). Tragic negativity involves opposed moments that are not identical but *entangled*—bound up with each other, perhaps inextricably so, but not implicitly identical. Should they become disentangled and should one subordinate the other to itself, this would only be the result of force, since they are symmetrical and neither is in-itself the means for the other to realize itself.[89]

As I argued in chapter 2, De Boer's raising of tragic negativity is very helpful in those parts of Hegel's work where the transition to a resolution has been too quick or cursory, and one moment has received short shrift. In such cases the most honest thing to do is to go back and rediscover the way two opposed moments implicate each other, without forcing a reading in which the result was foreordained. However, I do not think Hegel's treatment of gender is one of those instances. I acknowledge that Hegel does not give us a tragedy in which there is no resolution of the conflict, yet I disagree that Hegel has one of the opposed moments integrate the other. What Hegel shows rather is that Creon's position is determined by its exclusion of Antigone's: I take this as Hegel's final statement on the matter, not his portrayal of how it appears only for the understanding. If we examine the larger trajectory of the anthropology, the resolution does not come with a modification of the universal (e.g., a political change in Creon's governance) but with its dissolution: the passage into feeling is Hegel's proof that the masculine pseudo-universal of §397 is a fraud; and with the passage into insanity, the masculine awakening shows it was always implicitly identical to dreamy subjectivity. The masculine thus does not absorb the feminine as its presupposition, but rather each is reduced to a moment in a soul generating its own form of mediation. More proximately however, the gender conflict is "resolved" in sleep and waking, subjectivity and activity together as equally valid moments of one and the same soul.

Sleep as a Transcendental Condition of Waking Experience

As the feminine is the foundation for the masculine (which only appears independent), so the household is the foundation of the state: the state is a union of households and could not exist without them; the households first produce the people (which some women themselves literally bear) that will fill every office of the state.[90] Though it is difficult to recognize at first, the same is true of sleep and waking.[91] This seems not to be so because sleep and waking life seem to alternate but never overlap, such that one spends one-third of the time in sleep, and two-thirds awake. At most, it seems that sleep serves to recreate the energies used for waking experience. However, Hegel's notion of sleep is more subtle than that: while the time spent lying in bed, eyes closed, totally insensible to one's surroundings, and lost in vivid dreams provides the clearest example of it, "sleep" should be interpreted more broadly, and as a regular feature of what we are used to considering our waking life.

Sleep generally involves one losing the ability to distinguish what is internal to one's own mind and what belongs to the external world, and the failure to make this distinction itself induces sleep. Thus monotonous sounds or repetition of the selfsame activity cause one to drift off to sleep.[92] However, there are two major ways that "sleep" can have a broader meaning: (1) in forms of consciousness with decreased awareness of all or part of one's environment; (2) in the immersion in our own bodies that first grants us sensible access to external objects. The first is seen in loss of attention and daydreams, which though not an utter collapse into total unconsciousness are a lower degree of wakefulness and thus a passage to some degree into "sleep." Looking out the window of a train, the images blur together and the rhythmic rattling sound of the train on the track puts one in a kind of trance: one forgets where one is, what one is doing, even momentarily who one is. In those cases, if one is shaken out of this "sleep," one might well say that one was "somewhere else" or "miles away." While it is not true that this person was located anywhere but the train seat, the clouding over of the soul that sends the mind wandering far and wide is a kind of displacement insofar as one loses touch with the objects around oneself, no longer hearing the conductor announcing the stops but instead seeing and hearing—in a way that is not really willed—all sorts of other things. These experiences are presumably a part of everyone's life, but they would not be possible without the precise relation the human mind has with its world, which Hegel associates with the "natural soul."

Another example of a kind of low-grade sleep is the way we navigate familiar surroundings, like one's home, or one's route to work. Entering one's home, going to the pantry to get something to eat, one does not apprehend all the parts of the domicile even though the light continues to reflect off all manner of objects into one's eyes, giving visual data, and one's footsteps and the sound of the pantry door creaking open all create sound waves that strike the eardrum. The truth is that we pass a good part of our waking lives in some higher or lower level of "sleep."

If this kind of description of unreflective moving around in the world has a Heideggerian flavor, it is because both Hegel and Heidegger take their inspiration (to an extent that is hard to overstate) from Aristotle, who so outshone all of his predecessors (and nearly all of his successors) in sensitively discerning the grades of life and the soul in nature. The difference between sleep and waking is not one of dealing with imaginary fabrications or factual reality: to consider the mind as a theater in which representations or images are presented, some of which are the effects of real objects and some of which are not, is to lose sight of how sleep underlies all of our sensible experience. Sleep is the foundation of waking life not only in the physiological need to rest in order to be conscious later, but in the fact that even at your most alert, for instance, as you, with furrowed brow and intense gaze, focus very hard and deliberately on the tweezers as you position them in just the right way to remove a tiny splinter from your finger, you are asleep with regard to so much of your environment (the ground beneath your feet, the tightness of your shoes, the cold, etc.)—and you *must* be so in order for anything at all to be presented to you as "a real object of waking experience." To take a phrase from phenomenology, it is as if the horizon for the attention and "objectivity" characterizing waking life were a more encompassing state of immersive subjectivity.

We can also turn to what Hegel says about Hinduism in the philosophy of religion and India in the philosophy of history to aid us in understanding what he means by "sleep" and dreaming, insofar as Hegel takes Indian culture to be characterized by the sort of subjectivity that he associates with sleep. Of course, his reductive and condescending attitude is unfortunate and we cannot take his evaluation of India seriously. Nonetheless, these remarks are helpful in showing what Hegel was thinking. Of the spirit of India for instance he says:

> In a dream, the individual ceases to be conscious of self *as such*, as over against objective existences. Once awake, I am for myself, and the rest of creation is external, fixed in opposition to me, as I myself am for it. As external, objectivity expands itself to a rationally connected whole; a system of relations, in which my individuality itself is a member—an individuality integrated into that totality—this is the sphere of the understanding. In dreams on the other hand, there is no such separation. Spirit has ceased to exist for itself in relation to objectivity, and thus the separation of the external and individual ceases to be before

its universality and its essence. The dreaming Indian is thus all that we call finite and individual; and, at the same time, as infinitely universal and unlimited, in himself divine. The Indian perspective is a universal pantheism, but a pantheism of the imagination, not of thought. It is one substance, and all individuations are directly vitalized and animated into particular powers. The sensuous matter and content are in each case simply and unceremoniously taken up, and carried over into the sphere of the universal and immeasurable, and are not liberated into a beautiful form by free spirit or idealized in spirit so that the sensible world would be only the fitting expression of spirit. Rather, the sensible is enlarged to the immeasurable and indefinite, and the divine is rendered bizarre, confused, and ridiculous.[93]

In Hegel's presentation of Hinduism, the precise relation between universality and particularity has not been worked out: the universal appears in a dizzying array of determinate forms, but all vanish and are absorbed into the same simple unity, which is their foundation.[94]

Just as for men (in the standard version of Hegel's theory of gender) the feminine domain of the home is a place of relief, relaxation, and reinvigoration from the outside world, so is sleep for the soul of any gender. And as the family is the essential power[95] over the masculine state, which the latter cannot destroy or even disrespect without destroying its own foundation, so sleep is the absolute power[96] over the clear and orderly world of waking life. But it is precisely this order that makes waking life appear superior to sleep, since it is in waking life alone that we are in contact with what is real. Indeed, clarity and orderliness are emblematic of waking life: in response to the well-worn philosophical question of how we know that we are not dreaming all of our experience, Hegel answers that we find no justification for this certainty in this or that representation.[97] That is, I cannot be certain that I am awake now merely because I seem to be interacting with quotidian objects like a pencil and notebook rather than fantastic ones like unicorns and centaurs. The visual experience of seeing the pencil write on paper and the tactile sensation of writing can be (and often are) given in a dream. Nor can I be certain if I were to see a unicorn that I am dreaming: it would certainly be surprising, but mutations occur, and there are optical illusions as well. It is not impossible for light to be genuinely reflecting off objects onto my optic nerve in such a way as to produce the image that looks like a horse with a horn on its forehead. No single representation and no group of representations examined singly can assure us that we are either awake or dreaming. What assures us we are awake is rather the connection and order of our representations, over a long enough time (that random things are not happening, bodies are obeying physical laws, people are behaving as if the course of human history were what it has been, etc.).

And yet, for all this, sleep remains the foundation for waking life because it is "sleep," or more properly that with respect to which we are "asleep" or insensibly absorbed (viz., our bodies), that grants access to the reality we know in our waking experience (this is the second and more important way sleep has a broader meaning for Hegel). As I see something and reach out to grab it, my visual and tactile experience project me into the external object and its qualities: my body does not appear to me as an instrument that I point and control to experience objects, but rather as something with which I am immediately identified but do not feel. All sensible experience occurs through my body but *in* the experience my body vanishes, yielding all attention to the object.[98]

It may help to consider Heidegger's notion of the primordial phenomenon of truth as "being-uncovering," the original access we have to things themselves, which is distinct from the derivative notion of truth as agreement between different kinds of mental representations (e.g., perceptive and linguistic),[99] or Aristotle's point that perception is always true because it is our point of contact with reality, which makes it distinct from belief and imagination.[100] Heidegger's point and Aristotle's point are the same as Hegel's point: that the way we are used to thinking about how experience occurs and truth is given in experience overlooks the most crucial aspect, because our typical way of thinking about truth involves relating things without turning our attention to that which makes the relation possible by furnishing the *relata* and delineating the terms of the relationship. It is no surprise that sleep is not recognized as the foundation of waking experience, since this failure to recognize its importance is in truth the surest sign of its fundamental character.

But there is no avoiding this failure to recognize that waking experience is founded on sleep: in tragic fashion, it was destined to occur. The outrage that drives the tragedy is waking life's tendency to forget entirely its immersion in nature and its immersion in its own body (which is itself a part of nature): the pathos that results from this hubris is madness itself, a form of the feeling soul, the examination of which belongs to chapters 6 and 7. Even when I understand that waking life is founded on sleep—even as I affirm it in writing here—I have to constantly remind myself of this fact because my continuing waking experience imposes on me an unshakeable forgetfulness of this fact: in my experience I am focused on the objects in their difference from me, and to that extent I cannot but fail to attend to what in the experience is *unfelt* (and must be so).

In the three paragraphs on natural changes Hegel aims to show that the individual human being is in-itself spirit: but insofar as it remains a form of natural soul, it is spirit *only* in-itself. In natural qualities (the object of chapter 3) spirit appeared immersed in nature, with no account taken of how this absorption in diversity raises problems for spirit's claim to be identical to itself as the truth of nature: these difficulties are acknowledged here and in the next chapter on sensibility, which completes the paragraphs on the natural soul. Though in spirit all natural differences become merely ideal differences, to be something *actual* spirit still must exist in some particular flesh and blood person bearing all sorts of natural properties.

Often when the natural and not-merely-natural sides of humanity are discussed, they are roughly thrown together: it is said that we are animals, yet we are *also* rational, with a spark of the divine. An enormous explanatory burden is thus shifted onto that hapless word "also," which is utterly incapable of shouldering it. Hegel is more subtle. If reason is going to be housed in a natural body—if it will *be* in some sense a natural body—it will not do to pick out the sharpest animal in the menagerie and mutter cryptically that it is an animal, but also rational. Reason, after all, does not burst on the scene as from the barrel of a pistol: there are intimations of it, as in animal life developing from a state of immaturity to maturity, and in a newborn baby, which yet cannot *be* spirit in the full sense, lacking as it is in all self-awareness. But this means that concrete spirit, as this or that natural individual, can only ever present a limited image of spirit. The course of development in a human life is one in which what is inner gains outward expression even as the outer world works on human interiority, kneading it to make it appropriately supple and responsive. Any concrete existence of spirit, any actual human being, will have an inner world that may differ markedly from the outer world. The absorption in one's inner world and the engagement with the outer world are expressed, Hegel thinks, in the two types of human being, male and female, whose combination ever reproduces this duality.

Yet there is a dynamic in this relationship that propels the account past natural changes and eventually out of the natural soul: the inner world, the world of sleep, and the feminine supports the engagement with exteriority, the awoken state of masculinity. The more this inner world escapes attention, the more powerful and decisive it is. Two aspects of the natural soul are clear and distinct here: that which experiences and that *through which* we experience (which itself is experienceable). Yet these two aspects are separable only in thought: the reality of the natural soul is that it is at once an object and that which knows objects—or better, it is an object and, by virtue of this objectivity, it can experience objectivity but always only in the form of *other* objects. This is the soul as sensation.

5

Sensation and the Oblivion of the Body

> The eye sees not itself.
>
> —Shakespeare, *Julius Caesar*

In this chapter I explore how the soul's sensible knowledge of nature is undergirded by its insensibility toward its own body. Hegel understands sensation in an Aristotelian way, as the soul sensing only qualities that vary from the way its own organs are determined, such that the soul fails to sense its own self. Sensation takes the soul as its object only indirectly in the emotions, whereby a spiritual content (e.g., joy or anger) becomes embodied and is thereby *felt*. In this chapter I also include the critique (up to this point largely unnoticed) of crude empiricism and epistemological foundationalism that can be reconstructed from the anthropology's paragraphs on sensation and parts of the philosophy of nature. For Hegel, there is no mystery of how a "natural" object can produce an "intellectual" impression on the soul, because nature *renders itself* intelligible, offering itself up to the soul to be known. In a parallel process, the soul incarnates itself, giving its emotions physiological expression in its body (e.g., smiling, blushing): this allows the soul to *feel* an emotion such as anger, which would otherwise be an abstract thought of a disagreement between what is and what ought to be.

Seeking a Middle Term

To say that the senses "mediate" between the soul and nature is to say that the senses are the "middle term" that renders a "syllogism" what was previously a "judgment." These terms are usually used in formal logic, but Hegel uses them ontologically such that not only can you utter judgments or construct syllogisms *about* actual things, but the things themselves can be ontologically structured in the manner of a judgment, or a syllogism. For instance, the sans-culotte in revolutionary France was a Frenchman in the manner of a judgment. That is, this individual related to the universal (France) by *immediately* identifying with it just as in a spoken judgment ("S is P") the individual subject and universal predicate are immediately identified.

But group identification as a judgment is unstable: thus each sans-culotte identifies immediately with France and takes himself to speak for the nation itself such that his enemies are the nation's enemies. Any political disagreement between people thus becomes high treason and the Reign of Terror results. Identity is more stable if it functions as a "syllogism," with a middle term uniting the universal with the individual. The articulation of state institutions for citizen participation would be the middle or "particular" term in the preceding example. The particular term stands between universal and individual but facilitates their relationship rather than hindering it. Thus with legally defined procedures for citizens voting, holding office, petitioning government, and so forth, an individual Frenchman can identify with the nation in a way that does not at the same time exclude all other individuals from the same identification.

For a particular term to do this job, it must be immanent within the universal. The universal term in a judgment appears utterly undifferentiated, which is what makes its identification with the individual term unstable. And the particular term cannot be ad hoc: if the two are to reach a mediated, stable relationship, an immanent principle of differentiation must be identified within the universal itself. For revolutionary French politics, this would mean a conceptual analysis of French national political life to see what forms of exercise and expression are already implied in this concept.

In the sections on natural qualities (addressed in chapter 3 of this book) the soul (as universal) is related to the various (individual) parts of nature more or less in the manner of judgment, immediate identification. Particular ("racial" and national) cultures were the closest thing to a middle term given there until talent, temperament, and character, which are really the transition from natural qualities to natural changes. I showed in chapter 4 that in the paragraphs devoted to natural changes forms of mediation begin to emerge with greater complexity and adequacy. The ages of life, gender, and interwoven states of sleep and waking present a more ordered way that human life recognizes itself in nature, but while in chapter 4 the human being somehow displays what belongs to the concept of spirit in its plenitude, in other ways the person is not exactly what spirit should be, or not yet, or not in the right way. The senses are a better mediation because, barring unnatural mutations or random accidents, all people not only have the five senses, they have them from the beginning and in their entirety. These are the obvious candidates for such mediators since they do grant the soul access to nature and allow nature to go beyond mere existence to being known.

Yet finding a middle term is not the same as finding an adequate solution. What appears at first to be an effective middle term may for instance serve only to concentrate the tension between the universal and individual, rather than relieve it. Thus in politics the antagonisms of society may simply be transmuted into a state apparatus that festers in deadlock or unabashedly promotes a particular interest. The problem with sensibility as a middle term is the same as what recommends it: the senses are at once faculties of the soul (sight, hearing, etc.) and corporeal parts belonging to the natural world (eyeballs, ears, etc.). The senses bring together body (nature) and soul, sensed and sensing,[1] but only "externally" as Hegel would say, that is, without resolving their deeper opposition. If the senses are genuinely to serve as a mediating term, we cannot separate these contraries from each other, locating the sensing subject in the soul and the sensed object in the body. Insofar as spirit is the identity of subject and object, it is entirely appropriate that a theme of the philosophy of spirit should be both subject and object, yet there are many ways in which subject and object can be identified, and some, like sensation, involve implicit difficulties. It is fortunate then that Hegel devotes more paragraphs to sensation than to any other moment of the natural soul.

This chapter will proceed in the following way. First, I will introduce the five senses and explain how Hegel understands each of them. Subsequently, I will isolate certain nuances of Hegel's treatment of sensation generally, discussing them in turn. The first of these will be the relation of each sense to those phenomena deduced in the philosophy of nature that are its object(s). I will examine briefly the object(s) of each sense in the initial presentation of the five senses, turning subsequently to examine the object of sensation in greater depth in order to draw conclusions about what precisely in nature is sensed. The second nuance I will examine is what I have called (following Aristotle) the "mixing" of the soul with the body, which characterizes Hegel's understanding of sensation.[2] This "mixing" gives the soul certain determinations in the same way that merely natural objects have them (since the body with which the soul is mixed is in some sense natural), and the soul's possession of these determinations will render the soul insensible to them, thereby limiting what the soul can sense. This insensibility intertwined with sensibility is carried over from the last chapter, where the female and male character and the states of sleep and waking showed the mutual implication of "subjectivity" and "activity." This theme will continue to inform subsequent chapters as well. Finally, I will examine the corporealization of the emotions, which for Hegel is a phenomenon of sensation insofar as it is this corporealization of a spiritual content (e.g., anger) that allows it to be *felt*.

The Five Senses

Sensation generally can be defined as the form of mediation between the soul and the outer world of nature. This form of mediation is provided by nature itself insofar as one is born with the senses already inhering in one's flesh. Specifically of course, there are five different forms of mediation between the soul and its externally received content: sight, hearing, smell, taste, and touch. And different senses sense different objects: colors, sounds, odors, tastes, temperature, texture, shape, and weight. Yet Hegel is not satisfied with such a list of apparently only externally related terms. The speculative method requires him rather not only to find the unity among the senses (to understand what sensation is generally) but also to identify the principle of the differentiation of sensation into precisely these senses.

Accordingly, Hegel groups the five senses into three classes in accordance with the moments of the concept. The first class is that of "physical ideality."[3] This class includes sight and hearing, and it is characterized by the fact that in it "difference appears as *variety*."[4] That is, the object's unity is seen or heard in abstraction from its materiality or self-externality. The second class is that of "*real difference*,"[5] which includes smell and taste. In these senses an object's self-externality (the material separateness of its parts to each other) receives its due, insofar as the object is broken down in the very sensing of it. The third class is that of "*earthly* [irdischen] *totality*"⁶ or "*concrete* [konkreten] totality."⁷ This final class has only one member, the sense of touch. The tactile sense is the only one that senses its object as a totality (and not ideality abstracted from difference or difference with no unity).⁸

This schema can seem to be an a priori construct arbitrarily forced on reality, but its contours result from steps taken earlier in the *Encyclopedia*. Take for example sight and hearing. These are called the senses of physical or simple "ideality" because in sight and hearing the object's difference from itself is rendered *merely an ideal* difference.⁹ That is, in sight and hearing these differences are subordinated to an overarching unity (and are thus not *real*, i.e., unsublated differences). To be sure, if I am too close to a massive object, I do not see the whole thing: I see only a part, and it would seem that the unity of the object, its ideality, escapes me. However, this failure to see the whole has to do with the particular circumstances involved (my position relative to the object and the object's massiveness) and not with sight as such. Additionally, the fact that when I see something I see only the side of it presented to me does not alter the character of sight as the sense of physical ideality. The ideality of the seen object does not consist in seeing in an instant the entire surface area of the object—and still less does it consist in seeing every material part, including those internal to the object. Rather, this ideality consists in the object's presentation of itself to the sense of sight as a certain color through the medium of light.

Light for Hegel is a sort of universal element,¹⁰ shining on all bodies and illuminating them. As visible (i.e., in relation to light), an object presents itself as *one*, a single phenomenon. In Hegel's discussion of light in the *Philosophy of Nature* he says: "In shaped corporeity the first determination is its *self-identical* selfhood [mit sich identische *Selbstischkeit*], the abstract self-manifestation of it as indeterminate, simply individuality—*light*. But shape as such is not luminous; rather, this property is [. . .] a *relation* to light."¹¹

Just as shape is not by itself luminous but must be brought into relation to light, light by itself illuminates nothing: it requires the presence of matter. Bodies as such are outside of themselves: but in relation to light, the externality of a body's parts is rendered ideal, and it manifests itself in a single phenomenon, its color. Thus what is seen is indeed light, but it is not pure, unadulterated light. Rather, it is color, the effect of light's interaction with matter,¹² that is, light's idealization of the asunderness of matter and matter's "darkening" of light. Were light to relate to something immaterial, no visible phenomenon would be produced. Such a thing would have no color, being instead completely transparent.[13] When light relates to something material, the self-externality of the body's parts to each other is sublated in the manifestation of the body's color through the medium of light.[14]

That the differences of the body's parts are rendered ideal means that the object does not break apart when we see or hear it, as it does when we smell or taste an object. Nor do we feel in our seeing and hearing that the object resists our corporeal sense organs. Rather, in sight and hearing we may forget altogether that we have sense organs, as we lose ourselves in the pure witnessing of an object. It may be argued that an object's visibility *also* shows its *difference* from other objects. Yet this differentiation is contingent: another body may be the same color as the first, and to that extent the two bodies can be indistinguishable.[15] *As visible*, an object is only unified with itself. Visibility does not guarantee the manifestation of the object's difference from other objects (this occurs only in the *tangibility* of objects).

Just as sight presents an object's unity with itself as a single visible phenomenon, so in hearing we sense a body's unity with itself in a single sound: and just as in sight the *determinate* color of an object distinguishes it from other objects, so in hearing a *determinate* pitch and timbre of an object differentiate it from others. Likewise, just as in the object of sight (viz., color), a body's physical ideality emerges only through a body's relation to something outside of it (viz., light), so in the object of hearing (sound), a body's physical ideality emerges only in relation to another object that strikes it, producing the sound.[16]

A full explanation of sound however requires a brief digression into gravitation. All bodies are extended, taking up a determinate space. Since such determinacy requires that the end of one be the beginning of another, the concept of mechanism implies a number of particular bodies. The relations between these bodies are governed by gravitation.[17] The body's extension and weight determine its ability, when in motion, to repel other bodies. But bodies are at the same time set in motion by forces of (gravitational) attraction (forces that belong to *other* bodies)—which is equally a function of weight (or more precisely, mass) and its distance from other objects.

Now, this would appear to give us a stable, balanced world of corporeal interaction and mutual influence. However, since all bodies are extended, and all extended magnitudes are divisible in principle, any single body is a multiplicity of smaller bodies, each of which must have the same determinations (attracting and repelling all other bodies)—that is, since gravity is not a monopoly of immense planets, but even the tiniest body has its own *specific* gravity—the concept of the body itself threatens to break down. For, a condition for a single body to be a body at all is that it maintain unity with itself. However, this *maintenance* of the body's corporeal integrity is at once the *violation* of the corporeal integrity of its parts, insofar as the latter must cease to repel each other.[18]

That is, a body—any body—must *cohere* with itself in order to *repel* other bodies and maintain its independence, but this *coherence* of the whole body with itself is for its parts (which, recall, are themselves bodies in their own right) *ad*herence to a *foreign* body, the *failure* to repel this foreign body. The criteria for embodiment thus seem to contradict each other. Yet—and this is the important part—each of these criteria has been legitimately deduced from the concept of nature.

This conflict is resolved by positing bodies as sonorous. Hegel understands sound as "a body's inner oscillation within itself."[19] In sound, it is posited that the body's repulsion of all foreign bodies is an *abstract* independence, not a real, concrete independence. In other words, by understanding bodies as sonorous we can hold together everything that must belong to the concept of a body in a way that none of these different aspects rule out any of the others. Including sonorousness in our concept of bodies shows that "the repulsion of all foreign bodies" is too vague to be an adequate criterion of embodiment, and for that reason this criterion comes into conflict with itself insofar as *each* body is already itself a union of smaller bodies that are foreign to each other. Thus bodily *coherence*, understood inadequately as "the repulsion of all foreign bodies," would be the same as bodily *disintegration* (since it would require the smaller parts of a body to repel each other).

Yet in being sonorous, the *parts* of a body lose their foreignness to each other (at least for a time) in their vibration (as they chaotically move in and out of each other's spaces). These parts become one body in the "inner oscillation" (the unity being expressed in the sound), though this one body remains separate from other bodies, which it repels. Sound is thus the expression of the "ideality" of the differences among the parts of a body, the qualification of this difference in the expression of the unity of the body.[20]

Taste and smell, on the other hand, are the senses of difference. That is, the soul in taste and smell senses a body's real difference from itself.

Accordingly, the natural phenomena of odor (i.e., "particularized airiness"[21]) and taste ("particularized water"[22]) involve the sensed body literally breaking apart, becoming a gas or a liquid (respectively).[23] Given that in his deduction of the elements in the mechanics section of the *Philosophy of Nature* Hegel calls air the element of "undifferentiated simplicity"[24] (as opposed to the "elements of opposition," viz., fire[25] and water[26]), it can seem unclear why in the physics section he locates particularized *airiness* (i.e., odor) as a "property of opposition" until one considers the fact that odor is the result of a body's *combustion*, or catching fire (*Brennlichkeit*).[27] Indeed, Hegel notes in his paragraph on fire that air is implicitly fire (as shown in its compression),[28] that is, the power to decompose matter. As air is the element of matter's combustibility, so water is the element of its solubility.[29] In both cases, a body's difference from itself, the material externality of its parts to each other, is rendered a *real* difference when the body is brought into relation with these elements: the body physically breaks apart. This breaking apart of a body, the real manifestation of its opposition to itself, is at once an event in nature and a sensible phenomenon for the soul (either as odor or taste).

Hegel hardly mentions the sense of touch in the *Haupttext*: he merely lists it along with the others and gives its objects (weight, heat, and shape).[30] In the *Vorlesungen* from 1827/1828 Hegel has little more to say about it. As far as the different senses are concerned, he seems mainly concerned in these lectures to demonstrate how the different senses vary with respect to the extent to which the soul feels *itself* in its feeling of other objects: "In hearing and seeing we do not feel [*empfinden*] ourselves, in smell and taste we begin to, and in touch [*Fühlen*] as such the return [to the self] is completed, when I feel something, I feel it resist me."[31]

I will not dwell on the fact that the soul is able to feel itself more in touch than in the other senses because, as I will show later, the soul's "mixing" with its body (i.e., the fact that the soul feels *through* corporeal sense organs) means as a result that despite the relatively greater degree of self-feeling in touch, all sensation is characterized by a certain *failure* to feel oneself. It is worth noting however that an affective knowing of oneself belongs more to what Hegel calls "feeling" (*Fühlen* or *Gefühl*) than to sensation (*Empfindung*).[32] The term for the sense of touch is *Fühlen*, and Hegel seems in the 1827/1828 lectures on the anthropology (in the Erdmann and Walter transcripts) to think that the sense of touch is already implicitly self-feeling. This may be true. However, as this chapter will show, the sense of touch remains a form of *Empfindung* even if it is implicitly *Fühlen*. In fact, the sense of touch is, I think, the best example of *Empfindung*. I will return to this later in the chapter.

Here I will focus on how touch unites the ideality peculiar to sight and hearing with the difference belonging to smell and taste. As sight and hearing sense a body's unity with itself, and smell and taste sense a body's difference from itself, touch senses solidity and gravity, which Hegel understands to be a body's unity with and difference from itself. What is solid and has weight seeks its own center, holding itself together and repelling other bodies. Such a body's unity with itself is thus mediated by its difference from other bodies. But the physical properties allowing cohesion and repulsion enter into our sense experience in other ways as well: for example, sound is also derivative of corporeal cohesion. Why does sound not fall under the sense of concrete totality? The reason is that sound is only a momentary and inadequate overcoming of the difference of its parts, and this difference itself is not at all expressed in sound. The vibration that produces the sound subsides and the parts of the body return to their mutual externality, their mere embodiment. The body then once again returns to silence, no longer expressing its ideality. Solidity on the other hand is an expression of a body's ideality (perceptible for touch), the unity that the body has in its own right. An object's solidity thus does not require an outside object to strike it as its sonority requires, and solidity is not ephemeral like sound is. Sound is ephemeral precisely because it is an *abstraction* from the material separateness of its parts. This unsublated separateness eventually overcomes the sonorous expression of unity, imposing silence on the body. Solidity and weight on the other hand are expressions of a body's unity with itself that is mediated through its opposition to other bodies.

The visible body is also determinate (i.e., it is a *certain* color, different from other colors), but this determinacy is only implicit in the visible body. Only when it is juxtaposed with a body of another color does its determinacy appear, and even then, its determinacy is apparent for the observer only by reference to some *other* sensation. The same can be said of the sonorous body. It has a determinacy (of pitch and timbre), but this determinacy is only manifest when the body sounds along with other bodies. In touch, on the other hand, the body displays its "being-for-itself."[33] It has its unity by mediation with its other. In other words, it has reduced its other to a mere moment of its return to unity with itself. By concentrating in on itself, the solid object repels other objects, thus maintaining its identity and exhibiting what we might call a *differentiated* rather than a *simple* ideality.

Thus for Hegel a sense is a way of knowing that has a certain ontological structure (as, e.g., sight is a spiritual concretion of ideality in abstraction from difference) by virtue of which it is attuned to phenomena in nature that have the same ontological determination. This way of understanding knowledge's relation to nature is reminiscent of Plato's *Timaeus*. In the *Timaeus* Plato explains how the world soul and the human soul are both created by mixing the forms of identity, difference, and being.[34] That both the world soul and human souls are made from the same stuff (the mixture of these forms) accounts for the affinity between the intelligent human soul and the intelligibility of nature, that is, for how human beings can know these forms as they exist concretely in the world.

Similarly, in his philosophy of nature Hegel deduces natural phenomena that express a body's identity with itself (viz., light/color and sound), natural phenomena that express a body's difference from itself (odor and taste), and natural phenomena that express a body's being-for-itself, that is, its unity with itself mediated with its difference from itself and other objects (solidity, weight). These natural phenomena are the determinations of "the world's soul" as it were, which is "made of the same stuff" as the human soul. Thus the human senses of sight, hearing, smell, taste, and touch are able to perceive the various natural determinations of the world. Of course, what Plato understands by a "world soul" is not the same as what Hegel means by this term in §391. Hegel's world soul is not a subject, an independent self, as Plato's is,[35] but rather knows and thinks only in individual souls. Yet for both Plato and Hegel the world does have the same underlying structure as the ways of knowing belonging to the soul.

Setting the Stones in Motion

If sensation involves this homology between the soul and nature then the soul must be understood as always already attuned to nature, and nature must be understood as not only not resisting the soul's attempt to know it but even facilitating this knowledge. This does not mean that all "ideas" (taking this term in its usual sense of any mental content) are innate. The human soul would not be able to rely upon its own resources "before experience" (as if such a state were even conceivable) to derive from them any knowledge of the natural world. The path traced by Hegel's *Encyclopedia* (with ontological categories first, succeeded by forms of nature, and finally by forms of spirit) is not meant as a path any human being could take as a way of making progress in knowledge but rather as the systematic way that knowledge is presented in the highest form of spirit, philosophy. In our experience we still receive ideas adventitiously, but we should not imagine the mind as a camera that captures its "idea" as an imperfect photograph. There are certainly cases where one person's experience at one time gives a distorted impression that can be corrected later or by someone else, but there is no problem *in principle* with sense experience as knowledge of nature: that is, we need not worry that sensation necessarily distorts our knowledge and that nature in its reality is inaccessible to us. Hegel disposed of those objections in the introduction to the *Phenomenology*: here he wants to elaborate on how precisely nature presents its true self to our senses.

Our sensation is not a matter of *translating* natural properties into the language of our senses. No such translation is necessary because nature speaks our language. We do not need to rework nature into the form of knowledge, because it belongs to the essence of nature to make itself known to spirit. Thus Halbig goes too far when he describes Hegel's account of sensation as a "concession" to sensualism that supports a "foundationalist [*fundamentalistischen*]" theory of knowledge.[36] To be sure, spirit must still go to work on its sensible contents, negating them and working them up into thoughts,[37] but one must recognize that *even before it is sensed*, a natural determination (e.g., a sound) is in-itself comprehensible.[38] To see how this occurs it is necessary, as Hegel makes clear,[39] to look back to the philosophy of nature.

I have already discussed the natural phenomena that each sense perceives in the foregoing section. To illustrate my claim here that the sensing soul does not receive the sensation as a bare given, I must return to the account of sound and hearing. A sound is the expression of a body's ideality, its unity, in opposition to the differences between its parts. Since nature is defined as the externality of parts to each other,[40] and sound is precisely the momentary canceling of this difference, it seems that sound is in some sense not a natural phenomenon—or at least not *merely* a natural phenomenon. Indeed, Hegel's philosophy of nature shows that in the phenomena that are the objects of sense (color/light, sound, odor, taste, shape, weight), nature in some sense idealizes itself, makes itself into something that is perhaps more proper to spirit than it is to nature.[41] It would be too much to say that in these nature thinks itself, but it would not be inaccurate to say that nature, without any prompting from an investigating spirit, builds itself up and displays its essence as a kind of objective thought, or rationality.

Proponents of the soul as a blank slate typically explain the presence of abstract ideas in the mind by arguing that these ideas are the products of the mind's activity on the sense data received materially from nature (by some action of nature on our sense organs).[42] Hegel in contrast would reject the notion that nature impresses itself materially on the sense organs (by physically bombarding them, for example), externally introducing "sense data" into the soul, and that the soul is subsequently somehow able to alter the essential nature of this data by transforming it into immaterial "ideas." On the contrary, it is not in the knowing soul that the boundary between nature and spirit is traversed (i.e., that a natural body becomes a sensation). Rather, it is nature that works *itself* up into certain quasi-spiritual phenomena that can be sensed by the soul.

Thus while Hegel does speak of nature in the following way: "Nature is spirit alienated from itself, it is that in which spirit *lets itself go*, a Bacchic God, who does not restrain himself or hold himself together; in nature the concept's unity is hidden," thus giving the impression that nature is something alienated and distant from spirit, which spirit is at pains to know, he goes on to say:

> The thinking consideration of nature must consider how nature is in itself this process of becoming spirit and sublating its otherness—and how in each stage of nature the idea is present; alienated from the idea, nature is only the corpse of the understanding. Nature is however only in itself the idea, therefore Schelling called it petrified intelligence, and others have even called it frozen intelligence; however, God does not remain petrified and dead, rather the stones cry out and raise themselves [or, sublate themselves, *heben sich . . . auf*] to spirit.[43]

This latter quote presents a fuller picture of nature as something that is not only akin to spirit but that actually draws out of itself its intelligibility and presents it to spirit so that spirit may know it. At first glance Hegel seems to be referring here to Orpheus, the mythical poet who, it is said, gave the Greeks their religion[44] in songs that drew birds in the sky and fish in the sea toward him, and even set the trees *and the stones* in motion.[45] Yet Hegel is not pointing here to some poetic mediator between nature and spirit, who effects a transubstantiation by virtue of which mere nature becomes spirit or becomes amenable to spirit. His point is rather that Orpheus is not necessary because the stones *set themselves* in motion, sublating themselves to spirit, as nature offers itself up to be known as an ideality. Hegel's previous reference to Dionysus (the "Bacchic God") makes sense therefore, given that it was the maenads, the wild devotees of Dionysus, who killed Orpheus.[46] That the stones set themselves in motion is of course only a metaphor for nature's sublation of its mere materiality and its expression of itself in certain intelligible phenomena (color, sound, etc.). In chapter 3 I argued that the natural world has true anthropological significance, real human meaning. In the paragraphs on sensation Hegel moves closer to explaining one way that meaning can be found in nature by showing how our environment corporeally displays, in the manner of being, what we are able to sense and know.

When Hegel says that sound is "the negation of materiality"[47] he means that sound is the negation of a body's externality to itself, or that in it which is merely *natural*. Thus while a silent body is simply parts outside of parts, when struck and made sonorous, it expresses its unity (the *physical ideality* of its parts to the whole) in a single tone. Accordingly, as the *negation* of materiality, sound is the negation of the naturalness of a body, its transmutation into something more akin to spirit. Thus Hegel refers to sound as "the soul of matter"[48] and the "abstract soul"[49] of a body. He also calls sound "soul-like" (*Seelenhaftigkeit, Seelenhafte, Seelenhaftes, Seelenhaften*) several times.[50]

Certainly, dead matter, whether sonorous or not, has no soul in the proper sense. Sound remains strictly speaking a *natural* phenomenon, insofar as even in being sonorous a body does not *know itself* to be the idea. However, if it is permitted to use the term "soul" in a broader sense (as Hegel seems to do, at least in his lectures), as meaning simply the intelligibility of a body, the affinity it has to the soul by virtue of its ontological structure, then it would be accurate to describe something like sound as "the soul of matter." It is significant that both what merely passively possesses intelligibility and what actively knows (by sensing for example) can be called (in different ways) "the soul." Wolff likens Hegel's theory of sensation to Aristotle's in this respect:

> The sensing soul is the same as the one that is sensible (αἰσθητόν) of things; it is indeed not itself identical with sensible (material) things ("for, the stone is not in the soul"), but with the sensible form (τα εἴδη τά αἰσθητά) of things. Sensation (αἴσθησις) is nothing but the form of those sensible things (431b27–432a3). Hegel's conception of the soul as "ideality"

> takes up the matter as one sees here clearly, after and even terminologically directly from the Aristotelian conception of the εἶδος εἴδων. [. . .] The actuality of the sensible, i.e. the form, which the sensible thing first *makes* actually sensible, and the actuality of sensation, thus the form in which the actual sensing consists, is one and the same; "the being [*das Sein*]" however is not the same for the sensible and the sensation.[51]

That is, the sensing soul is the form of sensible things, and is thus identical with the sensible things themselves, except for the fact that these sensible things themselves are burdened with matter, and only passively *possess* a certain intelligibility, rather than *actively* thinking this intelligible principle. Yet insofar as ideal unity is one of the necessary moments of a body, then it is (in some sense) sonorousness that *makes* a body a body. And since Aristotle defines a soul as the *logos* of a thing, its principle, that is, that which makes it what it is,[52] then Hegel's theory of sensation and nature can be likened to Aristotle's. In the same vein, Ferrarin points out that when Hegel comments on Leibniz's dictum that "nothing is in the intellect which has not been in the senses" by adding "nothing is in the senses which has not been in the intellect,"[53] "he means that what is experienced even at the most elementary level is actually ultimately the *nous* itself as the principle of the world."[54]

The human soul and an aspect of intelligible nature such as sound are thus both "soul" in a sense, but in its sensation of this sound the soul communes with the sonorous body only in its (sonorous) *form*, but not its matter. It is not because of an inability or defect in the sentient soul that it does not commune with the sonorous body's matter. Rather, it is because in sounding, this body has temporarily canceled its own materiality. The difference between the sensation in the soul and the sensible principle in nature does not render the sensation that the soul possesses *only a defective copy* of the *real* object existing in external reality. What the body is most truly is how it presents itself as something capable of being sensed (here, a sound). Compared to the iron housing a bell's form, the sensation of the bell's tone is in fact *more* not less adequate to the concept of what the bell *is* most properly because the sensation is not burdened with materiality as the bell is. To be sure, the body's externality to itself is real, just as its unity is, but this externality does not escape sensation: as shown earlier, it is apprehended in smell and taste (the strangeness of smelling or tasting a bell notwithstanding).

Hegel's theory of sensation agrees with Aristotle's understanding of sensation as the soul's apprehension of the form presented to it materially (i.e., in an informed material object) and becoming this *form* alone, leaving the matter behind.[55] Those who try to respect nature and let it speak for itself, and so restrict their understanding of the soul to a blank slate, in fact fail to give nature enough credit. For, that position fails to appreciate that even nature is dignified enough to sublate its own self-externality and render itself intelligible. To truly honor nature requires recognizing this, rejecting the idea of the soul as a blank slate and the idea of nature as something substantially distinct from the soul.

Hegel also calls other natural phenomena the "soul [*Seele*]" of the body or matter, such as specific gravity,[56] heat[57] (as well as fire[58]), light,[59] and shape generally[60] (as well as specific determinations of shape: magnetism,[61] and crystal[62]). These are the *logoi* that nature *possesses* without contemplating them: it is by these phenomena that nature offers itself up to be known by the sentient soul.

Moreover, for Aristotle it is clear that both possessing knowledge and contemplation are entelechies of the soul, ways a body can be actual (i.e., can "have" a soul) because, as Aristotle says, both sleeping and waking depend on the existence of a soul, and waking is analogous to contemplation, while sleeping is analogous to the mere possession of knowledge.[63] Of course, Aristotle seems to mean in this passage by "the possession of knowledge" not the mere possession of intelligibility but the possession of acquired knowledge that is not currently being thought. Yet insofar as Aristotle also uses the term "soul" to describe the principle of an inanimate body,[64] the thinking of which constitutes knowledge of that body, such that the "soul" of such a body would be its intelligible principle, it would not be inappropriate to give the metaphor that a sonorous object is a sleeping sentient soul, while a sentient soul is an awoken sonorous object.

In fact, De Laurentiis argues that Hegel's theory of the soul is sometimes more Aristotelian than many Aristotle scholars are inclined to recognize, insofar as Hegel retains parts of Aristotle's theory that some have since wanted to excise as inauthentic, for want of seeing how they can be reconciled with Aristotle's broader approach.[65] In this vein, she notes the "double character of soul's logical-metaphysical status"[66] insofar as it is at once the formal principle of nature and the material ground of higher forms of spirit. It could be then that Hegel's Aristotelian theory of the soul (and also the way Aristotle is taken up in Neoplatonism, specifically in the presentation of nature as being drawn back on its return path to the One, with a continuum of natural beings achieving greater organization and cognition) preserves something important but easily overlooked in Aristotle's distinction between the first and second orders of the soul's entelechy. The emergence of sentient life would thus be the *awakening of matter* or *of nature* in some sense, when matter (in the form of the body with a sentient soul) begins not merely to possess the forms of nature but rather to perceive them.[67]

The Soul as "Mixed" with Its Body

In the last chapter I explained how I think sleeping and waking should be understood not only in the narrowest sense of a total lack of consciousness or the minimal state of consciousness needed for everything else. By defining sleep as "subjective" immersion in objects and waking as the "active" maintenance of a distinction between the self and its object, Hegel means to relate this pair back to his theory of gender and forward to sensibility. In sensibility the soul is awoken (perceiving objects it feels as different) but only by remaining sunken in a deep state of sleep with respect to its own body: not only does the soul not feel its own body (at least not anything of the quality it is sensing in the sensing organ itself), but only the numb slumber it has toward its own body allows it to be vividly awake to external objects at all. Thus if it is true that with sensation a part of nature is awoken, it is also true that this awakening has strict limitations.

In chapter 4 I explained Hegel's theory of gender by using the passive immersion in immediacy, which he associates with the feminine (and domesticity, the law of the netherworld), and the active differentiation of oneself from objectivity that he associates with masculinity (and the state and its laws). As in Hegel's study of gender in the "ethical world" and "ethical action" sections of the *Phenomenology*, the feminine household is silent and hidden, but it is the substantial foundation of the masculine state, which yet presents itself as the social reality *simpliciter*, so in sensation the body and its sense organs are the means for the experience of nature but themselves recede into the background of all experience, which instead presents the object in its distinction from the self as what is real. As a form of experience, sensation is thus like the masculine hubris in taking itself to be independent of the feminine and like awakening in contrast to sleeping. In the tragedy of *Antigone*, sensation resembles Creon's outrageous demand that the laws of familial piety and respect for the dead should be violated, that they must cede before the interests of the state.[68]

Waking consists in distinguishing oneself from objectivity, or, we might say as Aristotle does of the intellect, in being "unmixed [ἄμιγη]"[69] with corporeity. The soul for Aristotle must (in part, or somehow) be unmixed in this way in order to think apart from sensation. Yet sensation is most certainly "mixed" with the body. For an example, let us consider the sense of touch. What we call "room temperature" (the temperature of the skin, the tactile sensing organ) is simply the temperature to which we are insensible because it is felt as neither cold nor hot (and thus is not felt at all). We are insensible to a certain (range of) temperature because we sense corporeally, such that unlike Aristotle's intellect, our skin (the part of our body in which our soul senses heat and cold) is *not* "unmixed," since as corporeal, it is always already a certain temperature. In other words, because the soul is embodied, it passively bears certain determinations in the way merely natural bodies do. Because the soul is mixed with a tactile organ that passively possesses a certain temperature, it is unable to know itself as distinct from this determinacy. The soul instead only feels heat or cold when a temperature varies from the temperature by which it is determined. As Merleau-Ponty remarked: "Insofar as it sees or touches the world, my body can therefore neither be seen, nor touched."[70] An appropriate metaphor might be that for Hegel the naturalness of the body casts a shadow on our experience of the world: this shadow has the human form, and not only does it obscure part of nature but in this darkening *the human form* is itself obscure and the source of the obscurity.

Ferrarin makes a powerful case that activity is necessarily involved in sensation. The soul is not a purely passive and receptive Lockean tabula rasa on which natural objects imprint themselves but rather the activity of inwardizing and idealizing what is given, integrating it into an order first provided by the soul. In this way, Hegel retrieves a valuable part of Aristotle's legacy that was obscured by some of what were for Hegel more recent commentators (e.g., Tennemann).[71] I agree with this wholeheartedly, but I would also like to emphasize a passivity that the sensing soul retains: this passivity is not the inertia of a blank slate but rather the absorption in objectivity (rather than holding oneself apart from objectivity and experiencing it as an object) that is characteristic of sleep. Consider for instance how the very first event in any case of sensation is the meeting of two parts of nature (e.g., a human hand and a stone). There is sensation of the stone only because the soul is completely immersed in and passive toward the hand. In sensation the soul is so completely identified with the sensing organ that it even seems that the organ itself is doing the sensing. If it did not retain this passivity—if it did not fail to distinguish itself in some sense from the body it is given by nature—then it would not be a form of the "natural soul" at all.

Indeed, the shift to the second major part of the anthropology (the feeling soul) from the first (the natural soul, whose final form is sensation) is characterized by beginning to cease to identify with the body given by nature, taking this body instead as an object. Here in sensation, on the other hand, where the soul is mixed with its body, it senses only determinations that vary from its own, such that the soul at this stage does not feel *itself*.[72] The soul senses contents that vary from the determinations it passively possesses (in its mere naturalness) but not the determinations of its own body. In other words, though the soul knows other bodies, it is oblivious to its own body. Admittedly, in his lectures Hegel says that in smell and taste, and even more in touch, the soul begins to feel itself.[73] This is true and does not contradict the interpretation I am giving here. What I am saying is that in *all* sensation the soul is mixed with its body, that is, it senses through material sense organs that are already determined in certain ways. This prior determination of the sense organs renders the soul *insensible* to certain determinations in nature. The self-feeling the soul has in touch is only present when the ensouled body touches something that *differs* from its own natural determinacy. Room temperature is, I think, the best example of the sensible soul's obliviousness with regard to its own body, but there are others.

For instance, in order to see, the part of the body that receives light must be colorless. Were it to be a determinate color, that color would escape sensation. Of course, there are different colors of eyes (brown, blue, green), but these are the colors of the iris, not the pupil, and it is the pupil that receives the light. The pupil is black, which is not even a color at all. Or if it is a color, it is not one that we sense. What we call "black" is what does not reflect light at all but instead absorbs all light that it meets. Similarly, what we call green objects absorb all light except for a certain range of frequency that it reflects back into our eyes (viz., the one we call "green").

The same could be said of the other senses. If the eardrum were always already vibrating at a certain rate, such vibrations would not be heard, and thus the ear would never hear itself (or any body with the same auditory determination as itself), just as the eye does not see itself (or any body with the same chromatic determination as itself), and the skin does not feel itself (or any body with the same temperature as itself). Of course, I can look in a mirror and see (a reflection of) my face, including my eyes. And, I can see my eyes as represented in photographs. However, these are frivolous objections to Hegel's (and Aristotle's) doctrine of sensation. Hegel's point is that the soul must be embodied in order to sense. This embodiment is the only thing that grants it access to sensible objects. Yet, because it is embodied, the sensing soul is deprived of the ability to sense certain contents by the same stroke as it is granted the ability to sense others. The examples raised just now (seeing one's eyes in a mirror) do nothing to undermine Hegel's account. When I look at a mirror, I do see my reflection, including a reflection of my eyes. Yet I do not see that in my eyes which sees. The pupil appears to me only as black, a colorless void, reflecting no light at all back to me. I am only able to discern that there is a pupil at all because I see the surrounding tissue (which does not see), and the outline this tissue forms throws what remains unseen into relief.

Were the soul to sense incorporeally, it would not have such limitations because it would be "unmixed."[76] Since however the soul is embodied (and this body is always already determined in certain natural ways), the soul is limited in what it can sense, and its determinations (e.g., the temperature of its skin) determine for it *how* it will sense things (e.g., what will be sensed as cold, what will be sensed as hot, and what will escape sensation altogether). It must be said however that the section on sensation concerns *the senses* and only derivatively the (material) *sense organs*. The examination of the sense organs as features of merely natural life belongs rather to the philosophy of nature. Yet the section on sensation does direct its focus toward the material body in the discussion of the emotions.

The Embodiment of the Emotions

Emotions are not usually classed with sensations, even though both are affective, because sensation is usually restricted to sensitive awareness of external objectivity, whereas emotions are often thought of as feelings of one's internal subjectivity. Even if the stimulant is external, as, for example, if a person fifty feet from me in a park is throwing rocks at the ducks—an act that provokes in me a feeling of anger—it seems that the anger has more to do with me and my temperament than the other person. The sky presents the same sensible quality (blue) to all, and for each person it is presented to the same sense organ (the eyes), but others at the park see the same act of violence and are not angered; moreover, it is not as clear in the case of an emotion like anger as in the case of seeing or hearing an object which organ is doing the sensing. The act of violence is something *seen*, but I do not feel my anger in my eyes: I feel it in an only vaguely localized way in my chest, or perhaps deeper in my abdomen. My perception of the external world in emotions thus seems at once more intense and more arbitrary and subjective: I feel emotions powerfully in myself, but the connection between this sensation and the external object that may have incited it is tenuous.

In fact, emotion is a very different kind of sensation. It is a way the soul senses a part of the natural world, but the field of possible objects of sensation here is restricted to a person's own body. So, in the aforementioned case of anger, the part of nature sensed is my own chest, or abdomen, not the malefactor, the projectile, or the duck (though these too are perceived in cases of sensation that are not emotion). And this is what makes the emotions different in an important way from the other cases of sensation, which are characterized by external nature being sensed at the expense of an awareness of one's own sensing body: in emotion, the soul *senses itself* in its body insofar as it senses human, nonbiological content like anger, sadness, shame, grief, joy, and so forth.[75]

Of course, it is possible to give a biological account of the expression of emotion: the anthropological account is not meant to invalidate biological analyses. Take blushing from shame, for example. A dermatologist (who understands the human being as a mere biological organism) would say that the reddening of the face is caused by rushing of blood to capillaries in the face, and this is itself caused by hyperactivity of the nervous system, perhaps as a result of stress (stress of course being understood as something physical and empirically apparent for an outside observer). One could propose such a "naturalistic" explanation for hearing a sound as well (making the sound into a disturbance in the air and the sensation into a physical affection in the inner ear). And, of course, if one were to be truly facetious, one could claim that the human being is a mere extended body.

Any of these claims would be true, but only partially so. I argued in chapter 1 that while a human being cannot but be extended, extension does not exhaust what the human being is, not even what the human being is corporeally. Similarly, in response to the biological explanation of the reddening of the face, Hegel would not deny that such a series of causes and effects do occur, but he would deny that the phenomenon of blushing must be considered exclusively in terms of biology. What is missing in the biological account is the meaning behind the blushing. A complicated argument was needed in chapter 3 to defend the idea that parts of nature like the rain, blooming flowers, or falling leaves can have anthropological significance and thus not be reducible to only mechanical, chemical, and biological terms. But it is difficult to deny that there is meaning behind a person blushing: the meaning is shame, the emotion that is expressed in the expansion of cheek capillaries and that is felt by the ashamed person in her cheeks, face, and neck.

This material expression of an emotion is thus at once: (1) an expression for another, who can perceive the reddening of the ashamed person's face; and (2) an expression for the ashamed person, for whom the physical change involved in blushing makes possible the *feeling* of his or her shame. Hegel is primarily concerned with the second aspect of the corporealization of the emotions, namely, how this corporealization allows them to be felt by the person who has them. Emotion is thus a sort of transition between sensation and feeling insofar as, unlike sensation, feeling involves the affective awareness of *inner* contents (like shame) as opposed to externally received contents (like heat, a more typical object of sensation). But unlike feeling, the emotions perceive their contents *mediately*, through a certain part of the natural body. What part of the body is the mediating organ is less clear in emotion than in sight, hearing, smell, touch, and taste, but emotions are nonetheless always felt in the body. Thus for example the face and its capillaries are the mediating organ for the feeling of shame, allowing shame to be *felt* (corporeally), just as it is the eyes that allow colors to be seen.[78]

Without such mediating organs, emotions like joy, shame, grief, among others, could presumably still be known in some sense, but they could not be felt. In fact there are instances where an emotion really is known in some sense though it has never been felt. A child for instance, or even an adult who has had a very limited experience of life and the world may understand what a certain emotion is though he or she has never felt it. This "understanding" would be an abstract and inadequate understanding, but still, it would be inaccurate to say the person is totally ignorant of the emotion. For example, everyone young and old knows what shame is, both from feeling it and possibly also being able to give an abstract definition of it. But most often people think of shame as a feeling of inadequacy in front of their superiors, or their peers, yet there is also a way to be ashamed in front of those of lower status, such as one's dependents. Children at least, who have no dependents, have never felt this kind of shame. Likewise, many people who are never lonely could still define loneliness as "an unpleasant feeling of being isolated"; and many who have never lived in a foreign country could still figure their way to a definition of homesickness like "an unpleasant feeling of being far from one's home, family, friends, and familiar culture." This ability to define an emotion never felt could be the result of hearing or reading descriptions of it.[77] But the capacity for articulating definitions like these, and even the ability to contemplate them abstractly, is not the same as having *felt* them firsthand.

One who has only contemplated the concept of loneliness does not know how it feels, would not know for example that it can involve a feeling of coldness, and would not be able to understand why experiencing loneliness should feel cold rather than warm. Similarly, someone who has never been in love would not understand why it involves feeling warmth rather than coldness; and someone who has never been afraid (but who still has some intellectual grasp of fear as the worried expectation of some adverse circumstance) would not understand why *feeling* fear involves a prickly sensation rather than dull pressure. The precise feeling of an emotion is simply not something that can be known a priori. Analogously, someone who is blind might be able to understand that colors are a scale of determinacies varying in accordance with a certain measure called "brightness," but such a blind person would never be able to understand why the color blue is more soothing than the color orange, or why orange is more exciting than gray.

What is perhaps most noteworthy here is the very fact that emotions are materialized at all, that is, that a distinctively human, spiritual idea like shame should be corporealized and *felt* (rather than merely being an object of reflective thought). A complete account of these emotions may require relating them to the practical spirit section of the psychology.[78] Had Hegel given such a deduction there, we could refer to it to help us understand how emotions become embodied, just as reference to the sensed parts of nature as they are treated in their own right in the philosophy of nature helps in understanding the five senses. Unfortunately, Hegel did not give any such deduction; and it would be such a complicated project that it is impossible to attempt it here.

Though he does not venture such a deduction, Halbig does argue for a relationship between the corporealization of the emotions and another part of the psychology, namely, "attention [*Aufmerksamkeit*]"[79] in the section on theoretical spirit. Halbig presents attention as a sort of inverse of the corporealization of the emotions in sensation. Whereas in emotion mediated, spiritual contents are made to appear corporeally, or immediately, attention involves spiritual training that enables one to do the reverse, seeing *beyond* what is immediately present and discerning what underlies this immediacy (as for example a botanist not only knows more about the plant but, through attention, actually *sees* more than does the person unschooled in botany).[80] It is thus as if a natural phenomenon (e.g., a plant) were the embodiment on the part of the idea (or God) of what are properly understood as spiritual contents. That is, it is as if objects in nature are the creations from a divine poetic imagination, incarnations of the thoughts that lie at their heart; and it is by spiritual development that one is able to read nature the way one old friend reads the emotion on the face of another, seeing what the idea "means" in its expression in nature.[81] Halbig likewise relates the corporealization of emotions in the section on sensation to the role of "feeling" in the philosophy of religion,[82] but I will discuss this in the subsequent chapters.[83]

In closing I would like to note that at the end of the section on sensation, as the anthropology makes the transition from the natural soul to the feeling soul, Hegel notes again in his lectures that the individual soul must be understood as in some sense a world soul (*Weltseele*),[84] a soul with its own (inner) world. It was of course originally the universal soul that was called a *Weltseele*.[85] The significance of designating the individual soul in this way is that it is posited that the individual soul is a universal with respect to the contents of its own inner world. These contents are its sensations, which are the collected *logoi* of all of nature. It remains unclear at this point what it means that the individual soul is somehow lord over all of nature, yet also a determinate individual. The resolution of the incongruity between the soul's status as "world soul" and its determinacy will be the object of the next part of the anthropology (covered in the next two chapters here) on the feeling soul.

6

Perverse Self-Knowledge

I remember things I do not want to remember, and cannot forget things I want to forget.

—Euripides, from a lost play

To remember everything is a form of madness.

—Brian Friel, *Translations: A Play*

There are forms of madness that spread like contagious diseases.

—François Duc de La Rochefoucauld,
Réflections ou Sentences et Maximes morales

In this chapter I show how Hegel understands "feeling" as the way the soul circumvents the naturally given forms of mediation (the sense organs) to know contents immediately. Hegel gives many examples of varying credibility. I argue against the most dubious but defend his general idea of feeling while offering a reinterpretation of certain other examples Hegel gives (by classifying them as hypnotism, which is legitimate) and some examples of my own that Hegel does not give (couvade syndrome, and sympathy pains generally, as well as certain social disorders).

From Sensation to Feeling

The investigation turns here to the feeling soul section, the second of the anthropology's three parts, the part Hegel calls "the most difficult, because it is the most obscure."[1] I am translating as "feeling soul" what Hegel calls "*die fühlende Seele*," which is to be distinguished from the soul as sensation (*Empfindung*). For common parlance in English there is no clear distinction between the meanings of "feeling" and "sensation." Nor, as Hegel notes, is there in German.[2] Yet since Hegel does give his own particular meanings to these terms, let us take a moment to review what special meaning Hegel gives to "sensation [*Empfindung*]" in order better to understand how it is different from what Hegel means by "feeling [*Gefühl*]."

Sensation is the final form of the natural soul, which means that in it spirit fails to distinguish itself from nature. The soul in sensation is immersed in its body, sensing external nature through its sensing organ in such a way that this organ disappears from experience, becoming the medium but never the object. As the last form of the natural soul, sensation is only partly absorbed in nature, "asleep" with respect to its own natural body, though this slumber makes possible an "awakening" with respect to external nature. However, sensation does not succeed in sensing all of external nature: if a part of nature bears the same determination as the relevant sensing organ of the soul's body, that part of nature will go unnoticed.

My preferred example of this is the way the soul is insensible to the temperature of anything which is what we call "room temperature," that is, the temperature of the skin (the tactile sensing organ). When the soul is "mixed" with the body, as it is in sensation, it has a "mean" in relation to which other objects will be felt as either excessive or deficient. In sensing temperature, this mean is the temperature of the skin's surface (perhaps 70–75°F): in excess of this mean, objects are sensed as warm or hot; in deficiency of this mean, objects are sensed as cool or cold. But objects determined at the mean are not sensed at all—at least not with respect to their temperature. It is as if the human body extends not just to the fingertips but beyond to all of nature, which is determined as the body proper is. This insensibility is so commonplace that it seems unremarkable in any way. Yet bearing in mind Hegel's account of the natural soul, it is clear that the failure of the soul to distinguish itself from, say, an object bearing the same temperature as its skin is the relic of the absorption in nature that characterized the universal soul, the very first shape of spirit.

Most importantly, the soul's absorption in its body in sensation means it does not feel itself. In sensing nature sensation is still spirit, since all of nature is the idea, and sensation is the idea's self-knowledge; but it is an imperfect kind of spirit. To be sure, there is a way the soul in sensation senses itself: by embodying (*verleiblichen*) its own inner contents in emotion. The emotion is then given physical expression in the affection of a certain material organ, and the soul *feels* the emotion. Yet even here the soul is able to sense itself only because part of the material sense organ that expresses the emotion (e.g., the face becoming flush with blood and reddening when the person feels shame) becomes determined in a way that varies from what would otherwise be its condition and varies from the way the rest of the sense organ is determined.

In contrast to the sensation of external nature and emotion (both of which involve mediation of the body), feeling involves bypassing any mediation whatsoever. In feeling, the soul relates directly to a content. Yet because of this immediate relation between the soul and its feeling, the soul is unable to distinguish itself from this feeling. This inability is a result of the abandonment of any mediation: it is the culmination of a trend beginning in the "natural changes" section (covered in chapter 4 of this book) in which the soul's "active" differentiation of itself from its objects becomes more and more prominent and takes itself more and more to be the true form of spirit in opposition to its "subjective" identification with objects, on which this "activity" nonetheless continued to depend. In the section on sexual relation (§397) these tendencies were associated with the male and female, respectively, and also in §398 with waking and sleeping. In sensation the soul is awake to external nature only by being in a state of sleep with respect to its own body. Like the male principle's dependence on the female, a dependence with which the male is constitutionally incapable of coming to grips, sensation necessarily involves not only the persistence of "sleep" but the persistent failure to bring this fact to consciousness. The passage from sensation to feeling occurs when waking finally succeeds in detaching itself completely from sleep: the masculine, or the state, has severed its relation to the feminine, or the household. In a tragedy, this is the obstinacy of Creon maintaining one law in violation of the other. The result is pathos, a disordering of experience, the vengeance of the Furies. And yet we must not treat feeling as just an aberration, something which should not exist. Feeling is a form of self-knowledge: a shape of spirit if a perverse one.

It is important to keep in mind that feeling is not a slide back into a more primitive state, that it constitutes a genuine advance on sensation, especially because in the first two parts of the feeling soul section ("the feeling soul in its immediacy" and "self-feeling") Hegel seems more concerned to show the aberrant nature of feeling. This is especially true of the section on self-feeling, which is how Hegel understands madness. Yet Hegel could have just as easily presented sensibility in a way that placed overwhelming emphasis on how it remains ignorant of its own particularity. As it is, he downplays this aspect quite a bit, though it must be highlighted in order to understand sensation properly, especially in relation to feeling. Additionally, the reader must attend to how feeling follows from sensation in order to understand how the problems that come up in the section on feeling were always already implicit in sensation.

One feature of sensation that can escape notice is that, with the exception of the sensing of emotions through their embodiment, sensation always concerns knowing contents received externally. But one might ask, what happens to these sensations once they are received? How does the soul relate to them once they are no longer being felt by mediation of the body and its material sense organs? If this form of mediation is removed, what takes its place? Hegel's answer is that, initially at least, *nothing* takes the place of the sense organs: in feeling the soul feels its contents without any mediation at all.

This immediacy is a problem because, by relating to any feeling it has *immediately*, the soul does not have the distance from its feelings that would allow it to distinguish even one feeling from another, and a fortiori the soul cannot integrate all of its various feelings into one coherent order. Accordingly, the feeling soul "has" an indistinct mass of feelings (or, the soul *is* this indistinct mass of feelings, since it does not even distinguish itself from its feelings[3]), with no order or mediation between them or between any one of them and the soul itself. Thus in the introductory paragraphs of the section on the feeling soul Hegel speaks of an "indeterminate pit"[4] into which are deposited all of the soul's feelings. This pit is not *in* the feeling soul; rather, this pit *is* the feeling soul. In its initial definition, the feeling soul is thus only a hodgepodge of sensible determinations that *we* (concrete human beings whose experience is not limited by the moments in play in the soul's sensation) know to have come from the mediation the various senses provided between the soul and external nature. Since however the senses do not function to mediate the soul's relation to feelings of which it is already in possession, the ordering the senses provided in the soul's original reception of the determinations is not maintained. This storehouse may be called the soul's *unconscious*, since it contains feelings of which the soul is in possession, but to which it has problematic and irregular access, and over which it has yet to exert effective control.[7]

That the access the soul has to its feelings is irregular does not mean the feelings are inaccessible. In fact, the feeling soul is remarkable mostly for how it draws up long-buried feelings to the surface, with no rhyme or reason. Feeling is at once a forgetting of all of its contents and an inability to ever forget anything. It is perhaps best understood as an absence of any *character*[6] by which the soul's contents might be ordered according to one pattern or another, such that some feelings would be given priority and maintained as readily accessible, while others would be discarded and all but lost. The feeling soul can appear amazing[7] (e.g., in a feverish state one might suddenly call to mind in vivid detail a song heard only once in early childhood), but in truth it is a kind of dementia in contrast with a more fully developed soul.

If the transition from sensation to feeling can be understood as the height of masculine-political hubris over its feminine-household foundation, and likened to Creon's blindness to the unwritten law of the unseen world of the dead and familial piety, then the "indeterminate pit" of the feeling soul can be likened to the tomb in which Creon buries the still-living Antigone. As the masculine principle demands that all of nature should be present to it as an external object, so Creon will not allow the dead body of Polyneices to be covered over in a ritual that affirms the body to be familiar, not irremediably foreign, even as he commands that the living body of his niece be hidden away, as if he is unable to bear an encounter with corporeity that cannot be completely reduced to an object.

I will provide examples of this later in the more detailed analysis of feeling. Here it will be enough to establish the necessity of such a common "pit" in which all of the various senses bury their feelings. This common storehouse of feelings is necessary because, as Plato said, it is not the eyes that see, or the ears that hear, but rather the human being (i.e., the soul) that sees and hears through these organs.[8] Thus despite the soul's differentiation into the different senses (and the mediation these senses provide), all of the differentiated content it receives in sensation is still gathered together as the content of the single (and in some sense still undivided) soul. This common pit must be indeterminate because no particular term has been deduced to mediate between the soul (as universal) and the indistinct mass of singular feelings. That is, no determining principle has been deduced for the feeling soul.[9]

In recent analytic "philosophy of mind" there has been some discussion about whether the mind is "modular," that is, whether the mind is composed of separate faculties that operate independently of each other and potentially at variance with each other.[10] That Hegel would be hostile to what is today proposed as "modularity" of the mind is clear from his disdain for the faculty psychology of his own time.[11] However, one might think that Hegel articulates a "modular" theory of the soul (or "mind"[12]) in his deduction of the senses. After all, one might ask, is not the determination of the soul into the different senses the soul's division into different and independent sensible faculties? Halbig correctly answers this question in the negative. Even in its sensation (which would involve a determinate sense and an ostensibly "modular" soul), the soul brings with it the "categorical determinations of thought."[13] That is, even in sensation there are structures of subjectivity that undergird the differentiation into distinct senses, thereby guaranteeing the more fundamental unity of the soul as sensation.

However, while it is true that lower faculties like sensation must be understood in the context of the higher ones such as thought, there is a simpler response to the objection Halbig raises (and one that does not give Hegel the appearance of a Kantian), namely, that feeling (which is clearly nonmodular insofar as it bypasses the mediation of the senses and thus effaces all distinction of "faculties" in the soul) and sensation (which can appear modular) are two sides of the same coin. While sensation concerns contents insofar as they are received and can be differentiated from the soul, feeling concerns contents immediately related to the soul, contents with which the soul identifies completely. Thus despite the apparent "modularity" of the soul insofar as it is divided into distinct senses, these sensations are all simply deposited into the one "indeterminate pit" of the feeling soul, such that even the apparent modularity of the soul in sensation presupposes a deeper nonmodularity. The examples of the feeling soul given later will further show the "nonmodularity" of the soul.

First, however, let me note that though I said that as feeling soul the soul feels itself in its contents, identifying with a determinate feeling, in its immediacy the feeling soul does not *consciously* identify its content as its own self (as it will later, in self-feeling). The feeling soul in its immediacy has not even achieved the minimal separation from its content that such a conscious identification would require. By describing the soul at this stage as "immediate," Hegel means precisely that between it and its content there is no relation properly speaking but only a naïve identification that is *simple* (i.e., distinctionless and thus relationless).

The Displacement of the Self

One phenomenon that for Hegel concretizes very well the identification of the soul with a determinate feeling is the relation the feeling soul can have to its "genius." Such a phenomenon can have various forms, but to understand any of them, it is necessary to understand what "genius" means for Hegel. The term "genius" is most commonly used today to describe someone who is especially bright or talented, an innovator in a certain field. This usage is not wholly unrelated to what Hegel means, but clarification is still required.

First of all, it is not appropriate to call someone a genius if this person simply follows a rule, applying it mechanically. Instead, a genius is one who inaugurates a completely new rule, in, say, painting or music. This is the way Kant describes the genius in the third *Critique*.[14] Because genius is not a matter of grasping a general rule and applying it to particular cases, the activity of a genius can be seen not to be the result of a clear, intellectual, and communicable grasp of, say, what is beautiful. For that reason, one cannot *become* a genius, either through study or technical practice. One simply *is* a genius, or one *is not*. That a given person should be a genius, that her work should be the result of such an uncanny power, is thus fortuitous and inexplicable. Indeed, even the genius herself cannot explain her work. Accordingly, geniuses are often said to be "inspired" (perhaps by a god) rather than "scholarly." A scholar wills to understand something and then puts in long hours of study to bring about this understanding, at which point she can communicate this knowledge to others. A genius on the other hand seems not to be in control but rather to be *subject* to her "passion," or "inspiration," which drives her, perhaps involuntarily or even unconsciously, to create. The kind of person we are used to calling a "genius" is thus not very different from her tools. Both the painter and her paintbrush are only instruments for the painter's "inspiration," which controls the painter and, through her, the paintbrush. The true "genius" in this picture is thus not the painter, any more than it is the paintbrush. Rather, it is the powerful force that takes control of her, when "she" creates her art. Thus we should not say, for example, "Beethoven was a genius," but rather "we owe these sublime pieces of music to Beethoven's genius," that is, to the passion that drove and inspired him.

This sketch puts us in a better position to understand what Hegel means by "genius" in the feeling soul section. By this term Hegel means the element within or outside of a person that controls her. The person under the control of a "genius" is in no position to resist this control since she is often unaware that this "genius" is different from her own self. Accordingly, Hegel defines genius as "the determining *particularity* of man, that which, in all situations and relationships, decides his action and his fate."[15] This "particularity" is the man's "basic interests, [. . .] the essential and particular empirical relationships in which he stands to other people and the world at large."[16]

In other words, a person's "genius" is that in her that controls her destiny and decisions (her "oracle,"[17] as Hegel calls it) in the same way that an artist's activity is dominated by her genius. The person's "genius" is her "feeling totality,"[18] that is, the sum total of her experiences, temperaments, relations, and so on, that make up the "indeterminate pit," which Hegel speaks of in the *Anmerkung* to §403 and which I mentioned earlier—that is, the *unconscious*.[19] The appearance of the unconscious here, and its determining role, was prefigured back in §398 when it was posited that awakening is mediated through sleeping. Waking life, which would separate itself utterly from nature (as modern culture has done in the procedures of the sciences and in the Enlightenment), still has its destiny laid out for it by the unconscious, where the human immersion in nature returns, with an influence that is unchecked and wild.

Previously, I used the example of creative, artistic genius to explain how Hegel uses the term "genius" and noted that genius in this sense is often thought of as simply possessed or not possessed (but not acquired in any case). It would be best however not to rely too heavily on this example, since Hegel also understands "genius" to include the unconscious, that is, the residue of experiences that the soul somehow still possesses, but to which it is not presently attending, and perhaps to which it may have difficult access. For example, mundane details that are experienced, "stored away" as it were, and forgotten, without exclusion of the possibility of their recall at a later time. The experiences that lie obscure in one's unconsciousness and that together constitute one's "genius" for Hegel are certainly *acquired*, unlike artistic genius. However, we can say that in both cases genius is an active force in a person, the arbiter of many of a person's decisions, but one which is not under the control of the person, either because the person was simply born with this or that "genius" (e.g., creative capacity), or because the "genius" lies inaccessible (or only problematically accessible) in (or rather *as*) the person's "unconscious." Taking the latter example, we could say that this "feeling totality" or "genius" constitutes the person's "character," provided that we also include the caveat that "character" here should not be understood as something deliberately cultivated (as in the case of free spirit[20]) but rather as something acquired haphazardly as a result of the unique combination of experiences that an individual happens to have had. Thus different individuals respond differently to the same circumstances because of their different "geniuses."

That the soul is controlled by its genius means that the soul is susceptible to being controlled by something in some sense outside of it. But this is not a case of an overpowering force, like being blown over by the wind, or having one's options circumscribed by one's biological constitution: here one acts *as if* one were free, and one feels free (to the limited extent that "freedom" is really possible at this level). The controlling power is, for the soul in question, not distinguished from itself. The genius here can either be the soul's own unconscious or another person. Insofar as this "genius" then controls the passive soul (i.e., the rest of the person or soul, apart from its "genius") without the slightest resistance (because there is not even so much as a relation between the two), the latter in a very real sense relinquishes its own self, displacing it into its "genius."[21] The soul is in principle susceptible to such external control because the difference and externality of nature are nothing for the soul.[22] Just as the healthy, fully developed soul permeates its entire body (the material separateness of its parts constituting no obstacle for it), so the soul at this primitive stage is able to be extended over bodies that are different spatially, and even biologically.[23] In such a condition, the person is not in possession of the soul's genius. Rather, the genius lies *outside* of the feeling soul, in *another* (even if this other is the feeling soul's own unappropriated unconscious).

In chapter 3 I wrote of how the "natural soul" can unreflectively take itself to be the soul of all of nature, such that geographical phenomena are reflected in its mood.[23] Thus for the natural soul, the darkness enshrouding the world at night, or the shortened hours of daylight in winter can lead to a morose, *dark* disposition. These two are similar insofar as they are both cases of unreflective sympathy. Yet they differ in that in chapter 3 the individual soul sympathetically identified with the external world, whereas in feeling the soul loses itself rather in its own *inner* world. Why should the text have come around again to such a similar structure?

The course of the text from "natural qualities" to the "feeling soul in its immediacy" involved going from trying to understand the relation between the diversity of nature on the one hand and the "universal soul," which is the ideality of this diversity (but which has actuality only in individual souls), on the other, to trying to understand the relation between the diverse feelings making up the "feeling totality" on the one hand and the (individual) feeling soul, which is the ideality of this diversity (but which has actuality only in individual feelings), on the other. It is for this reason that Hegel calls the feeling soul "monadic."[25] A monad[26] is at once a part of all of nature[27] and internally a mirror of nature, reflecting ideally all of the diverse relations of nature.[28] Thus the feeling soul up to this point has not resolved the instability that characterized the natural soul. In fact, it has aggravated it, reinscribing it in the individual as such.

But if the feeling soul identifies immediately with an *inner* content, then how is it able to have its "genius" *outside* of it, in an *other*? This is possible because the feeling soul does not make the distinction between what is "inner" and what is "outer." In the *Enzyklopädie*'s first and second editions (1817, 1827) Hegel called the feeling soul "the dreaming soul [*die träumende Seele*]."[29] This term makes sense if one recalls Hegel's account of sleeping in the section on the natural soul. There he says: "We defined sleep as that state which distinguishes itself neither within itself, nor in relation to the external world. This definition [. . .] is justified by experience. For, when our soul senses or presents itself with always only one and the same thing, it becomes sleepy."[30] Sleep is the condition of the soul in which it fails to distinguish itself from the outer world. Because of this, the soul can identify immediately with something external to it, taking this externality to be its own self (rendering this content equally "inner" and "outer"), that is, relinquishing its selfhood utterly to this externality (viz., its "genius").

Examples and Analysis

Hegel gives three types of this relation to one's "genius." The first example is "dreaming [*das Träumen*]."[31] Now, in a figurative sense, every shape of the feeling soul is the soul "dreaming" insofar as it is the soul failing to distinguish inner and outer. Yet, besides dreaming, there are other phenomena that concretize the failure to make this distinction. Thus it could be that Hegel changed the name of this section from "the dreaming soul" to "the feeling soul" in order to avoid the confusion that is caused by naming a genus by one of its species.[32] In any case, the idea of dreaming has already come up as precisely this immediate absorption of the soul in its content. Yet one should not think of waking simply as occupation with the *external* world and of sleeping and dreaming simply as absorption in one's *internal* world. The true distinction between waking consciousness and dreaming is that the soul's contents in its waking life are mediated through each other in an orderly and coherent way, while in dreams this is not the case.[33] Accordingly, in his discussion of dreaming as a form of the feeling soul in its immediacy, Hegel speaks of the individual soul as being loosened from its determinate place in nature, experiencing things impossible to experience in waking life (e.g., phenomena that defy the causal order of nature, natural laws, etc.) and attaining "a profound and powerful feeling of the *entirety* of its *individual* nature, of the *complete compass* of its past, present, and future."[34] The soul's "genius" here is thus the whole world of its waking experience, disordered and condensed into a point.

Moreover, the feeling soul in its immediacy is as much pure waking as it is pure sleep and dreaming. The feeling soul is characterized by the attempt to circumvent the naturally given mediation of the body and its sensing organs, in which the soul in sensation is absorbed in a state of "sleep." The resulting disorder is an effect of the attempt to know the world without relying on any form of "sleep." If this disorder resembles the randomness and unpredictability of dreams, it means only that the state of radical enlightenment sought by the waking soul is only a different sort of obscure dream, or delusion. The parallels Hegel implies with the eighteenth-century Enlightenment movement are, of course, entirely intentional.

The second form of the relation to a "genius" is the relation between the unborn child and its mother.[35] The child here is separate from its mother spatially, but this spatial asunderness is nothing for the soul. Hegel was convinced that a pregnant woman was a single self spread over two bodies such that the fetus has its self only in its mother because the fetus has no being-for-itself. As Hegel showed in his analysis of the ages of life (§396), the fetus has only a vegetative life and knows no opposition. Whether the examples Hegel cites in his lectures (of the mother's emotions being transmitted to her unborn child) are to be believed is less important than his argument that spatial separation is nothing for the soul, and that one human can have its *self* in another. This principle is better illustrated in dreaming, or in the third example, which Hegel calls simply "the relation of the individual to his genius." Here is where Hegel gives one of the accounts of what "genius" means that I used for the explanation of the term, namely, that the genius is one's character, the totality of one's experiences that shapes one's decisions and acts—and hence one's destiny.

The relation between the feeling soul and its genius is still better presented however in cases where the genius is another person (though perhaps not in the relation already examined between an unborn child and its mother). Instead, I would like here to present some examples that Hegel does not use, but which I think demonstrate his point rather well.

Consider for example sympathy pains, or the development of sympathy symptoms (which are empirically verifiable by a third party). It is well documented that sometimes in cases involving two or more people who are very close emotionally (e.g., two people in love), when one is sick or injured, the other will feel his or her pain. Of course, if the illness in question is a communicable disease, then the second person may simply have caught the illness. But such a biological explanation is impossible when considering something like couvade syndrome.[36] This well-documented phenomenon involves men feeling symptoms of their wives' pregnancies, including food cravings, hormonal shifts, nausea, labor pains, and, in at least one case, "a swollen abdomen resembling that of a fairly advanced pregnancy."[37] Studies of the incidence of couvade syndrome among men with pregnant wives range from a low 11 percent[38] or 22 percent[39] up to 79 percent.[40] There is also the case of what is called *folie à deux* (double madness, or *folie à plusieurs* if more people than two are involved), in which delusions (often paranoid delusions) can be transmitted from one person (the "inducer" or "principal," i.e., the genius) to another merely by close emotional association.[41] It has been suggested that cases of mass hysteria, shared religious fanaticism (as for example in murderous or suicidal cults), and Saint Vitus's dance (which Hegel also mentions[42]) are properly cases of *folie à plusieurs*.[43] Phenomena like this are inexplicable for a biologist, that is, one who considers the human being to be simply a form of organic life. They can only be explained by an account of *the soul*, that is, of a form of spirit that remains indeterminate with respect to natural (including biological) distinctions.

There are many other cases of very close spiritual bonds between people that engender the displacement of the self of one person or the selves of many people into a "genius." For example, the relation between a leader and his or her followers in a social or political context. Here we have a word for that which makes one person a genius, the self of others who are in her thrall: charisma. To be sure, leadership does not always involve charisma. Some people become leaders by soberly making the case for a certain course of action. In such cases, however, people consciously follow the policy rather than the leader, considering the latter only a more or less effective instrument for accomplishing the end (which alone captivates them). In other cases, however, it is the leader herself and not her policies that command a following. Such a person exercises a curious control over others, which can appear inexplicable to an outside observer who is not under her sway (as for example in the case of an observer from a different time or place).

This is not to say that the emotional hold a good orator can have on her listeners is necessarily perverse. It can be a noble, and indeed socially necessary, bond. Martin Luther King Jr. and Malcolm X were both stirring orators who were able to use the emotional and rhetorical power of their speech to rally others in a just struggle. The difference between them and a demagogue like Hitler or Mussolini lies in the fact that a reasonable person, when not under the spell of their rhetoric, would reject the goals of the latter. The emotional sway an orator can have on an audience is in itself neither good nor bad but only an enduring possibility for all ensouled beings. The modern reader thus need not be puzzled when reading about how the Athenians were enchanted by the speeches of Pericles and Demosthenes, or how they were spellbound even by Alcibiades, who more than anyone else led them to ruin. The power of an orator is not based on the logical cogency of her argument, or the prudence of her suggestions, but rather on her *charisma*: it is what Hegel called a "*magical* relation,"[44] that is, an immediate relation that a genius is able to establish between herself and another. This relation does not take place on the level of the abstract understanding, and it does not consist in offering propositions in support of a conclusion. Rather, it takes place on the level of *the soul*.

The Sophists famously claimed to be able to teach this kind of rhetorical sorcery, though it is doubtful (as many at the time recognized) that such a thing can be taught. Admittedly, there do seem to be certain general rules to effective rhetoric, rules that one could teach: alliteration, the stirring use of meter, building up to a phonetic and semantic cadence, and so forth. Yet these techniques cannot make a person a great leader any more than the similar mechanical application of musical rules can make one an ingenious composer. The speech of a charismatic leader must resemble what Kant considered the beautiful object: it must be purposive without purpose. That is, it must strike and appeal to the very heart of one's audience, without seeming contrived to do so.

Indeed, Hegel's description of the hero (the founder of a state) in his philosophy of objective spirit agrees with this completely. The hero does not think up an abstract constitution and then try to apply it to the world. Instead, he in some mysterious sense feels what needs to be done and brings it about without reflection or total awareness of what it is that he is accomplishing.[45] What makes him a hero (and not, say, a madman) is not so much a property that he possesses in himself, but only that his actions really are in tune with the needs of the time, and that the population as a result does come under his sway, assembling around him and following him, even to their deaths.[46]

I would suggest therefore that the hero, the charismatic national leader, exercises the power of a "genius" over his followers. Indeed, in his lectures on the philosophy of history, Hegel refuses to go too far in discussing the role of the hero in founding a state, or the constitution of a nation before it has been organized (by a hero) into a state, because, he says, such a topic belongs to the *poetry* of history, not its *prose*.[47] In other words, it belongs to mythology rather than history proper (which concerns only the succession of nation-*states*). Just as a state has its origin in the immediate relation established between a charismatic hero and the populace,[48] an association that however *ought* to go on to develop into a well-articulated state[49] (which has no room for such heroes[50]), so the individual is susceptible to coming under the sway of such a genius, but this is not the normal, developed human condition. That is, the individual person has this susceptibility but *ought* not to succumb to it; and in the life of a healthy, properly developed person, there is no longer any room for a relation to a genius—or at least no room for one's total submission to a genius.[51] And since Hegel does not consider it beneath the dignity of philosophy to take the individual feeling soul as its object, nor should it be beneath the dignity of philosophy to take as its object the prepolitical, "mythological" origin of states, the poetry of history.

So much for the examples of the feeling soul in its immediacy that Hegel does not mention but that I think qualify. It is best now to turn back to the text to analyze some more of the examples Hegel does give and see if they can be accepted. In discussing this kind of diseased condition in the section on the feeling soul in its immediacy, Hegel has much to say about "magnetic somnambulism" and "animal magnetism." These include various phenomena, some almost certainly legitimate, some almost certainly illegitimate. Aside from dreaming, and the examples I have provided of sympathetic pain and charisma, other cases that I would be inclined to accept as legitimate include sleepwalking (i.e., somnambulism), hypnotism, and various other mental disorders in which one may have hallucinations amounting to the disruption of the relation between their senses and their proper organs. I am inclined to reject some of the other examples, namely, clairvoyance, and metal and water divination (of which Hegel himself was rather dubious[52]).

It is no problem for an interpretation of Hegel's anthropology to jettison these unlikely examples, because all Hegel really need be committed to is: (1) that the lowest, most abstract level of spirit is the soul; and (2) for the soul natural division is nothing. These positions are not at all incredible. Indeed, it would be foolish to claim otherwise. How else would one explain that a single living, feeling subject is present throughout the whole body? When it comes to admitting other phenomena as concretions of this form of spirit, I would judge each case individually, deferring when appropriate to experts in the relevant fields.[53] Dreams belong to everyone's experience and thus need no proof. Sleepwalking, hypnotism, and various kinds of hallucination are well documented and are accepted as legitimate by the American Psychiatric Association. On the contrary, the preponderance of evidence seems to rule against clairvoyance, metal and water divination, and so on. But I must dwell a bit longer on hypnotism, insofar as many of the less credible phenomena Hegel discusses might be legitimated by reinterpreting them as cases of hypnotism.

Hypnotism, as its name suggests, is a form of or at least something resembling sleep (ὕπνος, *hypnos*), the collapsing of the distinction for the soul between inner and outer. Hypnosis is best known for its role in treating neuroses. For instance, Freudian psychoanalysis relies on hypnosis for the exploration of the "unconscious." For a patient who displays neurotic symptoms resulting from a past trauma that has been repressed, hypnosis is used to gain access to this repressed content. Hypnosis can be therapeutic only if the patient has such a repressed content that needs to be brought to light. Hypnosis is then effective in inducing the patient's regression to the level of the soul (which under normal circumstances would be undesirable), in order to efface the distinction for the patient between inner and outer, such that the patient will willingly divulge to the therapist the repressed memory she was concealing even from her conscious self.

The patient is "willing" to divulge this content under hypnosis precisely because, for the patient under hypnosis, nothing is being divulged. In hypnosis the patient loses the distinction between inner and outer. Thus, in (what is for the therapist) the *expression* (i.e., externalization) of the repressed memory, the patient recognizes no boundaries (and thus nor does the patient recognize the crossing of a boundary). If, as I said earlier, the genius is the same as the unconscious, then the *expression* of the content that has been repressed to the unconscious would amount to the *liberation* from the control of the genius. For the artist, it is the very creation of her art, the objectification of the content of her unconscious, or genius, that liberates her.[54]

Not only do I propose accepting hypnotism as a form of the feeling soul in its immediacy, I would propose amending what Hegel says of certain other phenomena (the details of which are given later) in order to understand them as instances of hypnotism. For instance, Hegel asserts that in "somnambulism" or "animal magnetism," the passive soul and its genius can share the same feelings.[55] In addition to being possible in cases of couvade syndrome (discussed earlier), this sharing of feelings would be possible under hypnosis, at least insofar as the hypnotist would be able to induce certain feelings in the patient through suggestion. The confusion between inner and outer induced in hypnotism allows a suggestion from the hypnotist to be grasped as coming from *oneself* rather than from another. As a result, the patient can be made to do or to feel what the hypnotist suggests (within certain limits). Not only can the hypnotist thus "share" her feeling with the patient, but also the patient's private feelings can be "shared" with the hypnotist by the kind of divulging of private contents previously described.

Now, in his lectures, Hegel seems to think that it is possible for one person to *immediately intuit* the feelings of another.[56] Hypnotism does not allow this, and I do not accept that such a thing is possible. Yet what I have described as being possible through hypnosis still meets Hegel's own criteria for being concretions of the feeling soul in its immediacy. These criteria do not require the immediate *intuition* of one person's feelings by another but only that the proper mediation of the senses deduced in the sections on the natural soul (§§399–402) be bypassed in favor of an "immediate" feeling of the private feelings of another person's soul. The proper mediation deduced in the section on sensation involves the corporealization of an emotion in one person (e.g., a person's corporealization of shame through the reddening of the face) and another person's apprehension of this corporeal manifestation through his own sensation (viz., the *sight* of the first person blushing). This is not how a feeling is communicated in hypnosis.

Winfield argues correctly that consciousness and language are necessarily involved here.[57] Certainly, through hypnosis the feelings of one person are transmitted to another through *some* mediation, namely, that of language (the hypnotist's suggestion to the patient, or the patient's verbal expression of a repressed content). However, this is not the mediation that was deduced in §§399–402, and so hypnotism *does* constitute a disruption of the proper form of mediation. Of course, feelings are also transmitted via language in more commonplace ways (as one person can simply describe an emotion and perhaps thereby evoke it in another), but this requires the hearer to actively interpret the verbal signs of an emotion and voluntarily reproduce the emotion in himself. The use of language in such a case would not amount to a disruption of the mediation deduced in §§399–402. Sounds known to be *external* are in this case simply heard and interpreted. In hypnotism, on the contrary, the hypnotist's suggestion is not sensed as an external sound, and it produces the feeling in the patient without mediation of the understanding or will. Thus there is good reason for holding hypnotism to be a genuine form of the feeling soul in its immediacy and moreover to interpret Hegel's description of other less credible phenomena to be more properly examples of hypnotism.

Additionally, Hegel finds credible the idea that there could be a "common feeling [*Gemeingefühl*],"[58] that is, a generalized sensation that operates either through a different organ than the one normally used (such that one sees with one's fingers and tastes through one's abdomen) or through the body generally. I propose that it is possible for hypnotic suggestion (and perhaps also psychosis) to produce such disordered sensations. That is, by such means feelings *for the patient* can be induced, such that, say, chocolate would be tasted at the same time as a chocolate bar is placed on the patient's abdomen. However, there is no reason to believe (and every reason to doubt) that anyone (even in such a hypnotic or psychotic state) could actually be stimulated in this way *by natural objects*, and through *another body part* acting as a sense organ, such that she would be able to tell what an object was merely by placing it on her abdomen and "tasting" it. The sensation of the taste of chocolate would be in truth produced by the hypnotic suggestion (or by her psychosis), not by the chocolate bar. Nor would the abdomen be acting as a mediating sense organ. Here I would add the same point as the preceding: the feeling here is mediated through language (in the case of hypnosis), but this phenomenon of disordered senses is still possible and still qualifies as an example of the feeling soul in its immediacy.

All of these cases are meant to show that the soul is able to bypass the mediation it has been given by nature (the sense organs) and know its content directly. In doing so the soul knows itself as something particular. In sensation, on the other hand, the soul knows particulars only insofar as they are *not* itself. In foregoing any mediation however the feeling soul loses the ability to hold itself apart from its content as something distinct. Thus it displaces itself into another, whether this "other" is another person or its own unwieldy unconsciousness.

The movement from sensation to feeling is guided by the masculine drive to attain a position from which all of nature (including one's own natural body) appears to it as an external object, under its control. Yet in tragic fashion this act of hubris amounts to the soul's surrendering of all control to its object: the awoken soul no longer submits unreflectively to the natural world, its moods reflecting the natural shapes in which it is immersed, but now has created the terms of a new submission to objects. However, whereas the natural world that the universal soul felt as its own body was a deeply meaningful one, the feeling soul is in the thrall of a nature that has become disenchanted. The parallels with the eighteenth-century Enlightenment are, again, entirely intentional.

The natural soul differs from the feeling soul precisely because the latter is "awoken" and distinguishes itself from all natural objectivity. Yet this dissociation also leaves the soul alienated from its own corporeal immediacy, its own body and natural environment, which had provided the general tenor according to which nature could be experienced as having some meaning and order. In the absence of some new form of mediation to replace what has been lost, the feeling soul descends into mental illness. However, the pathology here and Hegel's bizarre examples can make it easy to lose sight of the fact that the feeling soul is a form of spirit, one that provides something absent in the natural soul, namely, self-knowledge in which the self's particularity receives its due. In its immediacy this particularity is only implicit, but it comes to the fore in self-feeling, that is, "madness," or mental illness, which is the theme of chapter 7.

7

Mental Illness and Therapy

> Our waking sleeps more than our sleeping; our wisdom is less wise than our folly; our dreams are worth more than our discourse . . .
>
> —Montaigne, "An Apology for Raymond Sebond"

> If my present deeds are foolish in your sight, it may be that a foolish judge arraigns my folly.
>
> —Sophocles, *Antigone*

In this chapter I analyze mental illness as "self-feeling," that is, the soul's immediate awareness of itself in any feeling of an object such that it cannot distinguish itself from the object and becomes excessively, obsessively attached to it;[1] and as sickness of the soul, with a structure that recalls Hegel's account of the sickness of the living organism in his philosophy of nature (in which the life turns on its own embodiment, consuming and destroying it), such that madness is the soul's failure to "assimilate" its own embodiment (i.e., to create for itself a form of mediation that does not render its own body opaque to itself). I show how habit is not only the soul's inurement to its feelings, but rather is the construction of a form of mediation, that is, the soul's production of its own "body" insofar as this mediation is the body's function. The whole anthropology can thus be interpreted as a series of ascending stages of the soul's relation to its materiality (whether the natural world generally, the natural body the soul finds itself with, physiological processes the soul undergoes, or a separate person).

Let me also note at this point that I am examining Hegel's theory of mental illness for the sake of showing how it fits into his account of the soul and its body. I am not concerned with mental illness as such, and so while in some cases I have referred to studies in contemporary empirical psychology to corroborate what Hegel is saying (e.g., in chapter 6), I am not attempting to definitively situate Hegel's theory of mental illness within the field of psychology.[2]

What It Means to Say That Mental Illness Is Pathological

Mental illness is disturbing because it allows the fantasies typically associated with sleep to invade the lucid experience of waking life, which we think of as where the *real world* is experienced. Mental illness thus seems to be sleeping while awake,[3] though a study of its roots in sleep and waking shows mental illness is less a matter of sleep intruding on waking life than it is waking life detaching itself from its somnolent foundation, seeking to know nature immediately but thereby depriving itself of what gave order to its experience. The disorder involved in the experience of mental illness shows that it is pathological. Mental illness is not the proper way the human soul should function: not because it varies from statistical norms, and not because it prevents the sufferer from finding a productive role in the modern capitalist economy or behaving like an enlightened citizen of a liberal democracy. Mental illness is pathological because a life lived in its grip is only a shadow of what a human life can be. It is as if you saw that someone had a great work of literature—say, *Moby-Dick*—shoved under a short table leg to keep the table from wobbling. You might say, "Why are you using *Moby-Dick* for something you could use a block of wood for? You are destroying the book: don't you realize what this is?" The person might then respond: "I don't care about this book. I care about having a level table. Your use of the book is no better than mine." If you could keep from having an apoplectic fit, you might then try to explain to the person that your use *is* in fact better, that the potential contained in the book *as* a book for deepening and enriching one's life is practically boundless, whereas the good it does as a mere extended object is slight.

In an analogous way, the mentally ill experience of life is so much more restricted and fails to really appreciate what is possible in human life. This is not to say that some mentally ill people do not lead good lives, nor that a good many sane people do not waste their lives. It is not even to say that by being sane, a sane person lives a fuller life than any mentally ill person. There are innumerable ways to fail to live a life as full and rich as possible, and mental illness is only *one* of those ways. A life steeped in the most insipid parts of popular culture, a career driven by pettiness and vanity, familial relationships that are abusive, attempting to dignify one's bitterness and resentment by channeling them into reactionary politics—a person who lives in this way is not mentally ill but lives a wretched life[4] (one that is pathological in its own right). If we contrast this with an artist or saintly hermit who suffers from mania, it is clear that the maniac lives better than the bourgeois drone. Nonetheless, mental illness as such is still pathological and the one suffering from it would live better if relieved of this burden.

To say that mental illness is pathological does not mean that in it what is human is lost. Mental illness is, in fact, a form of spirit, and that is saying quite a lot.[5] By including it in his philosophy of spirit, Hegel takes the position that the way the world is experienced in mental illness is part of our *genuine* experience of the world. By diagnosing it as pathological Hegel is not denying what the mentally ill person experiences as unreal: he is only identifying its limitations and showing that it is not the most sophisticated or most human way to be embodied and relate to nature. The Hegelian response to this malady is not to reject it but to contextualize it: to incorporate it into our mental life by fashioning for it a form of mediation (a "body") between itself and its felt content.[6]

Of course, the soul already has a body, a form of mediation, in the flesh, blood, and above all the sense organs given to it by nature. Yet there are two problems with this natural body: (1) it fails to mediate between the soul and sensations that match the determinations of its sense organs; (2) it only mediates the soul's relation to its external contents (sensations), but not its inner contents (already possessed feelings). In other words, though the natural body regulates the soul's relation with the external world, the inner world of the soul has not been assimilated and ordered, but only repressed. In its awakening (§398) the soul distinguishes itself from external nature without ever exerting any control over the turbulent inner world of its sleep. Because the soul in sensation remains immediately absorbed in its own body, unconscious of it, and the soul is still, in a sense, *asleep*—and this not despite its awakening, but because of it. Mental illness is not a trespass of illusion into reality, the false into the true, or nonbeing into being: it is the revelation that the "reality" intended by waking life, a reality founded on the suppression of sleep and its dreams, is itself demented.

Understanding mental illness in its place in the anthropology means understanding it in relation not only to sleep and waking but to femininity and masculinity, with which sleep and waking are so similar in Hegel's account. As feeling is only possible because of the natural body that gives access to the external world, but the feeling soul attempts to bypass this natural mediation and know its content directly and independently, so the masculine world of the state depends on the feminine world of the household but in Creon's intransigence, attempts to articulate justice independently and without regard to the unwritten law of the netherworld. To be sure, the fault is not in Creon's idiosyncrasies but in the organization of Greek ethical life, which recognizes two distinct but fortuitously harmonious laws. The "intransigence" here is just that Creon finds himself already on one side of this conflict, knowing one law but blind to the other. And yet, part of the tragedy is in how the universal and particular coincide, and one can seem to take the place of the other. Thus Creon (and Antigone) defend a legitimate law, but they also enjoy their own particularity in doing so, just as surely as the expression of the contrary law not only violates for each his or her own law but also destroys his or her individual personality. For Hegel mental illness involves just the same "self-feeling."

Mental Illness as "Self-Feeling" and Sickness of the Soul

In the anthropology Hegel calls mental illness "self-feeling [*Selbstgefühl*]." The term "feeling" is a technical one for Hegel. In his lectures on the philosophy of religion he makes it clear that *all* feeling is—at least implicitly—self-feeling: "This is what feeling is: the place where my being and the being of my object [i.e., what is felt] exist as one. Here my being and the being [of the object] are posited as one"[7]; " 'having [some content] in feeling' is nothing other than having it as mine, and indeed mine as this particular individual—that it belongs to me, that it is for me, that I have and know it in its determinacy, and equally have and know myself in this determinacy. It is feeling of a content, and equally self-feeling. The content is such that my particularity is bound up with it."[8] It appears therefore that even if it was not until 1830 that Hegel differentiated between *Empfindung* and *Gefühl*,[9] he still had worked out an understanding of *Gefühl* as early as 1824, and until his death this understanding remained basically consistent (including with the text of the anthropology and the lectures on it).

What the lectures on the philosophy of religion contribute to our understanding of feeling is thus that in feeling something, one is also feeling oneself. With a religious feeling this means that whenever I have a feeling of God, I am not simply apprehending God but always also enjoying my own particularity (i.e., I am feeling God *in God's relation to me*, as a particular empirical individual[10]). In feeling I identify with my felt content; and in "self-feeling," I have at least some indistinct awareness that my own self is present for me as a determinate object. Self-feeling is thus not the same as feeling in its immediacy (where the incongruity between the subject and its object is not even felt), but nor is it consciousness, which represents the felt object as something objective and distinct both from the experiencing subject and from the subjective sensation.[11] Rather, self-feeling—mental illness—is sickness of the soul.

Accordingly, there are instructive parallels with the other kind of sickness, namely, sickness of the organism. The living thing is a complex of assimilative processes that, far from being simply material, are actually the *destruction* of matter: in their operation these processes take in matter and transform it into energy for the continuation of precisely these assimilative processes, evacuating the rest as waste.[12] The very presence of this waste, as enduring, unassimilated matter, is a sign that natural life is subject to disease and death. Disease for Hegel occurs when one part of the living being (this or that organ or process) begins to operate independently of the whole, thereby subverting the self-reproductive activity of the whole.[13] In natural life, it is the aforementioned inability of the organism to assimilate nature completely that precipitates its disease and the death.[14]

Likewise, insanity is a sickness of the soul, such that the relation between the sphere of the soul (*das Seelenhafte*) and the "*objective consciousness*" (the more developed spiritual capacities whose deduction follows the anthropology) is one of "*direct opposition.*"[15] That is, in insanity the most basic level of subjectivity, which we call "the soul," begins to operate independently, just as for the animal, disease involves one organ system operating at variance with the rest of the animal's organic functions. Similarly, just as organic disease is provoked by the failure to completely digest inorganic nature, the sickness of the soul is prompted by the "moment of corporeity" that has not been fully assimilated by spirit:

> On account of the immediacy within which self-feeling is still determined, i.e. on account of the moment of corporeity there which is still undetatched from spirituality, and since feeling

itself is also a particular [*ein besonderes*] and hence a specific embodiment, the subject which has developed an understanding consciousness [*verständigen Bewußtsein*] is still subject to disease in that it remains engrossed in a particularity [*Besonderheit*] of its self-feeling which it is unable to work up into ideality and overcome.[16]

To understand what this unassimilated "moment of corporeity" is, recall a key feature of sensation: namely, that as sensation the soul is "mixed" with the body. As "mixed," the sensitive soul is in a way corporeal, natural. That is, the soul passively has certain sensible determinations in the way natural objects do. For example, the sensitive soul (since it is a human individual) is covered with skin. And this skin, like everything material, is necessarily a certain temperature. In other words, this skin passively possesses a certain measure of heat. But by *being* this determinate measure of heat (i.e., as a result of this "mixing" with embodiment), the sensitive soul becomes incapable of *sensing* precisely that determination. Thus other objects that possess the same measure of heat are likewise not felt at all by the sensitive soul (at least not with respect to their temperature). In other words, the sensitive soul is "mixed" with a body (as is thus still "sleeping" to this extent) and whatever determinations the sensitive soul has (in the natural, corporeal sense of merely passively possessing it), it does not sense. Therefore the sensitive soul senses what varies from its own particular, determinate condition, but it never senses or feels *itself* and indeed is unaware that it is particular and corporeal in this way.

The "moment of corporeity that is still undetached from spirit" is thus the soul's own body,[17] that is, that which mediates between the soul and its content. It is only when the soul manages to detach itself (at least minimally) from this corporeal moment (i.e., its own body) that the soul begins to *feel itself*. It is thus only in madness that the soul "awakens" to its own natural embodiment, and this awakening is the first step in transcending this natural embodiment (by producing a spiritual body). However, when the feeling soul circumvents the body and its forms of mediation it leaves this "corporeal moment" unassimilated. That is, the soul has not provided a more adequate form of mediation in the place of the body and its sense organs. Hegel's theory of habit and the "actual soul" will make clear that the significance of "the body" here and "the unassimilated corporeal moment" is simply that of the mediator between the soul and its sensation or feeling. The task of the soul is to lose or detach itself from the body given to it by nature and to fashion its own "body" (i.e., form of mediation) for itself.

The relation of the feeling soul to nature can shed light on Hegel's social and political theory insofar as both are rooted in his theory of gender and the relation between domesticity and civil society that this theory involves. The disorder belonging to the feeling soul develops organically from the presuppositions of gender and the natural soul just as surely as a perverse sort of social life develops out of the same presuppositions, when placed in the larger context of an entire community of people giving objective existence to its culture. Indeed, the common pattern is distinct enough that if we understand what happens in the passage from the natural to the feeling soul in the anthropology, we can discern in objective spirit many of the social-political counterparts to the aspects in the anthropology's account.

For instance, that the soul only begins to "feel itself" in feeling and not in sensation (where it is "mixed" with, knowing no distinction from its natural body) is analogous to how in Hegel's theory of gender women remain in the household and may know justice and goodness only mixed with their emotional attachments to their family members (the natural community from which the feminine ethical disposition, in Hegel's view, fails to differentiate itself). It is only men who leave the household and enter civil society, coming to take on an identity different from their place in the family and thus to feel themselves as a professional or worker of some kind and with some skill and distinction. The development of skills, the focus on merit, are ways the male ethical disposition has separated itself from its natural attachments and begins to view identity, status, and justice itself outside of any emotional attachment to *natural* relations. Typically commentators focus on how this sets out unjust and arbitrary limits for women[18]—and that is indeed a large part of Hegel's social philosophy. Yet few recognize the deep problems of the male experience: the civil society created by this masculine, extra-familial interaction is a profoundly perverse one, riven by unresolved contradictions and unaccountable injustices. For example, it is inegalitarian in principle,[19] does not provide equal opportunities,[20] and renders the individual's economic viability extremely precarious[21] and even self-destructive, insofar as increased efficiency results in lower value for work.[22] As a result, part of civil society ends up permanently excluded,[23] and the nation is driven toward war with its neighbors[24]—and these not as a matter of unfortunate circumstance but according to the "normal" functioning of civil society.

Any recommendation a defender of the modern liberal order may offer for addressing these problems will be inadequate if it is limited to alleviating the symptoms (poverty, unemployment, alienation, war) while leaving intact the basic principle of this sort of civil society (viz., that social relations are "free" by being immediate). In other words, modern civil society—capitalism—is pathological because it is a flight from femininity and the household, leaving an unassimilated "moment of corporeity." As a flight from the household, where each member is valued and has his or her place (while still being deeply unjust in maintaining traditional hierarchies), civil society presents each man to himself as an atom among other atoms, entering into relations with others arbitrarily, guided only by principles of egoism,[25] or, to use the economists' euphemism, "enlightened self-interest." Men in civil society are (in their minds) strangers to each other, all natural, familial mediation between people having been circumvented in a *bellum omnium contra omnes*. In such a state, the deepest injustice is accepted as true justice, as men fail to recognize each other as anything but things, means to the satisfaction of their own private ends.

It is not that civil society as such is antagonistic in this way: the independence of people from their family environment and development of talents, abilities, and social identity outside of the home is a necessary moment of freedom. But the civil society *that we have*, civil society in the shadow of capital, is antagonistic because "freedom" is conceived simply as the severing of natural ties.[26] The resolution of this problem requires seeing that the abolition of traditional hierarchies among men and of all traditional ("natural") forms of social mediation is not by itself liberation: *new* forms of mediation must be fashioned in their place, to make modernity the establishment of a human civilization in place of traditional social life, rather than the mere destruction of traditions in a headlong return to barbarism.

The social and political problems of modernity thus result not just from one part of the culture trying to separate itself from the unwritten laws of the inherited way of life (this separation is a necessary aspect of freedom), but only when this separation is paired with the failure to provide any new forms of mediation. *Écrasez l'infâme!* Yes, that is good and well, but something must then be provided to replace it. Similarly, there is nothing pathological about striving to experience nature beyond the limitations of the naturally given body and its senses, but it becomes pathological in mental illness because no new mediation is created to replace the circumvented one. The soul has many feelings—it is a world unto itself—but the soul cannot stably identify tout court with each of these feelings. Each feeling in its immediacy is contingent and excludes other feelings—with which the soul in mental illness identifies nonetheless.

In the absence of any mediating principle, each feeling clamors for the attention of the soul, which feels compelled to identify *simpliciter* with each feeling singly. It is not only that the soul is torn between conflicting feelings. The soul has no power over *any* of its feelings but instead is controlled by them. That is, the soul is not the substance that has its feelings as its accidents; rather, the feeling (*each* feeling) is the substance, and the soul is its accident.[27] The soul thus recognizes its feeling as something particular, and in taking this feeling to be its own self, recognizes its own particularity; but in identifying with any given feeling *simpliciter*, it fails to recognize that it is not limited to this particular feeling. Thus it is perhaps false, but at least misleading, to say that in self-feeling the soul "knows itself as particular." The soul here identifies with a particular feeling, but it fails to grasp precisely *how* it is particular and thus identifies completely with any and all feelings, no matter how contingent or mutually incompatible.[28]

Mental Illness as Excessive Attachment

Hegel deduces three types of mental illness (the first being further subdivided into three kinds): (1) the spirit sunken into itself, which can either be (1a) imbecility (simple self-absorption in a state of spiritual paralysis),[29] (1b) absent-mindedness (inability to attend to the immediately present),[30] or (1c) rambling (the inability to attend to anything at all, inability to hold one's representations together);[31] (2) mental illness proper (in which the indeterminate self-absorption of the first type acquires a definite content, on which the soul then fixates, according to its objective reality);[32] (3) mania or frenzy (where the soul becomes aware of the disruption of itself but cannot rid itself of its fixation).[33]

I will not go through each of these in detail. I will merely point out first that these three moments give mental illness in its concept, and in its properly conceptual articulation: the absorption within oneself in abstraction from determinacy (imbecility, absent-mindedness, and rambling); the fixation on a particular content, which implies some minimal differentiation (mental illness proper); the soul's awareness that it is internally divided, that it is diseased, though it has yet to assert control over its complex of feelings overcoming this difference (mania or frenzy). In what follows I will focus on mental illness proper (*eigentliche Narrheit*). In fact, in describing self-feeling and mental illness thus far, I have been describing it as mental illness proper.

From a sane observer's perspective, mental illness appears as a kind of excessive attachment: the soul in such a state identifies with (what an observer knows to be) a limited, contingent feeling, which because of its limitation and contingency cannot be stably identified immediately with the soul. The healthy, "self-possessed [*besonnen*]" subject on the other hand is able to order all of its feelings into a coherent whole, qualifying its identification with each in accordance with the organizing principle of this whole.[34] This "self-possessed" subject is not the sensing soul with its mediated relation to the sensible determinations of natural objects (a mediation that is itself given by nature) but rather the more developed soul (deduced at the *end* of the anthropology), which has itself fashioned its own mediated relation to its inner feelings. The mentally ill person fails to do this for the lack precisely of such an organizing principle, that is, a way to mediate these feelings (thus we might say that such a person is not "self-possessed" but possessed by another).

Take for example a mentally ill person with a fixation on some public figure. One can admire this public figure or take an interest in her career without being a mentally ill person, but it is pathological to be completely absorbed in one's relationship with this person, especially if the relation is so distant that the object of one's fixation is not aware of one's existence or fanatical devotion.[35] It is insane precisely because obsessive attachment to this feeling excludes attachment to any other feelings of the soul, restricting the person to a much more narrow, impoverished life. Thus the ill person may lose his job due to frequent absences (as he stalks this public figure). His personal relationships may similarly fall apart, and he may find himself incarcerated or hospitalized. The overriding attachment to this one feeling thus prevents the sick soul from forming some coherent organization of all of its feelings. But if this unfortunate person were hospitalized, the therapist would have to realize the futility—and indeed, the wrongheadedness—of commanding him simply to *give up* his interest in this public figure. For the philosopher who understands self-feeling, and for the therapist, this public figure is only another human being: famous perhaps, but also distant and inaccessible, and certainly not the appropriate object of any deep emotional bond on our part. But for the soul in self-feeling, the object of its feeling is in a very real sense *its own self*, not something toward which it can adopt a detached attitude.

The political analogue of the Terror may be helpful. In a nation, each member of the nation is in some sense the nation itself, immediately existing. Thus each can speak for the nation, act on behalf of the nation, exercise the authority of the nation.[36] The nation here is "universal" (in the sense that it includes many singulars and communes only with itself) though each member is only a determinate, contingent singular (which *is not*, at least in some sense, the other singulars). If the universal and the singular are identified *immediately*, then each member of the nation arrogates to herself the *sole* right to represent the whole nation. But the singular citizen obviously has limitations, contingencies (e.g., particular interests at variance with those of other citizens), and inadequacies that the nation as such (as universal) does not have. As a result, the immediate identification of universal and singular is unstable. Thus during the Terror of the early 1790s, each citizen identified himself immediately with the nation. Consequently, any difference between one citizen and another was held by each to be *treason* against the nation itself, and the "traitor" was put to death.[37]

What is needed are institutions that are particular and differentiate the nation (as universal) from itself but do so according to a principle immanent in the nation itself. Then a difference in opinion between two singular citizens does not necessitate the destruction of the nation (in the person of one citizen) in order to preserve it (in the person of another). Instead, each citizen would be identified with the nation only in a qualified way, and there would be a clearly defined rationale for determining the extent to which a given citizen acts within the law. In other words, in a case of the universal and singular relating immediately, what is needed is a mediating particular. For a nation, this mediating role is filled by its customs (*Sitten*), which are the social *habits* of a people:[38] these may be formally expressed in laws that mediate between individual citizens, qualifying the claim of each to represent the nation in accordance with the degree to which his actions are informed by the national customs. Here, in the feeling soul, the particular term that mediates between the soul and its feelings is the *habit* (*Gewohnheit*) of the individual. Habit is a particularizing principle immanent within the soul, which qualifies the soul's identification with each singular feeling to the extent required for all feelings to be integrated together as a totality.

Habit as Therapy

It may seem strange that habit should cure madness, since madness is the soul's complete absorption in one feeling, and habit seems to be a process of becoming *more* intimately familiar with a certain feeling, rather than less.[39] To see how habit functions in its therapeutic capacity, it must be borne in mind first that Hegel is not saying that to be unhabituated in a certain way is to be insane; nor is he saying that to become habituated in any way at all is to cure one's madness. It is best to leave aside what we usually mean by "habit" and let Hegel tell us what he means by the term. Additionally, it must be remembered that insanity is intrinsically unstable. In its sickness, the soul identifies with one contingent feeling, its enjoyment of which could easily be upset by the most common of circumstances.[40] When the soul's enjoyment of its *idée fixe* is disrupted, it is faced with the exceedingly unfamiliar *absence* of this feeling. The loss of this feeling is of course experienced by the soul as the loss of itself and thus as an intense agony (or "infinite pain"). Endurance of this agony however, *habituation* to it, constitutes therapy for the soul.[41] As Chepurin argues, habit at once resists self-feeling and follows from it, as a method of tying every feeling back to its center in the soul as the soul's own feeling.[42] In this way self-feeling undermines itself, generating the habituation that will produce a more healthy state of the soul.

An analogy Hegel gives can make this clearer. The habituated soul is to its individual feelings as the pure intuition of space itself or time itself is to particular spaces or particular times.[43] This makes sense insofar as any particular space is indeed *space*, but no particular space is space itself *simpliciter*. Rather, each particular space is limited on all sides by *other* spaces, which the first space *is not*, but which are equally spaces in their own right. Likewise, each particular feeling has a claim on the soul (the soul does feel itself in each feeling); but no feeling is the soul *simpliciter*. Each particular feeling is limited by other feelings that it excludes but that have an equal claim on the soul. In habit, the soul identifies with the totality of its feelings, taking each as limited.[44]

The therapeutic process according to Hegel involves talking and working with the mentally ill person in an attempt to arouse an appreciation in him for the actual world, in contrast to his fantasy.[45] The difficulty of course is that it is this actual world that impedes the sick soul's pursuit of its fantasy, so it will likely be very hostile to such an approach. Even if one were not able to cajole the ill person along, however, his illness would likely, as previously noted, undermine itself, and in his suffering the person may be cured despite himself. Such an experience would be agonizing, but the very experience of this agony would temper it, insofar as it would show the sick person that he is *not* in fact identical *simpliciter* with that feeling in which he was previously absorbed, that he remains even as this feeling vanishes. The very cry of despair, "I have lost myself," can reveal to the sick person that he is something distinct from the feeling with which he formerly identified. This statement shows that which has been lost to be an object, "myself," which is different from that which has lost it, "I." Of course I am not claiming that the structure of language makes insanity curable, but only that this cry of despair can indicate to the sick person that his suffering of infinite pain is already his transcendence of it.[46]

One way that this trauma could be induced (and which Hegel describes) is for the person administering the treatment to enter into the patient's delusion ("*in ihre Einfälle* [or *Vorstellung, Verdrehtheit*] *einzugehen*").[47] Thus Hegel gives the example of a mentally ill person who claimed to be the Holy Spirit. To cure him, another simply had to enter into his delusion (viz., that any person whatsoever can simply *be* the Holy Spirit), saying, "How can you be the Holy Spirit? *I* am it."[48] This technique demonstrates to the delusional person the absurdity of the delusion by bringing it into open contradiction with itself. Thus while the belief that any individual whatsoever can be the Holy Spirit can in some sense justify the insane contention that one is oneself the Holy Spirit, it can just as easily justify the *opposite* contention (that one *is not*, because *another* person is). In this way it is possible to cure someone of madness simply through dialectic. Indeed, this is precisely what Socrates does to his interlocutors in Plato's dialogues. When Polemarchus claims that justice is helping one's friends and harming one's enemies,[49] Socrates does not present an opposing position. Instead, Socrates simply enters into Polemarchus's delusion and shows that if he is right, then the "just" person may just as likely end up hurting his friends and helping his enemies.[50]

Hegel does not note this, but the entry on the part of the therapist into the patient's delusion constitutes *therapy* in the most literal sense insofar as the term "therapy" comes from the Greek θεράπων (*therāpon*), which denoted the victim of a sacrifice that functioned as a ritual substitute for the one performing the sacrifice, and onto which the impurities of the latter could be transferred—in other words, a scapegoat.[51] The therapist functions as a "scapegoat" for the patient insofar as by entering into the patient's delusion, the therapist takes on herself the patient's illness, and this assumption of the pollution of the afflicted person makes possible the latter's purification. Thus in the aforementioned example Hegel gives, the therapist, who is not at all insane, abandons the correct, rational thinking of which she is capable, submitting to the delusions of the ill person that anyone whatsoever can simply *be* the Holy Spirit. By taking onto herself this sickness, the therapist allows the patient to see his malady from the outside, to see that it *is* a malady from which he is in principle independent, and thereby the therapist makes possible the patient's restoration to sanity.

For the therapist of course (and for the madman as well once he has shaken the grip of madness) no unimaginable catastrophe has occurred when the *idée fixe* has been wrenched from the diseased soul. A single feeling is always something determinate, excluding other feelings (which equally belong to the soul) and thus can be immediately identified with the soul only with deep instability. But for the person suffering from mental illness, the deprivation of his *idée fixe* is the loss of himself. In suffering this, he suffers "infinite pain" (the withdrawal of the subject from all objectivity). But in doing so, the soul *determines itself*: it shows itself to be not merely this or that singular feeling but rather a whole "particular world,"[52] a coherent collection of feelings that can be affirmed consistently. As Winfield puts it, the soul "*produce*[*s*] the unity of its feeling and its physical appearance instead of simply *having* feelings that are conjoined with physiological modifications."[53] Ferrarin similarly explains Hegel's point as follows:

> By possessing a permanent disposition that results in an immediate reaction to stimuli without any need to give it any thought, we preliminarily discriminate that toward which we orient ourselves in the present: not just what we direct our body toward, but also what we let ourselves be affected by and what we expose ourselves to receive. We reduce the externality of nature in and through our bodily nature.[54]

To see how this occurs, consider the example already referred to, someone obsessed with a certain public figure, his fixation on which eclipses everything else in his life. His fixation is based on his *total* identification with *one* feeling. Yet, this feeling is essentially something contingent and limited. Thus to lose his connection with this, the object of his affection (if, say, this public figure dies or behaves in a way that defies the deluded person's idealized image of her), is something that this person may very well suffer. Yet when deprived of what he feels to be his own self, the sick person still continues to exist. He persists not only as an extended body, a chemical compound, and a living being, but also as a form of self-feeling, self-knowing spirit, feeling itself now not in a positive phenomenon as before (the object of his fixation) but in a *negative* one, namely, the *absence* of this object (which for him is his own self), an absence in which he now *feels himself* no less than he earlier felt himself in the presence of his *idée fixe*.

Taking gender roles as an analogue, the male leaves the household and the feminine sphere to enter into civil society with other men. These men define themselves in opposition to women (and civil society itself is defined in opposition to the household, underscoring the internal connection and dependence of men on women, and civil society on the household), taking lack of attachment and "freedom" to arbitrarily enter into and withdraw from any contract as their defining feature. This circumvention of the social organizing principle given by nature is analogous to feeling generally.

The tragedy lies in the masculine repudiation of the household, which is the naturally given form of social mediation. In the household one is surrounded by others that are significant to oneself, such that otherness, or objectivity, and value are mixed together. In leaving the household the male seeks a separation of value and objectivity, such that those he encounters will have no intrinsic value but instead be regarded only as means for the satisfaction of his own private ends, which alone have value for him.[55] That is, in circumventing the naturally given form of mediation, the male encounters only enemies and rivals in civil society, and his life is one of conflict and anxiety rather than freedom. The masculine idea of freedom (from natural ties) is in truth mediated by its relation to the household (insofar as it is defined completely by its flight from the household). But this makes the masculine idea of freedom unrealizable: as masculinity is defined in opposition to femininity, so civil society cannot persist as a site of shared masculine freedom, because one man is free only by subordinating another. Thus while Antigone is compared to a man for her activities outside of the household,[56] Creon says: "I am no man if she is a man."[57]

In the same vein, the feeling soul lives within a multitude of feelings, each of which it would identify with utterly, but the identification with one excludes certain others. The feeling soul cannot come to some coherent way to relate to its feelings, each of which has an equal claim on it, just as Polyneices and Eteocles, both sons to Oedipus, had an equal claim to the throne but could not both occupy it: Eteocles's outrage was to seize the throne, while Polyneices rebelled against Eteocles and Thebes in an act equally justified and equally outrageous. Creon could not come to grips with the contradictions of the masculine notion of social life and considered Polyneices's act to be a monstrous aberration: he could not recognize it as a legitimate application of the very principle he himself lived by, just as he could not recognize his nephew's dead body as something grievous, meaningful, and close to his heart. He ordered instead that the human body of his own blood be treated as a mere object.

The remedy for this was Antigone's defiant act of burial. It is true that Antigone is willful just as Creon is, and that she is flagrant in how she breaks the law, but it would be misguided to evaluate Creon and Antigone in the same way. Antigone's act is more justified than Creon's (though this does not save her) because she sees the tragedy in Polyneices's act: that it was a crime, but that it was not an aberration, falling outside of the ethical order. Her burial of her brother is the ritual affirmation that transforms his act and death, "resolving this wrong such that what has happened becomes a *work* that has been brought about, and the mere existence of the thing, its final form may be something *willed*, and thereby something fitting [*erfreulich*]."[58]

In the same way, habit reaffirms the soul's independence of the mediation given by nature, insofar as habit greatly expands the possibilities of experience for the soul: through habituation one can make something one is biologically predisposed to experience as unpleasant into something bearable and even pleasant (e.g., hard physical labor, very spicy food, even mortal danger).[59] In my reading of Sophocles, Antigone does not insist on burying Polyneices out of mere stubbornness or knee-jerk promotion of the cult of the dead. If she did, she would be comparable to Creon. But burying her brother, not just after his death but after *his crime* means she takes what Thebes (masculine political life) has rendered an inert, meaningless object, worthy of no respect, and reintegrated him into the house of Laius and the city of Thebes on a new basis, expanding and deepening their meaning to include the departure from nature and its tragic consequence. Contrast this with Creon's act of burying Antigone alive, which only shows again his myopia toward Polyneices: Creon cannot get past the "awakening," or the masculine principle according to which all of experience is an external object with no inner meaning and no intrinsic relations to anything else. For Creon, the death of Polyneices is as meaningless as the life of Antigone.

Hegel and Foucault

Based on the account given here, much of what Foucault says about modern ideas of mental illness and its treatment could be taken as an attack on Hegel. For instance, Foucault compares the early modern take on madness unfavorably to that of the Renaissance: in the latter, madness was treated either positively as something higher than mundane knowledge or negatively as something radically alien and completely overpowering. But in either case, for the Renaissance, madness was unreason inassimilable to reason. Madness was the presence of death in life, not to be overcome by anything human beings can muster. On the other hand, beginning in the seventeenth century madness was presented as something ensnared in the dialectic of "reason": a temporary delusion that already points beyond itself toward the truth, the absence of reason that is however only a pretext for the triumphant return of reason.[60]

Foucault does not mention Hegel in *Madness and Civilization*, though some remarks of his may be oblique references to Hegel. He says for instance that in the seventeenth century madness "struggles beneath Minerva's gaze"[61] (alluding perhaps to Hegel's famous image for philosophy, the Owl of Minerva), and that it is brought into "the inevitable procession of reason."[62] Though there is no indication that Foucault was at all familiar with Hegel's discussion of mental illness in the anthropology, just as Hegel writes about the therapist "entering into the delusion" of the madman, Foucault similarly writes about therapy using "theatrical presentation." For instance, Foucault describes how one patient complains he has only empty space in the place his head should be. The doctor responds by offering to fill that space and places a heavy lead weight on the patient's head. The resulting discomfort prompts the patient to come to terms with his delusion and admit that he has a head.[63] Foucault argues that the modern age cannot recognize madness in its truth as radical nonbeing: by recognizing it as a perverted form of reason, reason transforms it once more into being.[64] Foucault's description of madness as presented in modernity parallels Hegel's description in other ways as well: madness is understood as the surrender to an image in its immediacy,[65] which must be cured by wrenching the madman out of his subjectivity and reintroducing him into the "real world."[66]

Yet there is good reason not to take Foucault's presentation as an argument against Hegel. First and foremost, madness for Hegel is not the presence in the soul of only a watered-down, pseudo-nothingness. It belongs to the concept of spirit to alienate itself from all objectivity, and even from its own self: this is what Hegel calls "infinite pain" and "absolute negativity."[67] Mental illness is not just a pretense for the return of reason for Hegel but rather a legitimate form of spirit: it is not the most adequate expression of spirit, but nor is what he calls "reason [*Vernunft*]" itself in the *Encyclopedia*. If the criterion for authenticity in presenting madness is that it be shown as impossible to integrate into human life, then a "history of insanity" (such as Foucault intends to give) would be every bit as impossible as Hegel's philosophical treatment of madness. Both the history and philosophy of madness would present it as something inassimilable for human subjectivity *determined in a certain way* but not radically alien to all comprehension, since if it were, it would be as opaque to the historian as it is to the philosopher.

The question is not whether unreason falls outside of reason, or reason draws unreason into itself and dissolves it: either of these would present reason as something devoid of spirit in Hegel's sense. If we consider "reason" as an abstraction from unreason, then unreason clearly escapes "reason." However, Hegel's concept of spirit is of subjectivity emptying itself out and overflowing into—among other things—madness. Perhaps Foucault might have objected to the claim that reason determines itself as madness because this makes madness into a form of reason. Yet recognizing that reason determines itself as madness is also recognizing that "reason" is not a faculty of abstract thinking that excludes and cannot come to grips with the nothingness that madness makes present. In fact, tracing the argument from the "awakening" to habit shows that for Hegel a knowing that in its brilliance is unable to encounter the darkness of "subjectivity"—which is how Hegel describes the waking soul—is not only unable to resolve the problems raised by madness but is actually superseded by it.

The position taken by Renaissance philosophers like Erasmus (1994) and Montaigne (1991) that "Christian folly"[68] is higher than the wisdom of the wise—a position endorsed by Foucault—is thus not only in line with Hegel's position in the anthropology but also permeates his work generally: the speculative leaps of *Vernunft* are unreason and madness from the more limited point of view of the *Verstand*, which is what many of "the wise" before Hegel and today uncritically identify as the intellect as such, the rational faculty, and the highest epistemic authority.[69]

Let me say it plainly: what Foucault calls "reason" is not like what Hegel calls spirit but more like what Hegel calls the awoken soul; and for Hegel, not only is the awoken soul unable to assimilate madness, it is actually *assimilated by* madness, which is a higher form of spirit. The sanity that Hegel recommends over madness is not one that is unable to bear the opposition between the soul's awakening and madness. Rather, sanity is characterized by the ability to make peace with a certain kind of contradiction—namely, that the soul is this feeling and also its opposite—

a contradiction that the sick soul, with its rigid separation of that with which it is identified and that from which it is different, is unable to allow.

Hegel's idea of madness is thus not the inauthentic idea that Foucault criticizes. Yet it remains true that for Hegel, madness is something to be overcome, which arouses the suspicion that he might be susceptible to another of Foucault's criticisms, namely, that modern prescriptions for overcoming madness really only involve internalizing external authority and enforcing bourgeois norms—that is, bringing the madman into line with dominant social attitudes, conformity with which is called "sanity."[70] If this is true, then the body that spirit gives itself would be only a prison for the soul. Hegel admits that habits are social, and they involve internalizing social codes of behavior. And, it is true that for Hegel the cure for madness is a kind of socialization. However, that is only because (pace Žižek[71]) madness for Hegel is not social critique. Hegel does justify social critique—he even commands it. And a madman may also be a legitimate social critic, and social critique may often be *called* "madness" by conservatives. However, legitimate social critique is not madness, and madness alone is not social critique.[72]

Mental illness is an individual condition. Critique, on the other hand, while carried out by individuals, is always a matter of contrasting a present, illegitimate social state of affairs to a more legitimate one still developing. The critic is present in the criticized culture, but in truth she belongs to the other culture, at least in spirit. Thus critique is always "idealist" in Hegel's sense of the term: the critic is able to grasp the idea developing in empirical "reality," and by virtue of this attachment, she is able to call this reality into question. The Catholic Church developing in the Roman empire is an example. St. Augustine was not an isolated madman when he announced his allegiance to the City of God instead of the City of Rome: he was a member of a community of believers whose emerging culture would in time overtake that of the Roman empire. The same is true of the philosophes of the Enlightenment who represented cities and salons in their critique of the feudal aristocracy of the countryside; it is true of socialists and communists who represent the working class in their critique of bourgeois society; it is true of those intellectuals of Africa, Asia, and Latin America who critique Eurocentrism and colonialism on behalf of globally marginalized cultures; and it is true of the demonstrators in the Arab world and elsewhere who in 2011 rebelled against the general neoliberal order for the sake of a world that has at the time of this writing still not arrived. In contrast, for a would-be social critic to try to find fault with the way of the world from a radically individual, asocial perspective would truly be an exercise in madness, presumption, and vanity.[73]

Yet it may still seem strange that Hegel, who more than anyone has drawn attention to the historical character of social phenomena, should present madness as something eternally rooted in the structure of the soul. Berthold-Bond considers it a weakness in Hegel that he defines madness purely ontologically, without situating it socially and historically (i.e., without defining it at least in part as only a designation or labeling of behaviors deemed unacceptable by a certain ethos, in the manner of Foucault and Szasz).[74] However, Berthold-Bond argues that Hegel's silence about historical conditions of madness in the anthropology does not exclude them: Hegel shows, for instance, that crime is socially determined.[75] This silence can be explained by Hegel's systematic treatment, in accordance with which he tries to avoid bringing into his account a concept or factor until it has been legitimately deduced (without the implication that such a concept or factor is not operative in what was discussed earlier).[76] Hegel's theory is thus still *compatible* with a form of labeling theory, though not that of Foucault and Szasz.[77] I agree that as a matter of historical fact, the "labeling theory" of madness does prove true in some cases: for example, the frequent diagnoses of "hysteria" in women in the nineteenth century, as well as the case of homosexuality, which was for many years pathologized and consequently criminalized in the United States. But that is only to admit that the general public and officials wielding scientific and legal authority can indeed misrepresent the psychological character of a behavior or disposition. I follow Berthold-Bond in denying the very questionable conclusion Foucault and Szasz seem to draw, namely, that psychological diagnoses and treatment can be completely reduced to the exercise of power.

That mental illness is "anthropological" for Hegel thus means that it is an enduring possibility for humans and cannot be reduced to a contingent, historical institution. However, that does not mean that the way madness shows up in a given case does not owe a great deal to the precise social and historical context. In response to the mass shootings that seem to have become a regular feature of American life, some have tried to argue that these events are the result not of the proliferation of guns but only of the mental illness of the perpetrator, and thus they cannot be well predicted or prevented, such that no major legislative changes are needed. Yet, though many mass shooters may well be mentally ill, mental illness, which is purely physiological and has no roots in our culture, occurs necessarily in all societies at the same rate; but few other societies ever suffer one of these kinds of attacks, and none suffer them with the shocking frequency of the United States. The only conclusion I can draw from this is that something about American culture causes mental illness to express itself more often than in other countries in the form of random mass killing, rather than in some benign eccentricity. There is therefore a social aspect to the forms of embodiment under examination here. In the next chapter I would like to focus on the social dimension of human embodiment: how the parts of Hegel's anthropology can help us understand the basic constitution of culture, diagnose its problems, and set about repairing them.

8

The Social Dimension of Human Embodiment

Negroes want to be treated like men: a perfectly straightforward statement containing only seven words. People who have mastered Kant, Hegel, Shakespeare, Marx, Freud, and the Bible find this statement utterly impenetrable. The idea seems to threaten profound, barely conscious assumptions. A kind of panic paralyzes their features, as though they found themselves trapped on the edge of a steep place.

—Baldwin, "Fifth Avenue, Uptown"

Democratic society is instituted as a society without a [natural] body, as a society which undermines the representation of an organic totality. I am not suggesting that it therefore has no unity or no definite identity; on the contrary, the disappearance of natural determination, which was once linked to the person of the prince or to the existence of a nobility, leads to the emergence of a purely social society in which the people, the nation and the state take on the status of universal entities, and in which any individual or group may be accorded the same status. But neither the state, the people, nor the nation represent substantial entities. Their representation is itself, in its dependence upon a political discourse and upon a sociological and historical elaboration, always bound up with ideological debate.

—Lefort, *Democracy and Political Theory*

Hegel's anthropology concerns the first glimmer of spirit in what would otherwise be nature; but there in spirit's most primitive incarnation is contained implicitly much of what is unfolded in the rest of the philosophy of spirit. A patient and sensitive study of the anthropology can thus shed light on problems emerging fully in the more complex and sophisticated phenomena of later parts of the philosophy of spirit. One especially complicated topic belonging to the philosophy of objective spirit, but having roots in the anthropology, is racial, ethnic-national, and gender identity. Since social identity is very often founded on notions of race, ethnicity or nationality, and gender, and since social conflict often takes place along these lines, a philosophical-anthropological clarification of these forms of identity promises rich rewards. Much of this chapter goes beyond exposition and into creative application of Hegel. I do not mean the critical theory presented here as anything explicitly found in Hegel but only as an extension of what Hegel offers in the anthropology that brings out unexplored possibilities of his path-breaking approach to individual and social identity. For Hegel individual habituation is homologous with social acculturation in "ethical life"—that much is immediately clear, as I will show. But since habit is itself the product of a series of precise logical steps, by which more abstract ways of assimilating contents are incorporated, we can expect to understand proper ethical life as sublating more abstract and inadequate forms of acculturation, which may exist in fact as deformations of true ethical life. I aim to expose these less adequate forms of acculturation, showing how an ethical community can be more or less well constituted,[1] and I use the social meaning of physiological characteristics (such as race and gender, commonly understood) to illustrate this.

Habit as a Social "Sense" with Unlimited Scope

When I say that habit serves as a body for the soul, I am not trying to be cute or clever. Habit is incorporeal insofar as it lacks the immediacy and tangibility of flesh and bone, but it serves as a body insofar as it genuinely mediates the soul's experience nonetheless. Just as the natural senses at once direct the soul's attention toward certain phenomena and prevent the experience of other phenomena, and this revealing and concealing occurs because of the natural determinations of the sense organ (e.g., the temperature of the skin), so habit not only inures the soul to certain experiences, making them unfelt, but also heightens the soul's attunement to certain other parts of the world—and this not because of the natural determinations of a region of one's body but because of the history of one's experiences. Just as the idea first displays itself in externality spread throughout the natural world, before returning to itself in reflection on the history of cultures emerging from those regions,[2] so it is with one's individual human body and the habits developed over the course of one's lifetime. In other words, habit is like the acquisition of new "senses" if we define "sense" broadly as the soul's possession of a form of mediation by virtue of which it is receptive to a special content (without stipulating that the sense must be natural and inhere in a tangible body part) or spectrum according to which opposite qualities can be distinguished; and these forms of mediation are "modular" insofar as they are domain-specific, that is, the contents of one sense are inaccessible by another.

The five natural senses would meet these criteria insofar as by virtue of each the soul is receptive to some special content: colors, sounds, odors, and so on. We are receptive to each of these contents though one sense alone, and the content is always a spectrum or several spectra: sounds range from high to low as well as from loud to quiet, whereas colors range only from bright to dark.[3] Yet my point is that in habit we can have "senses" that are not natural. By a sense being "not natural" I mean: (1) that what is sensed is not given to the soul by the facticity of the person's physiology; (2) that this "sense" is receptive to a content that is not merely natural—that is, a content that is neither a merely physical property (such as color is) nor strictly concerned with the promotion of survival and the perpetuation of the genus; (3) that the range or character of this experience is not limited by the physical state of any flesh and blood sense organ (as for example tactile sensation is limited by the temperature of the skin), though these organs may still be involved in the sensing; (4) that, because its tie to flesh and blood organs is looser, the nonnatural sense is not subject to weakening or degeneration through the aging of the natural body (rather, as time passes and more experience is gained, such a sense usually becomes ever keener); (5) that one does not find oneself with such a sense at birth, but rather it must be acquired; (6) there is no limit to the number of such senses one can acquire; and (7) it is entirely contingent that one will acquire any such sense at all.

Take for example the sense of humor. Clearly, this meets the criteria for being not natural: it is not given by nature; its object (the humorous) is not a natural one; the ability to detect humor does not inhere in a sense organ like natural senses do; the development of this sense over time is generally one of increasing sophistication, unrelated to the simultaneous degeneration of the physiological body; and some people seem not to have developed this sense at all. And the sense of humor also meets the criteria for being a genuine *sense*: one is not able to sense anything else merely by virtue of one's sense of humor; the possession of this sense allows one to distinguish the funny from the dull; and this sense is a *receptivity* insofar as it allows one to *feel* a series of sentences or images in a certain way (as more or less humorous).

It is important to note the distinction between *understanding* something as humorous and *sensing* or *feeling* its humorousness.[4] The intellect can grasp perfectly well what makes a joke funny, and it can even identify something like general rules for crafting humorous speech or images: two things not normally associated should be brought together; a premise should be presented that leads the audience to anticipate one thing, but something quite different must in fact follow; and this following must proceed organically. But, of course, these rules are not funny; and subsuming a joke under these rules as an instance of a concept deprives the joke of any feeling of humor. The greater part of humor is thus inaccessible to the intellect because what is funny must be *felt* as such, and it is habit that generates and cultivates in the soul a sense of humor. Accordingly, we can distinguish between a gross sense of humor and a subtle one. Most often age and experience allow the refinement of a sense of humor, though a sense of humor can just as easily degenerate from sophisticated to crude: the character of a person's sense of humor depends on her experiences.

To take another example, one can become habituated to the similarities and contrasts between pledges others make and what they do, and thereby one can acquire a "sense" of the trustworthiness of people. Habituation to the contrasts between what others say and what they still intend to be communicated gives one a sense for irony. If one were able only to experience colors, sounds, odors, tastes, temperatures, among others, one would have no idea of trustworthiness or irony. Of course, one could object that making the judgment that another person's words are meant only ironically, or are false with an intent to deceive, is not a matter of habit but of the understanding (apprehension of general rules under which particular utterances can be subsumed and thereby categorized as "ironic" or "sincere," or "trustworthy" or "deceptive").

Yet while the understanding is involved in the formation of an explicit concept of the ironic, in everyday experience one does not carry out such intellectual operations in judging irony or trustworthiness: one apprehends these qualities unreflectively—one *senses* them. Yet one does not sense them through a certain sense organ, but rather by virtue of a habit for that content built from previous experience. Neither trustworthiness nor irony is a *natural* object or quality, and thus the apprehension of them is not assigned to any part of the human body. Of course, to *hear* someone make a pledge or speak ironically is to use one's *naturally given* auditory sense. However, the object in either of these cases is not the sound as such but rather something else communicated by way of the sound: and this "something else" (viz., trustworthiness or irony) is not itself a natural object but rather something human, or spiritual. It is not that only sounds are sensed while trustworthiness is only thought. Trustworthiness *can* be thought, but when I hear someone lying to me, my *feeling* for her untrustworthiness is distinct from the intellectual *judgment* I may also make to that effect. If it sounds incredible that one could sense what can also be an object of thought, consider how sound too can be an object of thought (viz., as waves of a certain length and frequency), but it would be absurd to deny that we also have a *sense* for sounds that is quite distinct from our thinking of it. Habit is thus a way of developing a "sense" for contents without having a certain sense organ devoted to the sensation of such a content. As Magrì says, habits are "dispositions that broaden the spectrum of subjective capacities";[5] or, as Winfield puts it, they are "acquired patterns of feeling that now function as given endowments of the psyche, standing distinguished from its own [natural] body and the world," or "universal patterns of altered sensitivity produced by the psyche [or soul] itself."[6]

To be sure, one can become habituated also to purely natural contents (the objects of *Empfindung*): living in a cold climate, one becomes habituated to low temperatures; what is initially experienced as a very bright light can through habituation be stripped of its excessive brilliance; after a few minutes of hearing noises like rain falling or background chatter one becomes accustomed to them and ceases to be distracted by them. When giving examples in the anthropology Hegel restricts himself for the most part to cases of habituation to such natural contents (e.g., cold, heat, fatigue, sweet tastes).[7] However, he does give some examples there of habituation to contents that belong more to the spiritual side of the human being (e.g., habituation to misfortune, to renunciation of desire, to the skilled performance of a certain activity, even to the activity of thinking).[8] As Moland notes, habit even functions to establish a certain distance between a person and the mores of her community, allowing her to call them into question.[9] Indeed, habit figures largely in later developments of the philosophy of spirit (especially in social and political life), even if Hegel rarely notes it explicitly.

Internalization, Imagination, and Ethical Life

For instance, internalization and imagination (EPW §§452–460) cannot be understood without presupposing the operation of habit in the background.[10] Internalization (*Erinnerung*) is the process whereby the intellect (*Intelligenz*) creates for and within itself a general image based on its repeated experience of certain contents: that is, it is the transformation of external intuitions into an internal image.[11] Imagination (*Einbildung*) is the intellect's ability to wield its images (*Bilden*), giving them existence as symbols and signs.[12] Both of these processes depend on the ability of the soul to keep from becoming completely absorbed in each singular intuition because: first, a relation could not be recognized unless the contents could first be distinguished (from the soul and from each other); and second, the soul would have no "particular world" to serve as a horizon for the meaningfulness of its symbols and signs. Indeed, without habit imagination could not name objects or generate language at all insofar as the system of signs (including words) is for imagination something like a complex of habits, by virtue of which the spoken or written sign can be experienced as referring to an intuited object and integrated into an intelligible order (just as in the anthropology feelings are shorn of their immediacy by being subsumed under the habits that mediate their relation to the soul).[13]

As Moland and Magrì have recently highlighted, habit is also presupposed by what Hegel calls *Sittlichkeit* (which is usually translated as "ethical life").[14] This translation should be understood to refer to integration of the individual into the collective *ethos* of a people. The ethos of a people is expressed by its customs (*Sitten*): it is through these customs that the good is determined into definite and socially recognized practices, rights, and obligations. Customs mediate between the individual conscience and its action in the world, which are immediately united in what Hegel calls "morality [*Moralität*]." In the absence of customs (i.e., in morality as such), there is always a disparity between the act and the intention that it only ambiguously represents. Custom provides a set of ready-made actions that are intersubjectively recognized as representing certain intentions, at least as far as a certain culture extends. In other words, customs provide an index for actions and their meaning. Thus within a certain culture, an individual can express a friendly and nonthreatening intention by certain gestures with her face and hands, the posture of her body, and so forth. A foreigner who has read extensively about such a culture might through her intellect relate an observed act to its intended meaning; but without completely assimilating into the culture (adopting as her own its habits, its ways of unreflectively mediating received contents), she will never be able to *feel* respected or disrespected, amused or scandalized, in the way people of that culture can. Indeed, a foreigner can never even feel *excluded* from the culture in the way a criminal, a radical, or an eccentric who is yet a member of that culture can feel excluded from it. By the same principle, the criterion for being a full-fledged member of a culture can be identified as possessing the complex of habits defining the culture (whether or not one possesses the proper documentation and legal recognition required for citizenship).

Without a culture antedating the individuals who are born into it—a culture in which these individuals develop and first become thinking individuals at all—their actions and speech would be hopelessly ambiguous. Being born with the same rational capacities is not enough because: first, communication limited to abstract thoughts would leave out too much that is rightly held to be indispensable to a shared human life; second, even the communication of abstract thoughts requires language (signification), which is impossible except against a background of a shared "particular world" (by which Hegel means something close to what is commonly called a *Lebenswelt* or "lifeworld" today). I am not alleging that translation is impossible in any sense, nor that people from different cultures can never communicate in any way, nor that our attempt to understand "what it was like" for, say, the Iron Age Scythians is doomed to failure. I am saying however that the construction of a complex system of signs, such as a language, is not the fashioning of pure ethereal meaning. Rather, it is an incarnation, the building of a kind of "body" that can be shared by many people as their own flesh, through which they feel and know.

For instance, scholars struggle mightily to understand what the Greeks meant by *eudaimonia*. Taking what they have understood, they try to find words in languages like English that approximate it to a greater or lesser extent, or coin new words drawing on existing English morphemes to try to convey this foreign meaning. An English speaker can learn from these scholars if they have penetrated deeper into the Greek world than she has, and if they are ingenious enough to make the proper new use of English. Thus they and we English speakers can arrive at some more or less vague understanding of what *eudaimonia* means. Nonetheless, words stubbornly retain their corporeal side, to the delight of poets and children and the frustration of legislators and certain philosophers. In the end we do not know with much clarity how a fourth-century Greek heard *eudaimonia*.

It is possible that we have experiences that, if they could peer into our souls, the Greeks would confirm as relating to *eudaimonia*, but it is more likely that we lack even precisely such experiences, as these too would be a part of the culture that we do not share. We can translate this enigma as "happiness" or "human flourishing" and this certainly gets at the idea to a certain extent. But that is like saying we can translate "shame" flawlessly as *la honte* or *die Scham*. Admittedly, if we hollow out our idea of shame until it becomes something as desiccated as a dictionary definition, we could translate it into any language and use the understanding to express it as "a deeply uncomfortable feeling owing to witnessing other people witnessing oneself in doing or saying something violating social codes of behavior." While the thought expressed by this sentence can probably be rendered in any language, and can be grasped by anyone, of any culture and language, this definition certainly does not do justice to our word "shame." It is not that *language* is inadequate to express a feeling like shame: for us, the word "shame" *does* successfully signify this feeling. It is rather that the *thought* of shame (which can be articulated in a longer definition) fails to convey what we *feel* and say in the word.[15] To give another example, how close could anyone expect to get in explaining to a fourth-century Greek what an American of our time means by calling something "cool"?[16] We cannot give a definition we would be satisfied with because our deepest acquaintance with what it means for something or someone to be "cool" is not intellectual: we have a *sense* for what is cool, which we are able to effectively signify to each other by using the word.

Thus in the process of acculturation individuals become part of a social *body*, in the metaphorical sense of the term I've been using (viz., as a form of mediation). As a member of such a social body, an individual can feel as the social body feels, developing as her own habits the customs of the social body. This process involves exposure to the kinds of experiences necessary for the development of the kinds of "senses" (i.e., habits) mentioned earlier: for example, one becomes polite (i.e., develops a "sense of propriety") through exposure to the proper way people should act in a given society, that is, through habituation to the way of life proper to one's culture. Just as there are all sorts of unfortunate aberrations in the development of the organs of natural sensibility (such that some people lack some senses altogether, or have them weakly), so the process of spiritual, cultural development is fraught with deformities (such that some people remain unreceptive to the proper spiritual phenomena). For example, one's upbringing could be so sheltered that one fails to develop a sense for the deceptiveness of certain people (i.e., one could be the type we say lacks "street smarts," but perhaps we should say lacks a "street *sense*").

Despite the distance separating both our culture and Hegel's culture from that of the Greeks, this understanding of culture as such is fundamentally Aristotelian. For Aristotle, education is nothing other than the cultivation of the proper habits,[17] and the precise character of these habits should be appropriate to the culture to which one belongs.[18] Moreover, for Aristotle the cultivation of habit acquaints one with a certain dimension of the natural or social world that was always present but of which one was previously ignorant as a result of not having the proper attunement to this dimension, an attunement acquired through habit.[19] Similarly, for Hegel the cultivation of habits opens up a certain dimension of experience of which one had previously no idea, and of which one would remain ignorant unless properly educated. Much of Hegel's philosophy of objective spirit is occupied with this kind of acculturation: thus the family is (in part) concerned with "the upbringing of children,"[20] that is, the *spiritual* development of human beings (rather than merely the *natural* birth of children); civil society[21] and the state[22] are similarly concerned with this spiritual development.[23]

The *Sitten* of objective spirit are thus forms of mediation on the scale of an entire culture that resemble the habits of the individual soul. Moreover, these cultural customs themselves have their immediate reality in the habits that individuals cultivate during the process of their socialization.[24] That habit is integral in both imagination and ethical life means that it is necessary for the construction and interpretation of symbols and signs: that imagination is concerned with producing signs is obvious,[25] but it takes only a bit of reflection to see that ethical action (action in the context of social customs) is also the production of signs. Recall that customs establish the *meaning* of actions for a certain culture: thus in many or all Western cultures wearing black is understood as a *sign* of grief, while in China this meaning is expressed by a different action (viz., wearing white).[26] Indeed, the fact that the process of acculturation is called *Bildung* indicates that it is a matter of making the individual into a sign or an image (*Bild*) of the culture itself. Acculturation can thus be likened to imagination (*Einbildung*), though on a larger scale. It is appropriate that habit should play such an important role in sign-making in the psychology and in objective spirit, since habit has this function in the anthropology as well: it is habit that gives the soul *actuality* in its body, rendering the body a mere *sign* for the soul.[27] That is, habit is the mediation of all content that itself lacks any immediacy: one cannot apprehend the habits of another (the way she moves her hands when she talks, the expressiveness of her face, the way she shifts when she is uncomfortable) without relating them to her soul. Thus habit is a form of embodiment the soul gives itself, such that this spiritual "body" or second nature refers only to the soul and not to itself.

The Enduring Ambiguity of Nature

Part of what it means for a culture to function like a body for its members is that meanings are often culturally specific. There is no "objective" or acultural meaning for, say, a shaved head. It can be a badge of religious devotion (as in many strands of Buddhism), a sign of grieving (in Hinduism), a mark of shame (for female collaborators in France at the end of the German occupation), or an indication of allegiance to fascist thuggery (for skinheads). Similarly, in the context of individual embodiment there is no single temperature that is the most comfortable. Admittedly, extremes can be identified that apparently could never be comfortable, but what is felt as comfortable has less to do with what is objective in temperature (how quickly matter in the air moves) and more to do with the conditions of embodiment of the person in question, primarily experience and habituation to a certain range of temperature. In my own experience, when I lived in Chicago, 40°F did not feel cold, but anything over 80°F felt hot; yet after living a few years in Arizona, 100°F no longer feels hot, but anything under 60°F feels cold.

It is not that there is no sense or logic to individual sensation or cultural meaning, it is only that the sense and logic are rooted in the mediation by which contents are interpreted and given meaning, and these are individual habits and cultural norms. If we abstract from these forms of mediation then the contents in question have no fixed meaning. An immediacy (something considered simply as existing, showing up, and not grasped in its relation to the subject or to its immanent end), whether a certain part of nature (a mountain or ocean) or an image or sound, is fundamentally ambiguous, and the range of different meanings such a thing does assume in fact depends entirely on the cultural context.

In other words, such an immediacy can be a *symbol* but not a sign (without losing its immediacy). A symbol represents something else in a way that relies on the symbol's materiality and immediacy,[28] whereas a sign completely subordinates the representation to what is represented.[29] Thus for example a snake is the symbol in the Bible for the devil, and for the danger of sin generally. The symbolization here relies on peculiarities about the snake that make it a better symbol than, say, a bear. Both are dangerous, but a bear is large, clumsy, and loud: you can see a bear coming and try to run or fight the bear. A bear is an adversary you can pit your strength and cunning against in a way that a snake is not. A snake lurks hidden and attacks the unwary suddenly with a single, deadly strike; and once you are stricken by a poisonous snake, it is already too late. The only protection you have against a snake is to take great care and meticulously avoid any area where a snake *might* be found. The Bible represents sin as a snake because sin is not something to grapple with but something to avoid like the plague: once sin enters your heart, any power you might then summon against it is already corrupted with sin (e.g., the pride you might take in being virtuous). In contrast, the sound "sin" and the sequence of the three letters to write it in English have lost their immediacy and instead point directly to the intended meaning (or at least it requires effort and the ingenuity of a poet for an English speaker to restore to the letters and sounds their immediacy).

Nature is unlike language (or habits, or anything properly human) because nature can never be a sign (though perhaps nature can *seem* to lose its immediacy if a culture degenerates and begins to lose its living relation to nature). Nature is always to a certain extent opaque, resisting attempts to subordinate it completely to one precise meaning; but it is never totally opaque (in a way that does not permit finding meaning in it). The enduring immediacy of nature helps to account for cultural variety: it is only because the sea can be at once terrifying and a bountiful food source, a barrier to travel and a means to travel, a protection against invasion and exposure to invasion, beautiful and sublime, that cultures (and different strands of the same culture) can orient themselves toward it in such different ways. But contrary to what Hegel argues in his lectures on the anthropology and the philosophy of history, it makes no sense to try to pin down the meaning of a part of nature once and for all, and still less to order the various interpretations of nature into a hierarchy, ascending from the Americas to Africa, to Asia, and culminating in Europe.[30] Hegel's and any account of such an order can only be rife with arbitrary judgments. Moreover, even if there were a hierarchy in those interpretations of nature that have been given in various parts of the world, the enduring immediacy of natural phenomena allows for the ever-present possibility of progress in spiritual sophistication within *any* natural environment. Sublimity for instance, is everywhere in nature: the sea, the desert, the heat and cold, the sky itself.

By understanding nature as retaining this opacity, and cultural significance as a playful, creative interpretation of nature rather than mere reception of an unambiguous content, we can preserve an understanding of nature as having anthropological significance, while rejecting the notion of a hierarchy of races or nations. We can even accept the idea of an immanent end in history (viz., the development of a culture that recognizes itself in the unfolding of human history across cultures rather than the peculiarities of one part of nature), provided that we also understand that the ambiguity of any part of nature makes possible many paths (at least one within any legitimate culture[31]) to this immanent end.

Assigning Meaning to the Human Body

This way of understanding cultural interpretation of corporeal immediacy helps us understand modern social identities as well, including most prominently race and gender.[32] One disappointment the reader experiences in reading Hegel's comments on race and gender (besides Hegel's naïve and indefensible positions) is that Hegel seems to have little to say about the way race and gender are experienced in a person's physical appearance.[33] For the general public today race means not a relation to a certain natural environment but primarily skin color, hair texture, and eye, nose, and lip shape; and gender means not a tendency to grasp objectivity as separate or to be immersed in it but rather the shape of the body, especially the genitalia. The physical characteristics of a person's body are immediacies that are in-themselves meaningless but have been assigned meanings culturally. Social hierarchies are often established by making this assignment of meaning appear as rather the simple recognition of a meaning read in a transparent natural shape. Yet as immediacies, the accepted markers of race and gender have the same opacity as nature does, and thus the meaning of these is no more fixed than in the case of the natural environment.

I mean what I say in what follows to apply broadly to the cultural process by which one group in a culture attempts to establish a hierarchy positioning itself over other groups and appeals to physiological differences (and their ostensibly transparent meaning) to justify this distinction. Yet owing to the great abundance of analysis and interpretation that has been produced in the past two centuries, which takes as its particular point of departure the black experience in French colonies or the United States, I will speak in what follows mostly about the black identity and experience: thus Du Bois, Césaire, Damas, Fanon, and Gooding-Williams loom large in my exposition. I do not claim to speak authoritatively on the black experience and identity based on firsthand experience because I am not black. My understanding of the issue is rather based on my reading of those who do have this experience and have in their writing raised it to the level of poetic insight and philosophical comprehension.[34] Since these sources speak often in terms of colonization, I will as well: I intend my exposition to lend support to this usage by showing how racial and gender hierarchies generally, including those within a single polity (i.e., among those who share formal political liberties), can still be productively studied as cases of colonialism in a broad sense.[35]

The anthropology of race can be elucidated by reference to the path we have followed from sensation through the different forms of feeling. It is no wonder that there should be a homology between forms of individual experience like feeling in its immediacy and self-feeling and forms of cultural integration insofar as both concern how what is outside of and foreign to the (individual or social) self can be experienced and recognized as something other than the self, and further how the self can order its relation to its own form of mediation (its "body"). Bearing this in mind, it would be more surprising if there were no similar structure between the forms recognizing otherness in individual and social experience.

The first mode of experience is sensibility: the absorption in corporeal immediacy in such a way that only what varies from the way one's own body is determined is noticed. The passage to feeling involves abandoning the naturally given body in favor of another, immediate relation: here one first encounters one's own corporeal immediacy as an object, in a profoundly disordered form of experience, in which one is under the spell of a strange power with which one is identified. This perverse, unstable condition tends to undermine itself insofar as an immediate identification of the soul with one content is no more justified than an immediate identification with its opposite. Yet the experience of this rupture, in which the soul comes to feel what it took to be itself as in truth only something particular, having only a limited place in the life of the soul, constitutes therapy and treatment for mental illness. Therapy is also the beginning of habit, the soul's reestablishment of a mediated relation to its contents by fashioning its own mediating "organs" (its habits or customs).

If we transpose this schema onto racial and gender identity, the following analysis presents itself. The form of social organization corresponding to the highest form of the natural soul, sensibility, is the simple concept of ethical life: people completely absorbed in their culture, not feeling it at all as something objective or distinct, responding only to the felt influence of something foreign.[36] The culture is completely homogeneous, taking its cultural identity to be something as natural as its environment and its differences with other cultures to be natural differences.[37] That this is "natural" does not mean that it is ideal, but only that this is how culture is understood if we do not take into account the complicating factors corresponding (in the language of anthropology) to feeling in its immediacy, self-feeling and habit. In this basic form of culture the individual takes herself as a token for the culture and never dreams that she has a different relation to the culture than do other members. Maybe there are (or were) communities like this, but even if there never were completely homogeneous cultures with total integration of their members, it serves heuristically as an expression of the simple concept of ethical life.

"Double Consciousness": Feeling in Its Immediacy as Ideology

As feeling involves some privileged internal content to which the soul relates and with which it identifies immediately, bypassing any naturally given form of mediation, so the social analogue of the feeling soul must be a culture with internal diversity such that some are unreflectively identified with the culture as such, and others, while de facto members of the culture, nonetheless bear characteristics that mark them (according to cultural standards) as outsiders in some sense, as not full members of the culture. Take for example how in pre-democratic Athens the city had members of recognized autochthonous families, and everyone else (their clients, metics, slaves) had an ambiguous status as not true citizens but still "Athenian" in some unofficial sense, as deeply integrated into Athens economically, socially—even to a certain extent religiously—and as having no other home.[38] The case of women in a great many societies until very recently also shows how it may be that a group's members do not count as true, full members of a culture (not having the rights and independent status of men, or of some men) but still belonging to the same culture in an undeniable sense. In such a condition the culture almost inevitably becomes at least just reflective enough that it can be wielded as a lens to be turned back on the individual, whereupon it becomes dimly apparent that the culture (which was probably always internally stratified) expresses the perspective of some particular group and not others in the same way.

In this social analogue to the feeling soul we can see how race (or any physiological characteristic) is constructed and invested with meaning as a social class marker, distinguishing those immediately identified with the culture as full, official members, from *the others*. There has been much debate recently about the metaphysical, ethical, and political status of race: so much that I cannot give a general review of the discussion here,[39] but I want to show how Hegel's anthropology can contribute to the so-called theory of racial constructivism. In opposition to those who argue that because race has no biological basis it cannot be called "real" in any meaningful sense, racial constructivists argue that despite this lack of a biological basis, social attitudes and practices (which do take race seriously) end up creating such different experiences and opportunities for people according to their racial designation that race comes to have a *social* reality.

For instance, Americans generally understand their society to include people of different races, such as whites and blacks. This racial distinction is thought to be based on hazy (and biologically indefensible) ideas of essential physiological distinctions (e.g., between shades of skin, type of hair, etc.) but also to be indicated by stereotypically white or black names (e.g., Schneider vs. Washington), styles of dress and speech, and so on. Since this distinction is taken to be real by Americans generally, a person whose appearance or name designates her as "black" can expect to be treated very differently from someone designated as "white," by being denied jobs (or job interviews), housing, credit; by being denied admission to schools, professions, and professional organizations; by being subject to increased surveillance and scrutiny from law enforcement, merchants, and the general public; and, when circumstances are comparable with whites, being more likely to be arrested, charged with a crime, convicted, and receive a harsher sentence. Given this wide disparity in treatment, it makes sense to argue that race is "real," though as a social product rather than a natural kind.[40]

It is hardly news that those designated as white have an easier time than those designated black. The more interesting thing is what this "designation" involves. Since race has no biological basis, social attitudes about race cannot be based on physical differences. Even if there were hard and fast physiological distinctions between this race and that, such natural differences would still not generate any unambiguous meaning. It is misleading even to refer to social attitudes *about* race because these social attitudes are themselves entirely constitutive of race.[41] To understand how this constitution and designation works, an account must show how social pressure and culture can shape and distort not just a person's opinions (what she reflectively holds to be true) but even her own immediate experience (what she unreflectively senses and feels about herself, others, and the world around her).

For instance, American culture protects the privileged position of some members of the culture (e.g., whites) over others by assigning the meaning "dangerous" to young black and Latino men, and with increasing ferocity to Arabs and Muslims as well.[42] This is accomplished, as Alcoff says, through innumerable "microprocesses"[43] (images on television, movies, music videos, journalism, political and commercial advertising, school curricula, casual conversations and jokes, gestures, glances, etc.), which build up attitudes in individuals and reinforce customs in a culture. Individuals reaffirm and further entrench this racism with each new racist joke or television show, but as a feature of the culture antedating any individual, this racism has a life of its own. One finds oneself always already acculturated into racism, such that one is not free to choose whether to be racist any more than one can choose to have a language: the same acculturation that makes one unreflectively racist first makes one an individual at all. The culture here acts as the "genius" with which each individual (whether of the dominant group or not) immediately identifies as his or her own self (that which determines the social meaning of what is experienced). One can resist racism by trying to turn back on one's mind to root it out, and to a certain extent one can even be successful. But even this is only possible using the cognitive resources provided by the same racist culture. The social analogue of feeling in its immediacy is thus an ideological culture, one that brings about the kind of subjects it needs in order to perpetuate itself insofar as the subjects it creates fundamentally misunderstand the nature of the culture, as they must for its perpetuation.[44]

The immediate identification of people with the "genius," which is the mouthpiece of only a particular part of the culture, can even obscure the incompatibility of the traits ascribed to a subordinate group (e.g., as Mexican immigrants in the US are called both lazy and a threat to jobs held or claimed by whites) or twist undeniable virtues into vices.[45] The character of members of the subordinate group is treated as something merely natural, like a natural species, with no individuality or possibility of variation.[46] As Du Bois puts it: "most Americans answer all queries regarding the Negro *a priori*,"[47] such that even direct experience with people who clearly defy the culturally assigned stereotype often fails to create cognitive dissonance and to undermine this stereotype, but rather it is dismissed or explained away.

Because the principal aim of racism in a culture is to reinforce the meanings it creates and assigns to different bodies, our inability to distinguish between certain fetishized physical characteristics (skin tone, etc.) and the moral and intellectual characteristics culturally associated with them is an index of the pervasiveness and power of ideological racism in the culture. A critical theory of race must therefore distinguish between the way race is presented by a racist culture (as something natural and indelibly marked on people) and the unnatural way this culture constructs this notion of race. To give a critical race theory based on Hegel's anthropology would involve distinguishing the natural embodiment involving certain physiological features resulting from genetic and physical-environmental influence (in-themselves having no fixed meaning); from the "body the feeling soul gives itself," that is, the attitudes inculcated through repeated experience and acculturation, and which then designate a meaning for the features of natural embodiment by interpreting it as a racial characteristic. This distinction makes possible a genuinely critical race theory because it shows how an anonymous racism can pervade a culture so thoroughly that it becomes "the body" in a sense of both the dominant and subordinate groups, mediating each person's experience of herself and others.

For example, one of the most pernicious stereotypes of American racism is the association of blacks with criminality. The typical well-meaning response that whites should become more reflective and refuse to entertain this prejudice belies the universality of racism in a racist culture: sociological and psychological research has shown that white supremacist ideology permeates the attitudes of both whites and nonwhites. In one study a series of surveys of the same respondents were taken over time and, in the case of 20 percent of respondents, the interviewer reported them as being of a different race after a certain life change (such as going from not incarcerated to incarcerated, employed to unemployed, etc.). In these cases, when the respondent experienced a negative change (going to prison or becoming unemployed), the interviewer recorded their race as black, though earlier it was recorded as white.[48] The same study also found that funeral directors were more likely to list the race of bodies as black if the cause of death was homicide—even contradicting the reports the deceased's family members gave of his or her race—and to describe those dead from cirrhosis of the liver (which is often caused by alcohol abuse) as Native American. Most strikingly, respondents interviewed first as not incarcerated then later as incarcerated were more likely to describe *themselves* as black after this change. Thus, culturally inculcated attitudes actually determine our own "immediate" experience of skin color. Studies have also shown that not only whites but also blacks and Latinos perceive a neighborhood to be in worse condition based *solely* on increased presence of blacks in the neighborhood.[49]

No longer just a medium for viewing objects outside the culture while the culture itself, because of its total transparency, goes completely unnoticed, the culture now reveals its image and appraisal of oneself to oneself, making dimly visible the incongruities possible between the authoritative gaze of the culture and the particular perspective available from the position one occupies in the culture. An Arab American child for instance may begin to notice that Arabs are always the bad guys in American media, and the Arabic language itself is presented as something frightening. Watching such a movie while hearing his grandparents speaking in Arabic in the next room, the child will begin to feel uneasy, a bit guilty, and deeply disoriented due to the contrast between these two accounts of who one is and what is good.[50]

The most sinister effect of racism is thus not that one's racial designation will have a large effect on the experiences one will have in life, though this is true. The most sinister effect of racism is its anonymity: when it comes to the meaning a culture imputes to bodies in its creation of races, whites and blacks will experience them *in the same way*. That is, generally speaking (exceptions of course being granted), both whites and blacks will feel apprehensive when a young black man walks toward them at night; both whites and blacks may be more inclined to favor a white job candidate over a similarly qualified black one; both whites and blacks may imagine "a person as such" as being white, the hero of a story (where the hero's race is not given) as being white, and take their standards of attractiveness from white appearances. "Who," Memmi asks, "can completely rid himself of bigotry in a country where everyone is tainted by it, including its victims?"[51] Though whites and blacks may have natural bodies that are different (by virtue of skin tone, which is fetishized and invested with the power and significance of establishing racial difference), when they belong to American culture (or any other racist culture), the body they give themselves—the body that cannot be immediately experienced but makes possible a great deal of human experience—will be a *white* body.

For whites, their double white embodiment makes it almost impossible for them to even glimpse the profound racism running through American culture and society (the same holds, mutatis mutandis, for men and sexism). Without intense and steady mental effort, all they see wherever they look is confirmation of their most deeply held, least-examined prejudices. For nonwhites, on the other hand, this amounts to the most invasive colonization possible: not only are their actions watched and scrutinized, and their opportunities restricted, but their own thoughts and opinions—even their unreflective feelings and attitudes—are taken apart and refashioned to be put in the service of white supremacy.

This dual embodiment provides the best context to understand what Du Bois meant in remarking famously that black folks live with a "double consciousness": one black, and one white.[52] It is not just that intersubjectivity is required for self-consciousness: that would not require positing a racial difference or hierarchy. Rather, here the subordinate group must bear witness to the dominant group's superiority as a group identified by certain physiological traits, and to their subordinate place in the order as a group, based on different physiological traits.[53] Having such a double consciousness involves what Fanon calls an attitude of *comparaison*: the black person in a colonial situation knows himself through his or her place in the colonial hierarchy, as above some and below others based on the standards issuing from colonialism.[54] Whereas Hegel's famous presentation of the "master-servant" dialectic in the *Phenomenology* (often taken to establish the necessity of intersubjectivity for self-consciousness[55]) serves to radically decenter for both parties the substance of their self-consciousness, in the racial hierarchy it is only the subordinate group who loses this substance: the dominant group enjoys the authority of its gaze and remains peacefully in possession of its selfhood. As Fanon bitterly remarks, in the colonial situation the white gaze is "the only valid one."[56]

The same principle can easily be applied to gender.[57] To say that women in a patriarchal culture have a "double consciousness," one female and one male, is only to say that in a patriarchal culture the male gaze is normative. The influence of acculturation into patriarchy involves women as well as men seeing women as "the second sex," in Beauvoir's apt phrase, that is, as a deviation from masculinity.[58] An example of this is "gaslighting": the term is taken from the 1944 film of the same name to refer to the way the person occupying a culturally authoritative position (e.g., a man) can distort and invalidate the experience of someone occupying a subordinate position (e.g., a woman). The individual's sense of self is disordered because of her immediate identification with the culture that grants the other voice its authority.

To view this as simply a conflict between two individuals is to fail to appreciate how a culture, the body by which its members feel social phenomena like status and worth, can prioritize the perspective of some of its members while concealing this prioritization, presenting itself a neutral. What I am calling the cultural "body" shared by all members is similar to what Fanon calls the collective unconscious—though in contrast to Jung, Fanon argues that this unconscious is not naturally given at all, but rather created and inculcated in the manner of culture.[59] The individual is at great pains to free him- or herself from this influence because it is woven into the very structure of his or her personality. It is thus not a conflict between one individual and another, nor even between a large group of individuals (the majority) and a smaller group (the minority): it is a conflict between a group of people advantageously positioned at the apex of a culture, socially represented as the general person as such, and a group of people who are inside only as outsiders, identified with their particularity so as to hide the particularity of those at the apex. The terrain of the conflict is thus not on neutral ground but within the very personality of the colonized, or the oppressed: "An Antillean is white through the collective unconscious, through a large part of the personal unconscious, and through virtually the entire process of individuation. The color of his skin, which Jung does not mention, is black. All the incomprehension stems from this misunderstanding."[60] It is because despite their exclusion, blacks are still in some sense insiders in the white world that Du Bois could write of whites:

> Of them I am singularly clairvoyant. I see in and through them. I view them from unusual points of vantage. Not as a foreigner do I come, for I am native, not foreign, bone of their thought and flesh of their language. Mine is not the knowledge of the traveler or the colonial composite of dear memories, words and wonder. [. . .] Rather, I see through these souls undressed and from the back and side. I see the workings of their entrails. I know their thoughts and they know that I know.[61]

The liberal response to this is to disassociate oneself from the devalued body one may have: perhaps not to loathe it, but to consider it insignificant and to identify with a "true self" inside or beyond the body.[62] Thus as the feeling soul involves circumvention of the natural forms of mediation, so the liberal rejects the identification of the culture with any one ethnicity or gender, promoting instead the identification of all people as simply human in an attempt to prevent the law from recognizing socially fetishized physiological characteristics at all. The appeal of this is not hard to see, and the liberal approach has certainly had some success in combatting the effects of racism and sexism. However, the failures of liberalism have long been apparent, and Hegel's anthropology can make still clearer how, far from dissipating the ideology, liberalism is itself an expression of it.

In a bigoted culture that assigns pejorative meanings to certain physiological characteristics, the retreat into one's interiority, the "true self," with which liberalism encourages all to identify is not truly raceless or genderless but rather expresses the dominant perspective in the culture, thereby naturalizing and legitimizing the social inequalities in question. Williamson contrasts the conservative (open, virulently racist) attitude of white southerners with the liberal (patronizing, subtlety racist) attitude of northerners:

> In Reconstruction, northern tutors took the place of southern ones in the education of black people. Where southerners had said to blacks "So far and so high," northerners now seemed to say "There is no limit to your whiteness; you too can be as white as I am white." Black people were, it was often assumed, after all only white people with black skins.[63]

The case of sexism is similar: part of the historical subordination of women has involved restricting their roles as much as possible to catering to the desires of men. Thus the normative standard for a woman's value in a patriarchal society is often her physical attractiveness to men. Many men acculturated into patriarchy frequently address women, even those who are officially their peers, like coworkers, by demeaning, sexualized pet-names, like "honey" or "sweetie." Often men do not think it amiss to comment on a woman's—any woman's—attractiveness and consider that they are being kind when they tell a woman she is beautiful. A woman who adopts the liberal approach and ignores the social hierarchy and her place in it, identifying instead as a genderless "person as such" will cease recognizing the condescension involved in such treatment as condescension or as something unjust. After all, considered in abstraction from the social system in question (precisely the kind of abstraction liberalism requires), the social system where sexual roles express and reinforce unjust hierarchies, it is *a good thing* to be attractive, and it is *kind* to call attention to good qualities of another person. The liberal woman may then smile when "complimented" and take great care to appear attractive to men, looking down on other women who are not so careful of their appearance, and feel perfectly natural in congratulating a friend on having "a smart son" and "a beautiful daughter."

Damas and Fanon likewise relate how schools for the colonized in French Guyana and Martinique orient the students toward France and its Gallic identity, even in opposition to their own actual ancestry.[64] Memmi notes that in Tunisia the colonized would often change their appearance to look like the colonizer, out of a mix of admiration for the latter and self-hatred (adopting the clothing, hair color, and architecture typical of the colonizers),[65] and Malcolm X vividly described the same attitude among American blacks.[66] The condition is similar to a worker who defends the so-called right of *all* people to "economic freedom," such as purchasing labor for a wage and retaining the profit, though for the worker this freedom amounts to the right to be exploited. Rather than an attempted flight from racial or gender identity, what is needed is the exposure of the dominant perspective as *merely* a perspective, the point of view not of pure, disembodied human consciousness but of a particular social group with a particular place in the social system and particular interests (which include presenting itself as not at all particular). Rather than aiming at completing the assimilation of the colonized into the colonial culture, this culture itself is the moment of corporeity whose particularity has not been posited and that must now be assimilated.[67]

"The nation is sick, trouble is in the land, confusion is all around"[68]

Implicitly, the unease felt by the person occupying the subordinate position in the culture is a recognition of the limitations of this authoritative voice, insofar as it is alien to the subordinate person's own perspective and hence is something particular: this is the social analogue to the sickness of the soul, self-feeling. In self-feeling the soul suffers the most profound disorder, feeling itself in (identifying with) the dominant part of the culture, which increasingly shows signs of being something merely particular. The source of this disorder is that what is beginning to be recognized as a natural immediacy (a certain skin tone, for example) is assigned an apparently fixed meaning, and this ordering, which is supposed to anchor the entire social system, is seen to rest on an arbitrary judgment. Because the fetishized immediacy can no longer be taken as immediately identified as a matter of course with the culture as a whole, social intercourse threatens to break down: a cultural standard such as white supremacy, which was previously unreflectively accepted as natural, becomes a point of frantic, desperate insistence. Once the exclusion of the oppressed from the culture is made explicit, they lose the guiding basis for action, the horizon of meaning that ethical life is meant to provide.

Damas's poetry gives very good descriptions of this malaise, self-feeling as a social structure. In "Hoquet" (Hiccup) he describes being gripped by what is in some sense a natural, involuntary response but that, like a hiccup, makes it impossible to act in a natural way, making all movement and speech awkward. He describes how his mother inculcated French culture to him in the form of table manners, religion, the French language, and music: she says salvation can only be had in assimilation,[69] even as this assimilation is imposed as something unnatural.[70] Fanon makes the same point in describing the lived experience of the black man:

> In the white world, the man of color encounters difficulties in elaborating his body schema. The image of one's body is solely negating. It's an image in the third person. All around the body reigns an atmosphere of uncertainty. I know that if I want to smoke, I shall have to stretch out my right arm and grab the pack of cigarettes lying at the other end of the table. As for the matches, they are in the left drawer, and I shall have to move back a little. And I make all these moves, not out of habit, but by an implicit knowledge. A slow construction of my body in a spatial and temporal world—such seems to be the schema.[71]

Because the human body (for both Hegel and Merleau-Ponty[72]) cannot be reduced either morally or epistemologically to an object like other objects, the imposed identification of the soul with a single objective quality makes natural action impossible. Everyone has this experience in a mild or momentary version: being embarrassed in front of others by some blemish on one's body; in the common nightmare of suddenly appearing nude in front of one's peers; or, how for the unpracticed public speaker in front of a crowd, any way of positioning the hands is extremely awkward, and any chance taken to swallow makes the speaking sound stilted and harried. The more adroit one is the quicker one can recover and divert attention from one's objectivity, regaining a mode of behavior in which one's body becomes once again only a sign for one's soul rather than just a pulsating biological organism inelegantly spread out in public. But for a social code to systematically affirm—or even to be primarily based on—a pejorative meaning assigned to a feature of one's physiology that is constantly on display to everyone is to condemn such a person to a thoroughgoing alienation from others, society generally, and from him- or herself. It is difficult to overstate how profoundly disturbing and disorienting this social determination can be. Damas describes the colonial culture as a *disgust*, anchored in him "as deep as a beautiful Malaysian dagger."[73] The weapon that wounds him is foreign—but not just foreign to him as an Antillean, or more distantly as an African, foreign also to Europe: even his feeling of European influence as something alien is expressed with the disdain and paternalistic fascination colonial powers have for the "exotic" colonized.[74]

It would be inaccurate to view this anxiety as the simple result of the centripetal force of assimilation, drawing the colonized willy-nilly into the colonial culture, and which will abate when the assimilation is complete. Assimilation is indeed promoted by the colonial power as a goal, but halfheartedly: the onus is completely on the colonized to transform themselves, while the power to confirm that assimilation has taken place, that foreignness has been overcome, rests completely with the colonizers,[75] whose very identity and social prestige depends on always finding in the colonized a failure to measure up.[76] Thus Damas likens colonial assimilation to the body's assimilation of food, but reverses the sides of the relationship, speaking of his pain in trying to incorporate the colonial culture into himself, his "indigestion/ of each bite of French history."[77] He likens colonialism to quicklime, a substance used to trap birds, which makes free movement impossible once they have lighted upon it,[78] and he says his hatred grows "on the margins"[79] of the colonial culture, neither within it nor outside of it: outside in such a way as to make possible the inside as an inside.

Habit and the Unmooring of a Reified Culture

The dissolution of ethical life here occurs because of its explicit identification with a mere immediacy, but the weapon that wounds is also the one that heals.⁸⁰ To explicitly posit an immediacy *as* a mere immediacy is at once to move beyond it. The subject of the disorder here is not only this or that individual but the entire culture, and cultures are rarely changed by dispassionate argumentation. Accordingly, therapy consists not in presenting a comprehensive accounting of all of the factors and their place in the social reality, but rather of "entering into the delusion" of the disordered subject. This means that any natural immediacy can be invested with the power and prestige previously identified only with the dominant group's fetishized feature.⁸¹ A subordinate group can thus assert its own priority and claim for itself with equal justification the mantle of civilization that was previously monopolized by the colonial culture:

> The colonized accepts and asserts himself with passion. But who is he? Surely not man in general, the holder of universal values common to all men. In fact, he has been excluded from that universality both in word and in fact. [. . .] Very well then! [. . .] The same passion which made him admire and absorb Europe shall make him assert his differences; since those differences, after all, are within him and correctly constitute his true self.⁸²

As Césaire brazenly puts it: "Accommodate me, I am not accommodating you!"⁸³ The movement of negritude, of which Césaire is a primary voice, is precisely this kind of self-assertion of the colonized against the colonizer.

For a member of the dominant group who has not had to have a "double consciousness," and has not suffered from a discord between the official perspective of the culture and his own, this rise of the subjugated appears to be mere criminality or confusion and arouses the dominant group's bewilderment and rage.⁸⁴ Césaire is only too happy to play up this effect:

> Because we hate you, you and your reason, we invoke
>   precocious madness [*la démence précoce*] flamboyant
>   insanity tenacious cannibalism.
> Treasure, let us count:
> the madness that remembers
> the madness that screams
> the madness that sees
> the madness that is unleashed.
> And you know the rest
> That 2 and 2 make 5.⁸⁵

Césaire's poetry (which often deliberately refers to Antillean or African objects unfamiliar to Europeans) is as incomprehensible to the colonizers as is the actual insurrection of the colonized. Indeed, the poetry is meant to be experienced as an act of violence, or a natural disaster: "I would rediscover the secret of great communications and of great combustions. I would say storm. I would say river. I would say tornado. [. . .] Whoever would not understand me would no more understand the roaring of a tiger."[86]

Yet the true identity of the colonized is obscure—for the colonized themselves nearly as much as for the colonizer. Authentic self-assertion is fraught with problems when one's own deepest way of relating to oneself is inauthentic: colonization not only establishes a new relation between groups, but in the same stroke it alters the identity of the groups.[87] Memmi argues that "the most serious blow suffered by the colonized is being removed from history":[88] colonization deprives the colonized of their agency, rerouting the solutions to all social and political problems through the formal or informal institutions of the dominant group. The more the particular (sub) culture of the colonized is removed from ruling and deciding matters, from actual participation in life, the more it becomes merely formal, rigid, and dogmatic.[89] In a short while both the colonizer and the colonized regard this ossified culture as something antiquated: at best to be venerated as a museum piece, at worst to be forgotten.

Hegel himself gives as one of the central features of Africa its being removed from history,[90] but the eternal, unchanging character of colonized cultures is rather an *effect* of colonization, not a precondition, inviting colonization as the colonizer presents it.[91] In fact, in presenting the colonized as firmly rooted in tradition rather than the current of history, the colonizer knows precisely what he is doing: there is a long history of colonizers taking great pains to "protect" indigenous institutions as one would protect a relic, by removing it far from where the action is.[92] Where these native institutions do not already exist in the most convenient (moribund and toothless) form, the colonizer simply invents them.[93]

The problem is thus that while the black soul must assert itself, it can appear that "what is called the black soul is a construction by white folk."[94] If the therapeutic assertion of a counter-absurdity in opposition to the *idée fixe* is such that it confirms and strengthens the demented attachment, then rather than the therapy drawing the patient out of the illness, the illness has drawn the therapy into itself. Gooding-Williams finds an analogous problem in Du Bois, who he argues operates with two notions of African American group identity: as masses (disorganized, backward, and requiring leadership from the "talented tenth," the educated and cultured like himself); and as folk (a group internally united around a shared spirit and thus having within itself its own direction).[95] But if the spirit of the people in question is formed by their subjugation, it would seem that "Du Bois cannot have his cake and eat it: he cannot coherently endorse a politics that both uplifts the masses and expresses a slavery-based racial identity, for uplifting the masses requires the demise of that identity."[96]

The problem here is not peculiar to critical race theory but rather belongs to all social and political philosophy that follows from German Idealism: a mere immediacy as such (a thing as it is found in existence) is not the idea (the truth of the thing); but nor is this truth apart from the immediacies that characterize the thing's existence.[97] Accordingly, what an individual happens to desire or take pleasure in is not necessarily good, though nor is the good alien to the individual's desires and pleasures; and the political consciousness of the oppressed, such as it happens to exist at any given moment, is not necessarily identical with the promotion of true justice (what would truly end their oppression and is thus their authentic political orientation), but this consciousness cannot fail to glimpse something of true justice—and even something unrecognized by the prevailing oppressive order.

To grasp the truth of a thing one needs first of all to acknowledge the presupposed conceptual baggage (for humanity, the concept of spirit), and to see how the immediacy, allowed its full expression on its own terms, prompts the emergence of its contrary, which was always covertly determining it: the reinterpretation of each moment in light of the other yields the truth of both. Thus here the nationalism of the colonized can be viewed strictly as a mere moment (the contrary to colonial culture), or more generously as the prefiguring of the resolution of the colonial situation. But because this nationalism as such is one moment of a larger process, it need not have a perfectly elaborate understanding of true justice: the masses thus do not need to be philosophers in order to serve the cause of righteousness.

Still, the authentic perspective of the oppressed does not arise from an indelible racial identity, predating colonization but hidden underneath the colonial apparatus and the latter's ways of interpreting life and what is just: such a racial identity is fictitious, and itself a product of colonialism. The oppressed cannot just take off the mask of colonialism in order to get at their authentic selves because the discovery and promotion of their authentic selves is the first step in upending colonialism.[98] Yet there is no antinomy between promoting a particular racial identity and "uplifting" (changing the culture of) this race because the point here is not to promote a subaltern identity as something permanent but to express it so that it may be transcended. Certainly, this expression is inadmissible according to the prevailing norms of the culture: the dominant part of the culture resists recognizing the assertion of the subaltern cultural identity's primacy because it would dissolve the fantasy the dominant part has constructed around itself. But it is still possible, and the tension and precarity of self-feeling make this rebellious expression of subaltern identity constantly come up in ways that make confrontation inevitable.

The question of authenticity thus need not be limited to contrasting assimilation on the terms dictated by the dominant part of the culture to the stubborn adherence on the part of the oppressed to an identity abstracted from and imposed by that same part of the culture. Criticism of the kneejerk reversion to what Gooding-Williams calls "Afro-kitsch," namely, the "black-washing" that some undergo in a frantic attempt to bury themselves in what they imagine to be their natural African roots,[99] has indeed shown this sort of particularist, racial-nationalist identity to be thoroughly bankrupt. It involves a simplified version of African culture (papering over real differences among Africans), and presupposes a biological essentialism of Africanness in opposition to Europeanness.[100] In rejecting this, Fanon notes that as human, he is heir to the Peloponnesian War and the invention of the compass as much as to Africa: he is not imprisoned by his past, and in looking to the future he has better things to do than harp on injustices of the seventeenth century.[101] In this vein, Gooding-Williams argues against the very possibility of being inauthentically black.[102] He distinguishes between the monolithic condition of "being black" (being socially designated as black whether one wants it or not) and the various ways of "being a black person" (interpreting and assigning significance to this designation).[103] There is no inauthentic way of being black since one simply is black or one is not; and there is no inauthentic way of being a black person because it always involves a creative interpretation of a given, intrinsically meaningless natural circumstance.

Yet though there is no acultural significance to being black (and no authentic "black identity" in abstraction from any cultural placement), there is a limited range of black identities that may count as authentic relative to placement in a white supremacist culture. Just as the soul cannot stably be identified with a single feeling (though such aberrations occur), people cannot be free (i.e., spirit cannot be properly concretized) in a culture that ideologically misrepresents them to themselves. A certain way of appealing to the past and the gesture of celebrating the particularity of the colonized against the colonizer is thus therapeutically appropriate even though the disruptiveness of colonization precludes simply picking up the precolonial culture as it is found and using it as the basis for the continuing life of the culture throwing off colonization. Because the cultural interaction as such (even in colonization) probably always introduces for both parties some positive influences that it would be foolish to spurn, this appeal to cultural particularity should not be a rejection of peaceful intercultural cohabitation as such, but it must be "nationalistic" in the sense of rejecting assimilation on the terms set by the colonizer.[104] Because the therapeutic effect requires a rhetorical rejection of the colonial culture as a unit and hostility to the colonizers *en bloc*, it can appear to be a new form of chauvinism to match the colonizer's chauvinism, that is, "reverse racism." However, as Memmi argues, the enmity of the colonized toward the colonizers "is not based on a belief in the inferiority of the detested group but on the conviction, and in large measure on the observation, that this group is truly an aggressor and dangerous. [. . .] it is not aggressive but defensive racism."[105] Fanon is in agreement: though he wants simply to be recognized as human, when his humanity is denied, it is necessary to assert the dignity of the particularity that is denied:[106] before one can be free, there must be a struggle in which the subordination is forcibly overturned,[107] though this struggle is only an aspect of the therapeutic process, and so the hostility it involves need not be eternal.[108]

Césaire's way of responding to racial oppression is instructive: the avowal of *négritude* can seem to evoke an African essentialism (as, e.g., in the case of Damas[109]), yet even as Césaire rejects "the west" ("I make a systematic defense of non-European civilizations"[110]), he likewise rejects a return to precolonial Africa,[111] arguing for neither assimilation into colonial Europe nor African essentialism, but for Soviet communism, which he sees as a nonracial, egalitarian rebellion against the dominant trend in the West.[112] Negritude, he says, is just an assertion of the humanity of the colonized,[113] in the only way that this humanity can be asserted given the context of colonialism. The appropriate condition, the one aimed at, is one where this insistence no longer needs to be made: "a land—a thousand times more native and turned to a golden tan by a sun that no prism divides—a land where everything is free and fraternal, my land."[114] The land where colors are not separated (where no prism divides the sunlight) is a thousand times more his own true native land than either the colonial metropole or the colonized African land—and this sought-after country is the only one that can bear the lofty emblems of the French Revolution (*libre* and *fraternel*).

The appeal to the particularity of the colonized is thus a tactic rather than a firm belief in the permanent incompatibility of the colonized and the colonizer in their humanity. The assertion of this particularity is part of the therapeutic process whereby the particular group that has been passing its own perspective off as the general "obvious" perspective, and its interests off as the universal interests, is finally recognized as only one part of the social world, with no monopoly on goodness or truth. This therapy has as its goal the creation of a new form of mediation that will be explicitly a form of mediation: it will not vanish as it presents only the object (as sensibility did), nor will it adopt the ideological guise of a "true," raceless, and genderless self. Instead, it will be openly a work in progress, an institution not fallen from heaven but made and continually remade, wearing its historicity on its sleeve.

Racial Politics and Democracy

In other words, the needed social mediation must be a way of disrupting existing social relationships without giving a new foundation grounding social relationships in the same apparently natural way. The key feature of the "historicity" of the needed form of mediation is that the culture should not be founded on anything outside of culture itself and human history. Thus what is authoritative cannot be something totally removed from the current situation, to be mechanically applied to it. There is a tendency to think of habit as lifeless and mechanical: Magrì for instance notes that Hegel himself treats habit both as training that bestows new dispositions and abilities and as subjection to mindless, automatic inertia.[115] Habits orient us in a certain direction, and this does involve a certain inattention to alternatives, but it is important not to lose sight of how the natural soul and other forms of feeling confine the soul (identifying it immediately with some natural determinacy or inner feeling), and the emergence of habit liberates it. Habits integrate our current experience into the general pattern of meaningfulness that has been established, but this ordering always leaves the ordering principle itself, the "style" that is the habit's general stamp, as always subject to alteration. Analogously, properly historical institutions regulate our social life in such a way that what is currently happening in our social and political life also has an influence on the ordering principle giving it its shape.

This bears some similarities to the way Nancy describes an "inoperative community" that is engaged in "unworking the work" of existing institutions, that is, undermining the establishment of social identity that would present human identity and stratified social roles as a completely transparent fait accompli.[116] Nancy's differences with Hegel notwithstanding,[117] Hegel's appeal to habit and to history as a principle for social organization should be understood not as turning away from superficialities toward a deeper, unchanging foundation for human social order but rather as a revolt against this kind of foundationalism. In other words, Hegel's appeal to "habit" and "history" should not mislead one to thinking these are *foundations* for social identity.

To be sure, "the course of history" can itself be used rhetorically to attempt to ground a social order as something quasi-natural and immutable. "Democracy" too can be taken not as a disruption of reified culture but as itself a culture that can be founded, but that would be to misunderstand what is democratic in democracy, just as what is historical in history can be overlooked. Truly "historical" and "democratic" institutions in the sense I mean must disrupt unequal cultures: this disruption is only a part of what is needed, but it is an important part. Consider for instance how before the democratic reforms Athenian citizenship could be possessed only via membership in one of the powerful families, or tribes. Cleisthenes's reforms dissolved those natural institutions and replaced them with new tribes, which encompassed a great many of those who were not formerly members of the great families. As one might imagine, Athenian aristocrats were not happy about the upsurge of democracy and used to complain that in democratic Athens a gentleman, when out in public, had no way of knowing if the person approaching was another member of an authentically noble family, a common citizen, a noncitizen metic, or even a slave. The persisting undemocratic features of ancient Athens notwithstanding, it was because Athens tended toward democracy that there were no recognized social practices determining which men could walk in the street and which could not, which men had to give way before which others when their paths met, and so forth. When an Athenian aristocrat's path ran into that of another man in the street, he was at a loss for how to respond: if he knew this other man to be noble, he would address him with respect, announcing his lineage to see if they had a common ancestor; if the other man was common or not a citizen at all, the aristocrat would demand to have his way. The aristocrat expects social status to be fixed and visible unambiguously, politically validated and endowed with force of law, but democracy means precisely this disordering of social strata.[118] Democracy removes the foundation of aristocratic privilege so the aristocrat feels "exposed" (as Nancy says[119]) because his own identity is groundless.[120]

Similarly, Lefort argues that "the political" is not found in the sparring of various interests in the legislative process, but in what he calls the "symbolic dispositive": the originative gesture that founds a society, assigning social roles, distinguishing what counts as a genuine interest and what does not, what is a matter for "politics" and what is not.[121] The emergence of democracy is, he argues, a radically contingent and highly volatile event that happens only when a society deprives itself of any foundation that would fix social identities and make possible a smooth, machinelike functioning of a state where the people's political life consists only in working and exchanging goods, passing and enforcing laws. When democracy exists, however briefly, social roles and identities lose their unquestioned validity, the social body dissolves, revealing itself to be based on nothing given, no mere immediacy. The effect of democracy on social relations is to make possible a community to which we may "co-belong without any representable condition of co-belonging,"[122] as Agamben says.

This is much the same as the way Gooding-Williams describes Douglass's "no-foundations" model of black politics, in which black political unity is forged as a political project in its own right rather than presented as something given (even if only in the form of common black interests prior to political engagement) and appealed to a foundation of black identity.[123] If the phrase makes sense, a "no-foundations principle" might make possible not only black political unity but even a genuine transracial political unity (difficult as it would be to accomplish in fact) that does not surreptitiously present the prerogatives of one group as what is plainly of concern to humanity as such.

But the approach inspired by Hegel that I am arguing for differs from these recent philosophers: though the upsurge of habit and history have this effect of disrupting unequal and reified cultures (a disruption that has been presented by these recent thinkers as the primary political task), it is not an end in itself and is complete only with the creation of new and truly inclusive forms of mediation.[124] The yardstick for measuring whether the authentically "historical" and equal community is being established is the extent to which what is being appealed to as a principle for gathering people together and organizing them according to a certain pattern prioritizes the experience of what is only a *part* of the group, foreclosing the possibility of an authentic expression of the perspective of other parts by preemptively assigning their positions and roles.

Proponents of this "no-foundations" or "inoperative community" approach might reject the Hegel-inspired version I present as a reversion to a totalitarian community where humanity is presented as completely transparent to itself. However, history and habit allow for a dynamism that allows this Hegelian approach to avoid this criticism insofar as the "historical" community is always provisional: the "principle" governing its identity is constantly in a state of revision, just as a habit gives form to one's experience but is constantly being reshaped by those experiences themselves.[125] For instance, a perpetually undemocratic feature of the United States has been the assumption common among the native-born that American culture is something fixed, to which immigrants must assimilate. Needless to say, this image of American culture prioritizes those already occupying powerful positions. In contrast, genuine democracy and "historical" culture require that the appearance of immigrants or refugees at our border or in our country be one that makes the native-born American feel exposed, unsure of what American culture is ultimately, and should involve the recognition that what formerly appeared as a satisfactory summary statement of Americanness is in fact only something particular, only one episode of a history that has not concluded. *And* this feeling of exposure should stimulate the reinterpretation of American culture as something that was always developing toward the inclusion of this new immigrant group—and the preservation and integration of their particular culture into a larger culture that would be incomplete without that contribution. Such a community is a genuine community rather than anarchy: it has an organizing principle, a soul. But this organizing principle is not based on some immutable, natural given but rather on its continually developing historical experience: the presence and participation of its members, the native-born as well as those constantly arriving.[126]

For Hegel, justice is neither an impossible ideal, residing in another world, out of reach for the fallen like us, nor a phantom, a trace of what never was and can never be actually present in the way we would like it to be. Yet, nor is it a simple immediacy containing within it no tension or contradiction. Spirit is what is true in and for itself, such that it must and does determine itself concretely. The question then is, what is the manner of this determination? Consider once more the way a person has a habit: a habit is possessed, shaping experience and making certain kinds of activity possible, but it is never possessed in the way a sense organ is possessed; it is never present as a flesh and blood region of the body. Accordingly, a habit is always either waning or fortifying itself: because of this, a habit can seem to be always either something that was, but has faded, or something still arriving, still on the horizon. Being musical for instance is a habit that has been allowed to lapse and begun to atrophy, or a burgeoning strength, always promising to be still greater in the future. Habit is never present as a natural organ is but is rather present only as the greater or lesser limitation of the natural tendency of the body to lie still or move for the sake of satisfaction of animal needs. Yet despite its intangibility, habit is still a *reality* here and now, and it is even a more adequate explanatory principle for human experience and behavior than tangible sense organs, or the chemicals composing them.

The historical culture that Hegel calls "the Germans" is similar. The actual Germanic tribes of late antiquity were of course always either coming or going in their wanderings, but more importantly, the cultural shift of which they are *but one* example (identification with the development of human culture across history rather than with one narrow national culture hailing from one part of the natural world) is a tendency that can be seen advancing or retreating depending on one's vantage point in the world and in history. To this extent, Hegel would agree with the recent "left-Heideggerian" philosophers that a free culture is not *founded* in the way other cultures are: "modernity" for Hegel is still and will always be in the process of arriving, insofar as it is eroding what is merely positive, merely immediate in existing cultures, redirecting their energy toward something higher, which they would not otherwise seek.[127] That the "German" culture has its identity in its non-nationality means that the political form it takes lacks the foundation (in national identity and in nature) assumed by all others. Spirit's final self-determination in the social and political world thus cannot take the form of a nation-state. Rather, spirit determines itself in the self-knowledge that takes the political form of internal critique: identification of that which is merely national in one's political community, which makes one's state an imperfect one.

The modern culture or spirit in which Hegel rejoices is thus in a sense a specter haunting the world, insofar as it is not present as this or that nation-state: it will never become "founded" as a national basis for a state, any more than a habit for playing the piano well can become an immediacy in the flesh and bone of the hands. The habit, if maintained, can permeate the hands and make them into its instruments (its "presuppositions"), so that the behavior of the hands could not be witnessed without referring them to the habit of the soul. But the hands remain bodies in a lesser, natural sense, for which being ensouled is only a *possibility*, and not a necessity. Analogously, a national culture *can* be made into the vehicle for spirit in its most highly refined political sense, but this culture of spirit never becomes simply fused with the national identity in question, which rather always retains the possibility of inertia and ceasing to be a vehicle for the aims of spirit. Hegel's apparent ambivalence toward France illustrates this: as the country of the Revolution in which freedom wills itself into existence, Hegel exults in France and heaps praise on it; but when national peculiarities begin to appear in the form of excesses, he readily distinguishes *the Revolution* from the French national culture that it inhabited for a time.[128]

Yet despite being a specter haunting the world, modernity is also already here. That a free community cannot be "founded" as an immediacy does not mean that we should withdraw, tend to our own gardens, and let the world go its own way. The development of human culture gives us an understanding of justice that we can use to evaluate the states we live in, and struggle against the injustice we find. Our limitation is only that we cannot found a state that will be just according to its natural tendencies. In the world we have a certain number of national cultures to work with: each of which *may* be refined to the point of moving toward the eradication of injustice, and this movement can be represented within each national culture by its own indigenous images and symbols, which are always ambiguous enough to admit of greater and lesser levels of sophistication in interpretation. But we cannot manufacture a national culture that does not have the limitations of nationality so that justice will be assured as a matter of course.

Analogously, we can think within various languages, and each will be flexible enough (if we know how to make use of it) to express sophisticated, philosophical thought. But we cannot construct an artificial language that is automatically philosophical and permanently eliminates the dangers of ambiguity and misunderstanding endemic to all natural languages. Formal logic, for instance, is just a hollowed-out version of the natural language of the person using it, with a profusion of ad hoc rules to artificially simplify it, while the person making use of it still must do their thinking in a real language, be it English, Arabic, Korean, or whatever. Logicians should refine their concepts and uncover ambiguities and obscurities that they find in their natural languages, but this labor will not and cannot end in a logical language that a person can actually live and think in, any more than revolutionary politics can create a just national culture or practice singing can make one's throat into something that naturally emits beautiful sounds.

Spirit creates its own body for itself in its habits, but this body still must inhere in a flesh and blood, living body, just as life is possible in nature, but only by redirecting the tendencies of chemicals (which on their own are not alive) toward biological ends. That life is only the temporary holding together of a mass of chemicals that do not *have* to be so organized does not mean that life is an unrealistic goal and living things should not strive to continue in their lives and reproduce it. Life is not an impossible, imaginary ideal—that hardly needs to be said, but the reality of life is obvious only because living things are present to our senses in a way that the body of spirit is not. Yet the body of spirit is no less real. A human life of habit and culture, a community of true justice, seems to be just a lofty but unrealistic goal only for those who misunderstand the way spirit is present. Genuinely human life, culture, and justice are all very real and achievable, but only by laying hold of natural organisms and communities that must be *made* to develop in the human way.

Conclusion

Because the anthropological is that in human experience which is corporeal yet irreducible to categories belonging to philosophy of nature, a sophisticated treatment of anything anthropological must begin by recognizing that being human means being embodied and by laying out both the various forms of embodiment and cognitive relations toward embodiment. In addition to the three forms of embodiment characterizing nature (the mechanical, chemical, and biological) and us insofar as we are natural, anthropological embodiment involves cognitive relations to what is corporeal such as: (1) the naïve absorption in given natural forms and unreflective identification of meaning in them; (2) the explicit identification of oneself with a particular, limited content, a circumvention of naturally given embodiment without creating a new content-mediating body; (3) the wrenching of the self from any particular content alone in favor of a constantly developing, historically formed but open-ended pattern into which all particular contents admitted must be integrated. Distinguishing forms of and ways of relating to embodiment (both of which I take fully articulated from Hegel) allows the complex account of the place of humans in nature and society that I've given here (which is based on Hegel's approach but departs from Hegel's expressed positions in certain cases—and goes beyond them in others).

Because spirit is the idea in and for itself, the world it finds before it is not something that must be taken up and transformed into something else, assimilated into spirit as the animal assimilates nature biologically. To say that the world is meaningful to us may invite the assumption that there is a certain secret lying hidden in a given natural form, and to uncover this secret would be to know the truth of this part of nature. Hegel himself gives this impression (though he does not wed himself to the idea) when he presents the geography of a part of the world as "expressing" a principle that can be consciously grasped by a people in its culture. I object to the claim of a strict correspondence between natural form and spiritual meaning because, at least in its claim of determinate and clear meaning attached to a part of nature, it more properly characterizes the animal experience of nature, where comestible parts of nature, potential mates, and approaching predators are experienced in accordance with the instincts governing animal subjectivity. To be sure, Hegel's description of cultures finding meaning in nature differs from this animal experience in the latter's much greater diversity (there being a great many cultures) and depth (insofar as cultures apprehend the beautiful and the just in nature rather than just the biologically expedient or inopportune). Yet a key feature of the transition from nature to spirit, to which Hegel does not remain faithful in this case, is that in its highest form, nature appears to itself as meaningful only in ways that are given, unalterable and directed strictly toward natural ends, whereas spirit involves the liberation of the subject from the confines of these given parameters of experience. Accordingly, human experience of the meaningfulness of the world is characterized by ambiguity, allowing even for an experience of meaninglessness. Once what I have referred to as the "opacity of nature" (its resistance in our experience to reduction to a single meaning) is admitted, the anthropology can take in some instances a very different course.

I have been most interested in this book in charting how this departure leads to different conclusions in our experience of social classifications like race and gender. A sympathetic reader of Hegel cannot but be irritated by the arbitrariness of Hegel's comments on race and gender. I consider what I've offered here both a defense of Hegel's underlying approach and a criticism of his actual account: whether my account is called "Hegelian" or not depends on how closely one insists on restricting what is Hegelian to the positions expressed by G. W. F. Hegel. While we obviously must take Hegel as our principle source of what is Hegelian, I think it is distinctly unphilosophical to treat a philosophical account as emanating completely from the individual mind of a particular historical individual. Hegel did not fabricate Hegelian philosophy: he took hold of the same thoughts found in other philosophers, and available to us all, and worked them into a form that showed in what direction they might be taken to improve on the directions taken by his predecessors. It would be silly to call a philosophical argument "Hegelian" if it did not take its point of departure and its method largely from Hegel, but Hegelian philosophy is not limited to what Hegel wrote. I accordingly have submitted in this book what I consider a Hegelian critical theory of race and gender.

I have used Hegel's presentation of ways of relating to embodiment and ways of integrating it into a meaningful order (or failing to do so) as a model for how anthropological phenomena like race and gender (social classes for uniting and separating people into some meaningful order) have been understood and misunderstood in our time. I have been aided in this by the fact that Hegel is often already lurking in the background in much of the discussion of race and gender over the past century and a half. I aimed to show that race is biologically fictitious but has a social reality insofar as the enforcement of racial and gender grouping and hierarchy creates experiences different enough in those categorized differently to create a social class where one would not have otherwise existed. Yet these differences do not radically separate different social classes so much as enforce the perspective and privileges of one class by hiding its particularity and presenting its peculiarities as general human nature. This prioritization amounts to colonization by one class of the others: fostering a culture that is commonly held but in which some occupy an authoritative position due to their possession of certain fetishized physical features.

The fetishization of these features is an attempt to fix the social meaning of a certain part of nature in a way that is inadmissible, according to the concept of spirit, and inherently unstable because its arbitrariness invites equally justified, contrary ways of fixing the meaning of parts of nature. It is because spirit is a concrete universal, generating its own content from within itself (rather than requiring externally given provision of a content), that nature is spirit's *own* world (always already meaningful), but not in the way that certain parts of the world automatically answer to given urges in the animal. The concept of spirit forbids that the meaning of this or that natural feature be given for us as it is for animals. Rather, what space is for nature, time is for spirit; and what the spatial differentiation of organs (given ways of experiencing nature) is for the animal, the historical development of habits (created and revisable ways of experiencing both nature and the social world) are for us.

Our social world can never be legitimately based on fixed meaning simply found in this or that part of nature—including skin color and body shape. Contesting such an absurd social system may take the form of assertion of a counter absurdity ("*that* natural determinacy is not the privileged one, *this one* is!"), but ultimately such a challenge is a part of the dialectic that has its truth not in finally finding the natural determinacy that would truly ground a social order, but in rejecting any such natural foundation in favor of the one spirit generates from itself: spirit's constant transcendence of the natural forms in which it finds itself that is its history. The appeal to history is not a conservative appeal to the past as something which must be scrupulously carried forward into the future exactly as it was. History is neither this particular naturally founded culture nor the jumble of all naturally founded cultures, any more than time is the moments in their isolation from each other that make up the past, or a living body is the isolated atoms that compose it. To the contrary, to appeal to history is to appeal to the way spirit overcomes its initial immediate identification with this or that determinacy. This does not mean that spirit one day escapes nature altogether into an ethereal realm of Platonic ideas: it means that in spirit's development it renders mere nature only a moment of its return to itself in self-knowledge—not as a rocket escapes the earth in its flight to the moon but as humans transcend the savage need and brutal desire to consume in our rituals by which food is carefully selected, prepared (using not merely biological, nutritive criteria), and eaten at certain times, in certain places, according to certain manners, and together with other people as a meaningful cultural practice. Consider how a person understands her personal identity: not as something given at any point but something developing over the course of her whole life so far, apparent throughout, even in regretted moments of deviation from what is now willed as her identity. When she makes a decision she considers it in light of who she is, which always involves an expressed or tacit understanding of her life history as how she became who she is. The past is not a torch that illuminates the present and the future; rather, our reflection on ourselves (carried out now) as developing in history is the torch that illuminates both the past (showing where we excelled and where we failed) and the path we will take in the future.[1] Our identity is always already partially constituted along certain lines but also always susceptible to changes, whether degenerative or rehabilitative. The only sure guidance we have is that our knowledge that the world around us is always already open to being experienced as meaningful, but the determinate meaning we draw from it is contingent on our experience and how we orient ourselves toward it; and that accordingly no part of mere nature, nothing given (whether skin color, genitalia, or DNA), can enduringly establish our collective identity, or our social relations.

Notes

Introduction

1. By "subjectivity" here I do not mean the contingent and arbitrary (*willkürliche*) individual (the one championed by the romantics) or the external reflection of the understanding (as seen in Kant and Fichte). Düsing (1979, 1990) notes that Hegel distinguishes subjectivity in that sense from subjectivity proper, that is, thought that thinks itself yet still stands opposed to objectivity; or, it can refer to the idea that thinks itself and is one with objectivity (spirit, or absolute subjectivity). See also Jaeschke (1997).

2. That is not to say that others have not been able to draw out sophisticated approaches to embodiment in other parts of Hegel's work, such as Russon (2001, 2004) does from the *Phenomenology of Spirit*. But the anthropology is where Hegel chose to give his only account explicitly devoted to human embodiment.

3. For Aristotle, of course, all life has a soul, and humans are characterized by having the highest of capacities in their soul. Hegel too uses the word "soul" to refer to various nonhuman, natural phenomena, but it is clear that he means the human soul to be in a class apart and makes the human soul, which he there calls simply *die Seele*, the explicit object of the anthropology.

4. Mauss (1973).

5. It is, of course, anachronistic to say that Hegel intended to show that *evolutionary*-biological concepts could not exhaustively explain humanity, since he lived before the articulation of the modern theory of evolution, but nonetheless his work presents a sustained criticism of reductive naturalism generally.

6. Descartes (1964b) I.LIII.

7. Nuzzo (2008).

8. I do not intend to go in depth into these thinkers' theories of embodiment (nor into Descartes's theory), though I will have occasion to bring them and others (e.g., Aristotle, Plato, Rousseau) into the conversation where appropriate. I discuss them here to help situate the theme of this book into more recent approaches to embodiment.

9. Heidegger (1953) §12.

10. Merleau-Ponty (2002) presents this kind of argument frequently, for example, 65, 115.

11. Butler (1993) 30–35.

12. "[D]o we have a body—that is, not a permanent object of thought, but a flesh that suffers when it is wounded, hands that touch? We know: hands do not suffice for touch—but to decide for this reason alone that our hands do not touch, and to relegate them to the world of objects or of instruments, would be, in acquiescence to the bifurcation of subject and object, to forego in advance the understanding of the sensible and to deprive ourselves of its lights. We propose on the contrary to take it literally to begin with. We say therefore that our body is a being of two leaves, from one side a thing among things and otherwise what sees them and touches them; we say, because it is evident, that it unites these two properties within itself, and its double belongingness to the order of the 'object' and to the order of the 'subject' reveals to us quite unexpected relations between the two orders"(Merleau-Ponty [1968] 137).

13. "[W]e do not allow ourselves to introduce into our description concepts issued from reflection, whether psychological or transcendental: they are more often than not only correlatives or counterparts of the *objective* world. We must, at the beginning, eschew notions such as 'acts of consciousness,' 'states of consciousness,' 'matter,' 'form,' and even 'image' and 'perception' "(Merleau-Ponty [1968] 157–158).

14. EPW §10A, §41Z no. 1.

15. By the time he arrives at the anthropology, in volume 3 of his *Encyclopedia of the Philosophical Sciences*, Hegel has already presented his immanent critique, which begins in actual experience: this belongs to the Jena *Phenomenology of Spirit* (especially the first part on consciousness), which is a propaedeutic to the *Encyclopedia*. (An analysis of the *Phenomenology* lies beyond the scope of this work, but the reader is encouraged to consult Jean Hyppolite's magnificent and unsurpassed *Genesis and Structure of Hegel's Phenomenology of Spirit*.) Once one arrives at the *Encyclopedia*, concepts may be examined in their own right, without the kind of persistent reference to skeptical and generally epistemological problems that characterizes philosophy in the "reflective" Kantian tradition.

16. Merleau-Ponty (1968) 158.

17. Much of the attention given to embodiment in the past few decades has focused on gender and race. See for example: Spelman (1988); Butler (2006, 1993); Fanon (2008); Gooding-Williams (2006, 2009). I will have occasion to discuss how Hegel's anthropology can contribute in these areas in chapters 3, 4, and 8.

18. John Russon (2004). See above all chapters 5 and 11. What I mean by the body as an "expression of spirit" will be made clear over the course of the book.

19. Wolff (1992).

20. Aside from Russon and Wolff, the theme of embodiment in Hegel has been studied in certain very good journal articles, chapters in anthologies, and in

some excellent books. Articles and chapters include: Peperzak (1995, 1990); Siep (1990); Van der Meulen (1963); Bernasconi and Lott (2000); Harris (1993, 1971); Merker (1990); Lucas (1991); Pillow (1997); Dupré (1994); Moland (2003); Reid (2013); Testa (2013); Wenning (2013); Magee (2013); Nuzzo (2013); Lumsden (2013); and Magrì (2016). I would also mention Mowad (2013a, 2013b), but I leave it to others to judge their merit. Outstanding books on the anthropology and embodiment include: Peperzak (1991, 1987); Ferrarin (2001); Winfield (2010, 2011); Russon (2001); Halbig (2002); DeVries (1988); Lewis (2005); Berthold-Bond (1995). Greene (1972) gave a book-length study of the whole of the anthropology, and I am grateful to have been able to refer to it, but I think mine can offer some things his has not, like more thoroughly relating the anthropology to the philosophy of nature and the philosophy of objective spirit. I hope others will make further contributions to correct mistakes I've made here and explore what I've passed over.

21. VPG 280–281.

Chapter 1

1. Kant (1998) A7/B11.

2. In the logic Hegel calls these mechanism (*der Mechanismus*), chemism (*der Chemismus*), and teleology (*Teleologie*). Teleology immediately precedes the positing of the idea (*Idee*), whose immediate form is life (*das Leben*). In the philosophy of nature he refers to mechanics (*die Mechanik*), then physics (*Physik*), which culminates in the chemical process (*der chemische Prozeß*), and finally organic physics (*Organische Physik*). Despite the shifting names, throughout the relevant sections Hegel consistently explains the same triad: (1) terms related externally; (2) terms explicitly determined by relations to each other; and (3) the process developing and maintaining its identity as its constituents pass into the terms by which they are determined. For consistency's sake, and to get around the awkwardness and anachronism of Hegel's phrasing, I will call these "mechanical," "chemical," and "biological" or "living" bodies. I will refer to human bodies as such, or as "anthropological" or "ensouled" bodies. Though the chemical process is only the consummation of what Hegel calls the physical, I prefer the term "chemical" to physical for a few reasons: (1) it is the term used for the general ontological structure in the logic; (2) the term "physical" for many English-speakers is too broad, denoting simply "materiality," rather than a specific form of material embodiment; (3) the chemical process is the clearest expression of what Hegel calls "physical" in the philosophy of nature. There is clarity to be gained and, for the purposes of this book, nothing is lost by not invoking other concretions of "physics" (such as light in its relation to matter, the moon and comets, air, sound and heat, etc.) when I mean only to relate forms of embodiment to each other with the ultimate purpose of clarifying anthropological embodiment. See chapter 5 for a discussion

of certain parts of the physics section of the philosophy of nature that are relevant in their relation to sensation.

3. There is inevitably ambiguity in any succinct reference to what makes human bodies unique, including the reference to a soul. Aristotle looms large in Hegel's anthropology, and as Aristotle recognizes a certain kind of soul in animals as well as plants, so does Hegel at times give the impression of doing so. See Winfield (2018). In chapter 5 I explore how this ambiguity should be understood and note where Hegel even refers to a "soul" of inanimate parts of nature. However, one of my aims in this book is to nail down what exactly the "soul" proper should mean for Hegel, and this involves restricting it to humanity (by which I do not mean a biological species but participants in spirit, which is hypothetically possible for something other than a member of *Homo sapiens*).

4. See Kisner (2008) for a fine explanation of how a single entity is determined at once by the categories of life and mechanism.

5. Hegel would actually call what I am talking about not the "essence [*Wesen*]" of corporeity but the "concept [*Begriff*]" of corporeity. He uses the term "essence" a different way in his logic. But that does not affect the point here, so it is appropriate in this case to use the term "essence," which is more commonly used to denote what Hegel means by the "concept" of something (e.g., nature, spirit, right, etc.).

6. EPW §247. In Hegel's terminology, this is the "concept [*Begriff*]" of nature.

7. EPW §260.

8. EPW §261.

9. EPW §266. For a description of Hegel's criticism of mechanism in the form of Newtonian physics, see Ferrarin (2001) 201–209.

10. EPW §§326–327. Of course, there is much material separating mechanics (§§253–271) from the chemical process (§§326–336) in the *Philosophy of Nature*. Yet all of the intervening phenomena are basically governed by chemical relations (i.e., being explicitly determined by something outside of them and actually entering into relation with this other that cancels their abstract independence). "The chemical process" comes only at the end of what Hegel in the *Philosophy of Nature* calls "physics" because it concretizes chemical relations most clearly—and that is also why I speak of chemicals here. In the briefer account of what I have called here the "dimensions of corporeity" (which is found in the "object" section of the doctrine of the concept in the *Logic*), mechanism is succeeded directly by chemism, which is in turn succeeded directly by teleology (analogous to "organics" in the *Philosophy of Nature*).

11. EPW §§326–327.

12. EPW §§328, 334.

13. EPW §336.

14. As Winfield (2011) says: "Neither mechanism nor chemical process is inherent in their objects. In both cases, some condition must intervene before objects

undergo mechanical or chemical change. [. . .] For this very reason, they cannot exhaustively determine the objects that figure within them. [. . .] Consequently, objects can be mechanically and chemically determined and still have features and processes that are undefined by mechanism and chemical relations" (20–21).

15. EPW §352.

16. "For Hegel, the truth of the organic process is that it can reproduce itself and contribute to the continuation of the species, while this is impossible for all nonorganic processes—that is, in that they are not independent and self-sustaining. And this is only possible because organic beings are not aggregates of parts but overarching totalities whose particular functions are oriented for the sake of the whole" (Ferrarin [2001] 217).

17. EPW §359 & A.

18. EPW §§360–362, Hegel (1988) 132.

19. See EPW §§359–365 & A & Z.

20. For a brief discussion of animal perception, see Siep (1990) 205–207 and De Boer (2010) 138–142.

21. I will give an extensive treatment of this self-determination in chapter 2, though readers familiar with Kant will recognize something analogous in Kant's moral philosophy: the (human) will, reason, determines itself, generating its own content, whereas inclination, the other determining ground for action (and the one that is shared with animals), relies on stimulation from outside. Hegel's articulation of spirit's self-determination cannot be reduced to the way Kant describes the will, but the echoes of Kant are clear, and Kant's moral philosophy was certainly a major inspiration for Hegel.

22. EPW §371. I will leave unexamined which species are accurately described as "animals" in this way and which are not. It could be, as some claim, that not only *Homo sapiens* but all higher primates (and perhaps also dolphins, whales, and elephants) are able to experience the world and themselves in what Hegel characterizes as a "human" or "anthropological" way. If this is true, that would mean that a chimpanzee for example is not a mere animal but is "human" in a very real sense (though certainly not quite the same as us): and this would have obvious ethical implications. In other words, I am not trying to sort out which cases of living species belong to humanity and which do not. I am simply giving Hegel's account of the criteria for being embodied in a human way and contrasting these with the criteria for being embodied in other ways. Moreover, as far as the ethical implications of this kind of classification are concerned, even if (as seems clear) many animals would not qualify as human, that alone would not necessarily deprive them of moral standing. While Hegel never as far as I know explicitly recognizes moral standing among animals, it is clear that his analysis of life tends in this direction by showing how vastly different animal embodiment is from mechanism, and the mere thinghood of, say, a stone or a machine.

23. PG §32.

24. The representation of such an everlasting life is a *bad infinite*, to use Hegel's term: that is, it would be the indefinite prolonging of organic life, without doing anything to alter the fact that organic life is mortal in principle, that the processes that constitute organic *life* are equally the processes that bring on death (see EPW §§94–95). The deduction of the soul for Hegel is thus not an affirmation of the doctrine of the "immortality of the soul" if by this is meant the everlasting life of the individual human being.

25. EPW 362.

26. To be sure, there is a gray area where higher forms of animal life seem to have something like social customs, perhaps obligations, and so forth. At this point I am not interested in sorting out membership of species in the merely biological or the anthropological but rather in articulating the difference between the two forms of embodiment.

27. Geertz (1973) 48–49.

28. Geertz (1973) 50.

29. "We are, they say, the only animal abandoned naked on the naked earth; we are in bonds and fetters, having nothing to arm or cover ourselves with but the pelts of other creatures; Nature has clad all others with shells, pods, husks, hair, wool, spikes, hide, down, feathers, scales, fleece, or silk, according to the several necessities of their being. She has armed them with claws, teeth, and horns for assault and defense; and, as is proper to them, has herself taught them to swim, to run, to fly, or to sing. Man on the other hand, without an apprenticeship, does not know how to walk, talk, eat, or to do anything at all but wail"(Montaigne [1991] 509–510). Montaigne brings this thesis up to reject it, but his position here has not aged well.

30. EPW §247.

31. Epicurus (1926a) 85.

32. Plato, *Phaedo*, 64c, 67d; *Gorgias* 524b.

33. Plato, *Phaedo* 64a, 67e, 81a.

34. It is worth noting that just as Plato presents the emergence of philosophy through death (viz., that of Socrates), so Hegel presents the emergence of spirit (that thinking element that is distinctively human) through the death of the animal (EPW §§375–376). There will be occasion in chapter 4 to examine how Hegel understands death in animal life in contrast with something like death in the life of spirit. It must also be noted that Hegel does not think that the death that signals the emergence of spirit involves the *absolute* separation of the soul from the living body, but only the soul's transcendence of the conditions of organic embodiment. Analogously, when oxygen is inhaled by an animal and becomes not a mere chemical but part of the life of an organic being, this oxygen does not for all that *cease* to be chemical but only acquires a new role that cannot be understood through the concept of chemism.

35. To be sure, the human soul is not bodiless. It is still the soul of the distinctively human body (which has not yet entered into this investigation), and

it even retains in some lesser sense organic, chemical, and mechanical determinations. My point here however is only that the human body is not the animal body, that is, that the human body cannot be understood biologically. The experience of "practicing death" (understood in the Hegelian way as knowing oneself in the appearance of oneself to oneself as something external) would be proof for Hegel that the one experiencing it transcends the body understood as something merely biological, though there is certainly still a corporeity proper to being human.

36. Again, for Plato as well what from the unphilosophical and not properly human perspective seems to be death is in truth the life of the soul (*Gorgias* 492e).

37. EPW §360–362.

38. "Instinct is a *practical* relationship to it [e.g., the food], an inner stimulus tied to the semblance [*Scheine*] of an external stimulus" (EPW §361). In the *Zusatz* to §351 Hegel seems to recognize a higher, quasi-human capacity in animals to have a disinterested relation to nature when he contrasts animal life with plant life. I reject this as either an unfaithful recording or Hegel overstating his case. The general thrust of the *Encyclopedia*'s account of the passage from nature to spirit, and of Hegel's account of spirit generally, requires that spirit be identified with the explicit mediation of its relation to its other, which this disinterestedness involves. Hegel defends this position in the *Haupttext*, as well as, for example, in the *Zusatz* to §361.

39. Winfield (2010) explains it as follows: "the external determination of mechanical and chemical process is precisely what allows them to be enabling constituents of artifacts and living things, which have dimensions irreducible to physics or chemistry. Both mechanical and chemical relations depend upon some external conditions to get underway, such as an impulse in mechanical motion or a catalyst to precipitate chemical reactions. As a consequence, they can be instigated by something else which may act mechanically or chemically upon objects but do so as a part of a process having a different type of initiation and result. An end, for example, is distinct from an efficient cause in that what it brings into being is not something different from itself and devoid of any intrinsic relation to it. Rather, an end gets realized, relinquishing the subjectivity of being merely a prospective goal and gaining fulfillment in an objectification with the same content. An end, however, as something yet to be realized, cannot immediately be its own fulfillment. If it were, the end would have no subjective character and there could not be any teleological *process*. Something must therefore mediate the end's realization, a means that works upon objectivity to make the end objective. That working upon objectivity is external to objectivity and therefore comprises a mechanical or chemical process" (30). See also Winfield (2011) 23–24.

40. "It is an axiom for the body in physical mechanics that a body is only ever set in motion or comes to rest through an *external cause*, such that motion and rest are only *states* of a body" (EPW §264A).

41. EPW §364.

42. Here Hegel is in agreement with the account Aristotle gives in *On Generation and Corruption* 321a17–22, 322a10–13.

43. Winfield (2011) gives a very helpful exposition of why machines cannot be said to have minds, or souls. If the telos as such (rather than just a tendency based on situational influence) is removed from the account, and it were supposed that there were machines that made more machines, and that the form of these machines changes based on evolutionary pressure. However, the function we might impute to such machines would in fact be completely external to them, since their developmental processes would really be a series of blind mechanical responses (31–35).

44. See for example the mechanistic explanation of perception, locomotion, respiration, and circulation that Descartes gives in *L'Homme* (1964a 10:119–163).

45. Of course, Hegel would also object that light and electricity cannot be understood merely mechanically (EPW §§317–320, 323–325). Nor, he might add, can nerves and muscles (EPW §354). But to explain this would require a thorough survey of the physics and organics sections of the *Philosophy of Nature*, which is not my project.

46. Hans Jonas (2001), who argues persuasively against precisely this kind of interpretation of life as a function of mechanism, notes that there do seem to be some physical parts (viz., chromosomal DNA molecules) of the animal that do not take part in the metabolism characterizing animal life (97–98). Winfield (2011) responds that this "persistent core does not, however, alter the distinguishing feature of metabolism, that the individual active form of the organism sustains itself through some continuous exchange and assimilation of material with and from its environment, in contrast to the fixity of lifeless things, whose alterations are externally determined contingencies" (51). Indeed, it would be absurd to identify the animal (or human) with those enduring molecules rather than with the assimilative or metabolic functions. Chromosomal DNA does not think, feel, speak, eat, love, hate, and so on. To allege that DNA is the underlying code that ultimately makes possible all of those acts characterizing life would commit what Deacon (2012) calls the homunculus fallacy (48): we are at pains to explain how certain material bodies (viz., living ones) behave in ways that defy physical explanation, but to point to a certain part of the living thing and say, "this part has the plan for the whole thing, and tells the other parts what to do, and that is how purposiveness enters the scene," is simply to posit a "little man" inside the big one, explaining difficult properties in the big one by leaving them unexplained in the little one. The very description of DNA as having "information," a "code," or a "plan" imputes to it the kind of not-merely-natural quality that the mechanistic interpretation claims to root out. Similarly, Haraway (1997) argues that a gene is "not a thing" but "a node where many actors meet" (142). The field of epigenetics demonstrates that environmental influence on an organism can alter its DNA, and these changes can be passed down to future generations. Frost (2016) notes how chemical reactions can serve biological ends (58), and how biological phenomena can be given a merely chemical explanation (69). She laments the absence of a

telos in this kind of explanation (80–81), but in the end is unable to justify it (85–88). Yet this inability is due to her question-begging reliance on a chemical idea of what causality can be.

47. *Physics* 193a10–16.

48. EPW §360A.

49. "Man is an animal, but even in his animal functions he is not confined to the implicit, as the animal is; he becomes conscious of them, recognizes them, and lifts them [. . .]. In this way man breaks the barrier of his implicit and immediate character, so that precisely because he *knows* that he is an animal, he ceases to be an animal and attains knowledge of himself as spirit" (Hegel [1988] 80).

Chapter 2

1. See EPW §388 & A for Hegel's criticism of the reification of the soul. See also Wolff (1992) 59–61 and Nuzzo (2013) 11.

2. "*For us*, spirit has *nature* as its *presupposition*. It is the *truth* of nature, **and, therefore, its absolute prius** [*Der Geist hat für uns die Natur zu seiner Voraussetzung, deren Wahrheit, und damit deren absolut Erstes, er ist*" (EPW §381). This sentence and its paragraph are analyzed in detail later in this chapter.

3. Berkeley (1979). He frequently speaks of "sensible things" as what can be known, but by this he means only "ideas" (13).

4. Berkeley (1979) 36.

5. Kant (1998) Bxiii.

6. Kant (1998) A418–419/B446. See also (1997) 28:49.

7. Kant (1974a) 5:43. See also (1997) 28:257.

8. EPW §84.

9. EPW §87.

10. EPW §88.

11. EPW §112.

12. EPW §161.

13. Kant (1998) A76–77/B102.

14. Of course, Kant would respond that he took great care to *prevent* his theoretical philosophy from engaging in forays into the realm of reason. The way Hegel thinks of the understanding and reason is inspired by Kant but certainly departs from Kant's theory in major ways, which lead Hegel to his much more negative view of the approach he denigrates as *verständig* and a much more positive view of the speculative leaps of *Vernunft*. This departure is tangential to my project and so I will not get into it here.

15. In fact, willing (*Wollen*) is a form of the concept (EPW §§233–235).

16. It should now be clearer why in chapter 1 I said that according to Hegel, self-externality is what most people would call the "essence" of corporeity but what

Hegel would call the "concept." That self-externality is corporeity's concept means that it is not a characteristic latent in all bodies that the understanding is able to abstract and hold separately in thought—that would be an essence (*Wesen*). That self-externality is the concept of corporeity means that it diversifies itself into its content, namely, the various forms of corporeity apparent in the natural and anthropological worlds.

17. Spinoza (1992) Part I Proposition 18.
18. "*All things are a judgment*" (EPW §167).
19. EPW §171.
20. EPW §180.
21. Aristotle, *On Generation and Corruption* 325a24–325b5.
22. EPW §§195, 199.
23. EPW §201.
24. EPW §203.
25. EPW §205.
26. EPW §212. When someone is called an "idealist" for expecting justice to prevail, this is true to Hegel's use of the term only if the so-called "idealist" has discerned the developmental path of the society and so knows that the existing state of affairs is only a waystation on the way to a different (and more just) society. To call someone who imagines a state of perfect happiness and supposes that it will or can come about despite its impossibility in principle an "idealist" is simply to abuse the term.
27. "Matter longs for a center"(EPW §358Z p466).
28. The numbering of some of these sections differs in the first and second compared to the third editions of the *Encyclopedia*: the sex relation is §§368–369 in the first and second editions, §§369–370 in the third; genus and species (conflict between species) is §370 in the first and second editions, §368 in the third. The last moment, concerning disease, therapy, and the "self-induced destruction of the individual" is §§371–376 in all editions.
29. This everlasting perpetuation of finite members of a series is what Hegel calls a "bad infinite" (EPW §§94–95): the universal (life) is here perpetually unable to actualize itself in an appropriate form, such that the never-ending generation of new mortal animals is not a sign of life's infinite power, but of its *inability* to determine itself concretely. This is an example of "judgment": there remains a gap between the universal and the individual, such that the individual (in its individuality) is only ever a deviation from the universal, which hence remains something merely abstract and potential. A genuine universal, or a true infinite, would be concrete and syllogistic: it would bear within itself the principle of its own determination (the particular or middle term of the syllogism), such that the individual would be the existence of the universal itself (in a way—given by the nature of the particular term—that does not exclude *other* individuals from likewise being the universal).

30. Hegel does not "deduce" his concepts in a way most people would recognize. Yet, I consider it appropriate to use the term "deduction" because Hegel himself uses it (*Deduktion*) to describe the moves he makes in his system: see for example GPR §§2A, 141A. For Hegel, a deduction is a proof (*Beweis*) that begins not from empirical reality (and to this extent his meaning agrees with what most people mean by the term), but rather on the necessity of the concept in question (GPR §2A). For example, a certain concept being accepted (from having previously been deduced), it may be shown upon analysis of this concept that it has certain necessary implications. The analysis that brings these implications to light is the "deduction." See for example the way the concept of chemism is "deduced" from the concept of mechanism, as shown in chapter 1. It belongs to the necessity of the concept of mechanism that a body has relations to other bodies that are constitutive of its identity: the analysis that results in this insight is the deduction of the concept of chemism from the concept of mechanism. See also Peperzak (2001) 85–91.

31. EPW §216.

32. This is why the first moment of organics in the philosophy of nature is geology (which concerns inanimate things like mountains, rivers, oceans, etc.): geological nature is the sum total of nature insofar as it is merely *potentially* alive. A plant or animal is nothing but this very same nature integrated into a different order.

33. As Nuzzo (2013) says, "spirit's liberation *from* nature is more precisely its liberation *within* (and *with*) nature" (1).

34. This is obviously true of life, but Deacon (2012) shows how in thermodynamic processes, which typically serve to increase entropy, can in the right circumstances (given the right constraints), contragrade systems (processes or sets of interrelated processes that run against what would be expected given the second law of thermodynamics) can emerge (and do all the time). These include morphodynamic processes such as Bénard cells, which form in a heated liquid because spatial constraints prevent simple conduction of heat from dissipating the heat as fast as it accumulates heat, such that the liquid arranges itself in small, hexagonal cells to facilitate release of the heat (250). The right confluence of morphodynamic processes can result in a teleodynamic system, such as microtubules (a part of living cells) whose formation requires several parts maintaining themselves far from thermodynamic equilibrium, catalyzing other reactions that similarly run against simple thermodynamics (299–300).

35. *Gorgias* 492e.

36. For an excellent commentary on the same, from which I have learned a great deal, see Peperzak (2000) 121–135.

37. EPW §381. As a reminder, boldface indicates material added in the second or third editions. In German: "*Der Geist hat* für uns *die Natur zu seiner* Voraussetzung, *deren* Wahrheit *und damit deren* absolut Erstes *er ist. In dieser Wahrheit ist die Natur verschwunden und der Geist hat sich als die zu ihrem Fürsichsein gelangte Idee ergeben, deren* Objekt *ebensowohl als das* Subjekt *der Begriff ist. Diese*

Identität ist absolute Negativität *weil in der Natur der Begriff seine vollkommene äußerliche Objektivität hat, diese seine Entäußerung aber aufgehoben und er in dieser identisch mit sich geworden ist. Er ist diese Identität somit zugleich nur als Zurückkommen aus der Natur."*

38. Both are based on the verb meaning "to place" (*setzen, ponere*). For an interesting analysis of the term "expose" (also based on *ponere*) and its potential for making Hegel speak English, see Kolb (2000).

39. EPW §146.

40. De Boer (2010) takes issue with the way Hegel treats one moment as being already implicitly fulfilled in another, such that the second's appropriation of the first is not a violent seizure (227n46, 172). This is an objection that cuts to the heart of Hegel's whole project of speculative philosophy and is intimately bound to De Boer's criticism of Hegel's use of "absolute negativity," so I will discuss it later, in the context of absolute negativity.

41. Nuzzo (2013) 2.

42. Aristotle, *Politics* 1253a19–20.

43. Peperzak (2000) 123–124.

44. EPW §213A.

45. In discussing Thales, Hegel uses a phrase—"*absolute Prius*"—which lexically is nearly identical and semantically is completely identical to "*absolut Erstes*" to describe "the element (στοιχεῖον) and principle (ἀρχή) of all beings" (*Werke* band 1 p198).

46. Peperzak (2001) 122–123.

47. It is omnipresent in the Jena *Phenomenology of Spirit* without ever receiving an explanation anywhere in the book.

48. EPW §90.

49. EPW §§91–92.

50. See Winfield (2010): "The universal *determines itself* in the particular, rather than positing something else with a derivative, conditioned existence. This is what allows the universal to have individuality, with an intrinsic differentiation that is determined in and through itself. It is also what allows particulars to be individuals, exhibiting the same independent being endemic to self-determination. Mind, inherently embodied, will exhibit the true relation of the universal and the particular by being at one with itself in the body, provided the body, in its distinction from the mind, is so determined that it comprises the necessary vehicle of mind's own actuality. Then, mind, while not being just another bodily organ, will still exist nowhere else than in the body" (34).

51. EPW §382.

52. De Boer (2010) 185–202.

53. De Boer (2010) 126.

54. De Boer (2010) 90–91. See EPW §§94–95.

55. De Boer (2010) 123.

56. For instance, the way he lets his treatment of civil society be guided by the universal network established through private deals such that the needs of each person that should be satisfied by such arrangements get lost (GPR §§182–255).

57. De Boer (2010), writing of problems integrating a minority into a nation-state, writes, "If particularity and universality depend on one another in such a way that they can neither exclude nor incorporate their contrary, then I might try to affirm, finally, their unsettling entanglement. In this case I would not reduce the other to his or her particularity, nor to his or her universality, but recognize myself in his or her precarious attempt to respond to the contradictory demands that the entanglement of contrary determinations entails"(199–200).

58. This argument is mainly given in chapters 3 and 8.

59. EPW §383.

60. EPW §384.

61. EPW §383.

62. Peperzak (2000) 129–310.

63. EPW §§7A, 246A.

64. EPW §386.

65. EPW §386.

66. EPW §387.

67. There are also experts opposing this position, such as Peperzak (2000), who says that the philosophy of subjective spirit "is a theory of the characteristic possibilities of *human* life" (113, Peperzak's emphasis); Ferrarin (2001), who says that for Hegel "spirituality permeates all forms of man's physical nature" (225); and Chepurin (2018), who notes that what Hegel calls the "natural soul," the purview of which includes those anthropological phenomena that seem most closely tied to nature, is "only seemingly 'natural,' involving as it does resistance to natural immediacy and the incorporation of natural changes and qualities into a radically new whole where they acquire, as Hegel puts it, a 'spiritual meaning' "(103).

68. Wolff (1992) 29–30.

69. Nuzzo (2013) 2. See also 8. Winfield (2011) similarly claims that the anthropology concerns the "zoological" (94, 99) in humans, not the anthropological per se.

70. Nuzzo (2013) 7.

71. "Hegel gave an account of the non-occurrence of man in his 'anthropology' in the context of one place where the topic is the animal-human distinction. In §190A of the Philosophy of Right he says 'the concretum of the *representation* that one calls *man*' can only be the theme 'here from the standpoint of [social and socially produced] needs' and indeed '*only* [or first, "erst"] here.' Hegel clearly means that what it means that man begins and constantly progresses from an original state of savagery and so 'leaves [*hinauszugehen*]' the animal kingdom can only be understood as including the more defined, social and population-theoretical aspects of animal life. Man can only come to satisfy his needs in a simply pre-given, limited

'circle of means and ways' [by being] among a particular, determinate population ruled by social conditions. In the anthropology, as mental dispositions and activities of only the *individual* living being are considered. Therefore a conceptual explanation of the distinction between humans and animals cannot yet be expected here, insofar as this distinction shows a social aspect" (Wolff [1992] 30–31.

72. Nuzzo (2013) 8.
73. EPW §386.
74. EPW §213A.
75. EPW §247.
76. EPW §251.
77. Ferrarin (2001) says that in subjective spirit "[c]oncept and actuality are not thoroughly reconciled [. . .] but unlike in nature, which is an unsolved contradiction, in spirit they can be in principle. Spirit emerges out of nature and tries to return to itself from it. This means that understanding spirit as disembodied is no less abstract than understanding nature as dead otherness devoid of rationality. However, in nature the Idea is external to itself. The progression of its moments finds finite expression in particular existences and formations external to one another. In spirit, instead, concept and actuality do not fall asunder. While inner and outer, essence and manifestation can never be identical in nature, in spirit (*for* spirit) they can. Spirit can comprehend the idea's actuality in its concept [. . .] Spirit is not merely beyond nature's juxtaposition and externality; what nature lacks is the dialectic of inner and outer. Spirit is the inwardization of externality and of all otherness and the externalization of interiority" (237).
78. EPW §396Z p76. See also VPG 56 and PG §§251, 255, 258, and VPG 72 where Hegel contrasts an "instinct of reason [*Vernunftsinstinkt*]" with biological instincts.
79. See VPGes 12, 105–133, 217–218, 232–233, 256–259, 277, 287–288, 341–342, in addition to EPW §§393 & A & Z, 394 & A & Z. See also Mowad (2012a, 2012b, 2013).
80. VPGes 142.
81. EPW §517.
82. Hegel even says that mental illness is the privilege of humanity (EPW §408Z p168).
83. Ferrarin (2001) argues that on this point Hegel departs from Aristotle: for Aristotle man is a part of nature, with the sole exception of his ability to think. And while Hegel too identifies reason as what separates humans from animals, "this is because for Hegel thinking pervades the lower forms of spirituality [. . .]. What spirituality means in this context is the progressive overcoming and self-affirmation of form over matter" and "this overcoming begins already in the Anthropology" (253–254).
84. Nuzzo (2013) 8–9.
85. De Laurentiis (2006) 235.

86. Hegel makes comparably cryptic remarks elsewhere, such as in the lectures on the philosophy of religion he says that the most primitive form of religion, the religion of magic, is one from which we may want to withhold the name of religion (VPR 433, 435).

87. Ferrarin (2001) 238.

88. Premack and Premack (1994) 352.

89. Premack and Premack (1994) 353–354. This claim is disputed, but we need not get into the details here.

90. Premack and Premack (1994) 355–356. Montaigne (1991) errs therefore when he says, "You need still greater powers of reason to teach others than to be taught yourself. Democritus thought, and proved, that we had been taught most of our arts by animals: the spider taught us to weave and sew, and the swallow to build; the swan and the nightingale taught us music and many other animals taught us by imitation the practice of medicine" (519). Clearly, in these cases we intend to learn, but the animals do not intend to teach us, and so the degree to which reasoning must be present in animals is very slight.

Chapter 3

1. EPW §§90–91.

2. Of course, Hegel had already confronted these skeptical concerns directly with a lengthy and devastating critique in the consciousness section of the Jena *Phenomenology of Spirit*.

3. There is some evidence today that some forms of animal life (e.g., higher primates, perhaps elephants, whales, and dolphins as well) are more complex than Hegel allowed, though it is not clear that any nonhuman animal life rises to the level Hegel recognizes as characterizing human life. De Waal and Ferrari (2010), who are most enthusiastic in arguing that animal cognition is more advanced than commonly recognized, argue for instance that animals demonstrate some of the basic processes at work in the higher thinking characterizing human life, but not that there is no enduring difference between the two.

4. *De Anima* 412a10–12.

5. EPW §389.

6. Kirk Pillow (1997) has identified the soul not with the Aristotelian passive *nous* but with "prime matter" (184). It is true that for Aristotle a thing's materiality is its potential to be something else (*Metaphysics* 1032a20–23, 1039b27–30, 1050a15–17, 1060a21–22, 1071a9–12), and thus matter qua matter is actually nothing in particular (*Metaphysics* 1029a20–22) though it is potentially anything. This agrees with the way passive *nous* is described as being "potentially all things" (*De Anima* 429b6–9). However, not only is prime matter devoid of spirit, it is the most debased form of nature—to the extent that it can be accorded existence at

all. However, for Hegel the soul is *spirit*, its immediate existence "in" a body notwithstanding. See Ferrarin (2001) 265–267 for an illuminating exposition of Hegel's account of sleep, with a focus on how it relates to Aristotle's. I follow Ferrarin in understanding that Hegel holding the soul to be the sleep of spirit does not mean it is spirit collapsing into nature, but rather that the soul is the fundament—itself belonging to spirit—on which higher forms of spirit are built (265–266).

7. EPW §389. See Wolff's (1992) thorough dissection of this sentence (39–43).

8. Heidegger (1953) §41.

9. Hans-Christian Lucas (1991) remarks that if the term "life" was not already taken, referring to a stage in the philosophy of nature, it would be appropriate to refer to the natural soul (the first section of Hegel's anthropology) as the sphere of "human *life*" (278).

10. VPGes 105–133. See also 217–128, 232–233, 256–259, 277, 287–288, 341–342.

11. See VPR 4a 412, 446–447, 476–477, 481, 501–506, 579.

12. Hegel, *Vorlesungen über die Geschichte der Philosophie* III 303.

13. Mill (1998) 5–10.

14. EPW §392. Shannon (1995) in a bit of an overstatement denies that there is a world soul for Hegel (31–32). He argues correctly that Hegel's understanding of geography and geology does not support the so-called "Gaia hypothesis," namely, that the earth is itself a living organism. However, perhaps because he confines his investigation to the organics section of the *Philosophy of Nature* and does not comment on the anthropology, he misses the fact that there *is* a world soul for Hegel (Hegel even uses the term *Weltseele*) though the reality of this world soul does not mean that the world is a living organism, or even that it has a soul apart from our experience of it.

15. Winfield (2010) argues that over the course of the subjective spirit section Hegel shows that individuals can have awareness prediscursively, and prelinguistically (6–7). The emergence of language (in the psychology section) falls outside of the scope of this work, but I take this as support of the kind of awareness of meaning I am arguing for here.

16. This is the sentiment behind the lament of Wordsworth (1977):

> The world is too much with us; late and soon,
> Getting and spending, we lay waste our powers:
> Little we see in Nature that is ours;
> We have given our hearts away, a sordid boon!
> This Sea that bares her bosom to the moon;
> The winds that will be howling at all hours,
> And are up-gathered now like sleeping flowers;
> For this, for everything, we are out of tune;

> It moves us not.—Great God! I'd rather be
> A Pagan suckled in a creed outworn;
> So might I, standing on this pleasant lea,
> Have glimpses that would make me less forlorn;
> Have sight of Proteus rising from the sea;
> Or hear old Triton blow his wreathèd horn. (568–569)

17. Merleau-Ponty is in complete agreement with Hegel on this point. Both hold that things themselves can be genuinely experienced as happy or sad, that these emotions are not overlaid on natural stimuli by artificial memories. Merleau-Ponty (2002) alleges that though the empiricist can offer elaborate theories to explain how we experience nature in an emotional way, she must suffer from "a kind of mental blindness" (29) to be unable to see what Hegel would call the anthropological significance of nature. This kind of blindness can be caused by traumatic brain injury according to Merleau-Ponty, as in the case of the World War I veteran Schneider, for whom "sun and rain are neither gay nor sad [. . .] the world is emotionally neutral" (182).

18. Merleau-Ponty (2002) xx.

19. EPW §392.

20. David Abram (1997) represents the movement of humans away from this sympathy with nature as a fall of biblical proportions, initiated by the way alphabetic writing from Semitic cultures (originally from the Phoenicians of modern Lebanon, though Abram incorrectly implies it came from the Hebrews [100]) where letters were pictographs rooted in nature was transferred to the Greeks, who took these building blocks of true human subjectivity as objects received from without (93–113).

21. Hegel (1988) 131–132.

22. It is no wonder that it is in his work on aesthetics and teleology (or the hidden meaningfulness of nature) that Kant gives his account of the "higher meaning" of colors, expressed in "a language that nature brings to us" (1974b, 172), just as Hegel does in his anthropology (EPW §401Z pp108–109).

23. *Metaphysics* 1042b8–1043a27.

24. In each of these cases, something that is "normally" or habitually understood through a certain concept is understood to have a property inexplicable through that concept: oxygen is most often understood merely as a chemical rather than as a vanishing moment in a living thing's reproduction of its own life, just as space is usually thought of through the concept of extension rather than understood as something combustible (as a certain space may be) according to the concept of chemism.

25. Johansson et al. (2001); Lam et al. (2006).

26. EPW §§213A, 23Z no. 2.

27. EPW §381.

28. For example: VPGes 12, 105–133, 217–218, 232–233, 256–259, 277, 287–288, 341–342.

29. See EPW §§352, 360–362, & A.

30. Ellman and O'Clair (1989) 282.

31. Blake (1974) 109.

32. Blake (1974) 107.

33. Ponge (2000) 43. My translation.

34. This too is a position Hegel shares with both Heidegger (1953) §26 and Merleau-Ponty (2002) 422.

35. Bernasconi (2000, 2002, 2003), Bernasconi and Lott (2000), Gordon (1997), Hoffheimer (2001, 2005), and Parekh (2009) have all taken Hegel to task for his racism. Others, like Lucas (1991), hurriedly and with obvious embarrassment pass over the offending passages, dismissing them as a sign that Hegel too was a child of his time (280–281). Buchwalter (2009) very soberly argues against the most damning interpretation insofar as he opposes any contention that a single culture is intrinsically better than others (*Bildung* being constituted by self-examination and self-criticism).

36. EPW §393.

37. Oceania does not appear at all in the main text and only briefly in the published lecture material (VPG 39), where it is noted only to be dismissed as irrelevant.

38. EPW §393Z p58. In his *VPG* Hegel also discusses racial distinction but he only mentions that it has its roots in geography (39) without going into the details of the geography of the various continents.

39. EPW §394. See also VPG 45–48.

40. Benhabib (1996) 26.

41. Thus Hegel apparently viewed real or imagined physical differences in skull size, distance from outer ear ducts to the root of the nose, and from the frontal bone to the upper jaw, forehead arching and width, greater or lesser prominence of cheek bones, skin tone, hair texture, and eye shape all to be anthropologically significant (EPW §393Z p59, VPG 40–42). I use the qualifier "apparently" because these remarks are confined to the lecture material.

42. It is worth noting that the justices' reasoning in *Brown v. Board of Education*, the court case in the United States that authorized the desegregation of schools (and provided the impetus for broader desegregation), was based not just on the truth that so-called "separate but equal" public facilities were never genuinely of equal quality (such that African Americans were harmed by inferior schools), but also and principally on the truth that segregating races harms everyone by depriving them of the benefits of living in a racially diverse society. While those of lower social status would likely still be very familiar with the dominant culture due to its pervasiveness, desegregation would benefit those of higher social status by relieving them of their ignorance of their fellow citizens. It is precisely

this ignorance, due to lack of exposure to racial diversity, that clouded Hegel's normally more acute judgment.

43. That is the "monogenetic" account of races, which turns out to be false but was always more plausible than the polygenetic account, which held that different races have no common origin at all. To be sure, there are innumerable *populations* with a high degree of differentiation, but these are not what is typically meant by "race"—otherwise the Amish, due to their high degree of endogamy, would be one of the best contemporary candidates for a "race." It is also important to note that even populations with a high degree of genetic differentiation from other populations are not "pure" in any sense. As Reich (2018) argues, the genomic revolution has definitively put to rest any claim to genetic purity among populations: "mixtures of highly divergent populations have occurred repeatedly" (81) such that "today's [racial] divisions are recent phenomena, with their origin in repeating mixtures and migrations" (97, cf. 260, 268). Reich is keen to point out that there are real biological differences between populations, and even that in some cases these map easily onto the commonsense idea of race (252), but those we know of concern traits like "skin color, bodily dimensions, ability to efficiently digest starch or milk sugar, the ability to breathe easily at high altitudes, and susceptibility to particular diseases" (255). In contrast, it is by no means clear that there is anything like a genetic foundation for intelligence or moral behavior, though in some cases there may be a genetic basis for traits that *in the context of a given society* allow better for the behaviors we associate with these qualities, for example, as a genetic predisposition to have children later in life can be positively correlated with completing more years of education (257), though the social system in which child care is the burden of the individual parents is not by any means "natural."

44. Zack (2002) 89. Zack is featured prominently in what follows because she gives the most thoroughgoing account of the biological groundlessness of race. See also Bernasconi and Lott (2000) 100–107.

45. Zack (2002) 33.

46. Zack (2002) 39.

47. That is, genetic explanations of phenotypical traits fail. Phenotypical traits are those that are immediately apparent and may result not from genetic causes alone (i.e., they are not genotypical traits) but rather from interaction of genotype and environment.

48. Zack (2002) 41.

49. Zack (2002) 44.

50. Zack (2002) 60.

51. Zack (2002) 62.

52. Boas (1962) 29.

53. Appiah (1996) 72.

54. Harris (1971) 81. Harris was not speaking of Hegel's concept of race in the context of the criticisms of the biological notion of race mentioned earlier.

55. See chapter 8 for my account of how we can give an anthropological account of the social reality of race considered as defined by physiological differences in human bodies (such as skin color).

56. EPW §393Z p57.

57. GPR §57A. Similarly, he held that Christianity was the truest religion partly because in Christianity it is posited not simply that *one* is free, or that *some* are free, but that *all* human beings are in themselves free (VPGes 31, 134).

58. Miller (1994) 403.

59. See Durkheim (1995), who argues that social organization and stratification is mirrored by natural differences in nature (111–112, 141–147, 370), and even that our notions of classification of natural kinds originates in our understanding of social hierarchy (148). Hegel endorsed Montesquieu's view of the importance of national character in deciding what laws are appropriate (GPR §§3A, 261A, 273A) but not Montesquieu's (2008) statements on the effect of climate on national character (231–245): this is no surprise insofar as Montesquieu argues for a climactic influence that is physiological. Herder (1967a) does not reduce this influence to biology (257–258, 265–273) and so is a bit closer to Hegel, though Hegel does not mention him in this connection. Nor does Hegel mention Montaigne (1991), who argues for both a merely natural influence (of the air on character) and of certain topographies necessitating certain practices, which in turn engender certain character traits (648–649), or Aristotle (1962), who notes an isomorphism between climate and character without explaining its cause (1327b19–37).

60. Homer (1975) 2–14.

61. Homer (1990) 5:35, 874.

62. His own father, Zeus, notes that he hates Ares the most of all the gods, yet in the same breath recognizes his kinship with this detestable deity (Homer [1990] 5:1028–1041).

63. "That age had no doubt that man, when he was not subject to external coercion, was determined by inclinations and convictions. But these impulses do not point inward to some emotional center or basic will, but outward toward the largeness of the world. What we in a moment of decision experience as motivations are here, for the enlightened, the gods. With them, and not in the human heart, resides the depth and the fundament of everything significant that transpires in man. This means that he knows he is surrounded by a great being and its living forms. Who these forms are is the most important question. If he knows them he knows himself; for contact with them is that decisive event, which he experiences now in one direction, now in another. Far from limiting himself to the subjective, therefore, and persisting in the groove, becoming at once insecure and obstinate, he expands towards the objective and substantial, towards the being of the world and hence towards the divine. This applies equally to fortune and misfortune, to good and evil. Even when an objectionable and fateful sphere attracts him, it is the realm and form of a god, and if its fascination has seduced him from orderli-

ness and duty he may, in his sorrow for what has happened, refer to its power of compulsion and think of its greatness. However bitterly he may lament his action, his conscience need not torment him, for the decision was not defeat of submerged good intentions in a struggle with evil inclination" (Otto [1983] 178).

64. VPGes 339-342. See also *Vorlesungen* Band 4a 579-582.

65. Generally, everything Hegel writes about non-Western cultures is either grossly oversimplified or a bald-faced lie. He took at face value reports from traveling merchants and missionaries, though both of these likely remained outsiders to the cultures they were reporting on. His credulity in such cases would not have been possible for such a critical mind were it not abetted by deep-seated racism. Needless to say, I do not accept, nor should the reader accept, the judgments Hegel makes about non-Western cultures. I give some of them here only to illustrate how he understood the relation between geography and culture.

66. VPGes 95-96, 153-154, 160-161; *Vorlesungen* Band 4a 446-447.

67. VPGes 183-185, 207-208; *Vorlesungen* Band 4a 476-477.

68. VPGes 216-217; *Vorlesungen* Band 4a 501-505.

69. It is worth pointing out that Hegel did not present progress in history as anything like a natural law, without the possibility of exceptions. Moreover, the progress in question was progress in *freedom*. It was most emphatically not a progress in *happiness* (VPGes 41-42). Suffering *unjustly* is of course to lack freedom as well as happiness, but being free for Hegel is not the same as being happy and does not imply an end to suffering.

70. To be sure, Hegel encourages this interpretation in his lectures (VPG 42-43), but these are errors of judgment, to which he need not have committed himself.

71. Pinkard (2001) 236. That the liberalism championed by Napoleon had its own deep flaws is an entirely separate point from its manifest superiority to feudalism.

72. Herder (1967b) 333ff.

73. Hence the term "bioregion," which indicates that regions should be demarcated by the *natural life* in the area, or by other natural, geographical markers (rather than by arbitrarily established political boundaries). The markers usually given are watersheds (the land surrounding a network of bodies of water—and the water itself—that all drain into a common body of water). See Sale (1985) for an articulation and defense of bioregionalism (43ff.). Alexander (1990) has raised doubts about the possibility of establishing bioregions, pointing out that the different criteria used for establishing bioregions do not agree on where boundaries are to be established (165). But see also Thayer (2003), who acknowledges that the distinction of nature into bioregions has as much to do with human perception as with strictly geographical phenomena (35). Accordingly, Thayer discusses the distinguishing of bioregions not only by physiography (15) and communities of life (33) but also by human cultures (60-61) and forms of art (94).

74. I have addressed this elsewhere: Mowad (2012b).

75. Morocco and Algeria in the northwest have some mountains, the Horn of Africa in the east has more, there are a few isolated ranges in the Gulf of Guinea, some in Angola and Namibia in the southwest, and there are some internal ranges across Central Africa, but most of the continent's edges have no mountain ranges at all. Between Djibouti and Algeria (across Eritrea, Sudan, Egypt, Libya and Tunisia, most of northeastern Africa) there are no mountain ranges. Nor are there any on the eastern coast south of Somalia (spanning Kenya, Tanzania, Mozambique, and South Africa). Similarly, West Africa from Benin across Nigeria, Cameroon, Equatorial Guinea, Gabon, Congo, to the Democratic Republic of Congo there are no mountain ranges at all.

76. To be sure, some features of African geography contribute to isolation: low elevation in the north and west and high elevation in the east and south cause rivers in higher elevations to have waterfalls, which prevent entering Africa by boat where its rivers empty into the ocean (July [1974] 8, see also 96 and 123). North Africa has been in constant intercourse with both Europe and Asia for five thousand years (Erman [1971] 36–37), but Hegel treats this as part of Europe anyway (EPW §393Z p58, VPG 39, VPGes 120). However, large parts of Saharan and sub-Saharan Africa have likewise been in contact with extra-African civilizations for well over one thousand years—in some cases nearly three thousand: Ge'ez, the classical Ethiopian language originated in the southern part of the Arabian Peninsula, and the country itself was host to large numbers of migrants from Yemen who, mixing with the Cushite people there, formed the state of Axum before the third century BCE (July [1974] 50–51). The Sahel region was the site of several kingdoms and empires that maintained uninterrupted contact with the Arabian Peninsula, and through it, the entire Muslim world (69–92), and the entire east coast of Africa was similarly in perpetual contact with Oman (105–109). It is as unfair to claim that Saharan and sub-Saharan Africa were "isolated" simply because they lacked extensive contact directly *with Europe* as it is to attribute this isolation to an inborn African characteristic, when the collapse of these states of the Sahel, for instance, was in fact due to European commercial influence along the western coast (which diverted trade away from these desert polities) (205). Even in cases where no extensive contacts are known, as in the case of Great Zimbabwe, it is clear that African civilization did not stand in need of this external influence to rise to great heights (151–156).

77. Radhakrishnan and Moore (1957) 556.

78. Arnold (1994) 86–87.

79. Césaire (1995) 123, 125.

80. I take this to be largely compatible with the argument De Boer (2010) gives about the tentative way intercultural relations in many cases must be handled (199–201). For her this means refusing to disentangle and establish a definite order between universality (belonging to a larger culture such as a nation-state)

and particularity (having a particular racial or ethnic identity, gender, language, etc.), due to the uncertainty that the particular is really immanent in (and has its ends satisfied by) the universal. However certain it may be when looking at past cultures that one has successfully incorporated the other as a moment in it, satisfying the telos of the other in its own more comprehensive end (and I am not the least bit convinced that this is an easy thing to discern, or that Hegel did a good job in this task), it is so difficult as to be almost impossible to successfully carry this out in the present—to know that one's own culture is truly more comprehensive than another. It would seem that when people are certain that their culture is superior to another contemporary culture in this way, they operate with a superficial caricature of the other culture. Scholars commit this error almost as frequently as the general public, though for scholars the mistake usually involves reducing a culture to its current state, or failing to see how the culture has been distorted by recent events but still retains within it many other potential lines of development that can be actualized given the right conditions and leader(s) and that are completely native to the culture, even if they resemble a similar feature in the scholar's own culture. This has happened repeatedly in Western appraisals of non-Western countries, where colonialism has destroyed the native institutions of a culture, or, by taking over, have deprived them of the opportunity to develop as they otherwise would, such that they ossify and become rigidly "traditional." This traditional character, called perhaps "fundamentalism" or lack of aptitude to deal critically with history and institutions, is then read into the culture as if it were part of the eternal essence of the non-Western culture. See chapter 8 for a more extended discussion of this.

81. Alcoff (2006) 188.

82. I have written about this in an article: Mowad (2012a).

83. VPG 413–414, 424. Winfield (1991) notes the peculiar character those who would fill the role Hegel assigns to the "Germans" would have to have: "If [. . .] its [freedom's] universally valid structures of justice are to arise within history, there must emerge within history a point from which an unconditioned, free institution of practical relations can occur. Such a moment would first have to liberate itself from the hold of all natural determination, as it is embodied in whatever past traditions and given authority contravene the institution of freedom" (110). Hegel's refusal to laud the culture of the ancient Germans—and his positive disdain for it (EPW §80A, VPGes 424, VA III 347), mocking Germanness (*Deutschtum*) as German stupidity (*Deutschdumm*) (Pinkard [2001] 311)—should be seen as even more striking given how sanctimoniously Germanness was being treated around him (see Fichte [2008]).

84. In addition to EPW §§393 & Z–394 & Z, see VPG 12, 105–133, 217–218, 232–233, 256–259, 277, 287–288, 341–342, and also Hegel's enthusiastic endorsement of Montesquieu's position that the peculiar character of a people (which is connected with its geography and climate) has a determining influence on what

form of government they have, which laws they adopt, and how they are interpreted and applied (e.g., GPR. §3A, §261A, §273A).

85. Accordingly, he describes the "Germans" as having *Gemüt* (heart, soul, or disposition), which is open to all contents but fixated on none, rather than a particular national character (VPG 12, 422–424). The "Germans" have this openness because they are not rooted to one location in the world: thus instead of describing their geographical conditions as Hegel typically does when introducing a new nation, he describes their *migrations* from one place to another (VPG 419–428). Of course, there are many nomadic peoples in history: Hegel could with equal justification have called the summit of history "the Arab age" since the Arabs of late antiquity were (largely) nomadic, had no strong culture that could not be abandoned in accepting a pure (i.e., universal and not narrowly national) religion (whether Christianity or Islam). In fact, though Hegel seems not to have known it, Islam shares many of the features of Christianity that he thought qualified the latter as the consummate or absolute religion. For example, the consummate religion should not be particular but rather the completion of what preceded it, and that is precisely how the Qur'an presents Islam, and how it presents Muhammad as the seal of the prophets. Islam presents itself as the consummation not only of the Abrahamic religions, but of all. Just as St. Paul referred to the Greeks' temple to the unknown god to present Christianity as the consummation even of paganism, so a Hadith has it that God sent prophets to *all* nations, such that all cultures are ultimately reconcilable as being based on the same fundamental principles. In another Hadith, Muhammad enjoins Muslims to seek wisdom wherever they can find it, in all cultures ("going even to China," which in that context means to the very ends of the earth). And the Muslim intellectual tradition supports this: Al-Fārābī (1985) held that different cultures are based on the words of different prophets, using different images and symbols to express the same truths, though with unequal clarity and adequacy, but that philosophers in any culture have access to the truth independent of the symbols and images employed in religious discourse, and so are equal (279–281). The same point was more famously made later by Ibn Rushd (1987). One might allege that this is more of a Hellenization of Islam than an authentic presentation of it, but that would beg the question: the very fact that Islam, like Christianity, was open to Hellenistic influence bespeaks its authentic character as a universal religion. Yet, Christianity in Hegel's account does seem to be an especially apt expression of the ultimate truth, insofar as the Christian presentation of God as becoming incarnate, suffering, dying, and being resurrected in the Holy Spirit of the Church expresses in narrative form the very concept of spirit. It could be that the historical revelation of the Qur'an (as distinct from the eternal, uncreated Qur'an) can fill the role of incarnation that Jesus (the Word) plays in Christianity, and perhaps also that the revelation of the Vedas in Hinduism can as well, but pursuing these questions would take us too far afield. But I would also mention the account offered by Gilroy (1993) of the "Black

Atlantic," the community in diaspora of those in Africa or whose ancestors came from Africa in the last few centuries. This community bears strong resemblances as well to the role Hegel articulated for the "Germans," insofar as they share a culture (most strongly expressed in music) characterized by separation from their original land (through slavers or colonialism within Africa) and creating anew their culture on a nonnatural basis, as a "non-traditional tradition" (198) not appealing to an original site that is corrupted by interaction with its opposite, but rather in constant intercourse with its other, disrupting what can be presented as a rigid opposition between inside and outside. A characteristic feature of this music is antiphony (or call and response), which breaks down the barrier between performer and audience, inside and outside (200). But see also the criticism of Gilroy's position offered by Gooding-Williams (2009), who is skeptical of the unity of such a culture across Africa, Europe, and the Americas, and if it did exist, of its potential to fill the emancipatory role Gilroy suggests (219–223, 235).

86. EPW §§548–549.

87. Part of the reason this has not been generally understood is that Hegel uses the term *Staat* (state) to refer both to the individual nation-state and to world-history. So, while all human communities realize themselves in a "state" and are free in seeing this state as the reflection of their spirit, other peoples of antiquity realized their spirit in a particular *nation*-state opposed to others and willed its ends over those of other nation-states, but the "Germans" realize their spirit in transnational world history and do not will any particular national program.

88. Boas (1962) states, "In many ways the educated Americans, Englishmen, Frenchmen, Germans, Italians, Spanish and Russians have more in common with each other than each has with the uneducated classes of his own nation" (92). This would express my point if we expand this list beyond Europeans and Americans and understand "educated" to mean cultural sophistication (as seen in a nuanced understanding of justice for example) rather than what comes from access to prestigious schools, which is often simply a result of wealth. In the anthropology itself Hegel does not go into intercultural relations and conflict, nor does he give the presentation I have just reiterated of the "Germans" as a nonrace (this comes rather from his *Philosophy of Right*, and his lectures on the philosophy of history and the philosophy of religion).

89. "Social identities are part of our interpretive horizon and have an effect on what we perceive or notice, but it is incoherent to propose that horizons be 'overcome.' [. . .] bodies are positioned and located by race and gender structures and have access to differential experiences, and may also have some differences in perceptual orientations and conceptual assumptions" (Alcoff [2006] 114); "Racial and gendered identities are socially produced, and yet they are fundamental to our selves as knowing, feeling, and acting subjects" (126), and they are socially produced according to how people appear corporeally (102), though what counts as an appearance of one race or another is itself social (91); race has no biological

basis but a social reality (181) constituted countless times every day through various "microprocesses" (185) on the parts of both the oppressors and oppressed. Appiah (1996) earlier made much the same point (76–80).

90. Alcoff (2006) 201.

91. Alcoff (2006) 92, 95.

92. Alcoff (2006) 215–217.

93. Memmi (1991) does an excellent job of teasing out many subtle aspects of the relation between colonizer and colonized. Even a colonizer of goodwill, he says, cannot truly be a part of the liberation movement: "how could he visualize sharing in any future liberation, being himself already free?" (23–24). Such a person is politically ineffective, because she speaks for no substantial social base but is rather one of a small number of "misplaced heretics" (41–42): because of cultural differences, she does not truly understand the people she would speak for (42) and is unbearably awkward in trying to relate to them (43).

94. For an articulation of this idea, see Alcoff (2006) 192, 205–206. See also Fanon (2008) 95.

95. Thus while many universities have programs for African American studies or similar programs for the experience of minorities, there is no European studies program. Racists are keen to point to this as a sign that whites are in fact treated unfairly today. Yet the truth of the matter is that until recently and still often today the entire liberal arts program functions as a white studies program (yet without being *marked* in this way), where philosophy, history, sociology, and so forth, all draw exclusively or nearly from white sources alone.

96. Much of the *Zusatz* to EPW §394 is concerned with identifying these traits. See also his analysis of how the national peculiarities of the French led them to imperfectly carry out the Enlightenment (VPG 500–501, 525–526), how the Germans' (*Deutsche*) penchant for navel-gazing and random feelings (EPW §394Z) distorts their social life (*Vorlesungen* Band 4a 265–269), and how he similarly criticizes the English and Austrians (VPG 535–539). See also his dismissal of Scandinavian (and indeed, German) mythology (EPW §80Z p171, also in his *Vorlesungen über die Ästhetik* III 347). Granted, he uses a much lighter touch in discussing European particularities than in African or Native American peculiarities, for example. I am not defending his clearly unfair and unsympathetic reading of non-Western cultures. To say that the substance of Hegel's account is more enlightened than it appears is not to say that it is perfect—far from it. One glaring inadequacy in Hegel's account is that he paid too little attention to the social role of racial appearance. (Recall, for Hegel race was a matter of the soul's absorption in this or that geographical environment.) In this respect, Alcoff's account, as well as those of Fanon and DuBois, are especially welcome contributions. In chapter 8 I will offer a critical race theory that is rooted in Hegel's account yet also takes into account the appearance of race.

97. The individual soul is first introduced in EPW §395. The main text of the paragraph says very little: the fuller explanation belongs to the *Zusatz*. The *Vorlesungen* from 1827/1828 transcribed by Erdmann and Walter and edited by Hespe and Tuschling have very little on the material from §395, but they lend credibility to Boumann's *Zusatz* to §395 insofar as Erdmann's and Walter's notes do not depart at all from it. Comprising less than two pages, Erdmann's and Walter's notes on the individuality of the soul concern the differences that Kant established between the temperaments (viz., that generally a person is not wholly dominated by any one temperament) (VPG 48), and the fact that certain areas permit of talents (e.g., art and mathematics) and others (the essentially human activities, religion, reason, etc.) do not (VPG 49). See the preface for a statement on the use of lecture material.

98. Taking tool use as an example of a talent, a skilled dexterous performance with a natural origin, the anthropological literature is abundant but comes to no consensus about how such a thing emerges from nature, even among animals (who in so many cases make use of nature in an instrumental way that it can scarcely be denied that animals do indeed use tools: see Beck [1980]; Van Lawick-Goodall [1970]; Galdikas (1982), McGrew [1974]). Yet while the genotypical foundation for such skills can be identified and accounted for naturally, how exactly phenotypical behavior patterns arise from and "express" this naturally given foundation is unclear (see Beck [1980] 183ff.). Yet the talent under consideration here is a capacity and disposition to skilled action existing immediately in humans that serves no evolutionary purpose, or at least *need not* serve any such purpose, in the manner of what Gould and Vrba (1982) call "exaption": for example, though human hand shape evolved to grab and swing from branches, it can easily be spontaneously put to new and unexpected uses.

99. EPW §395Z pp71–72.

100. VPG 48–49. See also EPW §395Z pp72–73.

101. EPW §395Z p74.

102. See for example EPW §405A as well as VPGes 38.

103. EPW §395Z p74.

104. Hegel does not bring genuine character (a system of habits) into the discussion until the end of the whole section on subjective spirit, noting that character presupposes one's willed creation of a conception of happiness for oneself, in accordance with which some impulses can be consistently pursued and others consistently rejected, that is, one's creation of a pattern of desires and actions that are characteristic of oneself) (EPW §395Z p74).

105. (1) Africans are described as immersed in their own natural simplicity to the exclusion of difference (similar to the soul as "talent"); (2) Asians are described as unproductively oscillating between inert indifference and sudden activity directed outward (similar to the passing from one "temperament" to another);

(3) Europeans are associated with the unity of the two preceding determinations (similar to "character").

106. VPGes 89.

107. As Hegel will put it later: "The soul is in itself the totality of nature, as individual soul it is a monad; it is itself the posited totality of its *particular* world in such a way that this world, with which the soul is filled, is included in it, and the soul relates to it only as to itself" (EPW §403A). See also VPG 33–34 and Chepurin (2018) 104.

Chapter 4

1. Russon (2004) 18.

2. Of course, the very inaccessibility of the interiority of another makes it difficult to know where to draw the line between those who possess it and those who do not. I hesitate to commit myself to the claim that the more intelligent but still nonhuman mammals do not have this interiority, but there is less need for circumspection as one descends down the animal kingdom's part of the *scala natura*.

3. I believe this is how Hegel's remark that the soul is the "universal immateriality of nature" (EPW §389) should be interpreted. Wolff (1992) correctly interprets this line as meaning that while nature qua external world can only be considered self-external, it first achieves the status of simple totality as the *inner* world of the soul (43–45).

4. The degree of complexity that has been uncovered on this question in recent decades is extraordinary, but that also means I cannot go into contemporary debates without losing hold of my theme.

5. EPW §357.

6. EPW §§366–367.

7. In predation (EPW §370, or §368 in the third edition), animal life as such maintains itself by using one species as the raw material for the continuation of the species. In disease (EPW §371), a part of the individual animal body begins to operate at variance with the ends of the whole organism, such that the living body turns against its own corporeity, consuming and destroying it as it would in a state of health destroy external nature.

8. EPW §396Z p76.

9. See for example where Hegel says, "[T]hat which is animalistic in the genus process [*Gattungsprozesse*] belongs to the consideration of life as such in the philosophy of nature" (VPG 56), thus indicating that what plays the role of "the genus" in human life is not "animalistic," that is, not biological.

10. In the section on observing reason Hegel refers to an "instinct of reason [*Vernunftsinstinkt*]" (§§ 251, 255, 258) as what in human life plays a comparable role to the biological instinct animals have, by which their genus directs them toward its own goals. And, in the Erdmann/Walter transcripts Hegel draws the

same analogy, saying, "In the animal what it needs is good for it, existing in this felt way—instinct—[but] the human being has no instinct, its instinct is reason [*Vernunft*]" (VPG 72).

11. EPW §370 (§369 in the 1817 and 1827 editions).

12. EPW §396Z p76.

13. EPW §§467–468.

14. EPW §367. See De Boer (2010), who argues as well that the structure of judgment (though she does not use the term here) is present in animal perception, insofar as the animal is completely absorbed in whatever particular feeling it is experiencing at the moment; and in the next moment, it will be absorbed in a completely different feeling, the first having vanished for the animal completely (140–142).

15. EPW §396Z p76.

16. Hegel does not therefore follow materialists like La Mettrie (1753) in explaining the emergence of reason in the soul by classing it as an epiphenomenon of the growth and maturation of the body (296).

17. Hegel uses the masculine forms (boyhood, manhood), but there seems to be no reason what he says here should not apply to women and girls.

18. EPW §396Z p78.

19. EPW §396Z p78. See also VPG 52.

20. EPW §396Z p78.

21. EPW §344. Aristotle too (with whom, along with Rousseau, Hegel's anthropology is in constant dialogue) holds that the embryo lives only a vegetative life (*Generation of Animals* 736a27–736b13).

22. The interpretation I am giving, that the ages of life are truly spiritual phenomena and not biological stages, is confirmed in Hegel's lectures, where he says of the birth of an infant, "the physiological changes are not so significant" (VPG 52), insofar as the vegetative state continues to a certain extent beyond this physiological change into infancy (52). This shows that what is relevant in the ages of life is the way in which the human being knows itself and the world, and not so much the traversing of biological stages.

23. EPW §396Z p79.

24. EPW §343.

25. VPG 52. See also EPW §396Z p79. Compare this to Rousseau's (1932) account of how a child learns space and extension by learning that objects differ from himself (tome premier 75–76).

26. VPG 52–53. See also EPW §396Z pp79–80.

27. VPG 59. See also EPW §396Z p80.

28. VPG 53. See also EPW §396Z p80.

29. VPG 53. See also EPW §396Z pp80–81.

30. VPG 53. See also EPW §396Z pp80–81. It is worth noting that here Hegel departs from Rousseau, with whom his entire corpus in some sense but EPW §396 in particular seems to be in dialogue. The departure consists in how

adults should see to the upbringing of children. As is well known, Rousseau (1932) advises against lecturing children with abstractions they cannot understand. Instead, the educator should descend to the level of children, share their faults and their ignorance, experience what they experience and prompt children to learn the only appropriate way, from their own experience (tome premier 416–417). Yet Hegel in his lectures has nothing but opprobrium for "the pedagogues of play" (VPG 53, EPW §396Z p81), that is, those who "lower themselves" to the level of children for purposes of instruction. Hegel can only be referring here to Rousseau's disciples in the field of pedagogy.

31. VPG 54. See also EPW §396Z p83.

32. EPW §396Z p83.

33. EPW §396Z p76. Again, this point (stated differently) belongs not only in Boumann's *Zusätze* but also in Erdmann's transcription of the 1827/1828 lectures (VPG 56).

34. Wolff (1992) 33–34.

35. EPW §438.

36. EPW §396Z p83.

37. EPW §441 Z. It is not until thought reveals itself as syllogistic and hence as *will* that the universality *actually* determines itself in particularity (EPW §§467–468).

38. EPW §386Z p83. See also VPG 54.

39. For Rousseau (1932), the love that emerges in the breast of a youth is the love of a generalized chimera, in comparison with whom no real woman can measure up (tome deuxième 134).

40. VPG 55. See also EPW §396Z p84.

41. VPG 55–56. See also EPW §386Z p85.

42. This is how life is defined in the *Science of Logic*, where only its ontological structure is given, leaving open whether it is concretized in nature or in spirit (EPW §218).

43. EPW §375.

44. That is, the ages of life (the particular term) are a differentiation that is immanent in reason (the universal term), making possible the unity of reason with the individual human being (the singular term) that progresses through these ages. This is an example of the syllogistic structure that permeates all of Hegel's mature work.

45. EPW §375.

46. Ferrarin (2001) makes a similar point in contrasting human life to animal life, though not in the context of a discussion of EPW §396, or indeed of the anthropology: "For Hegel, man is not simply his natural life but can rise above it. By thought and action the individual human being can consciously carry out and actualize a spiritual content. Thus here the concept is no more an in-itself but becomes *for* him. This has the more precise consequence that man can objectify

himself in the universal medium of reality and make his individuality universal, part and parcel of spirit's history" (222). Ferrarin conceives of the difference between humans and animals here as involving not a difference in what counts as the "genus" for each but rather in the ability of humans to negate immediacy, transforming it into something that reflects their own subjectivity (222–223). See also Ferrarin (2001) 233.

47. EPW §142.
48. EPW §573.
49. GPR 28.
50. It is noteworthy as well that Hegel uses the ages of life as a metaphor for the epochs of world history in his lectures on that topic. There he identifies the East (viz., China and India) with the world's "age of infancy [*Kindesalter*]" (VPGes 135). In keeping with my translation of *Kind* in EPW §396 as "infant," *Kindesalter* would be rendered "age of infancy." He identifies Central Asia (viz., the peoples of the Persian empire, which includes not only Persians as such, but also Assyrians, Babylonians, Hebrews, and Egyptians) with the "age of boyhood [*Knabenalter*]" (VPGes 137, or as I've called it, childhood), the Greeks with the "age of youth or adolescence [*Jünglingsalter*]" (VPGes 137), Rome with the "age of manhood [*Mannesalters*]" (VPGes 138, or adulthood), and the "Germanic [*Germanische*, not *Deutsche*] realm" with "old age [*Greisenalter*]" (VPGes 140). That determinations that Hegel elsewhere assigns to distinct peoples are all already present (in some form) in the ages of life of the *individual* soul (regardless of race) should make us still more skeptical concerning the connection Hegel himself tried to draw between speculative philosophy and racism.
51. See also Plato, *Gorgias*, 492e–493d.
52. EPW §381.
53. EPW §397.
54. He takes this position as early as 1802 or 1803 in *System der Sittlichkeit* (12–13) and holds it consistently through the 1807 Jena *Phenomenology* (§451) in the 1820 *Grundlinien* (§§165–166) and all three editions of the *Encyclopedia*, that is, up to the year before his death.
55. Pinkard (2001) 298–299.
56. Pinkard (2001) 299.
57. Pinkard (2001) 449. See Berthold-Bond (1995) for a fuller treatment of this relationship.
58. Pinkard (2001) 321.
59. Pinkard (2001) 482.
60. EPW §369 (in the third edition), §368 (in the first and second) Z p518.
61. "*ein* Naturunterschied"(EPW §397), "*natürlichen Allgemeinheit der Gattung*" (EPW §518), "*natürlichen Geschlechter*" (GPR §161).
62. EPW §397.
63. GPR §166A.

64. PG §452.

65. Commentators have drawn much insight from this part of Hegel's work. A major theme is how Hegel here invests a natural distinction with ethical significance. See Russon (2004) 76ff.; Harris (1997) vol. 2, 221ff.; Donougho (1989); Ravven (1988); Hoff (2014) 27; De Boer (2010) 18; Lloyd (1995) 88–93. Since the anthropology generally concerns the way what might otherwise be considered something merely natural is in truth imbued with spiritual significance, I want to focus here on the more specific point, namely, that gender distinction in the *Phenomenology* is not the subordination of the feminine to the masculine.

66. Hegel contrasts tragedy with comedy by saying that in the latter there is a conflict of duties (*Pflichten*) in which the nothingness of this duty is revealed (PG §465). The tragic hero on the other hand acts in accordance with one law (e.g., that of the family or that of the city) and, pulled along by a foreseeable but unalterable course of events, is himself or herself destroyed, such that the hero's destruction bears witness to the enduring *validity* of the violated law.

67. Nearly alone among commentators, Starret (1996) has noted this (257), and how it presents a formidable obstacle to the tendency (admittedly abetted by Hegel himself) to interpret Hegel's social philosophy as uniformly conservative and shortsighted. Despite giving in many ways a very insightful and sensitive reading of this part of Hegel's work, Butler (2000) misinterprets the relation between the sphere of the household and that of the state as one where the former must simply "give way" to the latter (4–5). This is not how Sophocles presents Antigone, nor how Hegel understands it in the *Phenomenology*.

68. PG §466, cf. EPW §395.

69. Russon (2001) discusses this section in his examination of Hegel's theory of embodiment as articulated in the *Phenomenology* (81–91), and he comes to conclusions compatible with mine (a similarity that I take as a sign that I am on the right track). He has occasion to touch on the anthropology in the book as well, noting that there Hegel shows "that the subject of a more sophisticated spiritual life remains a corporeal subject, but not this simply natural one"(135). His interpretation of the ethical action section of the *Phenomenology* is likewise in agreement with the one I am giving here: see for example where Russon notes that the divine law and the human law are not to be taken as positive laws on which subjects may idiosyncratically take a position but rather each as an "a priori ground of experience" (83), that is, something that frames how the world is experienced.

70. Sophocles (1982) 127.
71. Sophocles (1982) 133.
72. Sophocles (1982) 127.
73. This is my paraphrase of a sentence in PG §468.
74. PG §469.
75. PG §471.
76. PG §472.

77. The frame of reference for his theory of gender is the tribal world of ancient Greece and Rome, not women in the bourgeois, noble, or peasant households of his own time, and certainly not our social world. While it is true that for most of human history, in most places, women have had their extra-domestic opportunities severely restricted, it was most properly in the Indo-European world of antiquity that the family was the primary social institution organized around a hearth devoted to household gods (the penates Hegel refers to at GPR §163A) and existing uneasily alongside a supra-familial state. For ancient Indo-European cultures generally the soul was thought to reside underground, which Hegel calls the *unterirdische* (Coulanges [1956] 15), and which gave these culture their most primitive and original notion of the divine (21). Every home was built around an altar to the family's dead (25), just as familial life (the most primitive and original form of social life) was built around the domestic religion (34). It would be absurd to deny that Hegel was a committed sexist. But it would be almost as unreasonable to overlook how little the social world depicted in *Antigone* resembles the social life of his native Germany even one thousand years before his birth.

78. There is no need for an exhaustive list, but a few examples are Plato (*Timaeus* 42b–c, 82a–87b, 90e–91a) and Aristotle (*Generation of Animals* 718a18–20; *Politics* 1252a25–1252b7, 1259a39–1259b4, 1259b29–1260a31).

79. PG §§452–453.

80. Butler (2000) 12.

81. Butler (2000) 35.

82. Butler (2000) 38.

83. On reading Butler's treatment of Hegel's theory of gender I am reminded of an anecdote I once heard. When the eminent Hegel scholar Jean Hyppolite heard what Alexandre Kojève was saying in his celebrated lectures about the *Phenomenology*'s master-servant section, Hyppolite remarked: "That is brilliant—but it is not Hegel."

84. Mills (1996) 62–63.

85. De Boer (2010) 22–24.

86. De Boer (2010) 90–91.

87. De Boer (2010) 24–25.

88. De Boer (2010) 90–91.

89. De Boer (2010) 126.

90. By calling sleep the "foundation" of waking, it can seem to reduce sleep to a moment of awakening, which is the truth of both, but this is not the case. Waking is equally the foundation for sleep: each presupposes the other, and the truth is in the consciousness of the waking-sleeping soul, the soul for which each is but a moment. I call sleep the foundation of waking only because the drama of the anthropology is such that awakening is led to take itself as independent, and to take sleep as only a moment of its return to itself—but the awoken soul is wrong in doing so.

91. The meaning of sleep and dreams is of course a topic with a long history in anthropology. In 1871 Edward Burnett Tylor (2016), widely considered the founder of cultural or social anthropology, identified the experience of sleep as the primary source humanity had in its early stages for beginning to conceive of a soul, as that which can separate itself from its body in sleep and travel the world, meet the dead, and so forth (vol. 1, 428–429).

92. EPW §398Z p92.
93. VPGes 176–177.
94. VPR 4a 476–477. See also 431–432.
95. "*wesentliche* [. . .] *Macht*"(PG §474).
96. "*absolute Macht*"(EPW §398).
97. EPW §398A.
98. As is so often the case, Merleau-Ponty (2002) is in complete agreement with Hegel on this point: "I observe external objects with my body, I handle them, examine them, walk round them, but my body itself is a thing which I do not observe" (105).
99. Heidegger (1953) §44.
100. *De Anima* 427b11–12, 428a11.

Chapter 5

1. As Merleau-Ponty (1964) says, "The enigma is that my body simultaneously sees and is seen" (162). This remark (from "Eye and Mind") can obscure the differences however between what Merleau-Ponty maintains in that essay and what Hegel wants to show in the paragraphs on sensation. Merleau-Ponty's point here is that being embodied puts him in touch with material things by situating him among them, making his experience of bodies unlike the way a Cartesian geometer conceives of them. Hegel would not deny this (and the two are much closer than is genuinely acknowledged), but his point here is that the body's naturalness stands in the way of both knowledge of parts of nature and of self-knowledge.

2. See *De Anima* 429a18. The term "mixing" is an infelicitous way of rendering the relation insofar as the soul and body must be understood together from the beginning. By using this term I do not mean to imply that either has its identity apart from the other, but only to indicate that in sensation the soul is for itself indistinct from its sensing organ ("mixed" with it) even as it senses another object as distinct from it.

3. EPW §401A, or "simple ideality [*einfachen Idealität*]"(VPG 76). I will explain what this means later in this chapter.

4. EPW §401A.
5. EPW §401Z p103. See also VPG 76.
6. EPW §401Z p103. See also VPG 76.

7. EPW §401Z p104.

8. This way of classifying the senses implies that we may imagine other ways of sensing, say, physical ideality that do not take the form of seeing or hearing. If there are nonhuman rational creatures (e.g., angels, or extraterrestrials) it is possible that they could have a sense of physical ideality that does not depend on light or sound waves.

9. See Michael Wolff's (1992) meticulous analysis of what Hegel might mean by calling the soul "the universal [or general, *allgemeine*] immateriality of nature" (39–45). He concludes that the soul's "immateriality" must be taken to mean that the soul is the particular way that the world (of nature) exists in a nonmaterial, nonexternal way—in other words that the soul is the "ideality" of nature (45). Of course, there are many ways in which this is the case, from the universal soul's absorption in nature through habit. Sight and hearing are only two such ways that what in nature is separate attains unity.

10. Hegel calls light "universal physical identity" (EPW §277), "immaterial matter" (VPG 77). See also his discussion of the Persian religion of light in the VPGes 215–216 and the VPR (1827) 504–506.

11. EPW §317.

12. EPW §320. See also VPR (1827) 510.

13. A crystal most closely approaches this transparency (EPW §317 & A).

14. Hegel leaves it unexplained how in its relation to light the precise material structure of *this object*, results in precisely *this color*. We know today that the physical characteristics of a colored object allow it to absorb light at certain wavelengths and reflect it at different wavelengths. Thus a green apple absorbs all wavelengths of light except the one which our eyes experience as green: this it reflects back, which is why the apple appears to us to have this color.

15. To be sure, two objects can be distinct even though they have the same color, but two such objects *are not* distinct for vision. If the color is the same, then for vision the objects are indistinguishable. Of course, shape is also visible, and using only vision a person can distinguish objects that are chromatically identical based on their spatial determinations (their precise figures and positions in space). However, this does not constitute an objection to Hegel. The fact remains that *we see only colors, and always only in the medium of light*. We can distinguish shapes by sight only on the condition that there is a difference *in color*. For example, we can distinguish a large red square from a smaller red square only if the area outside of the smaller red square is a different color, thus placing the smaller red square in relief.

16. Of course, some objects are able to render themselves sonorous, but by this ability the object nearly transcends nature altogether. See Hegel's fascinating remarks on the singing of birds (EPW §§351 & Z, 358Z, 365Z, 370Z).

17. For the sake of simplicity and brevity, in what follows I am combining the account of gravitation given in §269 and its *Anmerkung* (as the culmination

of the section on mechanics) and the deduction of specific gravity in §293 (in the second part of the physics section).

18. Thus the contradiction that was apparent on the level of the mechanical universe as a whole (viz., that each body at once attracts and repels every other body) here finds its way into the core of the most miniscule body, and thus is posited of the corporeal *as* corporeal.

19. EPW §299. In his lectures Hegel describes sound in the following way: "What is called hearing is the vibration of bodies in themselves. The body vibrates, i.e. each part [of the body] is displaced [*sich verrückt*] into the place of the others, and is immediately once again pushed out by the others which assert themselves" (VPG 77).

20. See also Hegel's (1988) description of romantic music as sound as the releasing of the ideal from its entanglement in matter (88).

21. EPW §321. The wording is strange, but to say that the object of smell is "particularized airiness" means simply that when we smell we are smelling a body that is breaking up (i.e., being particularized) and being released as a gas or vapor. Most of the scents that come to mind (various spices, wood burning, food or flesh rotting, flatulence, etc.) are thus of organic matter that is undergoing some kind of chemical dissociation.

22. EPW §322. See the preceding note.

23. I would therefore add sound and water to the list Stone (2005) gives of Hegel's three "fundamental natural elements" (108).

24. EPW §282.

25. EPW §283.

26. EPW §284.

27. EPW §321. Similarly, Aristotle says that the sense of smell consists of fire (*Sense and Sensibilia* 438b20–21), since odor is a smoke-like evaporation, and smoke-like evaporations arise from fire (438b24–25).

28. EPW §283.

29. EPW §322.

30. EPW §401A.

31. VPG 76.

32. Hegel discusses feeling in his lectures on the philosophy of religion and consistently makes the point that all feeling is implicitly self-feeling (VPR [1824] 175–176; VPR [1831] 123–124; VPR [1827] 285–286). Willem DeVries (1988) argues that Hegel must not have differentiated *Empfindung* from *Fühlen/Gefühl* until 1830, because in the 1817 and 1827 editions of the *Encyclopedia* the second section was called *die Träumende Seele* (the dreaming soul) and was only called *die Fühlende Seele* in the last edition of 1830 (71). I distinguish Hegel's use of *empfinden* from *fühlen* here because of his final decision in the last edition to separate the two.

33. EPW §96.

34. *Timaeus* 35a–36d.

35. *Timaeus* 30b–37a. Accordingly, Hegel's conception of the soul is closer to Aristotle's, who similarly recognizes a congruity between the form inhering in a part of nature and the soul that can become the same form in its knowledge of that part of nature.

36. Halbig (2002) 55.

37. Halbig (2002) 55–56.

38. As Ferrarin (2001) puts it, "Objects do not have to wait for the synthesizing activity of a mind or transcendental subject to be unities. They are unities and concrete universals, that is, not sums of features but self-specifying universalities that constitute the truth and essence of the objects they identify" (72).

39. Hegel says: "The general forms of sensations are related to the various physical and chemical determinacies of natural objects (which are proved as necessary in the philosophy of nature), and are mediated by the various sense organs" (EPW §401Z p103); also "we accepted the content of *external* sensations from the foregoing philosophy of nature as having been proven there in its rational necessity" (EPW §401Z pp110–111).

40. EPW §247.

41. When I say that nature "idealizes" itself, I mean the term in the genuine sense that Hegel uses it. An idea is not a copy in my mind of an externally existing object—that is a *Vorstellung*. An idea is more real than what is usually called "real": it is the inner telos or complete truth of the "real" thing, which may or may not be evident in immediate appearance, or what is often called "reality." In this respect, Hegel's understanding of *Wirklichkeit* (usually translated as actuality) is instructive, insofar as it is defined as the emergence of what is essential in reality. If the idea is not present in immediate appearance (or "reality") however, it can still be known if the thinker is sensitive and attentive enough. To be an "idealist" is not to oppose true reality to some attractive but impossible alternative. It is to discern the inner truth that is latent within the externally existing, so that the claim to "reality" on the part of what presents itself as immediately existent is highly qualified. That nature idealizes itself means that it brings this inner truth out of itself, making it apparent, so that while there are still certainly deceptive appearances, nature as such does not as a rule hide itself from us or give us only deceptive appearances.

42. Hobbes (1997) 21–27, 41–46; Locke (1997) book 2, chapter 1 §§1–4; Hume (2006) book 1, part 1 §§1–7 (1977) §§1–3.

43. EPW §247Z p25.

44. Pausanias (1971) 9.30.5.

45. Apollodorus (2007) I.14; Apollonius of Rhodes (1971) I.23–34.

46. Pausanias (1971) 9.30.5.

47. EPW §401Z p103.

48. EPW §307Z p196.

49. EPW §323Z p273.

50. EPW §300 & Z, §316Z.

51. Wolff (1992) 54. What I translate as "sensation" or "sensible," and so on, are various forms of *Empfindung, empfindbar*.

52. *De Anima* 412b10–12.

53. EPW §8A.

54. Ferrarin (2001) 252.

55. Aristotle, *De Anima* 424a17–23.

56. EPW §318Z.

57. EPW §303Z.

58. EPW §336Z.

59. EPW §325, and in the *Zusätze* to §§317, 324, 341.

60. EPW §307Z.

61. EPW §314.

62. EPW §315Z: here it is called both soul (*Seele*) and soul-like (*Seelenhafte*).

63. Aristotle, *De Anima* 412a23–26.

64. For example, *De Anima* 412b10–16.

65. For instance, that *nous poietikos* is supposed to be pure activity "art" rather than an "artisan," yet must be spoken of as a subject (De Laurentiis [2006] 230).

66. De Laurentiis (2006) 235.

67. Winfield (2011) says, "Waking [. . .] immediately ushers in feeling [in the form of sensation]. [. . .] To awake naturally from sleep is then equivalent to come to have feeling" (103).

68. That Creon's demand was outrageous does not imply that Antigone's actions were not equally outrageous. But Hegel's primary concern is to show the hubris of the sensing soul in taking itself to be independent of the experiencing body while remaining totally dependent on it, and the sensible soul is analogous to masculinity in the paragraph on gender in "natural changes" and with Creon in *Antigone*.

69. *De Anima* 429a18.

70. Merleau-Ponty (2002) 105.

71. Ferrarin (2001) 268–278. See also 205–251.

72. Magrì (2016) argues that for Hegel one can have sensations without being aware of them, but to be aware of sensations is to feel them (78). I would add that feeling is characterized not just by awareness of feelings but by awareness of feelings as the subject's *own*, such that the subject is aware of *itself* in its feeling, in such a way that it is not completely distinguished from the feeling. Magrì makes this point as well: "What Hegel outlines through the analysis of sensation and feeling is an account of self-awareness that precedes the very distinction between subject and object" (78).

73. VPG 76.

74. Of course, *spirit* does know things incorporeally, but such kinds of knowing are not under examination here.

75. EPW §401. See also VPG 75. This is much like the thesis William James (1884) later advanced, apparently taking it to be his own original idea. Cannon

(1927) raises doubts about James's theory, citing experimental research in the forty years after James's article. These experiments show that what appears to an observer to be the same emotions can be aroused without the physiological changes having taken place, and the same physiological changes can take place without emotion. Cannon acknowledges a major weakness in his counterargument: it is based on observations in animals (and thus can conclude nothing about the subjective experience of emotion, which is what both Hegel and James were referring to). Cannon also argues that in the particular cases James was concerned with, the viscera are relatively insensitive and the changes in them are too slow to explain the sudden arousal of feeling. This objection, if true, would damage only James's theory. Hegel is not so much concerned with identifying specific cases of emotion felt as a result of a readily identifiable physiological change, as with arguing that the feeling of emotion is not an abstractly mental process.

76. The fact that blushing is more apparent for an observer the lighter the skin of the person blushing has nothing to do with the relation between the actions of capillaries and the feeling of shame in people of all skin shades.

77. This is not to say that reading literature cannot give a true understanding of emotions: part of the miracle of poetry and novels is how they *can* produce those feelings in the reader, who is not actually undergoing the experience of the character. But it is also possible, in low forms of culture, to give watered-down depictions of an emotion that do not give the reader the lived-through knowledge of it.

78. Hegel says in his lectures that such a topic belongs to "psychology" (EPW §401Z p102). This makes sense insofar as the corporealization of emotions involves feelings of pleasure and pain (EPW §401A), and these belong to the "practical feeling" subsection of the psychology's practical spirit section (EPW §§471–472).

79. EPW §448.

80. Halbig (2002) 98–99. See also Hegel, EPW §448Z p250. Halbig's remarks on attention here notwithstanding, this "seeing beyond" may be fruitfully discussed with reference to other parts of the psychology as well, such as imagination.

81. If anthropological meaning is discernable in the flesh and cartilage of a human face, it is a comparatively small step to showing how it can be found in the rest of nature. There has however been some debate about whether it can be discerned at all, even in human faces. It was argued in the early twentieth century that the ability of people to recognize the emotions of others has been greatly exaggerated (Féléky [1914], Langfield [1918], Sherman [1927]). It has since been shown that the flaws in these earlier studies resulted from showing still photographs (when emotional is expressed over time, not in a single instant) (Michotte [1950]).

82. Halbig (2002) 100.

83. Barbara Merker (1990) correctly argues that the corporealization of the emotions in the sensation section must be understood in relation to habit (which belongs to the feeling soul section and which I will discuss in chapter 7) (232–233).

84. EPW §402Z p120.

85. EPW §391.

Chapter 6

1. VPG 88.

2. EPW §402A. See also VPG 69. DeVries (1988) argues that Hegel did not differentiate between *Empfindung* and *Gefühl* until the third edition (1830) of the *Encyclopedia* (71). What I have just cited from Hegel's lectures on the philosophy of spirit comes from the winter semester of 1827/1828.

3. As Winfield (2011) notes, "[I]n feeling, the psyche is nothing more than a feeling of what *it* immediately is. Everything else that may otherwise characterize the psyche is left out of account in the feeling it has. The psyche accesses through feeling only its current feeling in all its momentary atomistic givenness [. . .]. Nothing abiding and necessary about the psyche's own reality can be felt as such. Consequently, the 'self' with which the psyche communes in feeling is utterly singular and contingent in character. In order for mind to relate to itself as something having a universal, necessary, communicable character, more than feeling must be enlisted" (108).

4. EPW §403A.

5. "When we have forgotten something, we are divided [into] the one, which we are in ourselves [*an uns*], and the other, consciousness, the power over us" (VPG 88). This division is clearly the one which we today would call that between the conscious mind and the unconscious mind. Berthold-Bond (1995) argues that Hegel anticipates Freud in this respect (135). Van der Meulen (1963) too agrees that in the feeling soul section Hegel is concerned with what we today call the unconscious (260). On the other hand, Ferrarin (2001) calls this "indeterminate pit" "self-consciousness" (73), but by this he means only that in it the soul is identical with its content (which is true of the unconscious). Of course, to call it the "unconsciousness" may be misleading insofar as consciousness (*Bewußtsein*) as Hegel conceives it has not been deduced yet. The contrast here is thus more between the truly awoken mind and the mind that sleeps even in its waking state.

6. See the VPGes 38 where Hegel says, "Character [*Charakter*] comprises all inner particularities, the way one behaves in private relationships, etc."

7. "[T]he two natural ways of entering into the council chamber of the gods and to have foreknowledge of destiny are sleep and frenzy" (Montaigne [1991] 640).

8. *Theaetetus* 184b-d.

9. As here Hegel discusses feeling as an abstract moment of subjective spirit, so Rousseau (1932) discusses a similar form of experience as an abstraction, a stage to be surpassed temporally in an individual life. I give my own translation, but I am not sure it is better than the one offered by Bloom: "Suppose an infant had at its birth the size and strength of a grown man; that he emerged, so to speak, fully armed from his mother's womb like Pallas emerged from the brain of Jupiter; this man-child would be a perfect imbecile, an automaton, an immobile and nearly insensible statue: he would see nothing, he would hear nothing, he would

know no one, he would not know how to turn his eyes toward what he needed to see: not only would he not perceive any object outside of him, he would not even relate anything to the sense organ which made him perceive it; colors would be nothing in his eyes, sounds would be nothing in his ears, bodies he touched would be nothing for his own [body], he would not even know that he is one: the contact of his hands would be in his brain; all of his sensations would form around a single point; he would only exist as a common *sensorium*; he would have only one idea, that of himself, to which he would relate all of his sensations; and this idea, or rather this feeling [*sentiment*] would be the only thing that he would have in addition to what an ordinary infant has" (tome premier 71–72).

10. See for example Fodor (1983), especially 23–38.

11. See for example EPW §§379, 445A.

12. I hesitate to identify Hegel's anthropology with what in modern analytic philosophy is called "philosophy of mind" because what analytic philosophers generally mean by "mind" is what Hegel would call "consciousness [*Bewußtsein*]": an empty subjectivity relating to external, corporeal objects.

13. Halbig (2002) 129.

14. Kant (1974b) 5:306–310.

15. Hegel, EPW §405Z p131.

16. EPW §406A. See also EPW §405A, and §406Z p144.

17. EPW §405Z p132. See also VPG 37 (as well as EPW §392Z pp56–57) where Hegel contrasts the ancient Greeks and Romans with the people of modernity. The ancients relied on oracles to give them direction regarding what to do in this or that situation. Moderns on the other hand use their own subjectivity to prudently consider all of the circumstances and make their own decision. Of course, the mere feeling soul (whether of a person of the last few centuries or not) is not such a prudent calculator and only obeys an *internal* oracle where the ancients obeyed an external one. Hegel refers to the ancient use of oracles in the context of his discussion of the universal soul and the tendency of the individual soul (in its capacity as the actuality of the universal soul) to identify immediately with nature. Thus the flight or innards of birds can be taken as a sign of the course one should take. Even when Hector chided Polydamas (who argued that an attempt to capture the Argive ships was inauspicious at the time because a serpent had just escaped the clutches of an eagle flying overhead), repudiating him by saying, "Bird signs!/ Fight for your country—that is the best, the only omen!"(Homer [1990] XII 280–281), Hector advocated pressing on only because of trust in *another*, prior sign given by Zeus (XII 272–273, 278–279), not because of the strength of his own independent subjectivity. For the universal soul (in the individual soul, its actuality), the whole of (external) nature is its genius, its oracle, just as the "feeling totality" of the individual feeling soul's inner "indeterminate pit" of feelings is its oracle and genius.

18. EPW §405A.

19. Thus Hegel defines the genius as "sensation without consciousness [*der bewußtlose Empfindung*]" (VPG 89n.92).

20. EPW §481.

21. Winfield (2011) argues that in any actual case of this occurring, the feeling soul is embodied, subject to influence from its environment and generating feelings internally independent of the influence of the genius, so the influence of the latter on the former cannot be total (118).

22. EPW §389 & A.

23. It is insofar as the feeling soul extends over bodies without regard to difference on any merely natural level (mechanics, chemism, biology) that Van der Meulen (1963) characterizes it as the sphere of formal intersubjectivity (260).

24. EPW §392 & A.

25. EPW §405.

26. In other words, a "simple substance," or a "soul" (Leibniz [1900] §19).

27. Leibniz (1900) §3.

28. Leibniz (1900) §56.

29. As he also does in the lectures on the philosophy of spirit from 1827/1828 (VPG 87).

30. EPW §398Z p92. See also VPG where Hegel defines sleeping as that state in which "[t]he condition of being divided [viz., waking] is negated, sublated, such that the natural individual, which was divided, is identical with itself" (61).

31. EPW §405Z p130.

32. Moreover, it was probably this terminological change that prompted Hegel finally to explicitly differentiate *Empfindung* from *Gefühl*.

33. EPW §398A. See also VPG 62–63.

34. EPW §405Z p130.

35. EPW §405A. See also VPG 89–90.

36. See Enoch and Ball (2001) 95–108.

37. Enoch and Ball (2001) 100.

38. Trethowan and Conlon (1965) 57.

39. Lipkin and Lamb (1982) 509.

40. Clinton (1987) 59. See also Munroe and Munroe (1971) 11.

41. Enoch and Ball (2001) 179–206.

42. Hegel, EPW §406Z p139. Saint Vitus's dance was one of the "dancing plagues" of the Middle Ages, in which manic, ecstatic dancing in one person would spread to dozens or hundreds.

43. Enoch and Ball (2001) 201.

44. EPW §405A. This is perhaps an unfortunate phrase to use, as it seems to indicate some occult phenomenon, an implication that is inaccurate.

45. VPGes 46. Hegel even calls heroes here "the soul-leaders [*die Seelenführern*]" of their peoples.

46. For Kant as well, an artist qualifies as a genius only if an audience experiences his work as beautiful.

47. VPGes 83–84, 142.
48. VPGes 282–283.
49. EPW §549A.
50. GPR §150A.

51. The reason I say that the rhetorical hold a leader can have on followers is not necessarily pathological is that the world we live in is not yet just. It is not even substantially just, needing only some refinement around the edges. Accordingly, there is still room for heroes in our world—indeed, there is an urgent need for them. But this point is only tangentially related to an investigation into the soul, so I will not pursue it here.

52. Thus he recognized that a so-called clairvoyant may simply be deceiving himself about what he sees (EPW §406A).

53. That once the two speculative principles given earlier are accepted the admission of instances as genuine cases of the feeling soul in its immediacy is strictly a matter of *judgment* should prompt the twenty-first-century reader to take the feeling soul section seriously (despite the incredible accounts it contains). Hegel's errors in judgment do not at all besmirch the principles of speculative philosophy. The modern reader should also note that Hegel should be forgiven these errors, insofar as his articulation of the principles of speculative philosophy was quite good, and the mistakes he made in judgment are perfectly understandable given the information that was available to him at the time.

54. See EPW §448Z p251, where Hegel describes Goethe as doing precisely this in his literary creation.

55. EPW §406A & Z p150. See also VPG 97.

56. VPG 105.

57. Winfield (2011): "To be put in the hypnotic trance in the first place, the subject must have consciousness as well as linguistic intelligence, just as much as does the hypnotizer. This is because the hypnotizer acts consciously upon a conscious subject, using language to facilitate the immersion in hypnotic 'sleep,' commanding the subject to focus on an isolated, reiterated perceptual stimulus, in oblivion to the contextual relations that allow for conscious distinguishing of subject and object. Hypnotic suggestion then employs speech to influence the unconscious psyche, relying upon the submerged linguistic capability of the subject and the passivity of feeling. Although hypnosis relies upon the psyche's susceptibility to immediate influence, the hypnotizer exercises influence over another mediated by consciousness and intelligence" (119).

58. EPW §406A & Z p141. See also VPG 94–95.

Chapter 7

1. The abundance of lecture notes on this area is a boon and should not be scorned. Hegel published his *Encyclopedia* only in outline (*im Grundrisse*) to

guide students taking his courses. The published text was therefore always intended to be supplemented by his lectures. I will make use of all pertinent lecture material in our investigation into self-feeling and habit: both Erdmann's and Walter's transcripts from 1827/1828 and Boumann's *Zusätze*, while still giving the *Haupttext* its due precedence.

2. For a more focused explanation of this sort, see Berthold-Bond (1995).

3. This is how it is defined by Aristotle (*On Dreams* 458a26–28) and Kant (2006) 68.

4. "For the purely negative is dull and flat and therefore either leaves us empty or repels us [. . .]. Thus the devil in himself is a bad figure [. . .] for he is nothing but the father of lies and therefore an extremely prosaic person" (Hegel [1988] 222).

5. Thus Hegel says that madness is a privilege (*Vorrecht*) only of human beings (EPW §408Z p168).

6. As Magrì (2016) puts it: "Sanity is not necessarily opposed to madness, but rather calls for a proper cultivation of the mind" (78).

7. VPR (1824) 175–176. The same idea appears almost verbatim in the 1831 lectures (VPR [1831] 123–124).

8. VPR (1827) 285–286.

9. As DeVries (1988) says (71), and as is suggested by the change of the section's title from "the dreaming soul" to "the feeling soul" in 1830.

10. VPR (1831) 124.

11. VPR (1824) 182–183. He also says this in the 1827 lectures (VPR [1827] 287–288) and in the 1831 lectures (VPR [1831] 135), though he there says "I" instead of "consciousness." Of course, *das Ich* and *das Bewußtsein* are one and the same (EPW §§412, 413).

12. EPW §365A & Z pp489–492.

13. EPW §371.

14. EPW §§375–376.

15. EPW §408Z p164.

16. EPW §408. The whole quote was added in the second edition (here the text is from the third, with negligible modifications from the second). Rather than putting the whole thing in bold, I thought it more appropriate to make this note here. See also Hegel's lectures: "In illness, that which is not under the control of our conscious actuality emerges" (VPG 109).

17. "As self-feeling, we are identical with our corporeity" (VPG 109).

18. Butler (2000) 38; Mills (1996) 62–63.

19. GPR §§185, 195.

20. GPR §§200, 237, 241.

21. GPR §198, EPW §526.

22. GPR §245.

23. GPR §§185, 244.

24. GPR §§246–248.

25. GPR §§189, 193, 197.

26. "The bourgeoisie, wherever it has gotten the upper hand, has put an end to all feudal, patriarchal, idyllic relations. It has pitilessly torn asunder the motley feudal ties that bound man to his 'natural superiors,' and has left remaining no other nexus between man and man than naked self-interest, than callous cash payment" (Marx and Engels [1978] 475).

27. "**In this basic division [*Urteile*], the soul is subject in general, its object being its substance, which is at the same time its predicate. This substance is not the content of its natural life, but has being as the content of the individual soul, filled as this is with sensation**" (EPW §404). This quote does not belong to the section on self-feeling in particular, but it comes from the introductory paragraphs to the feeling soul section generally, so it is applicable. Wallace and Miller have mistranslated this passage by reading *noch* for *nicht*. Thus they render the second sentence quoted earlier in the following way: "This substance is still [!!] the content of its natural life"—as a result of this error, they must introduce the following locution into Hegel's text (indicated in italics): "[. . .] but *turned into* the content of the individual sensation-laden soul."

28. Hans-Christian Lucas (1991) has made the interesting observation that the logical basis for Hegel's understanding of the sickness of the soul must be in the quality section of the doctrine of being (284–285). Lucas makes much of a certain *Zusatz* in which Hegel says that quality is a determinacy that is identical with being. If something is defined by its quality, then its loss of this quality entails the loss of the thing itself (EPW §90Z). Thus, Hegel says, quality is a determination that belongs to nature rather than spirit. Or, one might say, quality pertains to nature and to spirit in its immediacy. Lucas's thesis that self-feeling is a concretion of "quality" is plausible insofar as madness does involve the soul's identification with a determinate particular content, and the resulting instability, such that with the loss of this content the soul loses itself.

29. VPG 114. See also EPW §408Z pp172–173.

30. VPG 115. See also EPW §408Z p173.

31. VPG 115. See also EPW §408Z p174. Petry translates *Faselei* as "desipience," but the term is so rare in English I've chosen to use Wallace's and Miller's "rambling."

32. VPG 115–117. See also EPW §408Z pp174–175. Petry translates *die eigentliche Narrheit* as "folly proper," but because the term folly is antiquated and when used today is nearly always meant only hyperbolically (to refer to something imprudent but not a sign of mental illness), I've chosen to avoid it and use simply "mental illness proper" instead.

33. VPG 117–118. See also EPW §408Z pp176–177. Here again I think Wallace's and Miller's translations are more helpful. Petry renders *Tollheit* and *Wahnsinn* as "madness" and "insanity," respectively. While it is true that these German terms

can be used in the broad sense of Petry's chosen English translations, these are distinct forms of mental illness for Hegel, and the use of these terms invites the supposition that these name the entire class of deranged phenomena. "Mania" better describes how Hegel treats *Tollheit*, namely, as a singular fixation on one thing, and "frenzy" conveys the desperation Hegel intends in *Wahnsinn*.

34. EPW §408A.

35. I said earlier, in this illness the soul "accords objective reality" to its fixed idea. This does not imply however that the object of such a fixation must not exist, but only that it does not exist as the ill person thinks it does. The object of such an obsession in this example can thus be a real person, but perhaps one who does not entertain any direct interest in the mentally ill person's affairs, or have the qualities attributed to her.

36. At least this is how the classically liberal state is organized: in Locke's (1980) view, each *individual* has the inherent right to execute the laws of natural right (§7).

37. PG §§584-589.

38. GPR §151. Patriotism too, the disposition to trust the state, is called *habitual* for the citizen (GPR §268). See Barbara Merker (1990), who traces the reappearance of habit in later parts of the EPW and GPR (233-243), and chapter 8 of this book.

39. When habit has been condemned by other philosophers, it is usually this slackening of the intensity that was meant. For instance, Rousseau (1932) has nothing laudatory to say about habit (tome premier 258-259). Herder (1967b, 454-461) and Nietzsche (1925, 13-15) were no more kind.

40. Of course, part of neurosis is the way the soul shields itself from experiencing this by suppressing certain knowledge and experiences, transference, and so on. But these neurotic activities only show in just how much danger the soul is of having its relation to its *idée fixe* disrupted.

41. Thus no insanity is incurable aside from what Erdmann records as "idiocy as such [*der Blödsinn überhaupt*]" (VPG 114) and Boumann has recorded as "*natural* idiocy [natürlichen *Blödsinn*]" (EPW §408Z p172) (Petry translates *Blödsinn* as "imbecility," which I have followed here). From Hegel's descriptions, this seems to be what we would today call mental retardation, and which is incurable because it stems from physiological causes.

42. Chepurin (2018) 111.

43. EPW §409A.

44. "Only because we have habituated ourselves through experience to dealing with situations in determinate ways are we able to face similar situations readily, without being overwhelmed by them, with the speediness of thought and movement that comes from training"(Ferrarin [2001] 280).

45. VPG 120. See also EPW §408Z p179.

46. Hegel often notes how the bare expression of a problem can point to

its solution: "Nothing is known, or even felt as a *limit* or lack until one is above and *beyond* it"(EPW §6A); "Insofar as we know something as limited, we are already beyond it" (VPR [1827] 317); "the very fact that we know our limitation is evidence that we are beyond it, evidence of our freedom from limitation" (EPW §386Z p36); "Even when *finite* reason is spoken of, it proves that it is infinite simply by determining itself as *finite*; for negation is finitude, lack only for that which is the *existing sublation* [*das* Aufgehobensein] of it, the *infinite* relation to itself" (EPW §359A).

47. Erdmann (VPG 121-122), Walter (VPG 119-120 and 122n line 845), and Boumann (EPW §408Z pp181-182) all describe this.

48. VPG 122n line 845. See also EPW §408Z p182.

49. *Republic* 332a.

50. *Republic* 334b-d.

51. The meaning of θεράπων is usually given as simply the "companion" or "servant" of a warrior. Yet etymological research has shown that the word came to Greece from Anatolia via the Hittites, and that it means most properly such a ritual sacrificial victim who takes the place of the one performing the sacrifice. See Van Brock (1959).

52. EPW §§403A, 404, 409.

53. Winfield (2011) 132.

54. Ferrarin (2001) 279-280.

55. GPR §187. Once again, civil society need not be this way, but without the introduction of some new form of mediation, it can only be the war of all against all. By the same stroke, the male also loses the ability to appreciate the alterity of those members of his household who are not adult males, who become in his eyes not valueless objects but *his own* in the most privative sense, for which no independence can be allowed.

56. Sophocles (1982) 228, 252.

57. Sophocles (1982) 128.

58. PG §462.

59. "[T]o maintain itself, society often needs to see things from a certain standpoint and feel them in a certain way. It therefore modifies the ideas we would be inclined to have about them, and the feelings to which we would be inclined if we obeyed only our animal nature—even to the extent of replacing them with quite opposite feelings. Does society not go so far as to make us see our own life as a thing of little value, while for animals life is property par excellence? Thus to try to infer the mental makeup of the primitive man from that of higher animals is a vain quest" (Durkheim [1995] 62).

60. Foucault (1988) 16-32.

61. Foucault (1988) 36.

62. Foucault (1988) 35.

63. Foucault (1988) 190.

64. Foucault (1988) 190–191. See also 95–100, 107.

65. Foucault (1988) 94.

66. See the account Foucault (1988) gives about therapy as a kind of "centrifugal movement" to bring the subject out of itself (175–177).

67. Hegel, EPW §381.

68. See I Corinthians 1:25.

69. Schelling (2000) as well held that madness must be integrated into subjectivity if one is to avoid being a shallow "intellectual" (*Verstandesmensch*) (337–338 in the German edition, 102–103 in the English edition).

70. Foucault (1988) 247, 268.

71. Žižek (2009) 111–112. See also Chepurin (2018), who notes that Žižek goes too far in this respect (110).

72. This is not only the venerable position of a canonical philosopher such as Hegel: it is essentially the same position taken by Rancière (2011), who takes as a central aim the exposition of discourses that exclude certain unprivileged positions (and are constituted by this exclusion). As he notes in his explanation of his notion of "political dissensus": "Those who make visible the fact that they belong to a shared world that others do not see—or cannot take advantage of—is the implicit logic of any pragmatics of communication" (38).

73. Chepurin (2018) helpfully draws a connection between madness and Hegel's earlier presentation of the attitude of the youth, or adolescent, who similarly insists not on an ideal proper but on an abstraction in opposition to reality (while leaving open the intriguing possibility of a recuperation of madness in some sense as radical political activity) (113–115). See chapter 4 for my discussion of the ages of life.

74. Berthold-Bond (1995) 197.

75. Berthold-Bond (1995) 208.

76. Berthold-Bond (1995) 194.

77. Berthold-Bond (1995) 197.

Chapter 8

1. Hegel's deduction of ethical life follows other moments of objective spirit, or "right [*Recht*]," that is, justice: abstract right (relations between atomic persons and their property) and morality (the obligatory laws all agents *should* will as their ends). I do not mean what I offer in this chapter in opposition to this deduction of ethical life, but rather as a further refinement of it. The roots of ethical life are in the primitive, quasi-natural social groupings Hegel calls races and nations in EPW §§393–394. The ethical community is a *Nation* or *Volk* that is united by a religion. With the exception of Christianity (the "consummate" religion), each religion is "ethnic" or "determinate" insofar as it is the spiritual truth of a limited

part of the natural world. Accordingly, to properly understand ethical life one must trace it back to the anthropology. See EPW §552 & A, VPGes 69, GPR §270A, as well as Mowad (2013b) where I make this point at greater length. If it is granted that ethical life grows out of the anthropology, which also concerns how spirit can sink into primitive, pathological states, then it is natural to look there as well for material helpful in understanding defective forms of ethical life.

2. "World history, we know, is thus generally the unfolding of spirit in *time*, as the idea unfolds itself in space as nature" (VPGes 96–97).

3. There could be many more than the oppositions I have given here. For instance, there is certainly more to sound than pitch and volume. There is also timbre for instance (by virtue of which a trumpet playing a certain note at five decibels is still distinguishable from a piano playing the same note at the same volume), and this may be representable on some kind of spectrum as well. But in any case, the oppositions proper to the object of one sense are inaccessible to the other senses, such that however many ways we may distinguish sounds, colors are not high pitched any more than sounds are bright. Of course, we call sounds "dark" and "sweet," colors "loud," both colors and sounds "soft," and so on, but only metaphorically. Sounds can be "dark" only metaphorically because hearing and sight are senses inhering in corporeal sense organs each of which is uniquely receptive to phenomena of its domain.

4. Recall the discussion of corporealizing the emotions at the end of chapter 5, where I made a similar distinction.

5. Magrì (2016) 79.

6. Winfield (2011) 126.

7. EPW §410A.

8. EPW §410A.

9. Moland (2003) 149.

10. See Magrì (2016) 81–84 and Kirk Pillow (1997), who makes the case for a connection not just between habit and imagination as it is given in the psychology but also in between habit and the use of imagination in the creation of fine art.

11. EPW §§452–454.

12. EPW §§455–460.

13. Thus both habit and internalization/imagination are spirit's ability to create its own mediation between itself and its content. Hegel even uses the same language to describe them: just as habit mediates the relation between the soul and the feelings that would otherwise be buried in the "indistinct pit [*bestimmungsloser Schacht*]" of the unconscious (EPW §403A), so the production and use of images in internalization and imagination mediate intelligence's relation to its intuitions, which would otherwise be buried in the "night-like pit [*nächtlichen Schacht*] . . . without being in consciousness [*ohne daß sie im Bewußtsein wären*]" (EPW §453A). The difference between the unconscious proper to the soul and the unconscious proper to intelligence is that on the level of the soul, consciousness

(awareness of an object understood as *external* [EPW §413]) has not yet been posited at all, whereas on the level of intelligence not only is the externality of objects posited, but the interiority of spirit and the presence of external objects *within* spirit's interiority in the form of intuitions are also posited (EPW §445). Intelligence has an "unconscious" to the extent that the intuitions within it have not yet been sufficiently internalized (*erinnerte*) and thus are present within it as foreign contents, problematically accessible and not under intelligence's complete control. In this way, the formation and use of images by intelligence is a parallel process to the soul's habituation to feelings. See Winfield (2011) 130–131 for more on habit and memory.

14. Moland (2003) 155–164; Magrì (2016) 86.

15. We could say that *prosaic* language, the language of the understanding, is inadequate to express fully what we feel, but language can (and must) be poetic as well. A case can be made that Hegel would not agree with the limitations I am ascribing to the understanding: for instance, in the *Encyclopedia*'s psychology section the understanding (§467) succeeds the sign-creating imagination (§458 & A). Yet I have made it clear that I feel free to depart from Hegel's factual positions in pursuit of the spirit of his work—which I have no doubt he would expect scholars to do. It should also be borne in mind that for Hegel "intelligence" (of which the understanding is only the first shape) is fully realized only as *will*, which must realize itself in a social world of distinct cultures antedating the empirical individuals born into them.

16. The word of course has suffered from such overextension and overuse that often people of all stripes use it simply to express approval. But at its core it relates to someone or something that in the social sphere is not deceived by mere appearances and calmly rejects what ultimately is foolish but that is presented as the most serious thing by the dominant forces in the culture. Thus a teenager who does not take seriously the rules of high school, or anyone who sloughs off the drudgery and freely flouts the petty requirements of the workplace, is perhaps the paradigmatic image of someone who is cool. What is cool thus cannot be separated from some kind of counterculture. Probably the best way to explain what is cool to an ancient Greek would have been to point at Diogenes of Sinope, though what an American youth might rebel against was not even present in ancient Greece, so such communication would probably be impossible.

17. *Nicomachean Ethics* 1103b23–25.
18. *Politics* 1310a13–35, 1332b13–1334b28.
19. *Nicomachean Ethics* 1103b14–21, 1113a23–35.
20. GPR §§173–175.
21. GPR §239.
22. GPR §§268–270. See also GPR §153A.
23. There are of course, important differences between the two. Ferrarin (2001) explains: "As is the case throughout the Anthropology, the main differ-

ence between Hegel and Aristotle is that Hegel emphasizes man's pre-intentional and later explicit will, even in the lowest forms of his natural life. For Aristotle, instead, man's divinity is part of the cosmos, not symptomatic of a break with it" (283). Habit is the major step in humanity separating itself from nature for Hegel.

24. Hegel explicitly calls customs "habits" frequently. See for example EPW §§485, 486, GPR §151, as well as when he refers to the role of the ethical "disposition [*Gesinnung*]," which is simply another way of saying the same thing and even contains within it the connotation of "sense" (*Sinn*) (EPW §§486A, 513–515, 537–538; GPR §§268–269).

25. EPW §§457–459.

26. Of course, it is not as if there is a set of purely intellectual contents existing apart from any culture, as in a Platonic realm of ideas, that are then corporealized in different ways in such a way that whatever is expressed in one culture does or can find expression in any other culture. As a Westerner, I have heard that certain East Asian cultures wear white when mourning the loss of a loved one, and so I attach to their experience my word "grief." And while there is certainly something similar between what I feel when a loved one dies (and express by wearing black) and what a Chinese person feels when her loved one dies (and she expresses by wearing white), it is very plausible that notions of grief are shaped by culture. Thus I hesitate to assert that our feelings are identical while only the signs vary.

27. EPW §411. See Winfield (2011) 132.

28. EPW §456.

29. EPW §457. What Hegel calls a symbol is more like what linguists today (following Peirce [2011] 98–119) call an "icon." Linguists call a "symbol" what Hegel called a sign, which for linguists is a generic term for all semiotic representations, including the class for which Hegel gives no correlate, an "index," namely, a sign that draws its meaning from its physical relation to what it signifies (e.g., smoke signifying fire, or a footprint signifying the animal that made it).

30. See EPW §393 & A & Z, §394 & A & Z; VPG 39–48; VPGes 12, 105–133, 217–218, 232–233, 256–259, 277, 287–288, 341–342.

31. I realize the phrase "legitimate culture" opens a can of worms. I do not mean this in a very bold way. I only wish to exclude those short-lived, pseudo-independent, or miniscule social groupings that imitate a culture but lack the depth and richness to persist and provide a world of meaning for their members. For example, even if they declared independence, briefly had an army, printed money, and so on, the Confederate States of America was never a legitimate culture in its own right but rather a particularly lamentable faction of the culture of the United States of America.

32. Needless to say, I do not intend what I say here to sum up the social and political significance of race and gender. Rather, I intend only to show how the forms by which the individual soul recognizes and fails to recognize what is alien to itself, and how it recognizes its own particularity, can be identified as

operative on the level of an entire culture as well. In the process, I will make the case that a genuinely democratic culture has achieved socially what habit allows the individual soul to achieve with respect to its own experience.

33. Sadly, when he does speak of appearance, one wishes he had remained silent. See VPG 40–42.

34. Nor am I able based on firsthand experience to describe the female experience, though I will make reference to it relying on what women have written. I acknowledge this dependence and that what I write here is corrigible in a deeper way than that in which any exercise in philosophy is corrigible. If the reader finds that I have taken too great a liberty here or there, or that my lack of firsthand experience has skewed my presentation, I welcome efforts to identify such shortcomings.

35. This usage is not my innovation: Aimé Césaire (1956) explicitly argues that racial hierarchy in places like the United States counts as a case of colonialism (190), and this was generally the way racial hierarchy was treated at the two congresses of Negro writers and artists in the 1950s (*Présence Africaine* [1956]), over the objections of some American attendees. Adell (1994) however notes that Du Bois himself endorsed this usage (52–53); see also Du Bois (1999): "Can you imagine the United States protesting against Turkish atrocities in Armenia, while the Turks are silent about mobs in Chicago and St. Louis; what is Louvain compared with Memphis, Waco, Washington, Dyersburg, and Estill Springs? In short, what is the black man but America's Belgium, and how could America condemn in Germany that which she commits, just as brutally, within her own borders?"(20). Thus, by the 1960s Baldwin (1967) said that the policeman is hated in Harlem as a representative of "the force of the white world," and that there he is "like an occupying soldier in a bitterly hostile country" (361), and Newton (2002) likewise treated African American communities generally as colonized by occupying forces (135–136).

36. GPR §§147 & A–148 & A. Aristotle's presentation of the development of ethics and its politically integrative function can also be understood in this way, insofar as Aristotle gives no attention to the way critical divisions in a political culture call the perspective of the authoritative members into question. In contrast, Aeschylus's *The Persians* can be read as Greek culture that, stimulated by the jarring encounter with foreigners, turns back on itself, recognizing itself as something distinct. This national self-examination is carried out in the form of tragedy, such that Greek culture is the medium of examination and the object.

37. In the ethical "self-conscious *freedom* has become *nature*" (EPW §513).

38. Fine (1983) 34–43, 181–197.

39. A helpful overview is provided by Mallon (2006).

40. There is also vigorous debate about what it means to say that race is socially constructed. Piper (1992) gives an influential explanation for how these racial boundaries can be fluid in a certain sense, such that one can be of one race yet "pass" for another: that is, be taken or accepted by people as being of another

race (30–31). Michaels (1994) criticizes her, arguing that the very idea of passing presupposes racial essentialism, insofar as to be accepted as belonging to race X while one is *really* race Y means to invoke some criteria for true racial identity apart from the constructivist one of how one is socially categorized (767–768). Gooding-Williams (2006) defends Piper against this criticism, noting that Piper distinguishes between visual and cognitive identification: the former is how one is perceived, but the latter involves other criteria handed down socially as determining race but that may not be immediately apparent in a person. Thus the United States can adhere to the "one drop rule," that any black ancestry makes one black, while some people who meet this criterion for being black may still often be perceived as white due to light skin (91). Many commentators have also taken issue with the claim that socially constructed race really creates the same conditions for all members (e.g., men and women) designated as in the group: see Spelman (1988) 114–159, Gooding-Williams (2009) 228–235, Reed (1999) 12–16. The racial constructivist hypothesis I am advancing clearly rejects any racial essentialism in the biological sense, but I do not think it need involve the claim of invariant conditions across the membership of a race. Gooding-Williams (2009) for instance argues that there is no unitary antiblack racism and thus no unitary set of black political interests, insofar as black economic elites profit from a system that maintains poor blacks at the most abysmal level, where they cannot effectively compete with white workers and in turn inflame a hostility toward all blacks that might harm even black elites (229–230). I accept and appreciate the nuances of this "intersectional" approach, but I would also note that while all those designated as a member of a certain race need not have identical political interests, these political interests can vary *only because of* the intervention of factors that attenuate the adherence of certain members to their (designated) race. If a race is understood in a racist society as having quality X, but some members are admitted as not having this quality, this is only because those members are understood as acting in a racially uncharacteristic way, such that these are exceptions that underscore the broad legitimacy of the rule (as something with social force). André Breton offered what he thought was praise for Césaire in writing: "Here is a black man who handles the French language unlike any white man today" (in the original introduction to *Cahier d'un retour au pays natal*). As Fanon (2008) notes, there should be no surprise in this unless poetic skill in French is taken as a white characteristic (22). Césaire is here admitted into a higher class of blacks because of his poetry (introducing a gap between his objective interests and those of other blacks), but not because the social assignment of race is meaningless: to the contrary, Césaire is here exalted only in a way that reinforces the racial designation of blacks as inarticulate and not excelling in fine things like poetry.

    41. Accordingly, talking about "white" and "black" as real social categories, taking them seriously as the conventions that they are, need not involve endorsement of their claim to *natural* reality. Thus there is no reason to deny what Shelby

(2005) calls "the blackness of whites" (170), that is, that cultural influence originally coming from blacks has had a disproportionately large (if often unacknowledged) effect on what is thought of as the culture of American whites. The way this influence has been effected and its source concealed is very relevant for understanding how racial identity gets assigned and recognized, but the fact that racial definition loses its clarity very quickly once one begins to systematically examine it does not undermine the investigation of it *as a form of social consciousness*.

42. I know that to be an Arab is a linguistic classification (viz., to speak Arabic as one's native language), and to be a Muslim in principle has absolutely nothing to do with physical appearance. Yet Americans do treat both as a race, or as the same race, associating them with a certain physical appearance (see Beydoun [2013]) that, due to ignorance, actually blends stereotypes of Gulf and Levantine Arabs, Sikhs, and Hindu Indians.

43. Alcoff (2006) 185.

44. I am using the term "ideology" in a way that I believe is largely consistent with its general use in the Marxist tradition broadly speaking: from *The German Ideology*, through Althusser to Žižek, though I do not mean to commit my argument here to every detail offered in these critical elaborations of ideology.

45. For example, Arab hospitality is twisted by colonial regimes into lack of foresight or economy (Memmi [1991] 83–84).

46. That the colonized are never given individuality is what Memmi (1991) calls "the mark of the plural" (85). See also Said (1979), who makes a similar point (229–230), as well as Fanon ([2008] 138–140) and Memmi ([1991] 71), who argue that for whites the black man is always classified as something biological, in addition to Césaire (1995), who says mockingly: "Nothing could ever rouse us toward some noble desperate adventure./ So be it. So be it./ I am of no nationality ever provided for by chancelleries./ I defy the craniometer. Homo sum, etc./ And let them serve and betray and die./ So be it. So be it. It was inscribed in the shape of their pelvis"(106–107, amending Rosello and Pritchard's translation slightly).

47. Du Bois (1994) 61.

48. Sapperstein et al. (2014).

49. Sampson and Rudenbush (2004). Memmi (1991) identifies the same principle in the colonial situation, where the colonized "grant him [the colonist] more than those who are the best of their own people; who, for example, have more faith in his word than in that of their own population" (12).

50. See how Fanon (2008) describes something similar (124–125), and Memmi (1991): "Indeed, a man straddling two cultures is rarely well seated, and the colonized does not always find the right pose" (124).

51. Memmi (1991) 23. See also Douglass (2005) 126–127.

52. Du Bois (1994): The world "only lets him [the black person] see himself through the revelation of the other [white] world"; by being black one has a "double consciousness [. . .] always looking at one's self through the eyes of others" (2). See also 122. The concept of double consciousness has rightly occupied a central

place in discussions of race. In describing it I need to do little to relate it to Hegel's view of social relations and conflict because Du Bois was deeply influenced by Hegel. See Rampersad (1976) for how Du Bois studied philosophy at Harvard with the Hegelian George Herbert Palmer and spent two years of further study at the University of Berlin, arriving when it was experiencing a Hegelian revival and studying with Heinrich von Treitschke (19–47). This Hegelian background is often noted by commentators: see for example Gooding-Williams (2006) 76–77, 94, 107; Williamson (1978) 37, 40; and Adell (1994) 12–13. Adell (1994) also notes that Du Bois refers frequently to Hegel in his Philosophy IV notebook (13).

53. Du Bois (1999) expresses finely the point that part of what is distinctive about modern social systems is not that they are hierarchical, but that the modern hierarchy is presented as rooted in physical immediacies of people's bodies: "Such degrading of men by men is as old as mankind and the invention of no one race or people. Ever have men striven to conceive of their victims as different from the victors, endlessly different, in soul and blood, strength and cunning, race and lineage. It has been left, however, to Europe and to modern days to discover the eternal worldwide mark of meanness,—color!" (24). See also Henry (2005) 87.

54. Fanon (2008) 185–187. In explaining Du Bois's notion of double consciousness, Gooding-Williams (2009) says it involves "the sensation of measuring one's soul by the tape of a world that looks on in amused contempt and pity" (80).

55. Often commentators refer to the struggle for recognition from the *Phenomenology*'s self-consciousness section as the Hegelian background of Du Bois's notion of double consciousness (Gooding-Williams [2006] 76–77; Adell [1994] 16). See also Fanon (2008) 191. Given its ubiquity in the literature, it would be contentious to deny its usefulness, but the importance of this section for social philosophy has been overstated: it has a clear connection neither to anthropological phenomena like race and gender nor to the social and political philosophy proper belonging to objective spirit. I suggest that what I offer here from the anthropology can better tie Du Bois's notion of double consciousness to Hegel's work.

56. Fanon (2008) 95.

57. To be sure, racism and sexism are not just two species of a larger genus "oppression": each is distinct in how it operates and in its effects. I mean here only to highlight a certain similarity insofar as each involves a hierarchy established based on a fetishized physical characteristic, such that those who possess this characteristic are invested with the authority of being human as such, not a particular class but the generality such that their experience is at once human experience, their concerns are human concerns, and so on.

58. Beauvoir (2011) 26.

59. Fanon (2008) 165. See also Althusser's (2001) similar point about Freud's unconscious and his notion of ideology (108–109).

60. Fanon (2008) 169. As Douglass (2005) puts it: "Such is the power of public opinion, that it is hard, even for the innocent, to feel the happy consolations of innocence, when they fall under the maledictions of this power" (222).

61. Du Bois (1999) 17. It is also worth noting that Du Bois's (1994) image of "second sight" (2) and being "born with a veil" (2) are references to African American folklore in the nineteenth century, according to which, drawing on the notions of animal magnetism and mesmerism current at the time, the seventh son (which Du Bois associates with blacks, the first six being Egyptian, Indian, Greek, Roman, Teuton, and Mongolian) may see ghosts and the future. For Du Bois this second sight for blacks means having a second consciousness, seeing the world as whites see it in addition to from their own perspectives. See Gooding-Williams (2009) 78. Gooding-Williams (2009) also casts doubt on Hegel's anthropology as the source of Du Bois's references to animal magnetism and mesmerism (insofar as their vogue in the nineteenth century makes it likely that they would have been known anyway) (281n34), but even if Hegel's anthropology is not the source of Du Bois's images, I intend my presentation here to show the strong connections between the best that can be drawn from Hegel's anthropological social philosophy and Du Bois's account of racial hierarchy.

62. Jacobs (2001) contrasts the clergy who use Christian liturgy to browbeat slaves into accepting their oppression to a more liberal one (though she does not use the word), who says, "Your skin is darker than mine; but God judges men by their hearts, not by the color of their skins" (62–63). Rejecting this liberal attitude does not mean rejecting the equal moral status of people, but only rejecting the flight from particularity that it involves, and the way this flight often fails to really grapple with inequality: here for example the subtext of the clergyman's remark is that though his audience is black, he does not hold it against them (as the fault that he still deep down takes it to be).

63. Williamson (1978) 24. See also Baldwin (1967), who says the Northerner "never sees Negroes. Southerners see them all the time. Northerners never think about them, whereas Southerners are never really thinking of anything else. Negroes are, therefore, ignored in the North and are under surveillance in the South, and suffer hideously in both places. Neither the Southerner nor the Northerner is able to look on the Negro simply as a man" (363). See also Douglass (2005) 64, 252–253, 260, 262–263, 276, 295ff., 335–336.

64. "This education involves neither the history nor the geography of the American continent where the individuals receiving it live, nor anything about the origins of the individuals who live in that region, and still less of the tragedy at the source of the current reality. This education seems to have but one sole purpose: to hide certain lacunae and certain realities. This peculiar instruction relates in each case to a country called Gaul, to the inhabitants of this country, the Gauls, to their heroism in space, their uncontestable authority in time, to the respect they deserve, to their superior humanity, and to their mystical conception of race" (Damas [2005] 85, my translation). See also Fanon (2008): "In the Antilles, the black schoolboy who is constantly asked to recite 'our ancestors the Gauls' identifies himself with the explorer, the civilizing colonizer, the white man who

brings truth to the savages, the lily-white truth. The identification process means that the black child subjectively adopts a white man's attitude. [. . .] Gradually, an attitude, a way of thinking and seeing that is basically white, forms and crystallizes in the young Antillean" (126).

65. Memmi (1991) 121. He continues: "Just as people avoid showing off their poor relations, the colonized in the throes of assimilation hides his past, his traditions, in fact all his origins which have become ignominious" (122); "Must he, all his life, be ashamed of what is most real in him, of the only things not borrowed?" (123).

66. See Malcolm X and Alex Haley (1999) 54–58: "This was my first really big step toward self-degradation: when I endured all of that pain, literally burning my flesh to have it look like a white man's hair. I had joined the multitude of Negro men and women in America who are brainwashed into believing that black people are 'inferior'—and white people 'superior'—that they will even violate and mutilate their God-created bodies to try to look 'pretty' by white standards. Look around today, in every small town and big city, from two-bit catfish and soda-pop joints into the 'integrated' lobby of the Waldorf-Astoria, and you'll see conks on black men. And you'll see black women wearing these green and pink and purple and red and platinum-blonde wigs. They're all more ridiculous than a slapstick comedy. It makes you wonder if the Negro has completely lost his sense of identity, lost touch with himself" (56–57).

67. See EPW §408.

68. King (2001) 209.

69. "If your history lesson is not learned/ You will not go to mass"(Damas [2005] 36).

70. "Shut up/ Didn't I tell you that you must speak French/ The French of France/ The French of the French/ The French French" (Damas [2005] 37).

71. Fanon (2008) 90–61. He earlier quotes several lines of "Hoquet" (4). Contrast Fanon's description to the way I described in chapter 4 how normal experience occurs: "As I see something and reach out to grab it, my visual and tactile experience project me into the external object and its qualities: my body does not appear to me as an instrument that I point and control to experience objects, but rather as something with which I am immediately identified but do not feel. All sensible experience occurs through my body but *in* the experience my body vanishes, yielding all attention to the object." The condition of making one's own body an external object (which begins in the awakening and ends in individual mental illness, or the social pathology of white supremacy) makes normal experience impossible.

72. Merleau-Ponty (2002) 114–115.

73. Damas (2005) 26.

74. See also "En file indienne," where aspects of his native Antilles seem strange and are linked to another foreign culture (31), as well as "Regard" (69).

75. The relation is very similar to the one Hegel describes in the "Culture" section of the *Phenomenology*, where in order for the individual to *count* or to be worth anything (*gilt*), he must universalize himself, ridding himself of all particularity (PG §488), in return for which he should receive some recognition as having achieved this status, but this recognition is contingent on the arbitrary will of another (PG §§516–517). This leads to the "tearing apart" (*Zerissenheit*) of the human personality (PG §515). See the way Douglass (2005) describes how any behavior of a slave can be seen by the slaveholder as "impudent" (80, 88, 95, 100, 196, 240, 327).

76. Memmi (1991) 72–73. As a student I lived in Lyon, France, in la Guillotière, a neighborhood of French people with mainly Algerian heritage. It was abundantly clear to me then, and I have since become only more certain, that the French emphasis on *laïcité* (secularism) waxes and wanes to a great degree depending on whether or not it involves Muslims. People who would not bat an eye at seeing a crucifix worn in public, even by a public official, fly into a rage at any public display of piety among Muslims. People in Bretagne, le pays Basque, and Savoie can form more or less serious separatist movements, and Parisians chuckle and exult in this wealth of diversity in France. De Gaulle is said to have asked, "How can anyone govern a country that has 246 different kinds of cheese?"—and more than once a French person reminded me proudly that the number is closer to 350. But show these people a woman with a scarf over her hair and from out of nowhere the "deep-rooted" principles of republicanism and unity in a common culture come roaring back.

77. Damas (2005) 63.

78. Damas (2005) 27, 65.

79. Damas (2005) 60.

80. Hegel (1988) 8, EPW §24Z no. 3.

81. Recall the example of the mentally ill person who claimed to be the Holy Spirit. Therapy consisted in that case of having another retort: "How can you be the Holy Spirit? *I* am it." This counter-absurdity prompts the patient to vociferously argue that a single person cannot simply *be* the Holy Spirit, whereupon his mental illness begins to abate. See VPG 122n line 845 as well as EPW §408Z p182.

82. Memmi (1991) 132.

83. Césaire (1995) 100, 101.

84. Memmi (1991) calls this "the Nero complex": for the usurper to be shown *as* a usurper is to first posit that he has no right to what he claims: "This explains his strenuous insistence, strange for a victor, on apparently futile matters. He endeavors to falsify history, he rewrites laws, he would extinguish memories—anything to succeed in transforming his usurpation into legitimacy" (52). This can be seen for example in Israel's furious and mad attempts to deny that there is even such a thing as Palestinians, and in their systematic destruction of Palestinian

historical records and culture. See Khalidi (2007) xliii, Sheety (2014), Mermelstein (2011), and Dearden (2014).

85. Césaire (1995) 92, 93, amending Rosello and Pritchard's translation.

86. Césaire (1995) 86, 87, altering Rosello and Pritchard's translation slightly. See also: "In vain, twenty times over, in the tepid warmth of your throat do you ripen the same flimsy consolation that we are mutterers of words./ Words? As we handle quarters of the world, as we marry delirious continents, as we break down steaming doors, words, oh yes, words! but words of fresh blood, words which are tidal waves and erysipelas and malarias and lavas and bush-fires, blazes of flesh, blazes of cities . . ."(98, 99).

87. Accordingly, I reject outright any claim of an authentic racial identity, authentic interests apart from the relations with other groups and integration (in some sense) into a broader social system (relations that may not be emergent). When I refer to authenticity of a group I mean orientation against the group(s) and social mechanisms that oppress it, and toward ends that would relieve its oppression. Far from presupposing a prepolitical and enduring identity, what I mean by authenticity for an oppressed group is the disposition to act in a way that ends its subordination and terminates its identity as a subordinated group in opposition to other groups.

88. Memmi (1991) 91.

89. Memmi (1991) 99–100.

90. VPG 43, EPW §394Z p60, VPGes 120.

91. Césaire (2000) notes that there is no way to tell what would have become of a colonized country had colonization not taken place (45), and that the innovations of which colonists claim to be the only source can arise outside of Europe and without colonialism (45–46). Memmi (1991) makes the same point (112–113).

92. Hourani (1991) notes that in Memmi's own Tunisia the French *colons* pressed for annexation to France, dominating indigenous Tunisians by force, shunting them instead into a "traditional" culture that would keep them away from the levers of power (290).

93. The British used this most notoriously, and perhaps even invented it: Frederick Lugard, a colonial administrator, pioneered the method of "indirect rule" in what is today Nigeria. There he played on fears of French invasion to secure agreements from Yoruba, Hausa-Fulani, and Ibo ruling powers that their systems of government would be changed minimally, provided they agreed to fall under British "protection": this meant their foreign policy—and, de facto, a great deal of their domestic policy—would be decided by Britain, with the erstwhile rulers as the middle men. These authorities became at once extremely traditional (since the native culture ceased to develop and became rigid) and completely dependent on and deferential to the colonial power whose officers they were. See Gailey (1972) 123–124. In some cases, the British fabricated "native" institutions that had no

traditional basis at all, in order to use them as instruments of colonial control (180). It is telling then, that the push for decolonization ended up coming not from these supposed indigenous authorities, ostensibly representing Africans through African institutions, but from outside these leaders and institutions, and in opposition to them (July [1974] 585). The British later used indirect rule in Palestine as well: Khalidi (2007) notes that Palestine had a functioning Palestinian Arab Congress under Ottoman rule (41), but the British would not recognize it (42), instead designing a constitution to exclude national self-determination for the Arab majority (while carefully securing it for the Jewish minority [32], which the British groomed as their agent in the region). The British attempted to divide the native Palestinians into separate Muslim and Christian camps (arguing cynically that this was a traditional, indigenous division), but the Palestinians rejected this, defiantly forming Muslim-Christian associations (55). To undercut Palestinian efforts at self-determination, the British then created ex nihilo the Supreme Muslim Council in Palestine: a body that never existed previously in Palestine or anywhere in the Islamic world (55), as well as the mufti of Jerusalem, which had existed in Ottoman times but the British institution had much greater powers (56), and was occupied by Hajj Amin Al-Husayni, who received the fewest votes of the four candidates from the Jerusalemite Islamic leaders (56–57). Since the British withdrew, the Israelis have shown themselves to be the United Kingdom's apt pupils in imperialism, propping up the conservative fundamentalist group Hamas, providing funding and support over the years in order to weaken the Palestine Liberation Organization, which was secular and committed to principles of democracy (Sale [2002]). Khalidi cites a similar article (220n13) and also cites further evidence in interviews he conducted (220–221n19). See also Césaire's (2000) criticism of Tempels, the Belgian cleric in the Congo (today's DRC, then under Belgian colonialism) who promoted what he called "the black man's own particular spirit" and "Bantu philosophy"(58) as a counterweight to the influence of communism, which posed a genuine threat to Belgian colonialism. Reed (1999) relates how a relationship similar to the system of colonial "indirect rule" has prevailed with the rise of a black political class in the decades since the end of segregation.

94. Fanon (2008) xviii.

95. Gooding-Williams (2009) 132–133. See also Reed (1999) chapter 1.

96. Gooding-Williams (2009) 132.

97. In criticizing this call to begin from "the concrete," Marcuse (1969) says that it "illustrates a decisive truth about modern philosophy, that the standpoint of the concrete is frequently farther from the truth than the abstract. The reaction against German idealism saw an intellectual tendency gaining momentum, to merge philosophy with the concreteness of actual life. The demand was made that man's concrete locus in existence should replace abstract concepts in philosophy and become the standard of thought. But when his concrete existence bears witness to an irrational order, the defamation of abstract thought and the surrender to 'the

concrete' amounts to a surrender of philosophy's critical motives, of its opposition to an irrational reality" (370).

98. This is Du Bois's answer as well: Du Bois considers that white prejudice and its historical effects are the cause of the backwardness, and so black leaders must organize blacks to fight this prejudice in order to effectively allow the expression of the black ethos. The very self-assertion, the fighting of prejudice is what reforms the black masses into a coherent body fit to take its equal place in the nation (Gooding-Williams [2009] 19–65). This involves, Gooding-Williams (2009) argues, certain problems, such as how the leaders are able to appeal to the backward masses without sharing their backwardness (143ff.). In what follows I will argue that the ambiguity of anthropological speech, which can include poetry as well as cultural and political rhetoric, allows for it to function on higher and lower registers at the same time and may go some way to providing an answer to this difficult question.

99. Gooding-Williams (2006) 99. See Gilroy's (1993) similar criticism (188) of Asante (1989).

100. Gooding-Williams (2006) 99.

101. Fanon (2008) 200, 203. See also Douglass (1997b): "We have to do with the past only as we can make it useful to the present and to the future" (123).

102. Gooding-Williams (2006) 95.

103. Gooding-Williams (2006) 91.

104. Class division in the black community is indeed an impediment to ending racism (as many, e.g., Gooding-Williams [2009] 229–230) are right to point out), but I do not think this division amounts to the dissolution of the very idea of a coherent black social subject seeking liberation, leaving only disparate groups with similar complexion but contingently aligned interests. If we attend to class division not as the attenuation of racism (by at least allowing *some* blacks to rise into the middle and upper classes) but as its adaptation to the broad coalition that antisegregation activism made possible (splitting the movement), then it is clear that the struggle against racism is equally a struggle against the nonpolitical or antipolitical notions of success and thriving that animate the bourgeoisie (whether black or white). The issue then is not how to understand and organize truly antiracist and liberating politics without a coherent subject to be liberated, but rather how tactically to dispel the bourgeois ideology of individual professional success or constant consumption as the primary orientation for a person's actions in life in order ultimately to win the battle against racism.

105. Memmi (1991) 130. See also where he says: "though the xenophobia and racism of the colonized undoubtedly contain enormous resentment and are a negative force, they could be the prelude to a positive movement, the regaining of self-control by the colonized" (131–132). Malcolm X also makes the point that hostility of the colonized toward colonizers is not a blind prejudice but a hard lesson drawn from painful experience: "Unless we call one white man, by name,

a 'devil,' we are not speaking of any *individual* white man. We are speaking of the *collective* white man's *historical* record. We are speaking of the collective white man's cruelties, and evils, and greeds, that have seen him *act* like a devil toward the non-white man" (X and Haley [1999] 271).

106. Fanon (2008): "I wanted quite simply to be a man among men. [. . .] I wanted to be a man, and nothing but a man" (92), but in the face of degrading colonialism he declares, "I made up my mind [. . .] I will assert myself as a BLACK MAN" (95).

107. Fanon (2008) 196. See also Fanon (1963) and Douglass (1997a) 47–50 and (2005) 82, 187.

108. Shelby (2005) contrasts classical nationalism exemplified in Delaney (but which is more familiar to most people in Garvey, or Malcolm X before his hajj) to "pragmatic nationalism" (27–30). Classical nationalism involves an appeal to racial essentialism and an indelible racial identity and thus favors permanent separatism. Pragmatic nationalism (which is not meant to invoke the pragmatist school of American philosophy) rejects racial essentialism and separatist ideals in favor of appeals to racial identity only as a means to achieve social justice on matters where race is a factor. Shelby favors pragmatic nationalism insofar as, he says, classical nationalism has proved incapable of overcoming intraracial class division, and organizational centralization and institutional autonomy fail to embrace struggles of other oppressed people (such as the women's movement) both because of an obligation to support for them own sake and by spurning the opportunity to win allies (136–137). He holds up the Congressional Black Caucus and its relations to the varied constituencies of its members as an example of how black political solidarity can be maintained. The CBC champions legislation that will improve the lives of blacks and counteract the effects of racism by uniting many black legislators, sometimes with the cooperation of sympathetic nonblack legislators, even as it responds to criticism and petitions from blacks in civil society (activists, academics, figures in the media, etc.) (138–140). I appreciate Shelby's incisive analysis and his prescription is not dissimilar to mine. Yet I believe that in rightfully rejecting what he calls classical nationalism, his approach goes too far into liberal individualism, despite his protestations to the contrary (141, 154). He responds to the heterogeneity of the African American population (class division, etc.) by treating it as a boon rather than an obstacle, endorsing decentralization and "broad division of labor" (139), with some serving as elected leaders, others as intellectuals, some as wealthy benefactors, still others as activists, and so on. Circumstances set these different groups into action, with each prompting certain responses from the others and serving as a check on them, thereby achieving tangible political goals that elude classical nationalist organizations. Yet this decentralization, and the implied acceptance of class division as legitimate, appears to eliminate the possibility of a perspective from which this process may be critically examined. To avoid the pipe dreams of Black Power political groups, Shelby appears tacitly

to define success as the result of the give-and-take of these actors in civil society, their representatives, and the other parts of the government, such that if activists were pressing for more substantial changes, their position should be understood as only a moment of the truth, pushing the government as far to the left as was appropriate despite the way they understood their aims. The unachieved would thus be retrospectively interpreted as the impossible and naïve, in a perverse version of Hegel's equation of the true with the whole. Divisions between groups (such as powerful legislators who are cozy with funders hostile to ending racism, a constituency suffering the effects of racism, and activists who may articulate the interests of the constituency though without the power to enact it) are thus naturalized, as is the veto those with power have over those without. I am arguing for a kind of pragmatic nationalism as well, but the pragmatism here must not allow splitting the difference with the party of white supremacy in political haggling. I am certain that Shelby rejects this kind of compromise, but nonetheless I think his approach as he has articulated it can in some circumstances allow for it. The nationalism I endorse is pragmatic insofar as it serves to expose the contradiction implicit in the white supremacist position (that it illicitly attaches an "obvious" meaning to an intrinsically meaningless natural determinacy): once this therapeutic move is accomplished (which involves the implosion of white supremacy), the nationalism may "wither away," as Marx says of the state once the dictatorship of the proletariat has accomplished the effacement of class division. Accordingly, both Shelby and I call for pragmatic nationalism for the sake of eliminating the effects of racism and understand this to involve some sort of interracial cooperation, but I see a more positive (though temporary) role for autonomous racial institutions.

 109. Damas (2005) presents his Africanness as indelible, impossible to change, which is in fact the colonialist view of Africa: "The days themselves/ have taken the form/ Of African masks/ Indifferent/ To any profanation"(27); this African core makes it impossible for him to feel natural in a European covering: "I feel ridiculous/ in their shoes/ In their tuxedo/ In their dress shirt/ In their collar/ In their monocle/ In their bowler hat/ I feel ridiculous/ With my toes that were not made/ To sweat from morning until undressing in the evening/ With swaddling that weakens my limbs/ And lifts from my body its loincloth beauty" (41). See also 61.

 110. Césaire (2000) 44.

 111. Césaire (2000) 44.

 112. Césaire (2000) 52.

 113. Césaire (1995): "Haiti, where negritude for the first time stood up and declared that it believed in its humanity" (90).

 114. Césaire (1995) 86, 87.

 115. Magrì (2016) 75, 79–80. She goes on to show very deftly that habit is deeply involved in more advanced activities of the mind like memory, discipline, and self-cultivation (81).

 116. Nancy (1998) 31–32.

117. Nancy (1998) seems often (though not always) to express a low opinion of Hegel as someone who "brings about a totality" (2) and forecloses the possibility of a critical attitude. I do not think Nancy's position is quite so different from the most charitable interpretation of Hegel's social philosophy, but there is at least a difference in emphasis: Nancy is more preoccupied with showing the groundlessness of human identity, while Hegel's account places equal emphasis on the lack of a natural or biological ground and the need for some mediation to replace the aberrant, pathological destruction of all mediation. I will say more on this later.

118. That is why the term "democracy" was originally a term of opprobrium coined by aristocrats, meaning little more than chaos and mob rule.

119. Nancy (1998) 26.

120. I believe Winfield (1989) understands democracy in a compatible way and argues this is in line with Hegel's political philosophy. Democracy, he says, cannot be merely a political procedure to establish or protect some extra- or nonpolitical content (such as "natural" human rights), because then political life would be unfree, accepting as it would its content dogmatically (272). Justice cannot be prepolitical and instituted by democratic procedures: rather, justice and democracy must be *self*-grounding, acts of self-determination in the strongest sense (244). This involves the articulation of conventional institutions and the roles they involve (father, mother, official, civil servant, juror, et al.) (247). To confine politics to the promotion of this or that extra- or nonpolitical end is what Winfield (1991) calls a "deformation of politics" (171).

121. Lefort (1988) 11–12.

122. Agamben (2009) 86.

123. Gooding-Williams (2009) 237. "As pictured from a no-foundations perspective, black politics is constituted through controversy [. . .] 'all the way down' "(238). This is not inconsistent with my previous denial that black politics should be understood as having no authentic orientation because: (1) having skin of a certain shade has no fixed meaning but is only assigned a meaning through social and political relationships and processes (including both white supremacy and the rejection of it in negritude or "pragmatic nationalism"); (2) in the context of an oppressive system such as white supremacy, the authentic orientation of blacks and of all people (insofar as we are spirit and our "nature" is only to be free) is to work to destroy it, in a political movement analogous to the therapeutic "entrance into the delusion" of the disordered social subject; (3) the accomplishment of this therapy involves undermining any immediate identification of a natural determinacy with a fixed meaning anchoring the social system and replacing it with a foundationless "historical" or "habitual" social identity.

124. Winfield (1991) correctly identifies the major problem with modernity (liberalism and capitalism) as its failure to reconstitute some self-determining form of human interaction to replace what it has destroyed (108, 132).

125. In arguing against the "new orthodoxy" (e.g., Rorty, and I would add Nancy), which calls for corrigible, historical reason only and calls everything else foundationalism, Winfield (1989) notes that the very claim that reason must be understood as restricted in this sense is itself not a historical, corrigible claim, and that the criticism of articulations of reason in history presupposes the historical emergence of foundationless knowledge, though this foundationlessness does not predetermine how knowledge questions will be answered (20). His account is based on his reading of Hegel, and I believe it is compatible with the Hegelian account I am giving here. When I say that the historical and democratic ethical culture is open-ended and shaped by experience, I mean to exclude the same appeal to ahistorical cultural foundations that Winfield (1991) proscribes (232, 244–247). Winfield emphasizes the ability of reason to ground itself and provide a way to criticize shortcomings of existing cultures and states, but this self-determination is effected through the historical articulation of institutions and the progressive refinement of these institutions to purify them of the merely contingent and arbitrary aspects they would have owing to their precise origin in a certain part of the natural world and a precise point in history. The important point is: (1) that nothing outside of spirit's own articulation of itself in history may be appealed to, to ground justice; *and* (2) that this historical articulation itself must not be taken up as something positive but as something intended as rational and accordingly subject to criticism and further refinement. As I do—and as Hegel does—Winfield (1989) draws an analogy between objective spirit (social and political institutions) and subjective spirit (forms of embodiment and ways of individual knowing): just as the structure of consciousness, intersubjectivity, or language are necessary conditions for knowing but do not predetermine the standards for objectivity (since this would presuppose an account—itself antecedent to this foundation—of how they play this founding role), institutions in history cannot be dismissed as entirely contingent, but nor must they be endorsed in the shape they assume and as they have been handed down to us (112–114, 274–275): "Hegel, unlike the new orthodoxy, grasps the true lesson of subjective spirit, that consciousness, intersubjectivity and language all leave thought free of any limits other than those it imposes on itself. [. . .] Hegel strictly demarcates the legitimation of these [historical, political] institutions from the historical process by which they emerge. What gives the institutions of right their exclusive justice is that they are structures of self-determination. As such, they have no antecedent foundations from which their character derives. Hence, the history from which they arise can contribute nothing to their validity, neither by providing prior standards for justice nor by imposing external limits upon what can count as right and wrong" (114).

126. Accordingly, being "modern" in the sense merely of occurring after the scientific revolution, or the French Revolution, does not assure us of having just institutions. As a span of time, our century is as subject to the natural uncritical

immersion in nature and contingency as any other. As Peperzak (1987) notes, the "objectivity" of the law is the objectivity of the concept: it is objective insofar as it is received as something external by the arbitrary subjective consciousness, but not in the sense of necessarily being adequately expressed in whatever system of positive law happens to exist (6). Peperzak (2000) also remarks, "Neither facts nor history—e.g. in the form of the venerable past—can guarantee the rightness of enacted laws; they are no substitute for a conceptual insight into the rational necessity of their content" (179), and he explains Hegel's criticisms of some of his contemporaries who argued for the historicist view that the legitimacy of laws was grounded in the historical conditions of their emergence (180–183). See also Winfield (1989) 274.

127. Contrary to the common opinion of Hegel (which he admittedly invites with the way he writes at times) as one holding that the world and history have been completed, when Hegel spoke about his own time he usually remained sharply critical (VPR [1827] 265–270; VPGes 524–539).

128. VPGes 535, EPW §394Z pp67–68.

Conclusion

1. To give another example, the Holy Spirit is present in the Church, not in the immediacy of these precise bishops and cardinals—or even in all of the parishioners as mere immediacies—but in the collaborative process of theological reflection and the social act of worship that maintain the institution as a living one. It is not detached from the past (since that would leave only some immediacy to serve as the principle, even if this were only the whims of its members, or the random, uncritically examined influences of the here and now), but nor is it unthinkingly pushed forward by the dead weight of a tradition taken as something immediate, simply given, and not needing reflection and interpretation to bring out its meaning.

Bibliography

Abram, David. *The Spell of the Sensuous: Perception and Language in a More-Than-Human World.* New York: Vintage Books, 1997.

Adell, Sandra. *Double Consciousness/Double Bind: Theoretical Issues in Twentieth Century Black Literature.* Chicago: University of Illinois Press, 1994.

Agamben, Giorgio. *The Coming Community.* Translated by Michael Hardt. Minneapolis: University of Minnesota Press, 2009.

Alcoff, Linda Martín. *Visible Identities: Race, Gender, and the Self.* New York: Oxford University Press, 2006.

Alexander, Donald. "Bioregion: Science or Sensibility?" *Environmental Ethics* 12, no. 2 (1990): 161–173.

Al-Fārābī, Abū Nasr. *Al-Farabi on the Perfect State.* Translated by Richard Walzer. New York: Clarendon Press, 1985.

Althusser, Louis. *Lenin and Philosophy and Other Essays.* Translated by Ben Brewster. New York: Monthly Review Press, 2001.

Appiah, Anthony. "Race, Culture, Identity: Misunderstood Connections." In *Color Conscious*, edited by Anthony Appiah and Amy Gutmann. Princeton: Princeton University Press, 1996.

Apollodorus. *Library.* Translated by R. Scott Smith and Stephen Trzaskoma. Indianapolis: Hackett, 2007.

Apollonius of Rhodes. *The Voyage of the Argo.* Translated by E. V. Rieu. New York: Penguin Books, 1971.

Aristotle. *De Anima.* Translated by D. W. Hamlyn. Oxford: Clarendon Press, 1986.

———. *Generation of Animals.* Translated by Arthur Platt. In *The Complete Works of Aristotle*, edited by Jonathan Barnes, vol. 1. Princeton: Princeton University Press, 1984a.

———. *Metaphysics.* Translated by W. D. Ross. In *The Complete Works of Aristotle*, edited by Jonathan Barnes, vol. 2. Princeton: Princeton University Press, 1984b.

———. *Nicomachean Ethics.* Translated by Terence Irwin. Indianapolis: Hackett, 1999.

———. *On Generation and Corruption*. Translated by H. H. Joachim. In *The Complete Works of Aristotle*, edited by Jonathan Barnes, vol. 1. Princeton: Princeton University Press, 1984c.

———. *On Sleep*. Translated by J. I. Beare. In *The Complete Works of Aristotle*, edited by Jonathan Barnes, vol. 1. Princeton: Princeton University Press, 1984d.

———. *On Dreams*. Translated by J. I. Beare. In *The Complete Works of Aristotle*, edited by Barnes, vol. 1. Princeton: Princeton University Press, 1984e.

———. *The Politics*. Translated by T. A. Sinclair. Baltimore: Penguin Books, 1962.

———. *Physics*. Translated by R. P. Hardie and R. K. Gaye. In *The Complete Works of Aristotle*, edited by Barnes, vol. 1. Princeton: Princeton University Press, 1984f.

———. *Physiognomics*. Translated by T. Loveday and E. S. Forster. In *The Complete Works of Aristotle*, edited by Jonathan Barnes, vol. 1. Princeton: Princeton University Press, 1984g.

———. *Sense and Sensibilia*. Translated by J. I. Beare. In *The Complete Works of Aristotle*, edited by Jonathan Barnes, vol. 1. Princeton: Princeton University Press, 1984h.

Arnold, Matthew. *Dover Beach and Other Poems*. Mineola: Dover, 1994.

Asante, Molefi Kete. *Afrocentricity*. Trenton: Africa World Press, 1989.

Baldwin, James. "Fifth Avenue, Uptown." In *Twelve Prose Writers*. Chicago: Holt, Rinehart & Winston: 1967. Rpt. from *Esquire*, July 1960.

Beauvoir, Simone de. *The Second Sex*. Translated by Constance Borde and Sheila Malovany-Chevallier. New York: Vintage Books, 2011.

Beck, Benjamin. *Animal Tool Behavior*. New York: Garland Press, 1980.

Benhabib, Seyla. "On Hegel, Women, and Irony." In *Feminist Interpretations of Hegel*, edited by Patricia Jagentowicz Mills. University Park: Pennsylvania State University Press, 1996.

Berkeley, George. *Three Dialogues Between Hylas and Philonous*. Indianapolis: Hackett, 1979.

Bernasconi, Robert. "Religious Philosophy: Hegel's Occasional Perplexity in the Face of the Distinction between Philosophy and Religion." *Bulletin of the Hegel Society of Great Britain* 45/46 (2002): 1–15.

———. "With What Must the History of Philosophy Begin? Hegel's Role in the Debate on the Place of India within the History of Philosophy." In *Hegel's History of Philosophy: New Interpretations*, edited by David Duquette. Albany: State University of New York Press, 2003.

———. "With What Must the Philosophy of World History Begin? On the Racial Basis of Hegel's Eurocentrism." *Nineteenth Century Contexts* 22, no. 2 (2000): 171–201.

Bernasconi, Robert, and Tommy Lee Lott, eds. *The Idea of Race*. Indianapolis: Hackett, 2000.

Berthold-Bond, Daniel. *Hegel's Theory of Madness*. Albany: State University of New York Press, 1995.

Beydoun, Khaled A. "Between Muslim and White: The Legal Construction of Arab American Identity." *New York University Annual Survey of American Law* 69, no. 1 (2013): 29–76.

Blake, William. *The Portable Blake*. New York: Viking Press, 1974.

Boas, Franz. *Anthropology and Modern Life*. New York: W.W. Norton, 1962.

Buchwalter, Andrew. "Is Hegel's Philosophy of History Eurocentric?" In *Hegel and History*, edited by Will Dudley. Albany: State University of New York Press, 2009.

Butler, Judith. *Antigone's Claim: Kinship Between Life and Death*. New York: Columbia University Press, 2000.

———. *Bodies That Matter*. New York: Routledge, 1993.

———. *Gender Trouble: Feminism and the Subversion of Identity*. New York: Routledge, 2006.

Cannon, W. B. "The James-Lange Theory of Emotion: A Critical Examination and an Alternative Theory." *American Journal of Psychology* 39 (1927): 106–124.

Césaire, Aimé. "Culture et colonisation." *Présence Africaine* 8-10 (1956).

———. *Discourse on Colonialism*. Translated by Joan Pinkham. New York: Monthly Review Press, 2000.

———. *Notebook of a Return to My Native Land = Cahier d'un retour au pays natal*. Translated by Mireille Rosello with Annie Pritchard. Tarset, Northumberland: Bloodaxe Books, 1995.

Chepurin, Kirill. "Subjectivity, Madness, and Habit: Forms of Resistance in Hegel's Anthropology." In *Hegel and Resistance: History, Politics and Dialectics*, edited by Rebecca Comay and Bart Zantvoort. New York: Bloomsbury Academic, 2018.

Clinton, Jacqueline. "Physical and Emotional Responses of Expectant Fathers Throughout Pregnancy and the Early Postpartum Period." *International Journal of Nursing Studies* 24 (1987): 59–68.

Coleridge, Samuel Taylor. *The Notebooks of Samuel Taylor Coleridge*. Edited by Kathleen Coburn and Merton Christensen. New York: Pantheon Books, 1957–1973.

Coulanges, Fustel. *The Ancient City*. Garden City: Doubleday, 1956.

Damas, Léon-Gontran. *Pigments—Névralgies*. Paris: Présence Africaine, 2005.

———. *Retour de Guyane Suivi de Misère Noire, et autres écrits journalistiques*. Paris: Jean-Michel Place, 2003.

Deacon, Terence W. *Incomplete Nature: How Mind Emerged from Matter*. New York: W.W. Norton, 2012.

Dearden, Lizzie. " 'Israel has stolen 80,000 Palestinian books and manuscripts since 1948' Head of Arab League Claims." *The Independent*. October 28, 2014.

https://www.independent.co.uk/news/world/middle-east/israel-has-stolen-80000-palestinian-books-and-manuscripts-since-1948-head-of-arab-league-claims-9823864.html. Accessed July 30, 2018.

De Boer, Karin. *On Hegel: The Sway of the Negative*. New York: Palgrave Macmillan, 2010.

De la Mettrie, Julien Offray. *L'Homme machine: Oeuvres philosophiques de Mr. de La Mettrie*. Amsterdam: [n.p.], 1753.

De Laurentiis, Allegra. "On Hegel's Interpretation of Aristotle's *Psyche*: A Qualified Defense." In *Hegel: New Directions*, edited by Katerina Deligiorgi. Montreal: McGill-Queen's University Press, 2006.

Descartes, René. *L'Homme*. In *Oeuvres de Descartes*, edited by Charles Adam and Paul Tannery, tome 10. Paris: J. Vrin, 1964a.

———. *Principia philosophiae*. In *Oeuvres de Descartes*, edited by Adams and Tannery, tome 8. Paris: J. Vrin, 1964b.

DeVries, Willem A. *Hegel's Theory of Mental Activity*. Ithaca: Cornell University Press, 1988.

De Waal, Frans, and Pier Francesco Ferrari. "Toward a Bottom-Up Perspective on Animal and Human Cognition." *Trends in Cognitive Sciences* 14, no. 5 (April 2010): 201–207.

Donougho, Martin. "The Woman in White: On the Reception of Hegel's Antigone." *Owl of Minerva* 21, no. 1 (1989): 65–89.

Douglass, Frederick. *My Bondage and My Freedom*. New York: Barnes and Noble Books, 2005.

———. *Narrative of the Life of Frederick Douglass, an American Slave, Written by Himself*. Edited by William L. Andrews. New York: W.W. Norton, 1997a.

———. "What to a Slave Is the Fourth of July?" In *Narrative of the Life of Frederick Douglass, An American Slave, Written by Himself*, edited by William L. Andrews. New York: W.W. Norton, 1997b.

Du Bois, W. E. B. *Darkwater: Voices From Within the Veil*. Mineola: Dover, 1999.

———. *The Souls of Black Folk*. Mineola: Dover, 1994.

Dupré, Louis. "Hegel Reflects on Remembering." *Owl of Minerva* 25, no. 2 (1994): 141–146.

Durkheim, Émile. *The Elementary Forms of Religious Life*. Translated by Karen E. Fields. NewYork: The Free Press, 1995.

Düsing, Klaus. "Endliche und absolute Subjektivität: Untersuchungen zu Hegels philosophischer Psychologie und zu ihrer spekulativen Grundlegung." In *Hegels Theorie des subjektiven Geistes*, edited by Lothar Eley. Stuttgart-Bad Cannstatt: Frommann-Holzboog, 1990.

———. "Hegels Begriff der Subjektivität in der Logik und in der Philosophie des subjektiven Geistes." *Hegels Philosophische Psychologie*. Bonn: Bouvier, 1979.

Ellman, Richard, and O'Clair, Robert, eds. *Modern Poems*, second edition. New York: W.W. Norton, 1989.

Enoch, David, and Hadrian Ball. *Uncommon Psychiatric Syndromes*. New York: Hodder Arnold, 2001.
Epicurus. "Epicurus to Menoeceus." In *Epicurus: The Extant Remains*, translated by Cyril Bailey. Oxford: Clarendon Press, 1926a.
———. "Principal Doctrines." In *Epicurus: The Extant Remains*, translated by Cyril Bailey. Oxford: Clarendon Press, 1926b.
Erasmus. *Praise of Folly*. Translated by A. H. T. Levi. New York: Penguin Books, 1994.
Erman, Adolf. *Life in Ancient Egypt*. Translated by H. M. Tirard. New York: Dover, 1971.
Fanon, Frantz. *Black Skin, White Masks*. Translated by Richard Philcox. New York: Grove Press, 2008.
———. *The Wretched of the Earth*. Translated by Constance Farrington. New York: Grove Press, 1963.
Féléky, A. M. "The Expression of Emotion." *Psychological Review* 21 (1914): 33–41.
Ferrarin, Alfredo. *Hegel and Aristotle*. New York: Cambridge University Press, 2001.
Fichte, Johann Gottlieb. *Reden an die deutsche Nation*. Hamburg: Felix Meiner Verlag, 2008.
Fine, John V. A. *The Ancient Greeks: A Critical History*. Cambridge: Harvard University Press, 1983.
Fodor, Jerry. *The Modularity of Mind*. Cambridge: MIT Press, 1983.
Foucault, Michel. *Madness and Civilization: A History of Insanity in the Age of Reason*. Translated by Richard Howard. New York: Vintage Books, 1988.
Friel, Brian. *Translations: A Play*. New York: Farrar, Straus and Giroux, 1995.
Frost, Samantha. *Biocultural Creatures: Toward a New Theory of the Human*. Durham: Duke University Press, 2016.
Fulda, Hans-Friedrich. "Idee und vereinzeltes Subjekt in Hegels Enzyklopädie." In *Hegels Theoriedes subjektiven Geistes*, edited by Lothar Eley. Stuttgart-Bad Cannstatt: Frommann-Holzboog, 1990.
Gailey, Harry A. *History of Africa: From 1800 to Present*. Chicago: Holt, Rinehart and Winston, 1972.
Galdikas, Biruté. "Orangutan Tool Use at Tanjung Putang Reserve, Central Indonesian Borneo (Kalimantan Tengah)." *Journal of Human Evolution* 11 (1982): 19–33.
Gilroy, Paul. *The Black Atlantic: Modernity and Double Consciousness*. Cambridge: Harvard University Press, 1993.
Gooding-Williams, Robert. *In the Shadow of Du Bois: Afro-Modern Political Thought in America*. Cambridge: Harvard University Press, 2009.
———. *Look, a Negro! Philosophical Essays on Race, Culture, and Politics*. New York: Routledge, 2006.
Gordon, Lewis R. *Her Majesty's Other Children: Sketches of Racism from a Neocolonial Age*. Lanham: Rowman & Littlefield, 1997.
Gould, Stephen J., and Elizabeth S. Vrba. "Exaption—A Missing Term in the Science of Form." *Paleobotany* 8, no. 1 (1982): 4–15.

Greene, Murray. *Hegel and the Soul: A Speculative Anthropology*. The Hague: Nijhoff, 1972.

Halbig, Christoph. *Objektives Denken: Erkenntnistheorie und Philosophy of Mind in HegelsSystem*. Stuttgart-Bad Cannstatt: Frommann-Holzboog, 2002.

Haraway, Donna. *Modest_Witness@Second_Millennium.FemaleMan_Meets_OncEMouse*. New York: Routledge, 1997.

Harris, Errol. "Hegel's Anthropology." *Owl of Minerva* 25, no. 1 1993: 5–24.

———. "Hegel's Theory of Feeling." In *New Studies in Hegel's Philosophy*, edited by Warren E. Steinkraus. Chicago: Holt, Rinehart & Winston, 1971.

Harris, Henry. *Hegel's Ladder*. Two volumes. Indianapolis: Hackett, 1997.

Hegel, G. W. F. *Enzyklopädie der Philosophischen Wissenschaften im Grundrisse (1830) Erster Teil. Wissenschaft der Logik*. In *Werke* Band 8. Frankfurt: Suhrkamp Verlag, 1983a.

———. *Enzyklopädie der Philosophischen Wissenschaften im Grundrisse (1830) Zweiter Teil. Philosophie der Natur*. In *Werke* Band 9. Frankfurt: Suhrkamp Verlag, 1983b.

———. *Enzyklopädie der Philosophischen Wissenschaften im Grundrisse (1830) Dritter Teil. Philosophie des Geistes*. In *Werke* Band 10. Frankfurt: Suhrkamp Verlag, 1983c.

———. *Grundlinien der Philosophie des Rechts*. In *Werke* Band 7. Frankfurt: Suhrkamp Verlag,1986a.

———. *Hegel's Aesthetics: Lectures on Fine Art*, vol. 1. Translated by T. M. Knox. New York: Oxford University Press, 1988.

———. *System der Sittlichkeit*. Hamburg: Felix Meiner Verlag, 2002.

———. *Vorlesungen über die Ästhetik III*. Band 15. Frankfurt: Suhrkamp Verlag, 1986d.

———. *Vorlesungen über die Geschichte der Philosophie I*. In *Werke* Band 18. Frankfurt: Suhrkamp Verlag, 2014.

———. *Vorlesungen über die Philosophie des Geistes (1827/1828)*. In *Vorlesungen* Band 13. Hamburg: Felix Meiner Verlag, 1994.

———. *Vorlesungen über die Philosophie der Geschichte*. In *Werke* Band 12. Frankfurt: Suhrkamp Verlag, 1986b.

———. *Vorlesungen über die Philosophie der Religion (1827)*. In *Vorlesungen* Band 4a. Hamburg: Felix Meiner Verlag, 1985.

———. *Vorlesungen über die Philosophie der Religion (1827)*. In *Vorlesungen* Band 5. Hamburg: Felix Meiner Verlag, 1984.

———. *Vorlesungen über die Philosophie der Religion (1831)*. In *Werke* Band 16. Frankfurt: Suhrkamp Verlag, 1982.

———. *Wissenschaft der Logik*. In *Werke* Band 6. Frankfurt: Suhrkamp Verlag, 1986c.

Hegel, G. W. F., and Michael J. Petry. *Philosophy of Subjective Spirit. 2. Anthropology*. Dordrecht: Reidel, 1979.

Heidegger, Martin. *Sein und Zeit*. Tübingen: Max Niemeyer Verlag, 1953.

Henrich, Dieter. "Selbstbewußtsein: Kritische Einleitung in eine Theorie." In *Hermeneutik und Dialektik* Aufsätze I, ed. Rüdiger Bubner. Tübingen: 1970.
Henry, Paget. "Africana Phenomenology: Its Philosophical Implications." *C.L.R. James Journal* 11, no. 1 (2005): 79–112.
Herder, J. G. *Ideen zur Philosophie der Geschichte der Menschheit. Sämtliche Werke.* Band 13. Hildesheim: Georg Olms Verlagsbuchhandlung, 1967a.
———. *Journal meiner Reise im Jahr 1769.* In *Sämmtliche Werke.* Band 4. Hildesheim: Georg Olms Verlagsbuchhandlung, 1967a.
Hobbes, Thomas. *Leviathan.* New York: Simon & Schuster, 1997.
Hoff, Shannon. *The Laws of Spirit: A Hegelian Theory of Justice.* Albany: State University of New York Press, 2014.
Hoffheimer, Michael. "Hegel, Race, Genocide" *The Southern Journal of Philosophy* 39 (2001): 35–62.
———. "Race and Law in Hegel's Philosophy of Religion." In *Race and Racism in Modern Philosophy*, edited by Andrew Valls. Ithaca: Cornell University Press, 2005.
Homer. *The Homeric Hymns.* Translated by Thelma Sargent. New York: W.W. Norton, 1975.
———. *The Iliad.* Translated by Robert Fagles. New York: Penguin Books, 1990.
Horkheimer, Max. *The Eclipse of Reason.* New York: Continuum, 1974.
Hourani, Albert. *A History of the Arab Peoples.* New York: Warner Books, 1991.
Hume, David. *An Enquiry Concerning Human Understanding.* Indianapolis: Hackett, 1977.
———. *A Treatise of Human Nature.* New York: Oxford University Press, 2006.
Hyppolite, Jean. *Genèse et structure de la Phénoménolgie de l'esprit de Hegel.* Paris: Aubier, 1946.
Ibn Rushd. *The Decisive Treatise Determining the Nature and Connection Between Religion and Philosophy.* In *Philosophy in the Middle Ages*, edited by Arthur Hyman and James J. Walsh. Indianapolis: Hackett, 1987.
Jacobs, Harriett. *Incidents in the Life of a Slave Girl.* Mineola: Dover, 2001.
Jaeschke, Walter. "Absolute Subject and Absolute Subjectivity in Hegel." In *Figuring the Self*, edited by David E. Klemm and Günter Zöller. Albany: State University of New York Press, 1997.
James, William. "What Is an Emotion?" *Mind* 9 (1884): 188–205.
Johansson, C., C. Smedh, T. Partonen, P. Pekkarinen, T. Paunio, J. Ekholm, L. Peltonen, D. Lichtermann, J. Palmgren, R. Adolfsson, and M. Schalling. "Seasonal Affective Disorder and Serotonin-Related Polymorphisms." *Neurobiology of Disease* 8, no. 2 (2001): 351–357.
Jonas, Hans. *The Phenomenon of Life: Toward a Philosophical Biology.* Evanston: Northwestern University Press, 2001.
July, Robert W. *A History of the African People*, second edition. New York: Charles Scribner's Sons, 1974.

Kant, Immanuel. *Anthropology from a Pragmatic Point of View*. Cambridge: Cambridge University Press, 2006.
———. *Kritik der praktischen Vernunft*. In *Werke* Band 7. Frankfurt: Suhrkamp, 1974a.
———. *Kritik der reinen Vernunft*. Hamburg: Felix Meiner Verlag, 1998.
———. *Kritik der Urteilskraft*. Hamburg: Felix Meiner Verlag, 1974b.
———. *Lectures on Metaphysics*. Translated by Karl Ameriks and Steve Naragon. Cambridge: Cambridge University Press, 1997.
Khalidi, Rashid. *The Iron Cage: The Story of the Palestinian Struggle for Statehood*. Boston: Beacon Press, 2007.
King, Martin Luther, Jr. *A Call to Conscience: The Landmark Speeches of Dr. Martin Luther King Jr.* Edited by Clayborne Carson and Kris Shepard. New York: Warner Books, 2001.
Kisner, Wendell. "The Category of Life, Mechanistic Reduction, and the Uniqueness of Biology." *Cosmos and History* 4, no. 2 (2008): 113–153.
Kolb, David. "Exposing an English Speculative Word." *Owl of Minerva* 31, no. 2 (2000): 199–202.
Lam, Raymond W., Anthony J. Levitt, Robert D. Levitan, Murray W. Enns, Rachel Morehouse, Erin E. Michalak, and Edwin M. Tam. "The Can-SAD Study: A Randomized Controlled Trial of the Effectiveness of Light Therapy and Fluoxetine in Patients with Winter Seasonal Affective Disorder." *American Journal of Psychiatry* 163, no. 5 (2006): 805–812.
Langfield, H. S. "The Judgment of Emotion by the Facial Expression." *Journal of Abnormal and Social Psychology* 13 (1918): 172–184.
La Rochefoucauld, François Duc de. *Réflections ou Sentences et Maximes morales*. Paris: Éditions Garnier Fréres, 1961.
Lefort, Claude. *Democracy and Political Theory*. Translated by David Macey. Minneapolis: University of Minnesota Press, 1988.
Leibniz, G.W. *La Monadologie: Oeuvres philosophiques de Leibniz*. Tome premier. Edited by Paul Janet. Paris: Ancienne Librairie Germer Baillière et Cie, 1900.
Leiner, Jacqueline. "Entretien avec Aimé Césaire." *Tropiques* 1, no. 1 (1978): 5–24.
Lewis, Thomas A. *Freedom and Tradition in Hegel: Reconsidering Anthropology, Ethics, and Religion*. Notre Dame: University of Notre Dame Press, 2005.
Lipkin, Mack, and Gerri Lamb. "The Couvade Syndrome: An Epidemiologic Study." *Annals of Internal Medicine* 96 (1982): 509–513.
Lloyd, Genevieve. *The Man of Reason*. Minneapolis: University of Minnesota Press, 1995.
Locke, John. *An Essay Concerning Human Understanding*. New York: Penguin Books, 1997.
———. *Second Treatise of Government*. Indianapolis: Hackett, 1980.
Lucas, Hans-Christian. " 'Die, souveräne Undankbarkeit' des Geistes gegenüber der Natur: Logische Bestimmungen, Leiblichkeit, animalischer Magnetismus und

Verrücktheit in Hegels 'Anthropologie.'" In *Psychologie und Anthropologie oder Philosophie des Geistes*. Stuttgart-Bad Cannstatt: Frommann-Holzboog, 1991.

Lumsden, Simon. "Between Nature and Spirit: Hegel's Account of Habit." In *Essays on Hegel's "Philosophy of Subjective Spirit,"* edited by David Stern. Albany: State University of NewYork Press, 2013.

Magee, Glenn Alexander. "The Dark Side of Subjective Spirit: Hegel on Mesmerism, Madness and the Ganglia." In *Essays on Hegel's "Philosophy of Subjective Spirit,"* edited by David Stern. Albany: State University of New York Press, 2013.

Magrì, Elisa. "The Place of Habit in Hegel's Psychology." In *Hegel's Philosophical Psychology*, edited by Susanne Herrmann-Sinai and Lucia Ziglioli. New York: Routledge, 2016.

Mallon, Ron. "Race: Normative, Not Metaphysical or Semantic." *Ethics* 116, no. 3 (2006): 525–551.

Marcuse, Herbert. *Reason and Revolution: Hegel and the Rise of Social Theory*. Boston: Beacon Press, 1969.

Marx, Karl, and Friedrich Engels. *The Manifesto of the Communist Party*. In *The Marx-Engels Reader*, second edition, edited by Robert C. Tucker. New York: W.W. Norton, 1978.

Mauss, Marcel. "Techniques of the Body." *Economy and Society* 2, no. 1 (1973): 70–88.

McGrew, W. "Tool Use by Wild Chimpanzees in Feeding upon Driver Ants." *Journal of Human Evolution* 3, no. 6 (1974): 501–508.

Memmi, Albert. *The Colonizer and the Colonized*. Boston: Beacon Press, 1991.

Merker, Barbara. "Über Gewohnheit." In *Hegels Theorie des subjektiven Geistes*, edited by Lothar Eley. Stuttgart-Bad Cannstatt: Frommann-Holzboog, 1990.

Merleau-Ponty, Maurice. "Eye and Mind." Translated by Carleton Dallery. In *The Primacy of Perception*, edited by James M. Edie. Evanston: Northwestern University Press, 1964.

———. *Phenomenology of Perception*. New York: Routledge, 2002.

———. *The Visible and the Invisible*. Edited by Claude Lefort. Translated by Alphonso Lingis. Evanston: Northwestern University Press, 1968.

Mermelstein, Hannah. "Overdue Books: Returning Palestine's 'Abandoned Property' of 1948."*Journal of Palestine Studies* 47 (2011): 46–64.

Michaels, Walter Benn. "The No-Drop Rule." *Critical Inquiry* 20, no. 4 (1994): 758–769.

Michotte, A. E. "The Emotional Significance of Movement." In *Feelings and Emotions*, edited by M. L. Reymert. New York: McGraw Hill, 1950.

Mill, John Stuart. *Three Essays on Religion*. Amherst: Prometheus Books, 1998.

Miller, Daniel. "Artefacts and the Meaning of Things." In *Companion Encyclopedia of Anthropology*, edited by Tim Ingold. New York: Routledge, 1994.

Mills, Patricia Jagentowicz. "Hegel's Antigone." In *Feminist Interpretations of Hegel*, edited by Patricia Jagentowicz Mills. University Park: Pennsylvania State University Press, 1996.

Milton, John. *Paradise Lost: A Poem in Twelve Books*. Edited by Merritt Y. Hughes. New York: Odyssey Press, 1962.

Moland, Lydia L. "Inheriting, Earning, and Owning: The Source of Practical Identity in Hegel's 'Anthropology.'" *Owl of Minerva* 34, no. 2 (2003): 139–170.

Montaigne, Michel. *The Complete Essays*. Translated by M. A. Screech. New York: Penguin Books, 1991.

Montesquieu. *The Spirit of the Laws*. Edited by Anne M. Cohler, Basia Carolyn Miller, and Harold Samuel Stone. New York: Cambridge University Press, 2008.

Mowad, Nicholas. "Awakening to Madness and Habituation to Death in Hegel's Anthropology." In *Essays on Hegel's "Philosophy of Subjective Spirit,"* edited by David S. Stern. Albany: State University of New York Press, 2013a.

———. "History and Critique: A Response to Habermas' Misreading of Hegel." *Clio* 42, no. 1 (2012a): 53–72.

———. "The Natural World of Spirit: Hegel on Valuing Nature." *Environmental Philosophy* 9, no. 2 (2012b): 47–66.

———. "The Place of Nationality in Hegel's Philosophy of Politics and Religion: A Defense of Hegel on the Charges of National Chauvinism and Racism." In *Hegel on Religion and Politics*, edited by Angelica Nuzzo. Albany: State University New York Press, 2013b.

Munroe, R. L., and R. H. Munroe. "Male Pregnancy Symptoms and Cross-Sex Identity in Three Societies." *Journal of Social Psychology* 84 (1971): 11–25.

Nancy, Jean-Luc. *Inoperative Community*. Translated by Peter Connor. Minneapolis: University of Minnesota Press, 1998.

Newton, Huey P. *The Huey P. Newton Reader*. New York: Seven Stories Press, 2002.

Nietzsche, Friedrich. *Also Sprach Zarathustra*. In *Gesammelte Werke* Band 13. Munich: Musarion Verlag, 1925.

Nuzzo, Angelica. "Anthropology, *Geist*, and the Soul-Body Relation: The Systematic Beginning of Hegel's *Philosophy of Spirit*." In *Essays on Hegel's "Philosophy of Subjective Spirit,"* edited by David Stern. Albany: State University of NewYork Press, 2013.

———. *Ideal Embodiment: Kant's Theory of Sensibility*. Bloomington: Indiana University Press, 2008.

Otto, Walter F. *The Homeric Gods*. Translated by Moses Hadas. New York: Octagon Books, 1983.

Parekh, Sûrya. "Hegel's New World: History, Freedom, and Race." In *Hegel and History*, edited by Will Dudley. Albany: State University of New York Press, 2009.

Pausanias. *Guide to Greece*. Translated by Peter Levi. Harmondsworth: Penguin, 1971.

Peirce, Charles S. *Philosophical Writings of Peirce*. New York: Dover, 2011.

Peperzak, Adriaan. "Existenz und Denken im Werden der Hegelschen Philosophie." *Scholastik* 38 (1963): 226–238.

———. *Hegels praktische Philosophie*. Stuttgart-Bad Canstatt: Frommann-Holzboog, 1991.

———. *Modern Freedom: Hegel's Legal, Moral, and Political Philosophy*. Dordrecht: Kluwer, 2001.

———. " 'Second Nature': Place and Significance of the Objective Spirit in Hegel's Encyclopedia." *Owl of Minerva* 27, no. 1 (1995): 51–66.

———. "Selbstbewußtsein-Vernunft-Freiheit-Geist." In *Hegels Theorie des subjektiven Geistes inder "Enzyklopädie der philosophischen Wissenschaften im Grundrisse*," edited by Lothar Eley. (*Spekulation und Erfahrung* II, 14). Stuttgart-Bad Canstatt: Frommann-Holzboog, 1990.

———. *Selbsterkenntnis des Absoluten*. Stuttgart-Bad Canstatt: Frommann-Holzboog, 1987.

Pillow, Kirk. "Habituating Madness and Phantasying Art in Hegel's Encyclopedia." *Owl of Minerva* 28, no. 2 (1997): 183–215.

Pinkard, Terry. *Hegel: A Biography*. Cambridge: Cambridge University Press, 2001.

Piper, Adrian. "Passing for White, Passing for Black." *Transition* 58 (1992): 4–32.

Pippin, Robert. *Hegel's Idealism: The Satisfactions of Self-Consciousness*. New York: Cambridge University Press, 1989.

Plato. *Apology*. In *Five Dialogues*, second edition. Translated by G. M. A. Grube and John M. Cooper. Indianapolis: Hackett, 2002a.

———. *Crito*. In *Five Dialogues*, second edition. Translated by G. M. A. Grube and John M. Cooper. Indianapolis: Hackett, 2002b.

———. *Phaedo*. Translated by Grube. Indianapolis: Hackett, 1977.

———. *Phaedrus*. Translated by Reginald Hackforth. In *Collected Dialogues*, edited by Edith Hamilton and Huntington Cairns. Princeton: Princeton University Press, 1989.

———. *Republic*, second edition. Translated by Allan Bloom. New York: Basic Books, 1991.

———. *Sophist*. Translated by Nicholas P. White. Indianapolis: Hackett, 1993.

———. *Theaetetus*. Translated by M. J. Levett and Myles Burnyeat. Indianapolis: Hackett, 1992.

———. *Timaeus*. Translated by Donald J. Zeyl. Indianapolis: Hackett, 2000.

Ponge, Francis. *Le parti pris des choses: Précédé de Douze petits écrits et suivi de Proêmes*. Paris: Gallimard, 2000.

Premack, Ann James, and David Premack. "Why Animals Have Neither Culture Nor History." In *Companion Encyclopedia of Anthropology*, edited by Tim Ingold. New York: Routledge, 1994.

Radhakrishnan, Sarvepalli, and Charles A. Moore. *A Sourcebook in Indian Philosophy*. Princeton: Princeton University Press, 1957.

Rampersad, Arnold. *The Art and Imagination of W.E.B. Du Bois*. Cambridge: Harvard University Press, 1976.

Rancière, Jacques. *Dissensus: On Politics and Aesthetics*. Edited and translated by Steve Corcoran. New York: Continuum, 2011.

Ravven, Heidi M. "Has Hegel Anything to Say to Feminists?" *Owl of Minerva* 19, no. 2 (1988): 149–168.

Reed, Adolph, Jr. *Stirrings in the Jug: Black Politics in the Post-Segregation Era.* Minneapolis: University of Minnesota Press, 1999.

Reich, David. *Who We Are and How We Got Here: Ancient DNA and the New Science of the Human Past.* New York: Pantheon Books, 2018.

Reid, Jeffrey. "How the Dreaming Soul Became the Feeling Soul, Between the 1827 and 1830 Editions of Hegel's *Philosophy of Subjective Spirit*: Empirical Psychology and the Late Enlightenment." In *Essays on Hegel's "Philosophy of Subjective Spirit,"* edited by David Stern. Albany: State University of New York Press, 2013.

Rousseau, Jean-Jacques. *Émile, ou de l'éducation.* Paris: Éditions Lutetia, 1932.

Russon, John. *Reading Hegel's Phenomenology.* Bloomington: Indiana University Press, 2004.

———. *The Self and Its Body in Hegel's Phenomenology of Spirit.* Toronto: University of Toronto Press, 2001.

Said, Edward. *Orientalism.* New York: Vintage Books, 1979.

Sale, Kirkpatrick. *Dwellers in the Land.* San Francisco: Sierra Club, 1985.

Sale, Richard. "Analysis: Hamas History Tied to Israel." *UPI.* 2002. https://www.upi.com/Analysis-Hamas-history-tied-to-Israel/82721024445587/. Accessed July 30, 2018.

Sampson, Robert J., and Stephen W. Rudenbush. "Seeing Disorder: Neighborhood Stigma and the Social Construction of 'Broken Windows.'" *Social Psychology Quarterly* 67, no. 4 (2004): 319–342.

Sapperstein, Aliya, Andrew Penner, and Jessica M. Kizer. "The Criminal Justice System and the Racialization of Perceptions." *The Annals of the American Academy of Political and Social Science* 651, no. 1 (2014): 104–121.

Schelling, F. W. J. *The Ages of the World.* Translated by Jason M. Wirth. Albany: State University of New York Press, 2000.

"Second Congress of Negro Writers and Artists." *Présence Africaine* 24–25 (1959).

Shakespeare, William. *The Complete Works*, second edition. Edited by Stanley Wells, Gary Taylor, John Jowett, and William Montgomery. New York: Oxford University Press, 2005.

Shannon, Daniel. "A Criticism of a False Idealism and Onward to Hegel: Objections to the Gaia Hypothesis." *The Owl of Minerva* 27, no. 1 (1995): 19–34.

Sheety, Roger. "Stealing Palestine: A Study of Historical and Cultural Theft." June 17, 2014. http://www.middleeasteye.net/essays/stealing-palestine-study-historical-and-cultural-theft-1001196809. Accessed July 30, 2018.

Shelby, Tommie. *We Who Are Dark: The Philosophical Foundations of Black Solidarity.* Cambridge: Harvard University Press, 2005.

Sherman, M. "The Differentiation of Emotional Responses in Infants." *Journal of Comparative Psychology* 7 (1927): 265–284.

Siep, Ludwig. "Leiblichkeit, Selbstgefühl und Personalität in Hegels Philosophie des Geistes." In *Hegels Theorie des subjektiven Geiste*, edited by Lothar Eley. Stuttgart-Bad Cannstatt: Frommann-Holzboog, 1990.

Sophocles. *The Complete Plays of Sophocles*. New York: Bantam Books, 1982.

Spelman, Elizabeth. *Inessential Woman: Problems of Exclusion in Feminist Thought*. Boston: Beacon Press, 1988.

Spinoza, Baruch. *Ethics*. Translated by Samuel Shirley. Indianapolis: Hackett, 1992.

Starret, Shari Neller. "Critical Relations in Hegel: Women, Family, and the Divine." In *Feminist Interpretations of Hegel*, edited by Patricia Jagentowicz Mills. University Park: Pennsylvania State University Press, 1996.

Stone, Alison. *Petrified Intelligence: Nature in Hegel's Philosophy*. Albany: State University of New York Press, 2005.

Testa, Italo. "Hegel's Naturalism or Soul and Body in Hegel's *Encyclopedia*." In *Essays on Hegel's "Philosophy of Subjective Spirit*,*" edited by David Stern. Albany: State University of New York Press, 2013.

Thayer, Robert L. *Life Place: Bioregional Thought and Practice*. Berkeley: University of California Press, 2003.

Trethowan, W. H., and M. F. Conlon. "The Couvade Syndrome." *British Journal of Psychology* 111 (1965): 57–66.

Tylor, Edward Burnett. *Primitive Cultures*, vol. 1. Mineola: Dover, 2016.

Van Brock, Nadia. "Substitution rituelle." *Revue Hittite et Asianique* 65 (1959): 117–146.

Van der Meulen, Jan. "Hegels Lehre von Leib, Seele, und Geist." *Hegel-Studien* Band 2. Bonn: H. Bouvier und Co. Verlag, 1963.

Van Lewick-Goodall, Jane. "Tool-Use in Primates and Other Vertebrates." In *Advances in the Study of Behavior*, edited by D. Lehrman, R. Hinde, and E. Shaw. New York: Academic Press 1970.

Wenning, Mario. "Awakening from Madness: The Relationship between Spirit and Nature in Light of Hegel's Account of Madness." In *Essays on Hegel's "Philosophy of Subjective Spirit*,*" edited by David Stern. Albany: State University of New York Press, 2013.

Williamson, Joel. "W.E.B. Du Bois as a Hegelian." In *What Was Freedom's Price?*, edited by David G. Sansing. Jackson: University Press of Mississippi, 1978.

Winfield, Richard Dien. *Freedom and Modernity*. Albany: State University of New York Press, 1991.

———. *Hegel and Mind: Rethinking Philosophical Psychology*. New York: Palgrave Macmillan, 2010.

———. *The Living Mind: From Psyche to Consciousness*. Lanham: Rowman & Littlefield, 2011.

———. *Overcoming Foundations: Studies in Systematic Philosophy*. New York: Columbia University Press, 1989.

———. *Universal Biology After Aristotle, Kant, and Hegel: The Philosopher's Guide to Life in the Universe*. Cham: Palgrave Macmillan, 2018.
Wolff, Michael. *Das Körper-Seele Problem: Kommentar zu Hegel, Enzyklopädie (1830) §389*. Frankfurt am Main: Vittorio Klostermann GmbH, 1992.
Wordsworth, William. *The Poems*, vol. 1. New York: Penguin, 1977.
X, Malcolm, and Alex Haley. *The Autobiography of Malcolm X*. New York: Random House, 1999.
Zack, Naomi. *Philosophy of Science and Race*. New York: Routledge, 2002.
Žižek, Slavoj. "Discipline Between Two Freedoms—Madness and Habit in German Idealism." In *Mythology, Madness, and Laughter: Subjectivity in German Idealism*, edited by Markus Gabriel and Slavoj Žižek. London: Continuum, 2009.

Index

Africa, 57, 73, 74, 82, 83, 84, 187, 201, 214, 216, 218, 219, 220, 385, 252, 255, 256, 257, 286, 289, 290, 293
Agamben, Giorgio, 222
Alcoff, Linda Martín, 87, 89–90, 206
Althusser, Louis, 284, 285
Antigone, 113–120, 142–143, 155, 172, 183–184, 262–263, 268
Appiah, Anthony, 76, 256
Aristotle, xiv, xxii, 21, 37, 38, 56, 57, 58, 60, 66, 67, 81, 122, 124, 130, 139–143, 145, 199, 231, 234, 237, 244, 245–246, 250, 259, 263, 266, 267, 274, 281, 282
Arnold, Matthew, 85
Awakening, 116–126, 142–143, 152–153, 158, 169, 170–172, 174, 184, 186, 263

Baldwin, James, 191, 282, 286
Beavoir, Simone, 209
Benhabib, Seyla, 74
Berkeley, George, 27
Berthold-Bond, Daniel, 188, 233, 261, 270, 274
Biological characteristics of a body, xiv, 3–23, 61–72, 75–77, 100–109, 130–136, 284
Blake, William, 71–72
Boas, Franz, 76, 255

Butler, Judith, xviii, 87, 119, 274

Capitalism, 170, 176, 212, 294
Césaire, Aimé, 86, 203, 215–216, 219, 282, 283, 284
Chemical determinations of a body, 3–23
Chepurin, Kirill, 180, 243, 258, 278
Civil Society, 41–42, 48, 81, 112, 175–176, 183–184, 199, 243, 292–293
Coleridge, Samuel Taylor, 55
Concept, 25–53

Damas, Léon-Gontran, 203, 212, 213, 214
De Boer, Karin, 119–120, 262
De Laurentiis, Allegra, 141, 268
Death, 11–12, 14–16, 71, 100–109, 173
Democracy, 170, 220–226
Descartes, René, xvi, 20, 60, 231
Disease (*see* Illness)
Douglass, Frederick, 284, 285, 286, 288, 291, 292
Dreaming, 117, 120–126, 160–161, 165, 169, 171
Du Bois, W. E. B., 207, 209, 210, 215–216, 285–286

Elliot, T. S., 71

Emotion, 145–149
Epicurus, 14–16
Erasmus, 186
Ethical Life, 49, 172, 179, 192–200
Euripides, 151
Extension (*see* Mechanical determinations of a body), xvi, 1–23, 30

Family, 13, 80, 93, 109–120, 175, 176, 199
Fanon, Frantz, 203, 209, 210, 212, 213, 284, 285
Feeling, 151–189, 151–189, 204–214
Feeling in its Immediacy, 151–168, 204–212
Ferrarin, Alfredo, 49, 140, 143, 182, 233, 234, 243, 244, 246, 260, 261, 267, 270, 280
Fichte, Johann Gottlieb, 231, 253
Foucault, Michel, 87
Friel, Brian, 151
Frost, Robert, 85

Gender, 109–120, 142–143, 153, 175, 183–184, 211–212
Genius, 95, 157–168, 206, 271, 272
Gooding-Williams, Robert, 203, 216, 218–219, 222, 232, 255, 283, 285, 286, 291

Habit
  Habit and character, 95
  Habit and politics, 214–226
  Habit and therapy, 179–184
Halbig, Christoph, 137, 148–149, 156, 233
Harris, Errol, 76
Hegel, G. W. F.
  Travels and experience with diversity, 75
  Views of women, 109–110

Heidegger, Martin, xvii, 122, 124
Herder, J. G., 83, 250, 276
History, 44, 48, 59, 79–80, 87–88, 164, 186, 192–193, 202, 216, 220–226, 295–296
Horkheimer, Max, 55

Idea, 25–45
Illness
  Illness in the animal, 173–174
  Mental illness, 157–189

Jaeschke, Walter, 231
Judgment, 29, 101–102, 128–129

Kant, Immanuel, xiii, xiv, xvi, xix, 2, 13, 27–29, 66–67, 74, 156, 157, 163, 191, 231, 232, 235, 257, 272, 274
King Jr., Martin Luther, 163, 212

Lefort, Claude, 191, 222
Leibniz, 140
Life, 3–4, 8–23, 31–35, 46–53, 56–80, 100–109, 172–177

Madhva, 84–85
Madness (*see* Mental Illness)
Magrì, Elisa, 195, 196, 220, 233, 268, 274, 279
Marx, Karl, 98, 191, 275, 284, 293
Mauss, Marcel, xiv
Mechanical determinations of a body, 3–23
Memmi, Albert, 208, 212, 215, 216, 219, 256, 284, 289
Mental illness, 117–220, 151–189, 203–220
Merleau-Ponty, Maurice, xvii–xx, 62, 143, 213, 247, 248, 264
Mill, John Stuart, 60
Mills, Patricia Jagentowicz, 119, 274
Milton, John, 25

Moland, Lydia, 195, 275, 233
Montaigne, Michel, 169, 186, 236, 245, 250, 270
Morality, 196, 278

Nancy, Jean-Luc, 221–222, 295
Nature
    Nature and race, 73–92, 202–226
    That nature is meaningful, 59–73, 136–142, 200–202
Nuzzo, Angelica, xvi, 36, 46–49, 231, 233, 239, 241

Otto, Walter, 79

Peperzak, Adriaan, 37–38, 43, 233, 241, 243, 296
Plato, 14–15, 30, 35, 56, 57, 81, 85, 136, 155, 181, 230, 231, 237, 263, 281
Poetry, 65–66, 71–72, 85–86, 138, 149, 164, 203, 213–220, 283, 291
Ponge, Francis, 72
Premack, Ann & Premack, David, 52

Race, 73–92, 95, 202–226
Religion, xvii, xxi, 26, 43–45, 56, 59, 77, 79–80, 82, 87, 93, 108, 114, 122, 138, 149, 172–173, 186, 213, 245, 254, 257, 263, 265, 278, 286, 290
Rousseau, Jean-Jacques, 56, 231, 259, 260, 270, 276
Russon, John, xx, 98, 231, 232–233, 262

Schelling, Friedrich Wilhelm Joseph, 138, 278

Self-Feeling, 169–189, 212–214
Sensation, 127–149, 151–156, 203
Shakespeare, William, 127, 191
Shelby, Tommie, 283–284, 292–293
Sickness (*see* Illness)
Sleep, 160–161, 169
Smell, 130, 133–134, 140, 144
Sophocles, 86, 97, 113–114, 119, 169, 184, 262
Sound, 130–134, 138, 145, 195, 200
Spinoza, 29
Spirit
    The concept of spirit, 25–53
    Objective spirit, 45–46, 111, 163–164, 175, 191–202, 295
    Spirit in contrast to nature, 25–53
    Spirit as the idea, 25–45
    Subjective spirit, 45–46, 246
Syllogism, 29–30, 101–102, 128–129

Taste, 74–75, 130, 133–134, 140, 144, 167
Touch, 130–131, 134–135

Winfield, Richard Dien, 165, 182, 195, 233, 234, 237, 238, 242, 243, 246, 253, 268, 270, 272, 273, 280, 281, 294, 295, 296
Wolff, Michael, xx, 46–47, 105, 139–140, 232, 239, 246, 258, 265
Women, 109–120, 142–143, 153, 175, 183–184, 211–212

X, Malcolm, 163, 212

Žižek, Slavoj, 187, 284

www.ingramcontent.com/pod-product-compliance
Lightning Source LLC
Chambersburg PA
CBHW030127240426
43672CB00005B/57